Tibet
a travel survival kit

Robert Strauss

Tibet – a travel survival kit

2nd edition

Published by
Lonely Planet Publications
Head Office: PO Box 617, Hawthorn, Vic 3122, Australia
Branches: PO Box 2001A, Berkeley, CA 94702, USA and London, UK

Printed by
Colorcraft Ltd, Hong Kong

Photographs by
Robert Strauss (RS)
Garry Weare (GW)
Ray Vran (RV)
Ngawang Choephel (NC)
Jolieske Lips (JL)
Front cover: Avalokitesvara - the patron saint of Tibet (RV)

First Published
April 1986

This Edition
February 1992

National Library of Australia Cataloguing in Publication Data

Strauss, Robert
    Tibet – a travel survival kit.

    2nd ed.
    Includes index.
    ISBN 0 86442 139 7.

    1. Tibet (China) – Description and travel – Guide-books.
    I. Title.

915.1504

Mail Order

Lonely Planet guidebooks are distributed worldwide.They are also available by mail order from Lonely Planet, so if you have difficulty finding a title please write to us. US and Canadian residents should write to Embarcadero West, 155 Filbert St, Suite 251, Oakland CA 94607, USA ; European residents should write to Devonshire House, 12 Barley Mow Passage, Chiswick, London W4 4PH; and residents of other countries to PO Box 617, Hawthorn, Victoria 3122, Australia.

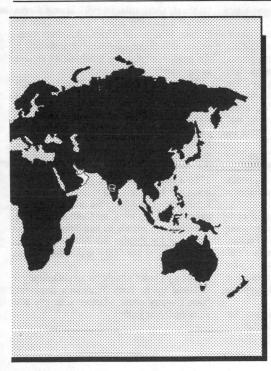

Indian Subcontinent
Bangladesh
India
Hindi/Urdu phrasebook
Trekking in the Indian Himalaya
Karakoram Highway
Kashmir, Ladakh & Zanskar
Nepal
Trekking in the Nepal Himalaya
Nepal phrasebook
Pakistan
Sri Lanka
Sri Lanka phrasebook

Africa
Africa on a shoestring
Central Africa
East Africa
Kenya
Swahili phrasebook
Morocco, Algeria & Tunisia
Moroccan Arabic phrasebook
South Africa, Lesotho & Swaziland
Zimbabwe, Botswana & Namibia
West Africa

Mexico
Baja California
Mexico

Central America
Central America on a shoestring
Costa Rica
La Ruta Maya

North America
Alaska
Canada
Hawaii

Europe
Eastern Europe on a shoestring
Eastern Europe phrasebook
Finland
Iceland, Greenland & the Faroe Islands
Mediterranean Europe on a shoestring
Mediterranean Europe phrasebook
Poland
Scandinavian & Baltic Europe on a shoestring
Scandinavian Europe phrasebook
Trekking in Spain
USSR
Russian phrasebook
Western Europe on a shoestring
Western Europe phrasebook

South America
Argentina, Uruguay & Paraguay
Bolivia
Brazil
Brazilian phrasebook
Chile & Easter Island
Colombia
Ecuador & the Galápagos Islands
Latin American Spanish phrasebook
Peru
Quechua phrasebook
South America on a shoestring
Trekking in the Patagonian Andes

The Lonely Planet Story

Lonely Planet published its first book in 1973 in response to the numerous 'How did you do it?' questions Maureen and Tony Wheeler were asked after driving, bussing, hitching, sailing and railing their way from England to Australia.

Written at a kitchen table and hand collated, trimmed and stapled, *Across Asia on the Cheap* became an instant local bestseller, inspiring thoughts of another book.

Eighteen months in South-East Asia resulted in their second guide, *South-East Asia on a shoestring*, which they put together in a backstreet Chinese hotel in Singapore in 1975. The 'yellow bible' as it quickly became known to backpackers around the world, soon became *the* guide to the region. It has sold well over half a million copies and is now in its 7th edition, still retaining its familiar yellow cover.

Today there are over 100 Lonely Planet titles – books that have that same adventurous approach to travel as those early guides; books that 'assume you know how to get your luggage off the carousel' as one reviewer put it.

Although Lonely Planet initially specialised in guides to Asia, they now cover most regions of the world, including the Pacific, South America, Africa, the Middle East and Europe. The list of *walking guides* and *phrasebooks* (for 'unusual' languages such as Quechua, Swahili, Nepalese and Egyptian Arabic) is also growing rapidly.

The emphasis continues to be on travel for independent travellers. Tony and Maureen still travel for several months of each year and play an active part in the writing, updating and quality control of Lonely Planet's guides.

They have been joined by over 50 authors, 48 staff – mainly editors, cartographers, & designers – at our office in Melbourne, Australia and another 10 at our US office in Oakland, California. In 1991 Lonely Planet opened a London office to handle sales for Britain, Europe and Africa. Travellers themselves also make a valuable contribution to the guides through the feedback we receive in thousands of letters each year.

The people at Lonely Planet strongly believe that travellers can make a positive contribution to the countries they visit, both through their appreciation of the countries' culture, wildlife and natural features, and through the money they spend. In addition, the company makes a direct contribution to the countries and regions it covers. Since 1986 a percentage of the income from each book has been donated to ventures such as famine relief in Africa; aid projects in India; agricultural projects in Central America; Greenpeace's efforts to halt French nuclear testing in the Pacific and Amnesty International. In 1991 $68,000 was donated to these causes.

Lonely Planet's basic travel philosophy is summed up in Tony Wheeler's comment, 'Don't worry about whether your trip will work out. Just go!'

Robert Strauss

Robert Strauss was born in England. During the '70s he travelled for several years in Europe and Asia, including a visit to the Tibetan communities in Dharamsala (India) and Nepal. After completing a degree in oriental languages in 1981, Robert made several visits to China and spent his time teaching, travelling and writing between England, Germany, Portugal and China. He coauthored the first edition of this book and then steamed off to Siberia to write the *Trans-Siberian Rail Guide* (Bradt Publications). He returned to update *China – a travel survival kit* before preparing this new edition. His continued preoccupation with Asia led to his coauthorship of *Japan – a travel survival kit*. At present he is completing a lengthy stint in South America working on travel survival kits to *Bolivia* and *Brazil*.

Acknowledgements

The author was helped along by a host of travellers and others. He would particularly like to thank the Library of Tibetan Works & Archives, Dharamsala, for assistance with illustration material. Special thanks to Laurie Fullerton (USA) for listening and support; to Rocky Dang, Malener and the Phoenix crew (Hong Kong); Bing (UK); the convoy crew – Ed, Dave, Christine and Meghan (USA); Annette (USA); Jim (USA); Alexis, Thomas and Samuel (UK); Geoff Bonsall (Hong Kong); John Hammer (USA); Jolieske Lips (AUS); John Kendall (Traveller's Medical Services) (AUS); Jamyang Norbu (UK) for helpful suggestions and sections on Tibetan culture; Deanna Swaney (Alaska) for last-minute assistance.

From the Publisher

Back in the Autonomous City of Hawthorn dreaming of 'The Land of Snows', was a hard-working Lonely Planet team. The line-up follows: Katie Cody, Adrienne Costanzo, Caroline Williamson edited the book; Sally Steward helped with the language sections and organised the foreign script typesetting; Sue Mitra proofread and handled the production of the book; Valerie Tellini was responsible for design and maps; Chris Lee Ack and Ralph Roob did some additional map drawing, and Todd Pierce contributed some illustrations. Greg Herriman and Sharon Wertheim were patient teachers.

Thanks also to those travellers who wrote to us with additional information:

Ubaldo Alvarez Alguin (Mex), Cary Apprnzeller (USA), Geoff Bailey (Aus), Ingrid Bremer (D), John Callanan (UK), Ngawang Choephel (Tib), Stuart Dalton (USA), Virginie Dameron (F), Eddy DeWilde, Norbu Dhargay (Ind), Tim Donne (UK), Tamula Drumm, Charles Ellsworth (USA), Dr Patrick Frew (UK), Arvind Habbu (USA), Anders Helthen (Aus), Philippe Langlet (Sw), Pete Larrett (USA), Althea Maddrell, Wendy Paton (Aus), Mark Renwick (UK), Marina Reuter (Aus), Tanya Riefler (Aus), Susanna Scanziani (It), Lia A Sullivan (USA), Ruth Toff (USA), Anne Trenoweth (Aus), Greg Tripp (Aus), Helen Tworkowski (Aus), James van Vliet (USA), Gladys B Watts (USA), Margot Welsh (Aus)

Aus – Australia, D – Germany, F – France, Ind – India, It – Italy, Mex – Mexico, Sw – Sweden, Tib – Tibet, UK – United Kingdom, USA – United States of America

Warning & Request

All travel guides rely on new information to

stay up to date. Things change – prices go up, good places go bad, new places open up – nothing stays the same. Tibet is likely to change rapidly, so if you find things better, worse, cheaper, more expensive, recently opened or closed, or simply different, please write and tell us about them and help make the next edition even better. We love getting letters from travellers out on the road and, as usual, the most useful letters will be rewarded with a free copy of the next edition, or another LP guide of your choice.

Contents

Map Legend

BOUNDARIES

— · — · — · — .... International Boundary
— · · — · · — .... Internal Boundary
━━━━━━━━ .... National Park or Reserve
- - - - - - - - - .... The Equator
. . . . The Tropics

SYMBOLS

◉ NEW DELHI ....National Capital
● BOMBAY ....Provincial or State Capital
● Pune ....Major Town
• Borsi ....Minor Town
■ ....Places to Stay
▼ ....Places to Eat
≙ ....Post Office
✕ ....Airport
i ....Tourist Information
◉ ....Bus Station or Terminal
66 ....Highway Route Number
☪ ✝ ⛪ ...... Mosque, Church, Cathedral
∴ ....Temple or Ruin
✚ ....Hospital
※ ....Lookout
▲ ....Camping Area
⊓ ....Picnic Area
⌂ ....Hut or Chalet
▲ ....Mountain or Hill
 ....Railway Station
 ....Road Bridge
 ....Railway Bridge
 ....Road Tunnel
 ....Railway Tunnel
 ....Escarpment or Cliff
 ....Pass
 ....Ancient or Historic Wall

ROUTES

——————— ....Major Road or Highway
- - - - - - - - - .... Unsealed Major Road
.... Sealed Road
- - - - - - - - - ..... Unsealed Road or Track
════════ .... City Street
+++++++++++++ ....Railway
━●━ .... Subway
. . . .Walking Track
- - - - - - - - - .... Ferry Route
++++++++++++ .... Cable Car or Chair Lift

HYDROGRAPHIC FEATURES

.... River or Creek
.... Intermittent Stream
........Lake, Intermittent Lake
.... Coast Line
......................................Spring
.... Waterfall
.... Swamp

.... Salt Lake or Reef

..............................Glacier

OTHER FEATURES

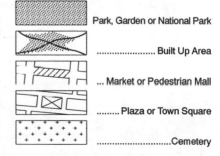

Park, Garden or National Park

.... Built Up Area

... Market or Pedestrian Mall

.... Plaza or Town Square

..............................Cemetery

Note: not all symbols displayed above appear in this book

Introduction

Prior to the 1950s, Tibet was a realm apart. The only foreigners who had visited were a tiny number of missionaries, explorers, wandering cranks and a British military force making a brief incursion to wave the flag.

Although these visitors gained admittance with varying degrees of success and some even survived the trip intact, they were all in awe of the rigours of travel in Tibet.

In 1959 the Chinese forcibly took control of Tibet but their Chinese experiment with tourism there only kicked off in the early 1980s with a trickle of tour groups dishing out thousands of dollars for the coveted cachet of being first into Tibet. At the same time a few independent backpackers wriggled past the red tape and outrageous prices. The Chinese officially opened the Roof of the World to foreigners in late 1984. More recently, Tibet has returned to the political agenda with a combination of rocks and faith against colonisation and Marx.

Today, obtaining a visa is a mere formality, but travelling inside Tibet can still provide a challenge. Foreign group tours are generally permitted access to Tibet, but the story for individual tourists is subject to change in line with the prevailing political wind. In 1991, the Chinese government was publicly proclaiming that individual tourists were again permitted entry to Tibet. However, the news obviously hadn't trickled down to local officials inside and outside Tibet who insisted on assigning individual foreigners to group tours with inflated prices averaging US$100 per day. The story for crossing into Tibet from Kathmandu was similar: visas were only issued to those travelling in an approved group, but the group can sometimes consist of only one person!

The environment of Tibet is tough with only the first signs of pampering for foreign travellers. Hotels with lifts and yakburgers have sprung up in Lhasa and beyond. Four-wheel drive vehicles cross high passes to crunch a path between Lhasa and the Nepalese border or even to the foot of Everest; the bank of Lhasa now handles plastic money; and direct flights connect Kathmandu with Lhasa. In the Barkhor, Lhasa's major market-cum-stock exchange the black market flourishes, pilgrims prostrate and Dalai Lama pictures and jewellery change hands.

For those prepared to rough it there are treks and bumpy transport further afield to places of great beauty such as Mt Kailas, mythical navel of the world.

Within Central Tibet there are reconstructed medieval monasteries and temples with small communities of monks which have survived the Cultural Revolution. In Lhasa there is the astounding sight of the 1000-room Potala, once the winter palace of the Dalai Lama, soaring above the city; nearby are the monasteries of Sera and Drepung, one of the largest monastic complexes in the world. Further afield is the eerie beauty of the devastated heights of Ganden Monastery or a visit to the massive Tashilhunpo Monastery, seat of the Panchen Lama, in Shigatse.

The natural beauty of Tibet includes the world's highest Himalayan peaks raised against deep blue skies; large clear lakes in startling colours; grasslands dotted with hundreds of yak; and towards Eastern Tibet the huge forests of Kham and vast windswept plateaus crossed by nomads on horseback.

There's only one drawback to visiting Tibet – once you've been up there, the rest of the world seems a step down.

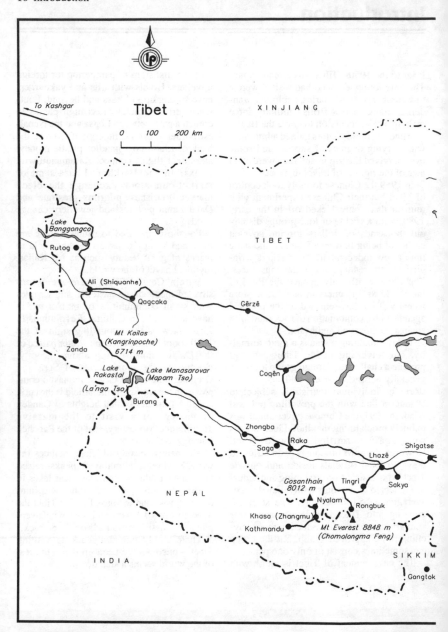

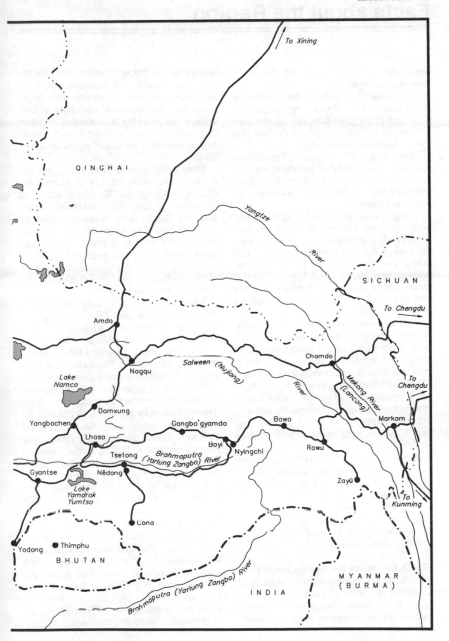

Facts about the Region

HISTORY

The Beginnings

Recent archaeological digs in many places in Tibet such as Chamdo, Burang, Tingri, and Chongye (Qonggyai) have unearthed traces of Tibetan culture dating from the late Old Stone Age and Neolithic Age.

According to Tibetan legend, Tibetans are descended from an ogress and a monkey who lived in the Yarlung Valley. From this region emerged the first line of Tibetan kings, the Yarlung Dynasty.

Songtsen Gampo the 33rd king in this line and the first for whom historians can unscramble approximate dates is also revered as the first great historical king of Tibet. During his reign (627-649 AD) he moved the capital to Lhasa (city of god) and continued to expand the territory of Tibet through military campaigns and alliances with border tribes.

Apart from marrying three Tibetan wives, he also improved political relations with his neighbours by marrying a Nepalese princess (Nepalese: Bhrikuti Devi; Tibetan: Trhisun) and a Chinese princess (Chinese: Wen Cheng, Tibetan: Munshang Kongjo). Both these princesses were strong Buddhists who encouraged Songtsen Gampo to actively support Buddhism. In Lhasa, the Jokhang and Ramoche temples were built at their request.

Since Tibetans still lacked an alphabet, Songtsen Gampo sent his minister Thonmi Sambhota to India to look for one. On his return, Thonmi Sambhota adapted a northern form of the Indian Gupta script Kashmiri script to form a Tibetan alphabet and so paved the way for translation of Buddhist literature into Tibetan.

Rise & Decline of the Tibetan Empire

From the time of King Songtsen Gampo until the end of the Yarlung Dynasty in the middle of the 9th century, Tibet gained and lost a vast Central Asian empire. From small-scale origins in the Yarlung Valley the Tibetan kings progressed with lightning speed to large-scale military campaigns over huge distances. The successful launching of this empire can probably be attributed to well-organised border alliances and rapid deployment of thousands of troops on horse-back.

During this period, Tibet conquered the oasis states around the Taklamakan (Kashgar, Khotan and Kuqa) and extended its influence deep into Turkestan, Nepal, northern Burma (now Myanmar), parts of northern India, the kingdoms of Swat and Hunza (now Pakistan). Much of northern-most India and large portions of China (including most of the modern provinces of Sichuan, Yunnan and Gansu) came under Tibetan domination.

Within the reign of Trisong Detsen (755-797), the second great historical king, the Tibetans annexed large portions of China and received tribute from the Chinese. In 763, Tibetan armies took the Chinese capital of Chang'an (modern Xian) and even temporarily installed their own puppet emperor.

With the help of two Indian teachers (Padmasambhava and Santarakshita), King Trisong Detsen established Buddhism as the official state religion. Not surprisingly, the followers of Bon, the indigenous religion of Tibet, were opposed to the favour shown to Buddhism and the resultant feuding contributed to the downfall of the empire.

The reign of Ralpachan, the third great historical king, saw even greater emphasis on Buddhism with the king becoming a monk. In 821, during a lull in the warring between China and Tibet, the two countries made a pact of nonaggression which was recorded on a pillar placed outside the Jokhang Temple in Lhasa. The text of the pact confirms that 'Tibet and China shall keep the frontiers which they now hold. All to the East is the country of Great China; all to the West is, without question, the country

The three great religious kings (clockwise from top):
Songtsen Gampo, Tri Ralpachen and Tri Songdetsen

of Great Tibet' and continues with the friendly phrase 'Tibetans shall be happy in the land of Tibet and Chinese in the land of China'. Unfortunately, even though chiselled in stone, this contract was to prove as flimsy as those made later on paper.

Under King Ralpachan, the rivalry between supporters of Bon and their Buddhist counterparts finally turned to bitter enmity. In 836, King Ralpachan was assassinated by men acting under the orders of his elder brother, Langdarma.

King Langdarma, a patron of Bon, reversed the religious pendulum and launched into a full-scale persecution of Buddhism. Buddhist teachings were burned, Buddhist temples destroyed and the monks either slaughtered or driven into exile.

In 842, Pelgyi Dorje, a Buddhist monk in hiding, received divine inspiration to descend from his mountain retreat in disguise and enter Lhasa where he put an arrow straight through Langdarma's heart. The assassination quickened the collapse of the Yarlung Dynasty and the decline of centralised authority. The Tibetan Empire was rapidly reduced to a loose grouping of small kingdoms and estates engaged in regional power struggles.

Revival of Buddhism

The revival of Buddhism started in Eastern Tibet with a small group of fugitive Buddhist monks who gradually returned to Central Tibet to restore and later establish monasteries. Meanwhile, the kingdom of Guge in Western Tibet (Ngari) sought to extend its support of Buddhism by inviting the great Indian teacher, Atisha, to Tibet where he became a driving force behind the revival of Buddhism.

By the middle of the 11th century, the nobility was sharing economic and political power in alliances with religious orders which had founded increasingly prosperous monasteries. The main orders of Tibetan Buddhism to become established were the Nyingmapa, Kagyupa, Kadampa and Sakyapa. The Sakyapa soon rose to a position of dominance with the support of the Mongols.

Enter the Mongols

When Genghis Khan threatened Tibet in the early 13th century, the Tibetans halted the impending invasion by offering to submit and pay tribute. In 1240, when the tribute failed to appear, Godan (a grandson of Genghis Khan) sent his forces to within striking distance of Lhasa before requesting the presence of Sakya Pandita, the head of the Sakyapa, at his headquarters in Koko Nor, just north of Tibet. Sakya Pandita then journeyed to Godan's court where he provided Godan with religious initiation, healed his illness and helped devise a Mongolian alphabet.

The political fortunes of the Sakyapa were later boosted by the patronage of Kublai Khan (another of Genghis Khan's many grandsons) who chose Phagpa, Sakya Pandita's nephew, as his personal priest and spiritual advisor. In return, the Sakyapa were granted the regency of Tibet. However, their supremacy had dwindled even before the fall of the Mongol Dynasty in China.

For almost three centuries Tibet kept control of its independence under a succession of Tibetan princes and kings who rose and fell on the support of competing religious orders.

In the 14th and 15th centuries the great religious reformer, Tsong Khapa (1357-1419), established the Gelukpa order (popularly known as the Yellow Hats) and founded the monasteries of Ganden, Drepung and Sera. On the death of Gedun Drub, Tsong Khapa's designated successor, a decision was made to select future heads of the Gelukpa according to a system of incarnation. In 1578, Sonam Gyatso (the third incarnation) visited the Mongol ruler, Altan Khan who gave him the title of Dalai Lama (Ocean of Wisdom) – a title which also applied retrospectively to the previous incarnations. The Gelukpa rapidly rose to importance as their ties with the Mongols strengthened.

In 1642, Gushri Khan, a prince of the Western Mongols, answered an appeal from Lobsang Gyatso, the Fifth Dalai Lama, and effectively crushed the opposition to Gelukpa rule. Lobsang Gyatso (1617-1682), traditionally referred to as the Great Fifth, was then able to exercise full authority over Tibet while the Mongols were content to provide military backing in return for nominal authority. During his reign, Lobsang Gyatso pacified and unified Tibet and the country experienced a surge in cultural and economic prosperity. On his orders, the Potala Palace was extended from Songtsen Gampo's original chapel into a soaring architectural masterpiece. Relations with the Manchu Dynasty in China remained on a diplomatic level; each side ruling its territory separately.

The early death of the Great Fifth was concealed for 13 years, but even so the behaviour of the constantly love-struck Sixth Dalai Lama did not inspire confidence. Neither did the attempt by the regent to play off rival and highly unstable Mongol factions; thereby alerting the Chinese to the threat of a Tibetan-Mongol combination.

With the approval of the Manchu Emperor

Kang Hsi the Qosot Mongol, Lhabzang Khan seized on this irregular conduct as a pretext for intervention. After marching into Lhasa, he executed the regent and set off towards China with the Sixth Dalai Lama who failed to survive the murderous journey.

Lhabzang returned to Lhasa to install his own brand of Dalai Lama, but the Tibetans spurned his choice preferring instead to wait, according to the Sixth Dalai Lama's prophecy, for a reincarnation in Litang (Eastern Tibet).

In 1717, the Dzungar Mongols invaded Tibet and ousted their Qosot rivals; Lhabzang was executed. However, the Tibetan rejoicing was cut short when the Dzungars showed no further interest in recovering the Seventh Dalai Lama (whom the cunning Manchu Emperor had previously nabbed) and turned instead to looting and pillaging Lhasa. The Tibetans set about ejecting their unwelcome guests while the Manchu Emperor also dispatched an army to counter the Dzungar threat.

Although the Emperor's first army was wiped out, his second army encountered less trouble since they arrived on the scene after the Tibetans had put the Dzungars to flight. But, most importantly, this army was assured of a friendly Tibetan reception because it was escorting to enthronement in Lhasa the prospective Seventh Dalai Lama.

Enter the Manchus

Kang Hsi had thus secured his Tibetan toehold. The city walls of Lhasa were demolished and the Emperor was represented by two Ambans (resident ministers) together with a sizeable garrison. Apart from stipulating a reversion to government under the Dalai Lama, the Manchu role in Tibet remained essentially protective. The Dalai Lamas from the Eighth through to the 12th were either unable or disinclined to govern; the high mortality rate can probably be attributed to the regents who relished power.

In 1792, the Gurkhas of Nepal flexed their muscle into Tibet and captured Shigatse. The Manchus answered an appeal for help from the Tibetans and threw out the invaders. This rekindled the Manchu fear of foreign intervention through the back door and Tibet was closed to the outside world. When the Gurkhas came back for a second bite in 1856, no Manchu assistance appeared and the Tibetans had to pay their invasive neighbours to stay out.

Although the fringe regions of Tibet (Amdo and Kham) had been loosely included in the Manchu Empire in 1724, the protective role of the Manchus in Central Tibet had faded completely by the fall of the Qing Dynasty in 1911.

Foreign Intrusion

Towards the end of the 19th century, as Britain and Russia were probing the limits of empire in Central Asia, Tibet became a focus of interest.

British suspicions of Russian meddling were aroused by reports of a mysterious visit in 1898 to the Tsar of Russia. The visitor was a Buryat Mongol monk called Dorjieff who was acting as an intermediary for the 13th Dalai Lama. Since Dorjieff was also technically a Russian subject, his subsequent visits were interpreted as a mounting Russian threat; the plot was stirred even thicker by the rumour of a clandestine Russo-Chinese Treaty on Tibet.

After securing Sikkim, the British launched a military mission under Colonel Younghusband into Tibet. The Tibetan forces with their outdated arms were no match for the weaponry which the British Army wielded with devastating effect. Younghusband entered Lhasa in 1904 to find that the Dalai Lama had escaped with Dorjieff to Mongolia. An agreement was signed with the Tibetan regent which opened Tibet to British trade, but, most importantly, put Tibet off-limits to foreign powers. The British then withdrew.

This demonstration of Tibet's vulnerability prompted the Manchus to invade Kham (Eastern Tibet) in the following year. When they reached Lhasa in 1910, the Dalai Lama had again escaped – in an interesting reversal of political direction – to the British in India.

Return to Independence

The 1911 Chinese Revolution marked the end of Manchu rule and the dismantling of their authority (exercised since the 18th century) over Tibet. The Chinese were expelled from Lhasa and the Dalai Lama returned from India to declare Tibetan independence in 1912.

Since border demarcation and claims to authority still needed to be settled, the British arranged the Simla Convention in 1914. The main proposals focused on the balance of Chinese authority and Tibetan independence which were to be applied to areas designated as Inner and Outer Tibet. Although negotiated on a tripartite basis, the agreement was not signed by the Chinese who consequently forfeited its benefits. Britain and Tibet did sign, Tibet thus retaining its independence and Britain the right to trade direct with Tibet.

The 13th Dalai Lama, Thupten Gyatso (1876-1933), proved an exceptional leader. Whilst manoeuvring Tibetan affairs around the chaotic disintegration of government in China, he also strengthened the Tibetan government's control in Eastern Tibet. Although reforms were attempted during his reign, they proved mostly experimental without the full support of the nobility and monastic institutions who felt threatened by change. Before his death in 1933, the 13th Dalai Lama gave a prophetic warning that Tibet was in great danger from 'without and within'.

The power of Tibetan government weakened as it was again passed into the hands of successive regents acting for the young 14th Dalai Lama, Tenzin Gyatso (born in 1935), who was installed in 1940. In 1947, Lhasa was shaken by an attempted coup d'etat and the death of the imprisoned ex-regent, Reting Rinpoche. In the same year, Tibet lost its last influential supporter when India regained its independence and the British retired.

The Chinese Move into Tibet

By the late 1930s, Chinese politics were dominated by two forces: the Nationalists and the Communists. After forming a brief alliance to fight the Japanese during WW II, both parties plunged into the Chinese Civil War which culminated with the Communist victory in 1949.

With the Nationalists out of the way, the Communists stated their intention to 'peacefully liberate' Tibet. In 1950, without further warning, the People's Liberation Army (PLA) was unleashed into Eastern Tibet where they captured the regional capital of Chamdo from ill-prepared and divided Tibetan forces; the governor-general of Kham, Ngabo Ngawang Jigme, surrendered soon afterwards.

Threatened by Chinese invasion, the Tibetan government directed an appeal to the United Nations, but their only supporter was the equally tiny country of El Salvador. Britain and India, from whom Tibet had expected assistance, mumbled unconvincing apologies before agreeing with other UN members to simply shelve the matter.

Without outside help, Tibet stood little chance of counteracting vastly superior military odds. When the captured Ngabo sent a request from Chamdo to negotiate with the Chinese, the Tibetan government agreed to send him to Peking at the head of a delegation. The negotiations, effected under duress, resulted in the 17-Point Agreement. Reportedly, the Chinese forged the Dalai Lama's personal seal in order to authenticate the document. In theory, this agreement covered key Tibetan issues such as maintenance of national regional autonomy, recognition of the status and power of the Dalai Lama, freedom of religious belief and protection of Tibetan culture. It never made it into practice.

Honey Proffered on a Sharp Blade

At first, the Chinese avoided direct confrontation in Central Tibet and were content to consolidate their position by moving in troops. The Dalai Lama, who had been officially given the reins of government at the unprecedentedly early age of 16, accepted an invitation to visit Peking in the hope that he could directly moderate Chinese policy. As he passed through China in 1954 he was

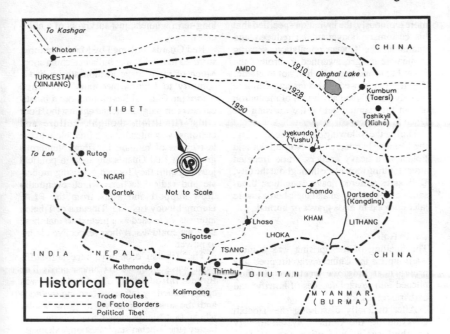

Historical Tibet
```
---------  Trade Routes
---------  De Facto Borders
─────────  Political Tibet
```

impressed by industrial development but noted the drab uniformity of daily life.

Talks with Mao Zedong in Peking seemed affable although Mao's parting comment to the Dalai Lama was clearly barbed:

I understand you very well. But of course, religion is poison. It has two great defects: it undermines the race and secondly it retards the progress of the country. Tibet and Mongolia have both been poisoned by it.

By 1955, the Chinese had tightened the noose on Tibet by forcibly incorporating Kham and Amdo (Eastern and North-Eastern Tibet) into their neighbouring Chinese provinces. These were the first Tibetan regions to be subjected to excessively hasty and brutal 'democratic reforms', the effects of which were disastrous.

The construction of roads encouraged a flood of Chinese settlers and secured military occupation which led in turn to food shortages and inflation; the imposition of taxes was soon followed by outright confiscation. Tibetan peasants were forced into collective farming and large numbers of Tibetan children were taken away for ideological 'schooling'. Monasteries became the focus of an attempt to undermine religion and monks who opposed the reforms were some of the first to be executed. Smouldering resentment was fanned to open revolt when the Communists tried to disarm the Khambas. Heavy fighting ensued all across Kham as the Khambas attacked PLA garrisons. When the first refugees from Kham trickled into Lhasa with news of Chinese atrocities, the tension started to build there too.

The Uprising

Early in March 1959, the Dalai Lama was brusquely invited to attend a theatrical performance at the PLA headquarters in Lhasa;

more ominously, the invitation specified that his customary bodyguard be reduced and unarmed. The Tibetan population, sensing immediate danger, swarmed to protect the Dalai Lama and persuade him not to attend. The friction between Tibetans and Chinese quickly outweighed any hopes of mediation and in the evening before the uprising the Dalai Lama escaped.

During the following days of the uprising, the Chinese hammered the Norbulinka and Potala with heavy artillery while frenzied street fighting took place throughout the city. Both sides suffered heavy casualties; thousands of Tibetans died and their bodies were later dumped in mass graves or burned.

Death Roll
The quelling of the uprising was a mere warm-up for the Chinese who dropped any pretence at kidglove treatment as they pitched into several decades of horrific and barbaric repression.

After officially dissolving the Tibetan government, the Chinese systematically crushed resistance with executions, imprisonment or deportation to labour camps. Monasteries were mostly emptied, their estates confiscated and any remaining monks put to work in the fields.

Tibetan society was divided into classes ranging from serf-owner to serf. This process was supported by 'study' meetings or the dreaded 'struggle sessions' (*thamzing*) which pitted Tibetans against each other in an atmosphere of utter terror.

In September 1965, the Chinese managed to mobilise a few photogenic smiles for the official inauguration of the Autonomous Region of Xizang (Tibet) – the actual region designated by this name was (and is) a truncated shadow of Tibet's former self. Within a year, the Cultural Revolution had arrived and there was no more smiling.

The Cultural Revolution & Its Aftermath
It is unlikely that a clear account of this period will ever surface since it was marked by diabolical chaos in which there were no long-term winners, just survivors of a holocaust.

Red Guards, inflamed by Maoist rhetoric, stormed into Tibet like bulls in a china shop. Much of the damage to monasteries had – contrary to Chinese accounts – occurred *before* the Cultural Revolution, but a fanatical new campaign launched against the 'Four Olds' (tradition, thought, culture and customs) was intended as a final blow to the last traces of religion in Tibet. Numerous groups of Red Guards engaged in political jousting until they formed opposing moderate and radical factions which eventually drew support and arms from the PLA. During bloody fighting, Tibetans or Tibetan interests were used as a pretext so that these factions could assert their respective claims to power.

The Tibetan economy, once self-sufficient, was subjugated to Chinese needs. The forced introduction of communes was accompanied by intensive farming methods and the absurd directive to grow winter wheat (a Chinese staple food) instead of barley (the Tibetan staple). Soon, exhausted soil and successive crop failures led to widespread starvation amongst Tibetans. As the economy collapsed, yet more campaigns were devised to reform thought or weed out counter-revolutionaries.

Although the PLA had officially regained control over the Red Guards by 1969, the abuse of power in Tibet continued unchecked into the late '70s.

Into the '80s
By 1979, the death of Mao and the break-up of the Gang of Four had produced a more liberal approach to government. Embarrassed by foreign news reports and the criticisms from visiting delegations of Tibetan exiles, the Chinese shipped off CCP General Secretary Hu Yaobang with a high-ranking entourage to inspect Tibet in 1980. What Hu saw shocked him into swift action: all policy requirements on taxation, agriculture and religious worship were immediately ordered 'relaxed, relaxed and relaxed again'. Hu also made a revealing promise to 'restore

the Tibetan economy to its pre-1959 level'. (It is ironic to note that Hu fell from grace in 1987 and became a Party scapegoat for the Tibetan unrest of 1988 which was partly blamed on his 'relaxation' policies.)

Between 1980-85, attempts were made to follow this softer line and redress the 'leftist errors' of the '60s and '70s.

The main nonevent of 1985 was the 20th anniversary of the Tibet Autonomous Region. Apart from banning the Western press from the region, the Chinese emphasised the peaceful nature of the event with a tight military blanket, including sharpshooters on the roof of the Potala. After defusing a bomb discovered in the local telex office, the festivities were orchestrated by and for the 200-strong delegation of Chinese officials who arrived in Lhasa to deliver speeches and gifts of tea, silk and no less than 90,000 alarm clocks for the Tibetan people (wake-up call for the Party?).

In a bid to counter criticism of their policies and, probably more importantly, to generate tourist dollars, the Chinese opened up Tibet not only to group tours but also to independent travellers. The resulting interchange taught Westerners a lot more about Tibetans and vice-versa.

In late 1987 the situation changed quite dramatically when Tibetans in Lhasa gave vent to their feelings about the Chinese and their policies. A series of demonstrations became a virtual uprising. Chinese security forces reportedly opened fire on the demonstrators, many of whom were monks from the monasteries around Lhasa. Both sides suffered casualties and at least one police station was reduced to a smoking pile of rubble. The response of the Chinese authorities was swift: Lhasa was swamped with plain-clothes and uniformed security, who put an abrupt end to the uprising. The embarrassment of foreign press coverage was neatly solved when all members of the foreign media covering events in Lhasa were unceremoniously booted back into China.

In March 1988 during the Monlam (New Year) Festival more unrest occurred with several deaths of Tibetans and Chinese. The outraged Chinese quickly clamped hundreds of monks in jail and started interrogating those responsible. In December 1988, there was an incident with more shootings in Lhasa.

On a brighter note, in June 1988 the Dalai Lama addressed the European Parliament in Strasbourg and made a proposal for a negotiated settlement with China over the Tibet question. Sketching what basically amounted to an autonomous Tibet within China, the key points of his proposal were:

• Tibet's foreign policy would still be Beijing's responsibility.
• Government would be based on a constitution or basic law.
• Government would comprise a popularly elected chief executive, a bi-cameral legislature and an independent legal system.
• Tibet would form part of a demilitarised zone, but China would maintain the right to keep military facilities in Tibet for defence purposes until neutrality was established.

The response from China was negative as was its response to an earlier Five Point Peace Plan presented by the Dalai Lama to the US Congress in September 1987. This plan called for the establishment of Tibet as a sanctuary of peace in the troubled Himalayan region, ensuring human and economic rights for the Tibetan people, and protecting the whole of the Tibetan plateau as an ecological preserve.

One chink of bright light was the news of the award of the Nobel Peace Prize to the Dalai Lama in 1989 which prompted a phenomenal outburst of Tibetan rejoicing – much to the chagrin of the perplexed Chinese government. The dismal pattern of riots, repression, and torture has continued into the early '90s.

There are still hopes for negotiation but the gap between the two sides is as wide as ever.

Tibet Today

Recent events, including the 1987-88 riots which have echoed into the '90s, have given the question of Tibet far wider coverage in the world media.

The Chinese continue to print fulsome praise of their achievements in Tibet while the Tibetans remain dissatisfied with their lot.

Economic reform has raised the average per capita income to between US$63 and US$110 per annum. Even by Chinese standards this is still low, but it does allow Tibetans enough food and even a bicycle or other consumer goods.

Certainly the most pressing problem facing Tibetans is that of the transfer of Chinese population into Tibetan areas. This sinocisation of the Tibetans is taking place at a rapid pace. Already, the population in Lhasa and Shigatse is predominantly Chinese and many parts of Eastern Tibet are heavily populated by Chinese. Settlers are encouraged with special loans, guaranteed jobs and housing, generous home leave allowance and higher salaries than in the rest of China.

Constraints on religion appear superficially to have been relaxed. Although several hundred monasteries are being rebuilt, the majority of these are being reconstructed through Tibetan efforts and these are subject to the approval of the Bureau of Religious Affairs. This bureau encourages a religious infrastructure to suit the needs of tourism and discourages the teaching that would lead to a serious propagation of religion.

Foreign Exploration

Tibet has always maintained a fascination for Western travellers. Apart from explorers and adventurers it has also attracted missionaries, map makers, plant lovers, panda hunters, military expeditions and cranks.

The first Westerners to appear on the scene were Portuguese missionaries who set up a mission in Tibet in the early 17th century. In 1661 two Jesuit priests visited Lhasa and were followed in 1716 by their colleagues Desideri and Freyre. Rivalry between Jesuits and Capuchins soon gave way to opposition from the Tibetan sects. By 1745 the Westerners had all been expelled.

In 1774, the Englishman George Bogle was sent by the British East India Company to Shigatse to research trade opportunities. Bogle met with the Panchen Lama and married one of his sisters.

The 19th century saw a tightening of the Chinese hold over Tibet. The Russian and British empires suspected each other of plans to invade Tibet. The Tibetan response was to shut the doors even tighter.

In the early 19th century the eccentric traveller Thomas Manning spent several months in Lhasa. Manning included in his baggage a pair of ice skates and spent much of his time trying his luck as an impromptu physician.

By 1865, the British were intent on mapping Tibet. Using specially trained Indian surveyors as spies, the terrain was mapped in secret. Disguised as traders or pilgrims, these pundits, as they were called, employed special rosaries and prayer wheels in their work.

Towards the turn of the century, Lhasa became a major goal for those intent on fathoming the unknown, writing a best seller or simply fulfilling a dream. The renowned Russian explorer Przwalski tried three times to reach Lhasa from the north but was unable to succeed. The American diplomat William Rockhill tried in 1889 disguised as a Mongolian, but was deserted by his guides.

Mr St G Littledale set off for Lhasa in 1895 accompanied by his wife, nephew and small dog. After braving severe storms and losing pack animals, the little band was stopped just short of Lhasa. Despite the offer of a bribe they were turned back.

The Japanese Buddhist, Ekai Kawaguchi, did manage in 1899 to reach Lhasa via Mt Kailas and later wrote his story in *Three Years in Tibet*. The Tibetans who helped him were either executed or imprisoned.

In 1903-04 the British expedition under Colonel Younghusband charged into Tibet and forcibly imposed a treaty on the Tibetans. The British withdrew leaving behind trade agents and political officers to keep a firm eye on their interests in Tibet to the exclusion of other nationalities.

Sven Hedin, the great Swedish explorer, made numerous attempts to enter Lhasa without success. Losing interest in Lhasa, Sven Hedin switched his attention to mapping southern and Western Tibet, particularly the region around Mt Kailas.

The first European woman to reach Lhasa was the French Buddhist, Alexandra David Neel, who disguised herself as a beggar. During WW II two Austrian mountaineers, Heinrich Harrer and Peter Aufschnaiter, escaped from a prisoner-of-war camp in India to Tibet and Lhasa where they spent several years. Harrer eventually wrote a best seller, *Seven Years in Tibet*.

Between the '50s and '70s the few foreigners who gained access to Tibet were mostly carefully vetted journalists. With the opening of Tibet in the '80s, various Westerners have begun to traverse the country on foot, on the back of a donkey or by yak. The blank spaces on the map are rapidly dwindling.

GEOGRAPHY

Almost as large as Western Europe in area, Tibet has borders with India, Nepal, Sikkim, Bhutan and Myanmar (Burma). The northern plateau of Tibet is called Chang Tang, a rocky, arid desert stretching 1300 km from west to east at an average altitude of 4000 metres and comprising nearly half of the country. It is bounded to the north by the Kunlun and Tanggula mountains beyond which lies the Qaidam Basin; to the west a barrier is formed by the Karakoram and Great Himalaya mountain ranges. The Chang Tang has no river systems; merely brackish lakes which are the remnants of the Tethys Sea which covered Asia Minor some 100 million years ago.

The south-eastern part of Tibet is closed off by mountain ranges running north to south and divided by three of the major rivers of Asia: the Yangtze (at 6300 km the longest river in China), which continues across China to Shanghai; the Mekong which enters Laos and Thailand; and the Salween which runs south into Myanmar.

The Kailas mountain range runs east from above Manasarovar Lake and is separated from the Himalaya by the Brahmaputra (Yarlung Zangbo) River, which flows east through the lowland valleys of southern Tibet. In the south-west, near Mt Kailas, are the sources of four major rivers: the Indus, which flows westward across Kashmir to Pakistan; the Brahmaputra, which flows east, joins the Lhasa River and drops down into north-eastern India; the Sutlej, which flows south to western India; and the Ganges, which flows south and across northern India. The Yellow River rises in the Bayan Har mountains in north-eastern Tibet (or rather Qinghai Province) and continues 5460 km across the north of China to empty just south of Tianjin.

The largest lakes in Tibet are Manasarovar, in the west; Tengri Nor (Nam Tso) in the north-west; Yamdrok Tso in Central Tibet; and Qinghai Lake (Koko Nor) in the north-east (Qinghai Province).

CLIMATE

In southern and eastern Tibet, the Himalaya act as a barrier against the rain-bearing monsoons, and rainfall decreases as you travel north. The central region of Tibet sees only 25 to 50 cm of rain a year (Sikkim, by contrast, sees some 500 cm). In the north and west of Tibet rainfall becomes even scarcer, but fewer than 100 days in the year are frost-free and temperatures plummet as low as -40℃. Northern monsoons can sweep across the plains for days on end, often whipping up duststorms, sandstorms, snowstorms, or (rare) rainstorms.

Temperatures can vary from below zero during the early morning and evening to a sizzling 38℃ at midday. Snowfall is far less common in Tibet than the name 'Land of Snows' implies, and the sun is quick to melt any snow that does fall. In the summer, the snowline in the north and east lies between 5000 and 6000 metres; in the south, even higher at 6000 metres.

FLORA & FAUNA
Alpine Zone
This zone, from 5000 metres up to the permanent snowline, has plenty of hardy plant and animal life. Among the plants are saussurea, gentian, rock-jasmine and sandwort which are rare flowers with special forms and structures. Rock-jasmine and sandwort are cushion plants. A cushion plant has crowded stems and leaves, is wind-resistant, can keep and accumulate heat quicker under direct sunshine, and loses heat slower at night.

Lower forms of plants such as snow algae, glacial-lake algae, moss and lichen are well adapted to the alpine environment. Lichens can survive extremes of climate fatal to other plants and excrete acids to break down rock substances for a foothold. It takes lichens about 25 years to grow to a diameter of two cm and some have been known to live up to 4500 years. Known as the 'pioneer plant', the lichen forms large colonies and prepares rock surfaces and soils for colonisation by other plants, especially the mosses. The acid excreted by the usnea, a low-altitude lichen, is an excellent antibacterial substance. Lichen acid is also used as a fixer to control the evaporation of industrial perfumes.

Animal life in this zone includes the alpine wild goat or ibex and the Himalayan marmot (its local name is 'snow pig') which scurries around satisfying an enormous appetite for food (which is stored as fat in preparation for hibernation). Brown bears roam this zone in search of marmots which they catch by digging into their burrows with their strong forelegs. The snow-grouse stays up around the snowline even during the most bitter winters.

Among the insects is the sandwort noctuid, a tiny moth, clothed with fluff, which is a bad flier. During high winds it folds its wings and lies on its side in the shelter of cushion plants. There is also an alpine grasshopper with defunct wings. Highly prized in Tibetan and Chinese medicine, the Aweto (Chinese Caterpillar Fungus or Cordyceps) is a brownish caterpillar three to four cm long that looks like a silkworm. A precious tonic made from it is supposed to be good for debility, coughing, lumbago, and other complaints.

Although it was believed for a long time that no birds flew over the high peaks of the Himalayas, griffon vultures have been seen flying at 9000 metres near the summit of Everest. Yellow-billed choughs are often seen at Everest base camps at about 7000 metres. Snow pigeons and bar-headed geese have also been sighted flying over peaks at 8300 metres.

Grassland Zone
The grassland zone extends up to 5000 metres and the vegetation varies according to the soil moisture. In the grassland, 4500 metres and upwards, apart from spear grass, glacier sedge and big-ear sedge, there are other plants such as dune blue-grass and pennisetum which are found on the sand and gravel deposits of dried lake basins. Rushes are often found in the marshlands near rivers or lakes. On the dry slopes, the drought-resistant pea-shrub develops into large clusters of cushions. On scree slopes there are cold and wind-resistant plants such as dwarf stone pines, rock-jasmine and sandwort.

Saltwater lakes of the grasslands contain a scaleless carp (known locally as 'naked carp') and several species of stone loach, also scaleless. During the summer many of the islands in rivers and lakes are visited by birds like the bar-headed goose, ruddy shelduck and brown-head gull which breed in large numbers. The most common birds in this zone are the snowfinch and the Tibetan rosefinch.

Wild asses (*kiang*) and gazelles graze the pastures together with marmots, pikas and other rodents.

Forest Zones

The dwarf-twisted forest is a zone which occurs at approximately 4000 metres and has different types of vegetation depending on exposure to sun and moisture. The higher this zone extends, the stronger the wind – which leads to the predominance of dwarf-like rhododendrons which hug the ground with twisted branches. On the shady and wet slopes evergreen rhododendrons bloom in vermilion, pink and yellow in May and June. An essence made from Himalayan rhododendrons (of which there are at least 300 species) is an excellent cure for bronchitis. On the sunnier slopes there are species of juniper.

The snow grouse inhabits these dwarf-twisted groves as does the pika, a rodent a little smaller than a hare. Pipits, robins and wheatears are birds typical of this zone.

From about 4000 metres downwards there is a zone with needle-leaved and deciduous trees. Different types of trees favour different altitudes. From 3700 to 4000 metres birches, rhododendrons and other deciduous trees prosper. In the lower part of the needle forest, the Tibetan fir is abundant until the zone grades off into mountain ashes, campbell maples and other broad-leaved trees. In the needle-leaved areas the forest is inhabited by musk deer and in the broad-leaved areas by the Asiatic black bear.

A mixed needle and broad-leaved forest zone occurs between approximately 3100 metres and 2500 metres. The predominant tree species are the Chinese hemlock (a needle-leaved tree) and the broad-leaved oak. Other species include the mountain ash, campbell maple, birch, hornbeam maple, holly, and wild peach. Shrubs and herbs

growing here include daphne (a shrub which provides pulp for high quality paper), Chinese magnolia vine, Jack-in-the-pulpit and ginseng.

In the warmer climate, monkeys (such as rhesus macaques and langurs) swing around the trees, and brilliantly coloured sunbirds extract nectar from blooms.

An evergreen broad-leaved forest zone occurs from approximately 2500 to 1600 metres – the upper part of the forest is dominated by the tropical oak, and the lower part has an abundance of lianas and specialised plant-forms. Species of medicinal herbs which thrive in this environment include seven-leaved grass, figwort or mock ginseng, and solomon seal. The roots, stems, leaves and flowers of the epiphytic fern (which grows on the daimyo oak) are all used for medicinal purposes. There is a tree which yields industrial oil, and a tree which produces varnish. The Machilus (laurel family), tropical oaks and camphor trees are prized for their fine timber. In the clearings, bamboos and Euphrates poplars thrive while red-abdomened squirrels, monkeys, rhesus macaques and langurs leap around. Red pandas and barking deer are also found here.

A recent survey by Chinese zoologists in Tibet pointed out the urgent need for nature reserves to conserve the top 12 protected species which include the wild yak, Asiatic wild ass, snow leopard and black-necked crane. Apparently the black-necked cranes have been decimated by the practice of collecting their eggs for use as a delicacy; only 1000 cranes remain.

The Wild & the Woolly

For many years there have been reports in the Himalaya of strange humans, under such aliases as the Yeti, Wild Man, *Yeren* (in Chinese), *Migyu* (in Tibetan), Abominable Snowman, Hairy Man, and Big Foot.

China now has its very own Wild Man Research Society which staged a successful exhibition in September 1985 of a Hairy Man which was, in fact, a rare macaque or short-tailed monkey (the first captured in 100 years), 1.06 metres high and weighing 92.5 kg. This Hairy Man was caught in Xining County (Hunan Province) after harassing two girls and was then taken on a tour of neighbouring counties as a curiosity. The Wild Man Research Society recently published a report which considered the natural habitat of the Wild Man to be the virgin forests of the Himalayas at about 4500 metres. The Abominable Snowman may be a Wild Man who occasionally forages above the snowline. The report cites several eye-witness accounts.

Nai Qiong, a 40-year-old Tibetan from Chengtang Village near Dinggyê in Southern Tibet, went on a hunt in the forests in 1968. One evening he decided to stay overnight in a cave large enough to accommodate four people. After his meal he lay down next to a fire. At about midnight he was awakened by shouts and somebody/thing throwing stones at him. At the entrance to the cave stood an extremely tall animal with a body covered in white fur and its two eyes gleaming brightly in the light of the fire. The animal continued throwing rocks and emitting strange, menacing sounds. Somebody/thing was also throwing rocks from above and there was more grunting coming from the surrounding area. Nai Qiong, not surprisingly, was scared witless and threw all the wood he could find onto the fire. The animal was obviously scared of the fire and stayed away, finally departing at the first light of dawn.

Another story concerns an official at the village of Boqü which is close to Zhangmu at an altitude of 2300 metres and has a subtropical climate. In the autumn of 1976, this official was asleep in his wooden house when he was wakened at midnight. What he saw by the light of the moon, standing in front of his bed, was a tall Wild Woman covered in chestnut-coloured fur with two massive breasts. She was, according to the official, eyeing him with what was clearly a strong desire to mate. The frightened official leapt out of bed and ran to his colleague's room. They both returned and although the Wild Woman was exceptionally strong, she meekly submitted to capture and was tied to a post. In the morning she had slipped the ropes and fled.

In 1972, a group of PLA soldiers were out on patrol in dense forest when one member of the patrol became separated from the others, who suddenly heard his screams. When they raced back to look for him, he had disappeared. Various attempts to find him proved fruitless. Several months later, another group out on patrol suddenly heard shouts coming from a cave about 50 metres above them. At the entrance to the cave they saw a man shouting who, in desperation, then jumped and was killed instantly when his head hit a rock. The patrol examined the body and discovered it was their missing colleague. His uniform was in tatters and his hands and feet were covered with strips of animal skin. While they were examining the body, a Wild Woman appeared on the scene but swung off on a liana when she saw what had happened.

The report summed up its findings: the Wild Man is stronger than modern man and averages 1.8 to 1.9 metres in height. The body is covered with thick fur which can be 12 cm long and either chestnut-brown or golden-brown in colour. The face is not covered with hair. The feet measure 35 cm and the eyes are extremely bright. The body exudes a strong smell of garlic. The faeces occur in much larger quantities than that of modern man and contain animal bones, seeds and fruit peel. Wild Men climb trees, swing easily from branch to branch and can walk erect. They live in natural caves in the forests but do not know how to use fire and are scared by it. Their main sources of food are small mammals and forest fruits and vegetables. They possess feelings and express fear, satisfaction or anger with special noises. They appear to have an interest in including people in their sex life.

GOVERNMENT

Before the Chinese occupation, the Dalai Lama was the supreme religious and temporal head of the government of Tibet. During the Dalai Lama's absence or minority, a regent (*gyaltsab*) appointed by the Tibetan National Assembly, ruled on his behalf. Next in line were two prime ministers (*silons*), one a monk and one a layman. Beneath them was the secular administration, the Council of Ministers (*Kashag*), composed of four ministers (*kalons*), one of whom was a monk, the rest being secular officials.

Parallel to the Kashag was the ecclesiastical administration, the Department of Religious Affairs (*Tse Yigtsang*), headed by the Lord Chamberlain (*Chikyab Khenpo*) and four secretary-generals (*drungyik chemo*) – the entire departmental staff was composed of monks. The secretary-generals dealt with the affairs of all monastic officials from their selection, training, appointment and transfer, to dismissal. They also served, together with four heads (*tsipon*) of the Finance & Revenue departments, as joint chairmen of the Tibetan National Assembly (*Tsongdu Gyezom*), the highest deliberative body of the Tibetan State, composed of 350 members. The other assembly was the Working Committee (*Tsongdu Rakdhu*) composed of approximately 60 members of the National Assembly. The decisions of the assemblies were forwarded to the Dalai Lama for acceptance or rejection. At regional level there were seven major administrative units with individual governors. Below them there were more than 240 districts (*dzongs*) each with a district-commissioner (*dzongpon*).

Since 1965, Tibet has been administered as an autonomous region (*zizhiqü*) of China. The region is divided into five prefectures – Ngari (Ali), Shigatse, Shannan, Nagqu, Chamdo – and 71 counties with Lhasa maintaining the status of a municipality. The old provinces of Amdo and Kham have been divided up into Qinghai Province and autonomous prefectures in Gansu, Sichuan and Yunnan provinces. The most important bodies, effectively in charge of Tibet, are the Communist Party Committee and the People's Government. The Political Consultative Committee is little more than a rubber stamp outfit.

In December 1988, Mr Wu Jinghua, first party secretary since 1985, officially retired for 'health' reasons after the unrest in Tibet, but other sources hint that he was considered to be a 'rightist deviationist'. He was replaced by Mr Hu Jintao, a former party leader of the Communist Youth League.

ECONOMY

The events of the '60s and '70s – the formation of communes, the redistribution of land and animals, the ban on barter, and the attempt to grow winter wheat (a Chinese food) instead of the traditional barley – brought about economic collapse in Tibet. The Chinese reluctantly started to admit this in 1980 after a visit by top-ranking Hu Yaobang, who was clearly shocked. As a result, new policies were formed: the household has been restored as the basic unit of production; 90% of agricultural families have been given land leases for between 30 and 50 years; communal animal stocks have been broken up and 95% of families have received animals to raise; the winter wheat policy has been abandoned and barley, the crop Tibetans have grown for hundreds of years, reinstated; and free markets, tourism and cross-border trade with Nepal and India have been encouraged.

At present, a massive capital works programme is in progress, requiring over US$215 million to be spent on 43 special building projects including generating stations, hotels, libraries, schools, art museums, trade centres and children's centres. Nevertheless, economic policy in Tibet was blasted in a critique which appeared in a Shanghai economic journal in 1985. It stated that Tibet had received more than US$3 billion in subsidies since 1952 and now had nothing to show for it. Like an anaemic patient requiring constant blood transfusions, Tibet has become totally dependent; every yuan created in Tibet swallows 1.2 yuan in subsidies. Together with the soaring costs of bureaucracy (dominated by Han administration) this is hardly a recipe for recovery. The national target in China for the year 2000 is to quadruple output; in the case of Tibet, this would require, at the present rate, more transfusions of state funds to the tune of US$1.53 billion.

Agriculture & Forestry

Tibet has about 228,000 hectares of farmland (limited by climate and elevation). The main crops are highland barley, wheat, rapeseed, broad beans, buckwheat, corn and rice. Although wooden ploughs and yaks are still used, mechanised equipment is being introduced. Estimates put the number of tractors in the region at 10,000. Irrigation systems and reservoirs are being built and proved their value during an unprecedented drought

in 1983. Strong sunlight produces extraordinary yields: cabbages weighing 28 kg; potatoes weighing two kg each; 6000 kg of barley per half hectare compared with a normal yield of 2000 kg.

The forestry industry is now concentrating on the extraction of lumber from the forests along the middle and lower parts of the Brahmaputra (Yarlung Zangbo) River, which cover 6.32 million hectares and represent 1.43 billion cubic metres of timber. The various vegetation belts contain a wealth of species including many varieties of pine, spruce and fir. The main load carried by truck convoys leaving Tibet is timber – in phenomenal quantities.

Animal Husbandry

Tibet is one of the largest pastureland areas in China with over 13.3 million hectares providing for 21 million head of livestock including yak, cattle, Tibetan sheep, goats, horses, mules and donkeys. Yaks, the 'ships of the plateau', are the mainstay of the traditional Tibetan economy. China has approximately 12 million yaks, 85% of the world's total. In the Tibetan Autonomous Region alone, there are four million. In China, the main areas where these comical creatures are found are on the Qinghai (Tsinghai)-Tibet plateau and in parts of Gansu, Xinjiang, Sichuan and Yunnan provinces.

There are three types of yak: the wild yak, the *dzo* (a cross between cattle and female yaks) and the domesticated yak. A wild, adult male yak weighs one ton, double the weight of a domestic one. The *dzo* is docile, strong and hardy so it is valuable for farm work, riding and as a pack animal. Yaks supply milk; a mature female yak (*dri*) produces milk for four to seven months of the year, with a higher fat content than cow's milk. Yak meat is tender and lean and is the principal meat eaten by Tibetans in cooked, wind-dried, semi wind-dried and almost raw forms. Yak dung is collected and dried for use as fuel. The hair and the hide are used for making thread, blankets, clothing, boots, tents and boats.

Mining & Mineral Resources

Tibet has an extraordinary wealth of minerals which have hardly been exploited.

Tibet's untapped mineral resources include oil-shale, asphalt, coal, iron, manganese, magnesium, tin, copper, lead, zinc, salt, arsenic, borax, sulphur, mica, graphite, talc, gypsum, jade, radium, and titanium. The world's largest lithium mine is in northern Tibet with a lithium deposit amounting to half the world's known total. There are also deposits of uranium which are, naturally, of crucial importance.

Industry

Before the 1950s, industry was only really present in the form of a mint and an ammunition factory in Lhasa, and various regional handicraft centres which produced religious products. Tibet now has 215 small and medium-size industries employing 69,000 workers, producing over 80 kinds of products and accounting for 20% of total production in Tibet. The Chinese justify the high percentage of Han Chinese workers (between 30% and 50%) with the excuse that most Tibetans are illiterate and have no more than four years schooling, thus making it necessary for them to be trained by Han workers.

The Chinese government has recently announced plans for a massive drive to develop western China. One popular proposal is that western China (covering over 60% of the country's total land mass but supporting only 28.5% of the total population), should first provide the eastern part of China with raw materials to support eastern industry and then set up their own manufacturing industry later.

Linzhi, 440 km to the east of Lhasa, is a much vaunted industrial centre and its showpiece is the Linzhi Wool Textile Plant. This factory moved to Linzhi from Shanghai with 642 workers and technicians in 1966, and produces copious amounts of woollen blankets, woollen fabric and knitting wool. The present workforce numbers about 1300; about 50% are Tibetan.

The industry around Lhasa includes

power plants, machinery plants, printing shops, chemical factories, woollen textile plants, leather processing factories, grain processing factories and carpet factories.

The present emphasis is on light industry, individual businesses, free markets and more autonomy for management in order to produce goods for consumption by the region's own population. The handicraft industry, producing articles such as aprons, rugs, butter-tea urns and yak saddles, is provided with state subsidies for gold and silver, exemption from taxes and low-interest loans.

Energy

Hydroelectric power stations are presently under construction in many parts of Tibet to tap part of the enormous power generating capacity of rivers originating in Tibet. There are plans to build the world's largest hydroelectric power station, at the turning point of the Brahmaputra (Yarlung Zangbo) River, with a generating capacity of 40 million kilowatts.

The exceptionally high altitude in Tibet creates intense solar radiation. The solar radiation observatory set up on the East Rongbuk glacial basin at 6000 metres has measured a direct solar radiation coefficient seldom found in the world – 1.8 calories per sq cm per minute. If the solar energy striking a square metre was concentrated, it would boil 10 kg of water from 0°C to 100°C in less than an hour! Lhasa averages 3000 hours of sunshine annually and solar energy is already in use. Portable solar hot-water heaters and solar ovens are made and used locally.

High-temperature hot springs are found all over Tibet. At Yangbajain, three geothermal generators can now supply Lhasa with over 8000 kilowatt hours of energy. Wind energy is also being explored. Two wind belts have been identified and experimental wind power stations near Nagqu have proved successful.

The Military

A factor often missed by reports (particularly Chinese ones) on Tibet is the cost of the continued military presence. Estimates put the number of PLA troops in Tibet at between 100,000 and half a million. Roads used almost solely by gigantic military convoys and garrisons in border areas are a reminder of Tibet's strategic importance. There are at least nine military airfields (Gonggar, near Lhasa, functions as the sole civilian one), 11 radar stations and three nuclear bases. It is reported that Tibet has become one of China's largest Inter-continental Ballistic Missile (ICBM) bases, capable of targeting India and other areas near the Indian Ocean. In August 1990, Swedish seismologists detected an underground nuclear explosion at Lop Nor, the Chinese nuclear testing site inside the borders of Xinjiang, but close to Tibet. This site has been repeatedly used for nuclear testing from the 1950s onwards and Chinese officials referred to 'severe atmospheric pollution' when Tibetans were evacuated after a test at this site in March 1982.

POPULATION & PEOPLE

Estimates for the population of Tibet vary considerably depending on which part of Tibet and which people (Chinese or Tibetan) are under discussion. One version sees 7.5 million Chinese facing six million Tibetans; another more credible version estimates the Tibetan population at four million, of whom nearly two million live within the Tibet autonomous region. The remaining two million Tibetans live in autonomous prefectures in Qinghai, Gansu, Sichuan and Yunnan.

An estimated 100,000 Tibetan refugees live outside Tibet, mostly in India, Nepal, Bhutan, Sikkim and Western countries like Switzerland, Canada and USA.

Figures for the Chinese presence in Tibet are impossible to verify, but should include a massive military contingent, construction squads, entrepreneurs and settlers.

Although the origins of the Tibetan people are uncertain, it's probably safe to assume they belong to the Mongoloid race. There are also several groups ethnically related to the

Tibetans: the Monba and Lhoba live on the Bhutan-Tibetan border; the Qiang live in northern Sichuan.

ARTS
Dance & Drama
One of the greatest spectacles in Tibetan performing tradition is the Cham, the sacred dance theatre of Lamaist Buddhism, which Victorian travellers disapprovingly referred to as 'devil dances'. The dances are traditionally performed in a monastic courtyard on special days such as Padmasambhava's birthday or the day before the Tibetan New Year's Eve. A number of stock characters like the Black Hat Priest, the skeleton-like Lords of the Cemeteries, the stag-headed messenger of Yama, Lord of Death, and often Yama himself, make their appearances in nearly all Cham performances. All the characters are masked except the Black Hat Priest. Most of the costumes are large and flowing with wide sleeves and are made of rich brocade and silks.

Like all good drama, Cham performances may be appreciated on a number of different levels. For the highest practitioner, they can be a kind of meditation in movement. By his actions, the dancer – aided by chants, music, and costumes – perceives himself as the deity he represents. Every gesture (*mudra* in Sanskrit) he makes is not only symbolic but is meant to have power in itself. Padmasambhava is said to have made rocks explode and set the Emperor of Tibet's robe aflame by the power of his *mudras*. The dancer could also consider his performance an offering to the Buddhist deities.

In contrast to Cham, the Tibetan folk opera tradition, *Lhamo*, was secular and performances were based on complete stories taken from history, legends, and biographies of saints and lamas. The stories of the plays are interspersed with comic interludes in which even sacred religious institutions like the oracle and monks are made fun of.

The opera troupes that toured Tibet at certain seasons of the year were, with the exception of a company from Lhasa, mainly recruited from the tillers of the soil. The Dalai Lama hosted an annual opera festival in Lhasa in the early autumn to which 12 different opera companies from all over Tibet came to compete.

Another such performing tradition came from Eastern Tibet. Known as *repas* (yogis), the men and women of these troupes performed fast acrobatic dances and brief scenes from the life of Milarepa.

For further information, see *Zlos-gar: Performing Traditions of Tibet* edited by Jamyang Norbu, Library of Tibetan Works & Archives, Dharamsala.

Music
Like most things in Tibet, Tibetan music can be conveniently divided into two categories: the secular and the religious. The differences between the two are distinct and unmistakable. Secular music was generally of a folk kind. There were specific songs not only for celebrating weddings, drinking beer, and courting women but also for ploughing, harvesting, building, begging, throwing dice, telling riddles, doing one's accounts (on the Tibetan counting table), or preparing for battle. These songs could be accompanied by the music of the Tibetan lute (*dra-nyen*), the two-stringed fiddle (*piwang*) and the spiked fiddle (*genja*). Other instruments like the hammer dulcimer (*gyu-mang*) and the transverse flute could also accompany singers but were generally confined to the music of the Lhasa *nangma* ensembles.

The singing and recitation of the famous Gesar epics was popular in Kham or Eastern Tibet. Roving bards could sing and recite the epic for days. Songs in praise of Buddhism, or holy men, or sacred mountains were popular with Tibetans. Similar to St Francis of Assisi who took the words of the gospel and incorporated them in the Jongleur songs of medieval Europe, saints and lamas of Tibet like Mipham, Milarepa and the Sixth Dalai Lama expressed their spiritual feelings in the melodies of the ordinary Tibetan.

A genre of song in Lhasa called 'Street Songs' (*trom-gyur shay*) served as an effective channel for open political and social criticism. These songs lampooned the vice, folly, and misdeeds of the mighty and summed up important political and social events, often with biting sarcasm and irony.

Over the centuries, the clergy have not only developed a rich body of sacred texts and ritual liturgical melodies, but also devised an ecclesiastical music which is tonally quite different from the secular. They have developed a notational system, *yang-yig*, as well.

A wide variety of musical instruments, very different from secular instruments which are mostly of the stringed variety, are used to accompany religious chanting and the sacred tantric dances known as Cham. The instruments generally used are the long trumpets (*dhung-chen*), double-reed oboes (*gyaling*), handled drums (*nga*), conch shells (*dhung-kar*), waisted drums (*damaru*), thigh-bone trumpets (*kang-ling*), and cymbals (*bub, silnyen, ting-shag*) of many sizes and tones.

Literature

Most ancient Tibetan literature is devoted to translations of Buddhist texts from India. These books are regarded as sacred since the book is a symbol of Buddha's word. Most of the books are written on local, handmade paper with illuminations in the centre or at the ends of the page. The wooden covers are carved on the outside and painted on the inside. Some of the most valuable books are written on black paper with gold or silver

script and are illustrated with miniature paintings.

The two most important collections of Buddhist scriptures are the Kanjur and Tenjur. The Kanjur, or 'Translation of the Buddha Word', contains works supposedly representing Buddha's words and is divided into six sections containing 1055 titles in 108 volumes. The sections are: Tantra, Prajnaparamita, Ratnakuta, Avatamsaka, Sutra and Vinaya. The Tenjur, or 'Translation of Teachings', is a collection of 225 volumes with 3626 texts divided into three groups: Stotras (hymns of praise), commentaries on Tantras, and commentaries on Sutras.

Other religious works include the *Collection of Sayings of the Kadampa Saints*, *The Jewel Ornament of Liberation* by Gampopa (a disciple of Milarepa) and *The Great Account of the Stages on the Path* by Tsong Khapa.

Popular literature includes heroic epics such as *Gesar* (reportedly the world's longest historical poem), legends of the saints, fairy tales and the *Hundred Thousand Songs of Milarepa*. Storytellers used to be a common sight. Lama-manis, a type of mendicant traveller, would move from place to place showing *thangkas* illustrating Buddha's life and reciting stories (sometimes also on popular themes) in a sing-song voice all day. Gesartellers were often illiterate but gifted with incredible powers of memory, and capable of reciting stories in minute detail for days or even weeks.

Architecture

The nomads (Tibetan: *drokpa*) live in yak-hair tents which are high and spacious with room for six or more people. Near the entrance is a stone kitchen range which serves as a campfire. The smoke is let out through an aperture in the roof. Some camps are protected by a low wall of stone.

A standard Tibetan house is one or two storeys high with a flat roof and floors of earth, beaten hard on a bedding of brushwood. Heavy logs and wooden pillars support the floors. The outside walls are made of earth or stone (round stones are not used) laid on mortar made from mud. Windows may use glass or waxed paper and are protected by wooden shutters. Living quarters are usually above the ground floor. A more opulent house could be three or more storeys high with panelled walls, and ceilings and pillars painted with ornate pictorial designs. ·

In areas in Eastern and Southern Tibet, such as the Chumbi Valley, where sloping roofs are constructed with pine shingles kept in place by stones, the houses bear a resemblance to Swiss chalets.

Painting & Sculpture

Tibetan painting and sculpture is religious in inspiration and is renowned for its *thangkas*, mandalas and statues. Patrons, usually monasteries or wealthy laypeople, employed painters and sculptors, who were often monks, to create artworks for ritual use or private devotion. The monks would often write commentaries on deities in the wide-ranging Tibetan pantheon and corresponding images were fashioned. The aim of the artist was not to be individually creative but to develop the traditional style he had learned. Many Tibetan works are anonymous; the painter worked according to iconographic pattern-books or consulted a lama who could locate the appropriate text.

The earliest influences on painting and sculpture in Tibet came with Buddhism during the reign of the Pala Dynasty in India creating the Pala-Tibetan style. Other influences, between the 14th and 16th centuries, came from Nepal and China and resulted in Tibeto-Nepalese and Sino-Tibetan styles.

The definitive work on the subject and an interesting read, as well, is *Tibetan Thangka Painting: Methods & Materials* by David & Janice Jackson.

CULTURE
Traditional Lifestyle

Marriage Traditionally, the compatibility of a couple was assessed by an astrologer and a lama. After the marriage contract was signed, there was an official ceremony at the bridegroom's home. The bride's family would then raise prayer flags on the roof of the bridegroom's home.

Amongst nomads it is customary for the parents of a son to start looking for a bride when he is about 18. Once a likely bride is found, a long series of visits are arranged and gifts like scarves, butter, cheese and meat are exchanged. If all goes well an astrologer is asked to fix an auspicious date for the marriage. On the day, the groom's family sends a group to the bride's home where her family pretends the visitors are unwelcome and uninvited. The bride's parents stay behind, while the bride leaves with the visitors to return to the groom's home on a specially decorated horse or even a white yak. On arrival at the groom's home, the bride pretends to be unhappy but finally accepts the gift of a pail of milk offered by her mother-in-law and flicks a drop of milk into the air for good luck. The marriage is concluded with a great feast. Snowfall during the marriage procession is considered an evil omen for the bridal pair.

The eldest brother's wife sometimes married the younger brothers as well, however, polyandry is rare now. It was practised previously on a limited scale, to ensure that a family's possessions and land remained undivided.

Burial Burial is performed, if possible, according to the advice of an astrologer who will assess which of the elements the body will return to – earth, air, fire, water or wood. Sky burial is the most common form. The body is blessed, tied up in a cloth in a sitting position, taken to a site out in the open on a mountainside and systematically cut up as food for the birds. The bones are pounded together with *tsampa* and this mixture is also left for the birds. Whatever the vultures leave uneaten is buried or burned. Burial in the earth is rare and is used only if the birds will not eat a body – a very inauspicious sign. Cremation is also a rare form of burial since wood is a scarce and expensive commodity in many parts of Tibet. Lamas may be cremated and their ashes placed in a chorten in their monastery. Water burial is reserved for small children and paupers. A wood burial requires the corpse to be placed in a hollow tree trunk. Embalming is reserved for high lamas.

Bardo Preferably before the moment of death, the dying person starts to receive last instructions for his passage towards rebirth, from a monk. According to the famous Tibetan scripture, *The Tibetan Book of the Dead*, between death and rebirth lies the world of Bardo which is divided into seven stages, each further subdivided into seven. During the 49 days of Bardo, the soul of the deceased, guided by monks, seeks to follow the right path towards liberation.

Jewellery & Dress Many Tibetans in Lhasa are adopting Western or Chinese clothing, but elsewhere traditional dress is still the norm and varies considerably from one part of Tibet to another. Men and women often wear the *chuba*, a heavy cloak made from sheepskin or woollen cloth which is tied at the waist with a broad cloth belt. Colourful boots of leather or felt with leather soles are also worn.

Nomad women often wear beautiful silver hair-bands studded with turquoise, coral and amber. Khampas normally wear their hair in two strands, plaited with red cord, wound around their heads. Head-gear varies regionally; felt stetsons (made in Tianjin) are popular, as are fox-fur hats.

Tibetans favour ornaments and wear pendants, necklaces, earrings (men normally only wear one), girdles, bracelets, charms, amulets and finger-rings made from a variety of materials such as silver, gold, coral, amber, turquoise, etc.

A popular talisman is the *gau* or portable shrine which houses the image of a deity, or mantras, or other small items. These miniature shrines can be found in nomad tents, monasteries, homes, and are often worn around the neck or fastened to a crossbelt, especially by travellers or pilgrims. The top is leaf-shaped, and through a window in the centre an image, wrapped in silk, of the owner's deity can be seen.

Popular talismans are based on the eight lucky Buddhist symbols: the Wheel of Dharma (the law), the Umbrella of Power and the Twin Golden Fishes (symbols of happiness), the Conch-Shell Trumpet (symbolising the spread of the doctrine), the Sacred Vase (containing the elixir of immortality), the Palbu (a mystic knot symbolising meditation), the Holy Lotus (symbolising Buddha and purity), and the Victory Banner (or canopy, symbolising the victory of Buddhism).

Tibetan Medicine

Tibetan medicine is an interesting combination of native healing tradition, ancient Indian medical theories, and Chinese apothecaric science. Ancient Greek influence has also been recognised.

Tibetan medicine is based on the central principle of maintaining the balance of the three 'humours' – wind, bile, and phlegm – in the human body. Imbalances in the humours are said to cause diseases. The most important diagnostic tools of a Tibetan doctor are pulse diagnosis and urine analysis. Pulse diagnosis in Tibetan medicine is an amazingly complex science involving the ability to distinguish the innumerable pulse types which provide information on every part and condition of the human body.

Moxabustion and 'Golden Needle' therapy, a kind of acupuncture, is also practised. Surgery was practised before the eighth century but was banned when the Emperor's mother died after an operation. Tibetan pharmacopoeia is also very rich. Many different kinds of plants and chemicals are used in Tibetan medicines.

Though China destroyed much Tibetan culture, it seems that Tibetan medicine has been made an exception. The old Tibetan Medical School in Lhasa has been expanded and various research and publication schemes undertaken. Tibetan medicine is only beginning to be known in the West though it is spreading in India and China. Two modern drugs based on old Tibetan formulae are currently being manufactured and distributed commercially in Switzerland.

For further information, see *Health through Balance* by Dr Yeshe Donden.

RELIGION

For centuries, Tibetans have followed their own forms of Buddhism which were a blend of Indian religion with an existing native religion. In spite of intense repression and persecution during the Cultural Revolution, religion is surfacing again as the focal point of Tibetan life.

Prior to the introduction of Buddhism, the native religion in Tibet was a form of shamanism called Bon, which relied on priests or shamans to placate spirits, gods and demons. According to Bon, the world was divided into three spheres: heaven, earth, and the underworld. Heaven was occupied by gods or Lha, Nagas were the masters of the earth, and the underworld was inhabited by a group of demons called Tsen. The centre of Bon religion appears to have been the Shang Shung Kingdom in Western Tibet.

Magic was a strong element of Bon and was used to control the spirits of mountain passes, soil, water and springs or sacred mountains. Animals and even humans were used in sacrificial rites; demonic forces were invoked or expelled through black magic.

With the arrival of Buddhism there began a long struggle for religious supremacy during which Bon adopted many Buddhist ideas.

The founder of Buddhism was Siddhartha Gautama, the son of King Suddhodana and Queen Mahamaya of the Sakya clan. He was born around 563 BC at Lumbini on the border of present-day Nepal and India.

In his 20s, Prince Siddhartha left his wife and newborn son to follow the path of an ascetic. He studied under several masters, but he remained dissatisfied and spent another six years undergoing the severest austerities. He gave a graphic account of himself: 'Because of so little nourishment, all my bones became like some withered creepers with knotted joints; my buttocks

like a buffalo's hoof; my backbone protruding like a string of balls...' Realising that this was not the right path for him, he gave up fasting and decided to follow his own path to enlightenment. He placed himself cross-legged under a Bodhi tree at Bodhgaya and went into deep meditation for 49 days. During the night of the full moon in May, at the age of 35, he became 'the enlightened or awakened one' – the Buddha.

Shortly afterwards, Buddha delivered his first sermon, *Setting in Motion the Wheel of Truth*, at the Deer Park near Sarnath. Then, as the number of his followers grew, he founded a monastic community and codified the principles according to which the monks should live. The Buddha continued to preach and travel for 45 years until his death at the age of 80 in 483 BC. To his followers, Buddha was also known as Sakyamuni (the sage of the Sakya clan). Buddhists believe that he is one of the many buddhas who appeared in the past – and that more will appear in the future.

Approximately 140 years after Buddha's death, the Buddhist community diverged into two schools: Hinayana (the Lesser Vehicle), and Mahayana (the Greater Vehicle). The essential difference between the two was that Hinayana supported those who strove for the salvation of the individual, whereas Mahayana supported those who strove for the salvation of all beings. Hinayana prospered in south India and later spread to Sri Lanka, Burma (now Myanmar), Thailand, Cambodia, Indonesia and Malaysia. Mahayana spread to Inner Asia, Mongolia, Siberia, Japan, China and Tibet.

Vajrayana Buddhism is a tradition associated with Mahayana, and is the form of Buddhism most often associated with Tibet. Vajrayana (the Diamond Vehicle, or Mantrayana, or Tantric Buddhism) recognises nirvana (the release from the cycle of mortal existence and rebirths) and samsara (the consequential succession of lives and rebirths) as propounded in the Mahayana tradition.

The aim of Vajrayana Buddhism is towards direct entry to nirvana within one

Top: Potala Palace - Lhasa (GW)
Bottom: Potala Palace - Lhasa (RS)

The 14th Dalai Lama (NC)

life rather than over the course of several lives.

The Introduction of Buddhism

Buddhism gained a firm foothold in Tibet during the reign of King Songtsen Gampo (circa 605-650 AD). Songtsen Gampo's two queens, Bhrikuti Devi from Nepal and Munshang Kongjo from China, were devout Buddhists. Their united persuasion led to the spread of Buddhist doctrine and the construction of the Ramoche and Jokhang temples. The king sent his minister, Thonmi Sambhota, to India to devise a Tibetan script and alphabet, thus opening the way to a systematic translation of Buddhist scriptures.

The Bon priests were not well disposed toward Buddhism although it had many similarities to their own practices and feared that their religion would be absorbed for this very reason. Skilful Bon interpretation of a smallpox epidemic in the 7th century, to which a royal queen had fallen victim, resulted in the expulsion of Indian Buddhist teachers and many of their Tibetan followers.

During the reign of King Trisong Detsen (755-797 AD), the power struggle reached a critical intensity between, on one hand, the imperial family and supporters of Buddhism, and on the other, the powerful alliance of the Tibetan aristocracy and the supporters of Bon. Although the Buddhist monks were superior to the Bon priests in doctrinal debate, they were no match for them when it came to magic. Seeing their power threatened by Santarakshita, an Indian scholar imported by Trisong Detsen, Bon priests seized on the occasion of the destruction of the palace on red hill (the early Potala) by lightning as a signal for violent opposition, and demanded that the new teacher return to India.

The Indian master who finally succeeded in introducing Tantric Buddhism was Padmasambhava (also known as Lopon Rinpoche). He founded Samye Monastery, with the first Tibetan Buddhist monks being ordained around 767 AD. Padmasambhava was said to have been born in a lotus bud, and then adopted by an Indian king. He renounced any claim to a throne, and was banished from his country. For many years he wandered, seeking religious knowledge from many centres and teachers, until he became a master of the tantric way, famous for his miracles. Padmasambhava spent many years travelling all over Tibet, preaching a type of Buddhism which appealed to Tibetans for certain similarities to Bon mystic practices.

Not long after Padmasambhava's death, a bitter political dispute developed between the Chinese and Indian Buddhists in Tibet. King Trisong Detsen decided to settle this issue and a debate was held at Samye in 792. The Indian Buddhist team prevailed and the Indian school (Mahayana) became the accepted one in Tibet.

King Tri Ralpachan (817-838) was the last of the three religious (Buddhist) kings. During his reign, translation work was continued on a huge scale under a commission composed of Indian and Tibetan scholars. In his efforts to promote Buddhism by force he alienated himself from his court, consisting largely of Bon followers, and was eventually assassinated by his brother Langdarma. Langdarma (reigned 838-842), was known as the 'Evil King' as he attempted to completely extinguish Buddhism in an orgy of persecution.

The rebirth of Buddhism, over a century later, was initiated by a small group of monks who fled via Western Tibet to Amdo. At the same time, in the kingdom of Guge in Western Tibet, Toling and Tsaparang became centres of Buddhist learning. Yeshe Ö, one of the kings of Guge, encouraged Rinchen Sangpo (958-1055) to revive Buddhism and sent him to India where he studied under many teachers, mastering Buddhist philosophy, various tantras, and the Kalachakra. He brought Indian scholars to Tibet, and with their cooperation, translated an immense number of scriptures into Tibetan. Rinchen Sangpo encouraged the construction and rebuilding of temples and monasteries in Western Tibet (notably Toling), Ladakh,

Lahaul and Spiti. He also cooperated with the Indian scholar Atisha.

Atisha (also known as Jowo Je) was born in Bengal, the son of a prince, and married early, becoming the father of nine children. He is said to have been almost 30 when he abandoned his princely rights and took his vows as a monk. He travelled as far as Burma and Afghanistan and studied in many different schools. After reluctantly taking his leave from the university of Vikramashila in India, Atisha reached Toling in 1042, and set about translating texts with Rinchen Sangpo.

Atisha attracted scholars and students from all over Tibet to whom he taught a disciplined path between intellectual and physical extremism. Through his work and that of his disciples, Buddhist doctrine was re-established.

From the 14th century onwards, increasing isolation from India, which had started during the Muslim invasions of the 12th century, led to the development of the separate sects attached to individual masters or monasteries.

Sects

There are numerous sects in Tibetan Buddhism, the most important of which are the Nyingmapa, Kagyupa, Sakyapa, and Gelukpa. Some Western scholars divide Tibetan Buddhism into Red Hat and Yellow Hat sects, according to the colour of the hats worn by the lamas. The Nyingmapa, Kagyupa and Sakyapa are referred to as Red Hat sects, while the Gelukpa are called the Yellow Hat sect. Some Tibetan scholars prefer the term 'old translation school' for the Red Hat sects, and 'new translation school' for the Yellow Hat sects thus illustrating the origin of the differences which are not as radical as the coloured hats might suggest.

These sects, although essentially religious, attained increasing political power. Intense rivalries often led to struggles for domination of the political field. In the 17th century, the Gelukpa sect, backed by the Mongols, assumed a dominant role in politics and effectively ruled Tibet through their leader, the Dalai Lama, from 1642 until the Communist occupation of the 1950s.

Nyingmapa Sect This is the oldest sect, dating back to the time of Padmasambhava who hid secret doctrines in different places during his wanderings in Tibet. These secrets (*terma*) were discovered by men such as Orgyen Lingpa (died 1379) who reportedly found the biography of Padmasambhava. According to this biography, Padmasambhava concealed 108 scriptures, 125 tantric images and five rare essences between the region of Mt Kailas and China.

Once discovered, these *terma* were compiled into books. The teachings of the Nyingmapa (ancient, old) are compiled in 61 volumes and are divided into nine sections or vehicles. The first three are dedicated to the 'Body of Emanation' and were proclaimed by the Buddha. The following three elucidate the doctrine of the lower tantras and are ascribed to the 'Body of Enjoyment in Heavenly Paradises'. The last three deal with the highest tantras.

Mindoling Monastery south of Lhasa near Tsetong (Zêtang) is one of the three most important monasteries of this sect and is now under renovation.

Kagyupa Sect The Kagyupa (oral transmission) sect was founded by Marpa (1012-1098) who was born in southern Tibet. After learning Sanskrit, he sold all his worldly possessions and went to India where he met Naropa, a disciple of Tilopa and a famous Vajrayana teacher, who initiated him into tantric doctrines. Marpa returned to India twice for spiritual guidance and to study sacred books of the Vajrayana tradition, which he translated into Tibetan.

Marpa's most famous disciple was Milarepa (1040-1123), Tibet's most revered poet. At an early age Milarepa became embroiled in a family feud. When his mother refused to marry her late husband's brother, the man became enraged and seized all their property, leaving her destitute. Milarepa's mother encouraged him to seek revenge by learning black magic from a sorcerer, which

Marpa

Dusum Khenpo, was the first incarnation and founder of the main Karmapa monastery at Tsurphu (near Lhasa) in 1189. (Another subsect, the Drukpa, is now found in Bhutan and Ladakh.) The 16th Gyalwa Karmapa (head of the Kagyupa sect) was born in Tibet in 1924. After fleeing Tibet in 1959, he founded Rumtek Monastery in Sikkim as his principal seat in exile. He died in Sikkim in 1981.

Sakyapa Sect For a description of the Sakyapa (grey earth) sect, and Sakya Monastery, refer to the separate chapter on Sakya.

Gelukpa Sect The origins of this sect can be traced to the Kadampa sect which was founded by Atisha. Tsong Khapa (1357-1419), also known as Je Rinpoche, was responsible for reforms which led to the founding of the Gelukpa (The Virtuous) sect.

Tsong Khapa was born of nomad parents in Amdo, at what is now the centre of Kumbum (Taersi) Monastery. At seven he took the vows of a novice and by the age of 16 he had learnt all his teachers could offer, so they sent him to central Tibet for higher studies. He showed special interest in logic and composed a famous work called 'Lam-rim' *(The Graded Path to Enlightenment)*. As his group of followers began to increase rapidly, he built the monastery at Ganden in 1409 to provide a base for his new sect, which required adherence to monastic discipline.

Studies at Ganden, where he was the first abbot, encompassed various Buddhist schools, non-Buddhist philosophical systems and tantras. The actual practice of these tantras was only open to those monks who had already mastered theoretical learning. Monks had to observe absolute celibacy (in contrast to the Sakyapa sect which required its abbots to marry) and abstain from liquor and narcotics. A system of 253 vows was introduced for the monks, leading gradually to higher levels of renunciation. Drepung Monastery (built in 1416) and Sera Monastery (built 1419), together with Ganden Monastery, formed the three main

he then used to kill his enemies and destroy their wealth. Although this pleased his mother, Milarepa was plagued by remorse and finally sought out Marpa to help him atone for his crimes. Marpa subjected Milarepa to gruelling tests before initiating him and giving him responsibility for transmission of the doctrine. Milarepa then spent six years in solitude, meditating in a cave. His only clothing was a light, cotton robe, hence his name Mila-repa, cotton-clad Mila. After returning home to find his mother dead, his home in ruins, and his sister dressed in rags, he decided to lead the life of a hermit and search for final liberation. The rest of his life was spent in the mountains where he achieved his goal of final liberation. The songs and poetry he left behind, known as *The Hundred Thousand Songs of Milarepa*, are revered by Tibetans.

Gampopa, a disciple of Marpa and Milarepa, founded a subsect of the Kagyupa; the Karmapa sect. Gampopa's disciple,

Tsongkhapa

Dalai Lamas

I	Gedun Drub	1391-1474
II	Gedun Gyatso	1475-1543
III	Sonam Gyatso	1543-1588
IV	Yonten Gyatso	1589-1617
V	Ngawang Lobsang Gyatso	1617-1682
VI	Tsangyang Gyatso	1683-1706
VII	Kesang Gyatso	1708-1757
VIII	Jampel Gyatso	1758-1805
IX	Luntok Gyatso	1806-1815
X	Tshultrim Gyatso	1816-1837
XI	Khedrup Gyatso	1838-1856
XII	Trinle Gyatso	1856-1875
XIII	Thupten Gyatso	1876-1933
XIV	Tenzin Gyatso	1935-

Sources do not always agree on the accuracy of these dates. The title originated in the 16th century, when the chief priest of the Gelukpa, Sonam Gyatso (the Third Dalai Lama) visited Mongolia and converted the Mongolians, for the second time, to Buddhism. The Mongolian ruler, Altan Khan, embraced Buddhism as the national religion and conferred the title of Dalai Lama on Sonam Gyatso. This title was applied retrospectively to the two previous heads of the Gelukpa who, like Sonam Gyatso, had been recognised as successive reincarnations of Chenrezig (Avalokitesvara).

'Dalai' is a Mongolian translation of the Tibetan *gyatso* meaning ocean, thus the full title means Ocean of Wisdom. In China and the West, this is the title used for the leader of the Gelukpa, but most Tibetans generally use terms such as 'Gyalwa Rinpoche' (Victorious One).

The present Dalai Lama is the 14th and although the Dalai Lama represents the highest bodhisattva, there are many other incarnations, called *tulku*, usually descended from the founder of a monastery. A *tulku* is discovered and verified through local oracles, omens and common opinion and, if necessary, a final decision is made by the Dalai Lama. There are four grades of *tulku*, the highest of which, a regent, is chosen to act during the minority of the Dalai Lama.

Discovery and verification of a Dalai Lama is a complicated process. Often the dying Dalai Lama will give an indication of

centres for the Gelukpa, and their influence on state affairs was emphasised by the term 'the three pillars of the state'.

Gedun Drub, who was the nephew of Tsong Khapa, became abbot of Ganden in 1438, and thus the supreme head of the Gelukpa. It was Gedun Drub who, to honour his teacher and predecessor Khedrup Je, founded Tashilhunpo Monastery in Shigatse, which later became the seat of the Panchen Lama (see the Shigatse chapter for details on the Panchen Lama). Shortly after the death of Gedun Drub (the First Dalai Lama) the Gelukpa introduced the system of reincarnation. Tsong Khapa had foretold that Gedun Drub would be the first of a succession of reincarnations of Avalokitesvara. At the same time he predicted that the abbots of Tashilhunpo would be the successive reincarnations of Amitabha.

his rebirth; sometimes children may come forward of their own accord or are recognised because of special powers or behaviour. Searches are conducted in secret to investigate predictions from oracles, strange signs and phenomena. Lhamo Latso, the oracle lake near Lhasa, famed for the visions seen in its waters, has often been consulted. Children chosen as likely candidates are subjected to a range of tests. In one test, for example, they are asked to select, from a variety of objects, those which once belonged to the deceased Dalai Lama. The child may well identify persons from his previous life or show knowledge of a different dialect. Another system, attributed to the Chinese, involved the use of a lottery, with a name drawn during a special ceremony.

Once selected, the Dalai Lama was brought to Lhasa around the age of six and trained at the Gelukpa colleges. He might, in time, develop an interest in the teachings of the other sects, which all accept him as temporal and spiritual head of Tibet. The Dalai Lama was expected to complete his Gelukpa training and take his final examinations at the age of 18. Thereafter he was ceremoniously put in charge of the affairs of government. Historically, the regents, who were in charge of the Dalai Lamas, could and often did exercise more than their fair share of authority. From the Sixth to the 12th Dalai Lama, the respective regents became so powerful that none of the Dalai Lamas even reached the age when they could assume control of state affairs.

The Fourth Dalai Lama, Yonten Gyatso, was born (as predicted by the Third Dalai Lama) as a son of the Mongol King, Altan Khan. This forged a strong link between the Mongolians and the Tibetans which was opposed by the Chinese during the Ming Dynasty.

The Fifth Dalai Lama (Ngawang Lobsang Gyatso), also known as 'the Great Fifth' is renowned for his political astuteness which was backed up by the military expertise of his patron Gushni Khan and his minister Sonam Chospal. This combination preserved Tibet's independence against Chinese and Mongolian pressure. Under his rule the Gelukpa sect assumed a dominant role which maintained religious unity in Tibet until occupation by the Chinese in the 1950s. The Fifth Dalai Lama started construction of the Potala, which was completed many years after his death. It was kept secret to ensure its completion. During his reign, out of gratitude to his teacher, Lobsang Chogyan, he created the office of Panchen Lama. The Fifth Dalai Lama bestowed land and farms on the Panchen Lama, near Shigatse, where Tashilhunpo Monastery was founded.

The Sixth Dalai Lama, Tsangyang Gyatso, was a strange combination of spiritual and earthly attributes. As a young man he developed an eye for the ladies and is said to have slipped out of the Potala at night to visit the brothels in the village below. The Lukhang (House of the Serpent), on an island in the lake behind the Potala, was one of his favourite secret meeting places. Clearly though, his love, as portrayed in his poetry, was not merely physical but also contained a higher element derived, perhaps, from tantric practices. His death remains a mystery. Some accounts say he had a son by a special love and the high monks, fearing the office of Dalai Lama would become hereditary, drove him into exile in Inner Mongolia and imprisoned his lover and their son. Other accounts maintain that the Chinese used his unorthodox lifestyle as an excuse to intervene and invited him to Peking. On the way he disappeared at Litang (some say at Gunga Nor near Qinghai Lake). This explains the absence of a tomb for the Sixth Dalai Lama in the Potala.

The seventh Dalai Lama, Kesang Gyatso, was born in Litang, as prophesied by the sixth Dalai Lama. He was quite different in nature to his predecessor and retreated further and further into a saintly life of solitary contemplation. He left most affairs of state to the regent, the Panchen Lama and the Chinese who used this chance to obtain a tighter grip on political affairs – a precedent which can be followed to present times.

As a result of intrigue and dissension between the Tibetans and Chinese, from the

Seventh to the 13th Dalai Lama, only one reached his majority. Many of them were poisoned, but the strangest death was that of the 12th Dalai Lama, whose regent organised the collapse of his bedroom ceiling on his head.

The 13th Dalai Lama, Thupten Gyatso, was a shrewd reformer and proved himself a skilful politician when Tibet became a pawn in the Great Game between Russia, China, and Britain. He was also responsible for restoring discipline in monastic life and increasing the number of lay officials to avoid excessive power being placed in the hands of the monks. Legislation was introduced to counter corruption among officials, a national taxation system was established, and a police force was created. As a result of his contacts with foreign powers and their representatives he showed an interest in world affairs and introduced electricity, the telephone and the first motor car to Tibet. Nonetheless, at the end of his life in 1933, he saw that Tibet was about to enter a dark age:

Very soon even in this land of the harmonious blend of religion and politics...acts may occur forced from without or within. At that time if we do not dare to protect our territory, our spiritual personalities including the victorious Father and Son (Dalai Lama and Panchen Rinpoche) may be exterminated without trace, the property and authority of our Lakangs (residences of reincarnated lamas) and monks may be taken away. Moreover, our political system, developed by the three Great Kings will vanish without anything remaining. The property of all people, high and low, will be seized and the people forced to become slaves. All living beings will have to endure endless days of suffering and will be stricken with fear. Such a time will come.

The present Dalai Lama, the 14th, was born on the fifth day of the fifth month of the Wood Hog Year of the Tibetan calendar (6 June 1935) in Amdo near the monastery of Kumbum (Taersi, in Qinghai Province). Many portents led to his discovery. The head of the deceased 13th Dalai Lama, lying in state, had turned toward the east. Three letters, a monastery with a jade-green roof, and a house with turquoise tiles were seen in the waters of the oracle lake (Lhamo Latso)

by the regent in 1935. Search parties scoured Tibet and one which had travelled north-east found a house with turquoise-green tiles near the monastery of Kumbum, which had a jade-green roof. The leader of the group disguised himself as a servant, but the moment he entered the house, the youngest child of the family jumped into his lap and requested his rosary – one which had belonged to the 13th Dalai Lama. On being shown a whole variety of religious objects (drums, rosaries, walking sticks) the young child selected only the ones which had belonged to the deceased Dalai Lama. The three letters 'ah', 'ka' and 'ma' seen in the oracle lake were interpreted as meaning Amdo (for the province) and 'ka-ma' for the monastery of Karma Rolpai Dorje, close to Taersi.

The Chinese governor of the area demanded a huge ransom to let the boy go to Lhasa; 300,000 Chinese dollars. After several years of bargaining, the money was paid and the child set off with his parents in a large caravan which took over three months to reach Lhasa. En route, the Tibetan National Assembly declared the child the 14th Dalai Lama and on 22 February 1940, the formal ceremony of instalment on the Lion Throne was held in Lhasa.

From the age of six, the Dalai Lama received strict religious training and learnt to read and write. At the age of 13 he was formally admitted to Drepung and Sera monasteries to attend debates and practice dialectical discussion at large meetings. He then continued with studies of Buddhist thought and took the preliminary examinations at each of the three monastic universities (Sera, Drepung and Ganden) at the age of 24. A year later he took his final examinations and received his degree as Master of Metaphysics. His time was divided between the Potala (winter residence) and the Norbulinka (summer residence) where he had time to tinker with a motor generator and cars which had belonged to his predecessor.

Although the accepted age for a Dalai Lama to assume control of the state from his

His Holiness The Dalai Lama consecrating a Tibetan settlement for Bonpos near Solan, Himachal Pradesh, India (NC)

regent was 18, the Tibetan cabinet, dismayed by the Chinese occupation of Eastern Tibet, made a special request for him to assume control at the age of 16. As the Chinese threat to Lhasa became clear, the National Assembly requested the Dalai Lama to avoid personal danger by staying near the Indian border at Yadong. After the signing of the Sino-Tibetan Agreement in 1951, the Dalai Lama returned to Lhasa. Within a few years the Chinese had firmly established themselves in Tibet. In 1954, the Dalai Lama and the Panchen Lama visited Peking. Smouldering resentment amongst Tibetans led to a series of revolts which culminated, in 1959, in a full-scale uprising against the Chinese in Lhasa. On 17 March 1959, the Dalai Lama, disguised as a soldier, escaped from the Norbulinka with members of his family and an armed escort, to start a long trek into exile in India.

Since then the Dalai Lama has formed a government-in-exile at Dharamsala in India and has become an eloquent spokesman for Tibet as well as a rallying point for Tibetan exiles and their culture. For the Chinese, he is a distinct embarrassment. The Chinese have made several offers for his return but are unwilling to grant him residence in Lhasa. They would prefer that he stayed in Peking, at a safe distance from the fervently dedicated Tibetans. In 1989, the 14th Dalai Lama was awarded the Nobel Peace Prize. As he said on receiving the Nobel Prize for Peace:

I...ask you not to forget Tibet at this critical time in our country's history. We too hope to contribute to the development of a more peaceful, more humane and more beautiful world. A future free Tibet will seek to help those in need throughout the world, to protect nature, and to promote peace. I believe that our Tibetan ability to combine spiritual qualities with a realistic and practical attitude enables us to make a special contribution, in however modest a way. This is my hope and prayer.

Gods & Saints

The Tibetan Buddhist directory of gods and saints, consisting of myriad deities imported from India and innumerable local creations, is so vast that it cannot be described in full detail here. The following is a broad outline of who's who at the cosmic party.

Buddhas Buddha Sakyamuni, the historical Buddha of this age, is generally ranked highest, but there are thousands of other Buddhas:

Buddha Sakyamuni is usually shown seated on a lotus throne, legs crossed, with the fingertips of his right hand touching the earth. His head reveals fixed marks of identity: a bump of wisdom on top of the head, often crowned with a precious jewel; three auspicious lines on the neck; ear lobes elongated and split; and a dot in the centre of the forehead, symbolising the third eye of spiritual wisdom.

Adibuddha is the Supreme Buddha, the source of all other Buddhas, but at least three separate forms are recognised depending on individual sects. The form recognised in the Gelukpa sect is Vajradhara.

Buddha Maitreya is the future Buddha (Tibetan: Champa), often depicted standing, or sitting on a throne, flanked by or holding the Wheel of Dharma on the right, and a libation jug with a plant, on the left.

Dhyani Buddhas, the Vajrayana deities from India, are usually divided into five basic families, each with a Buddha at its head. There are five Celestial Buddhas, each with a Shakti (female consort) and an attendant bodhisattva. Amitabha (Tibetan: Opame) is the Buddha of Boundless Light, the Great Buddha of the West. Amitabha is often seated in a contemplative pose, holding a bowl of ambrosia, with peacocks in attendance below. The Panchen Lama is a reincarnation of Amitabha. The other Celestial Buddhas are: Akshobya, the Buddha of the East; Ratnasambhava, Buddha of the South; Amoghasiddhi, Buddha of the North; and Vairocana, Buddha of the Centre.

Bodhisattvas

Bodhisattvas are beings who compassionately refrain from entering nirvana in order to save others. Some of the ones most commonly worshipped in Tibet are:

Avalokitesvara (Tibetan: Chenrezig) is the patron saint of Tibet. A form of Avalokitesvara is Shadakshari, of whom the Dalai Lama is an incarnation. Shadakshari is said to live in a paradise called Potalaka which is symbolised by the residence of the Dalai Lama in Lhasa which bears the same name. Avalokitesvara is represented with up to 11 heads and from two to 1000 arms. The many heads are said to have burst from an original head as a result of contemplating the suffering of living beings. In his cosmic form, he is given 11 heads (eight represent the cardinal directions and intermediate points; the other three signify the zenith, centre and nadir). The head at the top is that of Amitabha (the parental Buddha of Avalokitesvara). The 1000 arms which form a mandala around his body represent omnipresence. The palm of each hand is marked with an eye to symbolise the vision of the cosmic god.

Manjusri (Tibetan: Jampeyang) is representative of divine wisdom and is depicted with from one to four heads and from two to eight arms. He holds a sword and a book.

Vajrapani (Tibetan: Chana Dorje) is one of the oldest Bodhisattvas in the Buddhist pantheon. He bears a thunderbolt and a bell. He is often depicted clothed in a tiger skin, with serpents writhing around his arms and feet.

Tara (Tibetan: Dolma) is the spiritual consort of Avalokitesvara and possesses 21 forms. One form, Green Tara, is identified with Princess Bhrikuti, the Nepalese wife of Songtsen Gampo; another form, White Tara, is identified with Princess Wen Cheng, the Chinese wife of the same king (himself identified as a reincarnation of Avalokitesvara).

Mahasiddhas, Saints & Lamas

The cult of the Mahasiddhas (perfected beings) in Tibet recognises 85 *mahasiddhas*, all of whom were Indians. They are virtually always male historical figures; unorthodox teachers, yogis, or wandering mystics. *Mahasiddhas* are usually depicted wearing a loin-cloth, sitting on an animal skin, their eyes bulging with mystic power and their hair drawn up in a top-knot. The following are especially revered:

Nagarjuna, the 1st century AD founder of the Madhyamika school of Buddhism, is portrayed like a Buddha, with seven serpents forming a hood above his head.

Avalokitesvara

Padmasambhava was an 8th century tantric master. The patron saint of Nyingmapa, he is portrayed in the lotus posture, dressed in brocade, with a crown on his head. In his right hand is a *dorje* (thunderbolt), in his left is a skullcap, and in the bend of his left elbow he supports a flaming trident.

Rinchen Sangpo (958-1055) was a prodigious translator and religious master. He is depicted in the meditation posture, seated on a lotus, dressed in a long yellow robe.

Atisha (982-1054) was an Indian teacher, credited with the founding of the Kadampa sect. He is portrayed in red clothing with a monk's hat.

Marpa (1012-1098), a Tibetan guru, is shown with a book and a skull.

Milarepa (1040-1123), a great Tibetan mystic and poet, is shown with his right hand at his right ear. He wears a red meditation band over his shoulder.

Tsong Khapa (1357-1419) was the founder of the Gelukpa sect. He is shown dressed in red, with a yellow hat. The lotus flower on his left shoulder contains a book, the one on the right contains a sword.

Dharmapalas These gods are Protectors of the Faith (Tibetan: Chokyong). Some were imported from India and others, originally Bon deities, were conquered and transformed by Padmasambhava into Buddhist protectors:

Mahakala (Tibetan: Gonpo) is the most important *dharmapala*, with a shrine in virtually every Tibetan monastery. He is a form of the Hindu god Shiva, and is highly revered by nomads in Tibet as the 'Protector of the Tent'. Mahakala is usually depicted in a black or white form with six arms either cradling a staff with a severed head or holding the symbols of his power to defeat hostile demons: a snare, a trident, a rosary of skulls, a chopper to cut off the demons' life roots and a skullcap to hold their blood. His head is framed with a ring of fire (representing cromation) and his face is crowned with a shock of hair. He is the Sakyapa sect's patron deity.

Yama was originally an ancient Hindu god of death. Yama plays a more important role in the Tibetan pantheon, as Lord of the Dead and King of Religion. He is always shown in a terrifying pose, with the head of a buffalo, riding naked on a blue bull. His head is adorned with rings of severed heads and a diadem of skulls.

Yamantaka is the slayer of Yama, an angry form of Manjusri (divine wisdom). He is shown ringed with fire, with nine demonic heads (the principal one is that of a buffalo, the ninth, at the top, that of a benign Bodhisattva). His 34 arms swirl out in all directions holding emblems such as skullcaps, daggers, swords, choppers, and drums. His 16 legs trample on assorted creatures of the world as he indulges in the cosmic dance of destruction. Yamantaka is evoked and appeased during the New Year festivals in special ceremonies performed by both Sakyapa and Nyingmapa sects.

Lhamo is the protective goddess of both the Gelukpa sect and of Lhasa, usually depicted in blue or black, riding on a mule with a human skin thrown over its back. A Gelukpa text describes her as follows:

She is of dark-blue colour, has one face and two hands. Her right hand wields a club adorned with a thunderbolt, which she lifts above the heads of oathbreakers, the left hand holds in front of her breast the skull of a child born out of an incestuous union, full of substance possessing magic virtues, and blood. Her mouth gapes widely open and she bares her four sharp teeth; she chews a corpse and laughs thunderously.

Yidams Whereas *dharmapalas* are protectors of religion, *yidams* protect the individual in the role of guardian deities – a type of guardian angel. Each monastery, family or individual has a *yidam*. The Gelukpa sect adopted, as their *yidam*, Vajrabhairava (a cosmic and angry form of Manjusri), and the Sakyapa adopted Hevajra. Hevajra has the usual assortment of arms, legs and heads (16, four, and eight respectively). Although he has a fearful black countenance, and wears a skull necklace, his inner nature is tranquil when embracing Nairatmya, his consort. At the time of initiation, the lama will decide on an individual's *yidam* which the individual will then carry with him, often as an image on a *thangka* (scroll) or in a *gau* (portable shrine). *Yidams* are not restricted to a terrifying form, there are also angry and even benign forms.

Dakinis These are a class of demigoddesses, the female counterparts of male *dakas*. The Tibetan expression for *dakini* (Khandoma) means 'sky-walking woman', which explains the belief that they can fly. Since *dakinis* are also regarded as embodying wisdom, in both celestial and mortal forms, they play an important role as spiritual guides for *mahasiddhas*. In tantric initiation, the expression dakini is used to describe the female partner who thus takes on a human or superhuman aspect. *Dakinis* are usually depicted as naked virgins, often with a necklace of skulls around their necks.

Local Deities & Lokpalas Many of the local Tibetan gods which were already resident in the mountains, forests, lakes, rivers, sky and underworld were coopted into the Buddhist religion. Other common subjects of worship are the four demon kings, guardians of the four directions, known as the *lokpalas*: Vaishravana, the Regent of the North; Dhritarashtra, the Regent of the East; Virudhaka, the Regent of the South; and Virupaksha, the Regent of the West. They come from the slopes of Meru, the cosmic mountain at the centre of the universe (associated with Mt Kailas in Western Tibet).

Monasteries
Several centuries after Buddha Sakyamuni's death, wandering assemblies of monks in India started to settle in permanent monastic institutions which gradually served two important functions, as centres of learning and as places of retreat. In time, this form of cohabitation required organisation, rules and administration.

The establishment of Buddhism in Tibet would have been impossible without the establishment of monasteries which became a dominant element in political, religious and cultural life. Even today, monasteries (although most are ruined or under reconstruction) form focal points in the sweeping Tibetan landscape and appear to be gradually regaining a sad fraction of their former importance.

The Tibetan word *gompa* means 'place of meditation'. It is probable that small hermitages (some still exist) were the origins of some of the large monasteries. Other monasteries, such as Samye, were constructed on new sites, usually in solitary and lofty positions in the mountains, in accordance with the advice of astrologers. They varied in size from communities numbering a dozen monks to huge monastic cities such as Drepung, Sera and Ganden, inhabited by many thousands of monks.

Monasteries were usually endowed with estates which were farmed by tenants who, in return for use of the land, provided taxes and provisions. As a result, trading and commerce became vital sources of income. Devout pilgrims and visitors often provided offerings of money, and the monks could leave the monastery to perform rituals for which they received payment. Monasteries on trade routes also charged caravans for the provision of pack animals and guides.

The smallest monastery consisted of a single room which functioned as an assembly room, library and shrine. The larger monasteries consisted of several temples, meditation rooms, living quarters for the abbot, living quarters for the monks, storage rooms and outhouses. The design generally followed a standard pattern with a *lhakang* (a hall housing the principal deity), and a *dukhang* (a hall of assembly for the monks) which adjoined the *gonkhang* (an inner chapel, often underground) reserved for the Yidam and other guardian deities. The *gonkhang* is usually in total darkness, and has an atmosphere of awe and mystery: monks chant constantly to ward off hostile forces and images, painted on a black background, make everything seem even spookier. *Gonkhangs* usually contain images of *dharmapalas*, especially Yamantaka and Mahakala, and chortens containing the relics of abbots or lamas. Monasteries also have a library (*kanjur-lhakang*), a large kitchen, a courtyard (surrounded by a gallery) for religious dances, and other rooms to store ritual objects, dance masks, food and materials.

Monasteries are often surrounded by walls. On the roof are cylindrical victory banners (*gyaltsan*), often in the form of gilded metal cylinders filled with prayer slips. A common symbol seen on the upper walls or roof is the Wheel of Dharma flanked by two deer (signifying Buddha's first sermon at Sarnath in India). Often seen on the exterior wall is the *namchuwangdan*, an intricate monogram containing seven syllables surmounted by the crescent moon, the sun and the flame of wisdom. This is considered a mantra of great power as it represents the human body in microcosmic form.

The *lhakang* and *dukhang* usually have an entrance hall with the guardians of the four directions (*lokpalas*) on the wall facing the main shrine and other instructional wall paintings such as the Wheel of Life on the other walls. A set of steep steps usually lead into the main temple. Inside, opposite the entrance, a hall of pillars houses a large statue of the main deity (often Sakyamuni or Maitreya). These statues, often made from gilded bronze or copper, are consecrated by sealing mantras (prayers), jewels or coins inside. Right and left of the main statue are statues of bodhisattvas, saints, previous abbots or patrons. On the altar in front of the statues stands at least one butter lamp and seven offering bowls: the first, second and sixth are filled with water; the third contains flowers; the fourth holds incense; the fifth is a butter lamp; and the seventh holds aromatic substances. Other items include a large copper bowl filled with a mound of rice or barley (symbol of Meru, the cosmic mountain) and various dough effigies (*torma*) made from barley-flour, butter, honey or sugar. Pilgrims and visitors leave gifts such as money, greeting scarves (*khata*), bracelets or, as a sign of the times, digital watches!

Monastic Life At any age a male can join a monastery. A sponsor, who is usually a friend or relative, arranges for a teacher and residence. The entrant is then expected to take the pre-novice vows of a *rapjung* (the first of three grades of monk). He receives training, works, studies and takes part in ceremonies that start at dawn and may continue into the night. Between the age of 15 and 25 monks take 36 further vows to become a *getsul*. Full ordination as a *gelong* requires a minimum age of 20 and observance of 250 rules. The *rapjung* monk wears brownish-red robes; the *getsul* and *gelong* monks wear red.

Within a monastery only a small proportion of the monks are *gelongs* and even fewer are lamas. In Tibetan, the term lama corresponds to the Sanskrit 'guru'; strictly speaking, this term is reserved for 'perfect' teachers. Nonstudent monks can train as artisans, look after the monastery's land, do the accounts and handle the business and financial matters. Other monks work in the kitchens or perform general cleaning and maintenance duties.

The daily timetable, rituals, festivals and ceremonies of the major sects all follow the rules of the *Vinaya* (Sanskrit: that which leads) text. Every two weeks the assembled monks recite the rules, with a pause after each one, to allow any monk who has transgressed to confess and receive punishment. The most important rules, punishable with expulsion if broken, concern sexual intercourse, theft, murder and exaggeration of one's miraculous powers; other rules, in seven groups, deal with lesser transgressions such as lying and drinking.

The structure of administration varies from sect to sect but in general the *khenpo* (abbot) directs the teaching, presides over the assembly and liturgical acts, and monitors the education of the monks. The *kyorpon* checks whether students have memorised their allotted scriptural passages, and the *chotrimpa* is responsible for monastic discipline.

In the Geluk tradition, studies are divided into five groups, each requiring several years for completion. The first, *Namdrel*, is the study of logic; the second, *Parchin*, is a comparative study of Buddhist scriptures; the third, *Oumah*, is the study of the path between extremes; the fourth, *Sunyata*, is the study of nonexistence or voidness; the fifth, *Dzo*, is the study of metaphysics. Various classes of degrees are awarded by monasteries, the best known being the Geshe degree system of the three great monastic universities (Drepung, Sera and Ganden). The Geshe degree is conferred on supreme masters of the five major topics of Buddhist philosophy after passing through at least 17 classes in a minimum of 20 years.

Statistics for the number of monasteries and monks before the occupation of Tibet by the Chinese in the 1950s vary according to political viewpoints. Before the 1950s there were at least 2500 monasteries. No reliable statistics are available for the present status but reports indicate that at best only 10% of the monasteries (and monks) are still active. The Chinese Religious Bureau, a state-run agency that oversees all spiritual activity in Tibet, has 35 members – seven are Chinese, the rest are Chinese-appointed Tibetans. This bureau allocates funds for the reconstruction or renovation of monasteries and screens aspirant monks who also undergo literacy tests and background checks before permission is given. Since the quotas of monks fixed by the bureau for the monasteries are low, many aspirant monks are rejected. Today, it is too early to assess the veracity of a reported religious revival. Full restitution of the monastic system is one thing, showcase Buddhism is definitely another.

The Religious Life In tents, monasteries and private homes Tibetan Buddhism still has its place in the daily life and actions of most Tibetans.

Every altar has at least one butter lamp, which is supposed never to go out. On special occasions, or in large monasteries, there may be hundreds. The lamps are usually made of copper or brass, but sometimes they are silver, or gilded. They have a wide bowl to hold yak butter, and a twist of cotton for a floating wick. The bulbous stem rests on an inverted lotus. Butter lamps used to be a favourite gift to be offered to a monastery, and many of them are inscribed with details of the donor and the weight of silver used. The finest lamps were made in Dêgê.

Many pilgrims who come to Lhasa still travel incredible distances, performing *kjangchag* – prostrating themselves all the way. This is meant to be healthy and holy, and is popular during the fourth month of the year, the month of Buddha's birth (May). Travelling at the beginning of the century, F Kingdon Ward came across a prostrator:

...one of those extraordinary people of whom I had often read, who proceed by measuring their length on the ground over the entire distance, thus acquiring a vast amount of merit. He was a ragged-looking man, dirty and unkempt, as well he might be, with a leather apron over his long cloak, and his hands thrust through the straps of flat wooden clogs, like Japanese sandals. Standing up with his arms by his side, he clapped the clogs together in front of him once, twice, then slowly raised them above his head, and clapping them together a third time, stretched himself at full length on the ground with his arms straight out in front of him. Mumbling a prayer he again clapped, made a mark on the ground at the full stretch of his arms, and rose to his feet. Then he solemnly walked forward three steps to the mark he had made, and repeated the performance; and so the weary journey went on.

Korlam, or circumambulation of sacred places in a clockwise direction, reflects the religious belief that humans revolve around Buddha in the same manner as the planets move around the sun.

A tradition derived from the custom of offering garments to deities is the offering of a white ceremonial scarf, the *khata*, during visits to monasteries and shrines and as a greeting (it is also offered during marriage and death ceremonies). *Tsa tsa* are votive plaques, which used to be mass-produced in clay from bronze moulds. The earliest forms were used to consecrate *chortens* and were stamped with magic formulas. They are still common and can be found painted or unpainted on altars, chortens, or carried in a portable shrine. They are popular souvenirs for pilgrims visiting a monastery.

The *manichorkor* or prayer wheel, is a specialty of Tibetan Buddhism, and can be turned by hand, hot air, wind or water. Prayer wheels vary in size from the hand-held version to the huge wooden cylinders, sometimes numbering hundreds, in monasteries or temples. As they spin, the scrolls contained in the cylinders release several million prayers and invocations to the heavens, and gain the user merit.

Rosaries usually consist of 108 beads, the holy number, and are used to recite the name of Buddha 100 times (the extra beads are in case you become forgetful or lose some). The largest bead indicates the completion of the cycle. Rosaries are made from many materials: turquoise, amber, coral, wood, seeds and bone.

Prayer flags are seen gracefully fluttering from bridges, tents, rooftops, rock cairns at the top of high mountain passes, or virtually any high point. The prayers printed on the cloth are meant to soar into the skies.

Spirit traps are used to protect buildings against evil spirits or demons. They are usually made from the skull of a dog, sheep or goat supported by a willow-rod framework interwoven with straw and woollen threads in special patterns. Once the demons are caught in the threads of the trap, they are destroyed by burning the entire trap.

Water has a fundamental place in Indian mythology and Buddhism. In Tibet all lakes are considered sacred, the habitat of *lu* (water spirits) and are venerated by circumambulation. For washing, ritual initiation and offerings to deities, different types of water vessels are used. Visitors and pilgrims to places of worship who make offerings or present a *khata*, receive water in their cupped hands which they drink and rub on their foreheads.

Other Buddhist Devotional Objects

Mandalas The meanings and functions of a mandala are many. It is considered, primarily, to contain the essence of religion; it is a symbol of both the mind and the body of Buddha. The main use of a mandala is in meditation. Following the strict rules of a written description, a mandala usually depicts deities or symbols arranged around a central figure. The entire assembly is enclosed by a rectangular building with a door in each wall pointing to one of the four main points of the compass. The circular perimeters of the mandala include flames, thunderbolts, cemeteries and lotus petals. The person meditating contemplates the mandala according to his training, and perhaps follows the instructions in the written description until he temporarily occupies the place of the central figure, thus acquiring some of its attributes and powers.

Mani-Walls These walls are generally a metre high and can vary in length from a metre to several km. Slates, stones and boulders are carved or painted with inscriptions (often the *Om Mani Padme Hum* mantra) and images of deities (often that of Avalokitesvara), and piled on top of each other. The walls are considered holy objects pilgrims circumambulate or prostrate around them in a clockwise direction.

Thangkas *Thangkas* are rectangular shaped religious paintings, usually on cotton or linen that can be rolled up. Red or yellow silk is used for the border, and plain blue silk or Chinese brocade serves as a mount. Sometimes the bottom of the mount has a small, rectangular patch known as the *thang-so*, which serves as an 'entrance' to pass into the subject of the painting. Two sticks are attached to top and bottom so that the *thangka* can be rolled up and transported. Ease of transport was important for nomads and it's probable that Buddhist monks used *thangkas* as mobile illustrations of their religion. Special pattern-books give exact iconographic instructions for painting.

The colours were made from minerals and plants in complicated processes which were kept secret between master and disciple. Before use, *thangkas* were consecrated. Since they were not waterproof, a mirror image was sprinkled with water instead. A mantra, often written on the reverse of the *thangka*, was also part of the consecration ritual and on the reverse of some *thangkas* there is even the handprint of the officiating monk.

Chortens The *chorten* (Sanskrit: stupa) is a particularly striking symbol of Buddhism. The origin of this structure is traced to the death and cremation of Buddha. Buddha's ashes were divided among eight lords who took them home and built eight stupas to house the relics. In Tibetan Buddhism, a *chorten* generally symbolises the mind of Buddha, one of the 'three supports'; the other two supports are the book (symbolising the word) and the image (symbolising the physical plane).

Chortens vary in design and size from those a metre high to the many-storeyed structures such as the one in Gannets. In its standard form the rectangular base of the *chorten* represents the earth element; the spire represents the fire element; the crescent symbolises the air element; and the ball of flame on the top represents the ethereal element. The rings (either seven or 13) around the spire signify the seven or 13 stages of heaven. The *chorten* resembles a cosmic mandala: the central shaft represents Meru, the cosmic mountain, and each of the sides of the rectangular base respectively represent the four cardinal directions.

Religious Restrictions

The 1990s have brought little relief to religious persecution in Tibet and the general restrictive trend continues with limits on the numbers of monks at each monastery; prohibition of lay believers receiving religious instruction; requirement of permission from Party and government officials before young Tibetans can enter a monastery; and the insistence on government approval for all reconstruction projects. *Forbidden Freedoms: Beijing's Control of Religion in Tibet* (International Campaign for Tibet, 1990) covers this topic in detail.

TIBETAN LANGUAGE

Tibetan is generally considered to belong to the Tibeto-Burmese language group within the Sino-Tibetan language family. This classification, however, is based more on contemporary political and racial considerations than on any real linguistic similarities. In short, no-one is entirely certain to which grouping it is most related.

The Tibetan language is widely spoken throughout Central and Himalayan Asia. It is the language of the Tibetan Autonomous Region and is spoken in large areas of China's Sichuan, Yunnan, Gansu and Qinghai provinces as well as in parts of Sikkim, Ladakh and Nepal. Although there are many regional dialects and subdialects, they are mutually intelligible. The Lhasa dialect is considered the lingua franca and has two distinct, social levels of speech – ordinary and honorific – but the honorific form is now falling into disuse.

Although there may have been a Tibetan script in earlier times, it was the introduction of Buddhism in Tibet during the 7th century which created the need for a written language so that Sanskrit canonical texts could be translated into Tibetan. King Songtsen Gampo sent his minister Thonmi Sambhota with a delegation to India where he produced a script for Tibetan, based on the Sanskrit alphabet.

The Tibetan alphabet is written with 30 consonants and four vowels plus six symbols used for Sanskrit words. There are four types of script: two for general use, one for Buddhist textbooks, and one for ornamental use.

Lonely Planet publishes a useful *Tibet phrasebook*, which includes Tibetan script, in its series of language survival kits. Snow Lion Publications in New York have published their *Tibetan Phrasebook* complete with cassette tapes.

English is not commonly spoken in Lhasa, although there are a few Tibetans, often those who have been to India, who speak excellent English. Many Tibetans also speak Mandarin Chinese – less by choice than by force of circumstances, which includes the education system. Certainly, outside of Lhasa, you will find a knowledge of the Tibetan language invaluable. However skimpy your efforts may seem, it's still worth downing a couple of cups of beer (*chang*) and letting rip – the Tibetans love it.

The pronunciation provided for the following phrases is approximate and based on the Lhasa dialect. Accents used here indicate the following pronunciation: â, a short sound similar to the 'a' in 'alone'; ü, similar to the ü in German; and ö, similar to the 'eu' sound in French.

Personal Pronouns

I
  nga   ང་
you
  kayrang   ཁྱེད་རང་
he/she
  kong   ཁོང་
we
  ngandzo   ང་ཚོ་
you
  kaynandzo   ཁྱེད་རང་ཚོ་
they
  kondzo   ཁོང་ཚོ་

Some Useful Words

slowly
  kâliy, kâliy   ག་ལེར་ག་ལེར་
quickly
  gyogo   མགྱོགས་པོ་
big
  chembo   ཆེན་པོ་
small
  chunjun   ཆུང་ཆུང་
good
  yago   ཡག་པོ་
bad
  dukja   སྡུག་ཅགས་
cold
  thrang-mu   གྲང་མོ་
hot
  tshabo   ཚ་པོ་

Question Words

where
  kaba   ག་པར་
when
  kâdü   ག་དུས་
how many/much
  kâdzay   ག་ཚད་
who
  sû   སུ་
why
  kan yin-na   གང་ཡིན་ན་

Greetings & Civilities

Hello. (lit: good fortune)
  tashi delay
Goodbye. (when leaving)
  kâlishu

Goodbye. (when staying)
  kâlipay
Thank you.
  tujaychay   ཐུགས་རྗེ་ཆེ་
I'm sorry.
  gawn-da   དགོངས་དག
How are you?
  kayrang gusu debo yimbay?
   ཁྱེད་རང་སྐུ་གཟུགས་བདེ་པོ་ཡིན་པས་
I'm fine.
  nga debo yin   ང་བདེ་པོ་ཡིན་
I want tea.
  nga cha gaw   ང་ར་ཇ་དགོས་
I don't want this.
  diy mâgaw   འདར་འདི་མི་དགོས་
What is this?
  diy karay ray?   འདི་ག་རེ་རེད་
Is this ...?
  diy...rebay?   འདི་••••••རེད་པས་
Do you have...?
  ...yöbay?   ••••••ཡོད་པས་
Where is the...?
  ...kaba do?   ག་པར་འདུག
How much is this?
  diy gon kâdzay ray?
   འདིར་གོང་ག་ཚད་རེད་
Yes. (there is/are)
  du   འདུག
No. (there isn't/aren't)
  mindu   མི་འདུག
Yes.
  ray   རེད་
No.
  maray   མ་རེད་

Small Talk

What is your name?
  kayrang gi minglâ karay sa?
   ཁྱེད་རང་གི་མིང་ལ་ག་རེ་ཟ
My name is...
  nga minglâ ...sa
   ངའི་མིང་ལ་••••••ཟ
Where are you from?
  kayrang lungbâ kânay ray?
   ཁྱེད་རང་ལུང་པ་ག་ནས་རེད་
I'm from ...
  nga ... nay yin   ང་••••••ནས་
    Australia
    otaliy   ཨོ་ཏ་ལི་ཡ་

Canada
janada ཅ་ན་ད་
France
farensi or *fago* ཕ་རན་སི་ (or)ཕ་གོ་
Germany
jarman or *tago* འཇར་མན་ (or)ད་གོ་
India
gyagar རྒྱ་གར་
New Zealand
shin shilen ཤིན་ཤི་ལེན་
UK
injiy lungba དབྱིན་ཇིའི་ལུང་པ་
USA
âmerika ཨ་མེ་རི་ཀ་

Do you speak English?
inji-gay shing-giy dugay?
དབྱིན་ཇིའི་སྐད་ཤེས་ཀྱི་འདུག་གས་
I don't understand.
ha ko ma song ཧ་གོ་མ་སོང་
Go away!
pa gyu ཕར་རྒྱུགས་

Family
brother
pingya pu སྤུན་སྐྱག་པ་
sister
pingya pomo སྤུན་སྐྱག་པུ་མོ་
mother
amala
father
pala
son
pu པ་

daughter
phomo པུ་མོ་

Getting Around
I want to hire a ...
nga ... chig laygoyö
ངར་ཀྱང་ཀྱང་ཕི་ཕུ་གཅིག་གླ་དགོས་ཡོད་
bus
gong- gaw chidrâ
minibus
membow མ�འན་པའོ་
jeep
jiyp ཇིབ་
landcruiser
fengtian
taxi
thrudzu དལ་
truck
datrâ ད་ཕྲལ་
horse
da ད་
donkey
phung gu བོང་གུ་
yak
yak གཡག་

How much is the fee per ...?
... rayray laja kâdzay ray?
ཉིན་མ་རེ་རེ་ལ་གླ་ཆ་ག་ཚད་རེད་
day
nyima ཉིན་མ་
km
gongli ཀུང་ལི་

ཐ་ད་ན་པ་བ་བ་མ་ཙ་ཚ་ཀ་ཥ་ག་ང་ཅ་ཆ་ད་ཉ་ཏ་
ཤ་ ༑ ཏ་ པ་ ཕ་ བ་ མ་ ཙ་ ཚ་ ཀ་ ཁ་ ག་ ༑ ཐ་ ཌ་ ད་ ན་ པ་
ཤ་ ༑ ཏ་ པ་ ཕ་ ཝ་ མ་ ཙ་ ཚ་ ཀ་ ཁ་ ག་ ༑ ཐ་ ཌ་ ད་ ན་ པ་
ཤ་ ༑ ༑ ཏ་ པ་ ༼ ༽ ༼ ༽ ༼ ༽ ཙ་ ཚ་ ༼ ༽ ༼ ༽ ༼ ༽ ༑ ༑ ཐ་ ཌ་ ད་ ན་ པ་

Tibetan Alphabet – 30 consonants, plus four vowels (at right), written from left to right in four

How much will this cost?
laja kâdzay ray?
རྒྱ་ཆ་ག་ཚད་རེད་

Where are you going?
kaba payga?
ག་པར་ཕེབས་ག་

I'm going to Lhasa.
nga Lhasa dru-giy-yin
ང་ལྷ་སར་འགྲོ་གི་ཡིན་

What time will it leave?
chudzö kâdzay drugiyray?
.......ཆུ་ཚོད་ག་ཚད་ལ་འགྲོ་གི་རེད་

I am sick.
nga nâgiy
ང་ན་གིས་

Is it OK if I take a photo?
bar gyâbna digirebay?
པར་རྒྱབ་ན་འགྲིག་གི་རེད་པས་

Directions

here
day འདིར་

there
pâgay ཕ་གིར་

north
chang བྱང་

south
lho ལྷོ་

east
shar ཤར་

west
nub ནུབ་

straight on
shar-gya ཤར་རྒྱག་

(on the) left
yönjolâ གཡོན་ཕྱོགས་ལ་

(on the) right
yayjolâ གཡས་ཕྱོགས་ལ་

Accommodation

guesthouse
drönkang འགྲོན་ཁང་

I need a bed.
nga nyethri chig gaw
ང་ར་ཉལ་ཁྲི་གཅིག་དགོས་

How much is it per day?
nyimâ rayrayla laja kâdzay ray?
ཉིན་མ་རེ་རེ་ལ་རྒྱ་ཆ་ག་ཚད་རེད་

Is there a toilet?
sanjö dugay?
གསང་སྤྱོད་འདུག་གས་

Is there hot water?
chu tshabo dugay?
ཆུ་ཚ་པོ་

Food

I'm...
nga...giy ང་.......གིས་
    hungry
        throwgaw-dough གྲོད་ཁོག་ལྟོགས་
    thirsty
        ka gom ཁ་སྐོམ་

food
kala ཁ་ལག་

barley
nay ནས་

different kinds of script.

roasted barley
  dzambâ རྩམ་པ་
eggs
  gaw-ngâ སྒོང་
fish
  nyasha ཉ་
fruit
  shin do ཤིང་ཏོག
hot (spicy) food
  kala ka tshabo ཁ་ལག་ཁ་ཚ་པོ་
meat
  sha ཤ་
milk
  oma ཨོ་མ་
onion
  dzong ཙོང་
rice
  dray འབྲས་
tea
  cha ཇ་
vegetables
  tshay ཚལ་

I don't eat meat.
  nga sha dzani sâgimay
  ང་ད་ཤ་པ་ནས་བཟའ་གི་མེད་

Numbers

1	*chig*	གཅིག
2	*nyi*	གཉིས་
3	*sum*	གསུམ་
4	*shi*	བཞི་
5	*nga*	ལྔ་
6	*thru*	དྲུག
7	*dün*	བདུན་
8	*gyay*	བརྒྱད་
9	*gu*	དགུ་
10	*ju*	བཅུ་
11	*jugjiy*	བཅུ་གཅིག
12	*jung nyiy*	བཅུ་གཉིས་
13	*jogsum*	བཅུ་གསུམ་
14	*jupshi*	བཅུ་བཞི་
15	*jönga*	བཅོ་ལྔ་
16	*juthru*	བཅུ་དྲུག
17	*jupdün*	བཅུ་བདུན་
18	*jopgyay*	བཅོ་བརྒྱད་
19	*jurgu*	བཅུ་དགུ་
20	*nyishu*	ཉི་ཤུ་
30	*sumju*	སུམ་བཅུ་
40	*shipju*	བཞི་བཅུ་

50	*ngâpju*	ལྔ་བཅུ་
100	*gya*	བརྒྱ་ཐམས་པ་

Time

today
  târiy དེ་རིང་
tomorrow
  sânyi སང་ཉིན་
yesterday
  kaysâ ཁ་ས་
now
  tanda ད་ལྟ་
morning
  shawgay ཞོག་སྐད་
evening
  gawnda དགོང་དག

Days of the Week

Monday
  sa dawa གཟའ་ཟླ་བ་
Tuesday
  sa mingma གཟའ་མིག་དམར་
Wednesday
  sa lhagbâ གཟའ་ལྷག་པ་
Thursday
  sa pubu གཟའ་ཕུར་བུ་
Friday
  sa pasang གཟའ་པ་སང་
Saturday
  sa pembâ གཟའ་སྤེན་པ་
Sunday
  sa nyimâ གཟའ་ཉི་མ་

Some Useful Words

amber
  poshay སྦོས་ཤེལ་
backpack
  gyâb-pay རྒྱབ་ཁད་
beer
  chang ཆང་
black
  nagbo ནག་པོ་
book
  tep དེབ་
bridge
  samba ཟམ་པ་
candle
  yangla ཡང་ལར་

English	Tibetan (roman)	Tibetan (script)
cave	pugbâ	ཕུག་པ་
cheese (dried)	churâ gambo	ཕྱུར་ར་སྐམ་པོ་
chicken (meat)	chasha	བྱ་ཤ་
doctor	âmchi	ཨེམ་ཆི་
dog	kyi	ཁྱི་
east	shar	ཤར་
few	nyun-nyun	ཉུང་ཉུང་
gold	ser	གསེར་
green	jâng gu	ལྗང་ཁུ་
guide	lâmgü chay-ngen	ལམ་རྒྱུས་བྱེད་མཁན་
hat	shamo	ཞྭ་མོ་
hospital	men gang	སྨན་ཁང་
hotel	drönkang	འགྲོན་ཁང་
hot spring	chutshen	ཆུ་ཚན་
knife	thri	གྲི་
lake	tsho	མཚོ་
matches	musi	མུ་ཟེ་
medicine	men	སྨན་
monastery	gombâ	དགོན་པ་
mountain	riy	རི་
mountain pass	lu	ལ་
much/many	mâng gu	མང་པོ་
mule	thray	དྲེལ་
nomad	drogbâ	འབྲོག་པ་
north	chang	བྱང་
photo	par	པར་
rain	charbâ	ཆར་པ་
red	maamo	དམར་པོ་
restaurant	sagang	ཟ་ཁང་
road/trail	lang-ga	ལམ་འཕྲག་
rock	do	རྡོ་
sheep	lug	ལུག་
silver	ngü	དངུལ་
south	lho	ལྷོ་
spoon	tuma	གཏང་ཀྱུ་
snow	kan	གངས་
snow leopard	sap-sig	གཟིག་
star	garma	སྐར་མ་
store	tshong-gang	ཚོང་ཁང་
Tibet	pö	བོད་
Tibetan (language)	pögay	བོད་སྐད་
turquoise	yu	གཡུ་
vulture	gö	རྒོད་
water (boiled)	chu köma	ཆུ་འཁོལ་མ་
west	nub	ནུབ་
white	gabo	དཀར་པོ་
wool	bay	བལ་
yellow	saybo	སེར་པོ་
yoghurt	sho	ཞོ་

CHINESE LANGUAGE

Nothing reveals the role of the Chinese in Tibet more clearly than the sad necessity to include this section. Hotel staff, truck drivers, restaurant owners, shopkeepers, CITS officials, PSB officers and, of course, party cadres owe their positions either to the fact that they are Chinese or to their ability to speak Mandarin. In Tibet, where proficiency in Mandarin is a key to power and preferential treatment, linguistic chauvinism is alive and kicking.

Spoken Language

Although there are eight major dialects in China, the official dialect promoted as a lingua franca is the Beijing dialect, which the Chinese refer to as Putonghua and Westerners as Mandarin. Since many of the Chinese in Tibet come from provinces such as Gansu, Sichuan, Shaanxi and Guangdong, you will also hear dialects from these areas. However, Mandarin is understood by almost all the Chinese and, to a lesser extent, by many Tibetans, especially in towns. In the remote areas of Tibet – away from the roads – nomads and villagers are refreshingly ignorant of Mandarin and you will have to try your Tibetan.

Spoken Mandarin makes do with about 400 syllables which are provided with tones. These tones are crucial for meaning. Without mastery of tones, your efforts at mandarin will be unintelligible, so it is worth practising the tones in the phrases given here with someone who speaks Mandarin.

Written Language

Written Mandarin draws on a fund of approximately 50,000 characters which were originally pictographs. Literate Chinese have a command of at least 5000 characters and a knowledge of at least 1500 is required to read a newspaper.

Most of the characters used today have two components. The phonetic component provides a rough indication of pronunciation and the root component, also called the radical, provides the meaning. Modern Mandarin uses around 214 radicals and dictionaries usually list characters under these. For example, many characters connected with trees, forests and wooden products or structures contain the radical for 'tree'.

Characters are all written with a basic stroke system which makes use of up to 13 basic strokes. Some characters are written with just a few strokes, others require as many as 20. One further complication is the use within China (but not Taiwan or Hong Kong) of simplified characters intended to speed up literacy, particularly in rural areas.

Pinyin

A phonetic system known as Pinyin was introduced in China during the 1950s to Romanise the Chinese language. Mandarin uses four basic tones which are represented in Pinyin as follows:

— first tone	(high level)
´ second tone	(rising)
ˇ third tone	(falling-rising)
ˋ fourth tone	(falling)

So, for example:

mā	means mother
má	means hemp
mǎ	means horse
mà	means to scold

An unmarked syllable receives no stress and is skated over with no particular tone.

Although Pinyin helps foreigners get their bearings in the language, it is of little use unless tones and intonation are correct as well. The phrases given are provided with pronunciation and tones using Pinyin. For a more detailed language guide to Chinese, try Lonely Planet's *Mandarin Chinese phrasebook* which is part of a series of language survival kits.

Basically the sounds of Pinyin can be read as they are pronounced in English although the following are exceptions:

c	like the 'ts'	in 'its'
q	like the 'ch'	in 'choose'

x	like the 'sh'	in 'short'
zh	like the 'j'	in 'journal'
z	like the 'ds'	in 'zero'

Personal Pronouns
I
　wǒ　　　我
you
　nǐ　　　你
he/she/it
　tā　　　他
we
　wǒmen　我们
you (pl)
　nǐmen　你们
they
　tāmen　他们

Demonstrative Pronouns
this (one)
　zhèi (ge)　这个
that (one)
　nà (ge)　那个
these (ones)
　zhèi (xie)　这些
those (ones)
　nà (xie)　那些

Adverbs
slowly
　mànmàn de　慢慢地
quickly
　kuài kuàide　快快地
here
　zhèlǐ　这里
there
　nàlǐ　那里

Questions
where
　zài nǎr　在哪儿？
when
　shénmo shihou　什么时候？
how much (money)
　dūoshao qián　多少钱？
who
　shúi　谁？
why
　wèi shénmo　为什么？

Greetings & Civilities
Hello.
　nǐ hǎo　你好
Goodbye.
　zàijiàn　再见
Thank you.
　xièxie　谢谢
How are you?
　nǐ hǎo ma?　你好吗？
I'm fine, thanks.
　wǒ hǎo, xièxiè　我好，谢谢
Yes. (there is/are)
　yǒu　有
No. (there isn't/aren't)
　méi yǒu　没有
Yes.
　shì　是
No.
　bù　不
Sorry.
　dùi bu qǐ　对不起

Small Talk
I want...
　wǒ yào...　我要…
I don't want...
　wǒ bù yào...　我不要…
What is this?
　zhè shì shénmo?　这是什么？
Is this...?
　zhè shì...ma?　这是…吗？
Do you have...?
　nǐ yǒu...ma?　你有…吗？
Where is the...?
　...zài nǎr?　…在哪儿？
How much?
　yào dūoshǎo qián?　要多少钱？

Countries
Where are you from?
　nǐ cóng nǎli lái?　你从哪里来？
I'm from
　wǒ cóng ... lái　我从…来
　Australia
　　àodàlìyà　澳大利亚
　Canada
　　jiānádà　加拿大
　China
　　zhōng gúo　中国

France
fǎguó 法国
Germany
xīdé 西德
India
yìndù 印度
Nepal
nípō ěr 尼泊尔
Tibet
xīzàng 西藏
UK
yīng guó 英国
USA
měiguó 美国

Kinship Terms
mother
mǔqin 母亲
father
fùqin 父亲
parents
fùmǔ 父母
child
háizi 孩子
boy
nán hái 男孩
girl
nǚ hái 女孩

Getting Around
Where are you going?
nǐ dào nǎli?
你到哪里？
I'm going to Lhasa.
wǒ dào Lāsā
我到拉萨
When are you going?
nǐ shénmo shihòu qù?
你什么时候去？
What time are you going?
nǐ jīdiǎn zhōng qù
你几点钟去？
Have you got a spare seat?
nǐ yǒu kōng zuò ma
你有空坐吗？
Go ahead! (help yourself, don't stand on ceremony)
bù kèqi! 不客气

How much do you want from here to Golmud?
cóng zhèli dào Gě-ěr-mù nǐ yào duōshao qián?
从这里到格尔木 要多少钱？

Let's go! (Let's roll!)
zǒu ba!
走吧
Get out. (of the cab)
xià chē
下车
Get in. (the cab)
shàng chē
上车
Can I help?
wǒ nèng bu nèng bāng nǐde máng?
我能不能帮你的忙？
The truck's broken down.
chēzi huàile
车子坏了
We need to fill up with petrol.
wǒmen yào jiā yóu
我们要加油
Don't smoke.
bú yào chōu yān
不要抽烟
We need to fill up with water.
wǒmen yào jiā shuǐ
我们要加水
Let's eat!
chī fàn ba!
吃饭吧
Have a rest!
xiūxi ba!
休息吧
Wait a moment!
děng yīxià!
等一下
Where's the toilet?
cèsuǒ zài nǎr?
厕所在哪儿？
I want to take a photo.
wǒ yào zhào ge xiàng
我要照个相
Is this alright?
zhèli hǎo bu hǎo?
这里好不好

Here is just fine.
zhèli hǎo
这里好
Take it easy! (said to the person leaving)
mànmàn zǒu!
慢慢走
I don't feel well.
wǒ juéde bù shūfu
我觉得不舒适
I've got a headache.
wǒ toú téng
我头疼
altitude sickness
gāo shān fǎn yìng
高山反应
What's the name of this place?
zhèige dìfang jiào shénmo mingzi?
这个地方叫什么名字？
How far is it from here to...?
cóng zhèli dào...yǒu duōshao gōnglǐ?
从这里到…有多少公里

Hiring Transport
We want to hire a ...
wǒmen yào zū jià ...
我们要租架…
bus
gōnggong qìchē　　公共汽车
donkey
lú　　驴
horse
mǎ　　马
jeep
jípǔ　　吉普
landcruiser
fēngtiān　　丰田
minibus
xiǎo xíng gōnggòng qìchē
小型公共汽车
taxi
chūzū chē　　出租车
truck
kǎchē　　卡车
yak
máo niú　　毛牛
yak-hide boat
niú pí chúan　　牛皮船

We want to hire a taxi on Monday.
xīngqī yī wǒmen yào zū jià chū zū chē
星期一我们要租架 出租车
We want to stay at Gyantse overnight.
wǒmen yào zài Gyantse zhùsù
我们要在江孜住宿
One person wants to return.
yīge rén yào húi lai
一个人要回来
We don't want to return.
wǒmen bù yào húi lai
我们不要回来
What is the price per day?
měi yī tiān zūfèi yào duōshao?
每天租费要多少
kilometre
gōnglǐ
公里
What is the total price?
yígòng yào duōshao qián?
一共要多少钱

Train
hard seat ticket
yìngxí piào　　硬席票
hard sleeper ticket
yìng wò piào　　硬卧票
soft sleeper ticket
rǔan wò piào　　软卧票
I'm going to Xining tomorrow and want to buy a (hard sleeper ticket).
wǒ míngtiān dào Xīníng, xiǎng mǎi yī zhāng (yìng wò piào)
我明天到西宁
想买一张硬卧票

How much is it?
yào duōshao qián?
要多少钱？
When does the train leave?
hǔochē shénmo shíhòu kāi?
火车什么时候开？

Bus
I want to take the bus to Zêtang.
wǒ yào zùo gōnggòngqìchē dào Zétāng
我要坐公共汽车到泽当
When does the bus leave?
qìchē shénmo shíhòu kāi?
汽车什么时候开？

How much is the ticket?
chēpiào yào dūoshao qián?
车票要多少钱?

Places
Public Security Bureau (PSB)
gōng ān jú 公安局
China International Travel Service (CITS)
zhōnggúo gúoji lǚxíngshè 中国国际旅行社
Civil Aviation Administration of China (CAAC)
zhōnggúo mín yòng háng kǒng zǒng jú
中国民用航空总局
bus station (long distance)
(cháng tú) qì chē zhàn 长途汽车站
airport
fēijī chǎng 飞机场
post office
yóu jú 邮局
train station
hǔochē zhàn 火车站

Accommodation
hotel (hostel)
lǚshe 旅社
guesthouse
zhāodài sǔo 招待所
hotel
fandian/lǚgǔan 饭店/旅馆
hotel (higher grade)
bīngǔan 宾馆
I want a single room.
wǒ yào yí jiān dāng rén fáng
我要一间单人房
I want a double room.
wǒ yào yí jiān shūang rén fáng
我要一间双人房
I want to stay in a dormitory.
wǒ yào zài sùshè zhùsù
我要在宿舍住宿
How much per day?
měi tiān yào dūoshǎo qián?
每天多少钱?
I want something cheaper.
wǒ yào piányí de yí diǎn
我要便宜一点的
Too expensive.
tài gùi
太贵

Where is the toilet?
cèsǔo zài nǎr?
厕所在哪儿
Ladies
nǚ 女
Gents
nán 男
Is there any hot water?
yǒu rè shǔi ma? 有热水吗?
Is there a bathroom?
yǒu xǐzǎo jiān ma? 有洗澡间吗?
water (boiled)
kāi shǔi 开水
washbasin
liǎn pén 脸盆

Food
I'm hungry.
wǒ è 我饿
I'm thirsty.
wǒ kǒu kě 我口渴
food
fàn 饭
beancurd
dòufu 豆腐
beef
niú ròu 牛肉
beer
píjǔ 啤酒
duck
yā 鸭
dumpling (plain)
mántou 馒头
dumpling (filled with meat)
bāozi 包子
dumpling (filled with meat and vegetables)
jiǎozi 饺子
egg
jī dàn 鸡蛋
fish
yú 鱼
milk
niú nǎi 牛奶
mutton
yáng ròu 羊肉
onion
cōng 葱
pork
zhū ròu 猪肉

peanuts
  hūa shēng 花生
rice
  dà mǐfàn 大米饭
soup
  tāng 汤
tea
  chá 茶
vegetables
  shū cài 蔬菜
water (boiled)
  kāi shǔi 开水
yak meat
  maó niú ròu 毛牛肉
I'm a vegetarian.
  wǒ chī sù 我吃素

Time
today
  jīntiān 今天
tomorrow
  míngtiān 明天
yesterday
  zùotiān 昨天
now
  xiànzài 现在
morning
  shàngwǔ 上午
afternoon
  xiàwǔ 下午
evening
  wǎnshàng 晚上
the day after tomorrow
  hòu tīan 后天

Days of the Week
Monday
  xīngqī yī 星期一
Tuesday
  xīngqī èr 星期二
Wednesday
  xīngqī sān 星期三
Thursday
  xīngqī sì 星期四
Friday
  xīngqī wǔ 星期五
Saturday
  xīngqī lìu 星期六
Sunday
  xīngqī rì 星期日

Numbers
1
  yī 一
2
  èr 二
3
  sān 三
4
  sì 四
5
  wǔ 五
6
  lìu 六
7
  qī 七
8
  bā 八
9
  jǐu 九
10
  shí 十
11
  shíyī 十一
12
  shíèr 十二
20
  èrshí 二十
30
  sānshí 三十
40
  sìshí 四十
50
  wǔshí 五十
100
  yī bǎi 一百

Tibetan Geographical Terms
fort – *dzong* (also *zong*)
ice, snow – *kang* (also *gang*)
lake –*caka* (also *co, tso, ringco, yumco, nor*)
lamasery or monastery– *gompa* (also *gonpa*)
pass, hill – *la*
peak – *ri*
plain, plateau – *tang*
river – *zangbo* (also *chu*)
sand – *chema*
spring – *chumi*

Chinese Geographical Terms

basin, depression – *péndì*
desert – *shāmò*
island – *dǎo* (also *yǔ, zhōu, sha*)
lake, sea, wetland – *hǎi* (also *hú, yánhú*)
mountain(s), peak(s) – *fēng* (or *shān*)
municipality – *shì*
pass – *shānkǒu*
plain – *píngyuán*
(high) plateau – *gāoyuán*
province – *shěng*
ruins – *yíjī*
spring – *quán*
stream, section of stream, river – *hé* (also *gou, qu, shuǐ, yuán, jiāng*)
autonomous county – *zìzhìxiàn*
autonomous prefecture – *zìzhìzhōu*
autonomous region – *zìzhìqū*

Names

The Tibetans have not yet established a list of official place names in Roman script corresponding to their spoken form. Hence a simple phonetic spelling, culled from maps and major works of Western literature, has been adopted for Tibetan terms and monastery names in this book. This renders the sounds as closely as possible without the complications of exact transcription.

Finding the correct sound or transliteration for a Tibetan word is a tricky affair. Written Tibetan is derived from the Indian script of the 7th century, but the spoken language (much as has happened with English) has changed drastically over the years. So, for example, Tashilhunpo Monastery is transliterated as *bKra-shis-lhun-po* and Drepung Monastery becomes *hBras-spǔngs*.

To further complicate things, with the arrival of the Chinese in the '50s, place names were transcribed into Chinese characters which approximately represented the sounds, but not the meaning of the names. Since Chinese characters are transcribed into Roman script using several systems of tran-

scription, the gap between the spoken and the written name has become even greater. The official transcription system now used by the Chinese in Tibet is Pinyin. This Romanising of a Chinese character representing a Tibetan place name considerably alters the pronunciation. So, for example, Tashilhunpo Monastery comes out as *Zhaxilhünbo*.

The diacritical marks used in the Pinyin system in this book are the umlaut (as used in the German, über) and the circumflex which is equivalent to the 'e' in the French 'je'.

Monastery or Temple

The Potala
  Lhasa   རྩེ་པོ་ཏ་ལའི་ཕོ་བྲང་།
Jokhang
  Lhasa   ཇོ་ཁང་།
Ramoche
  Lhasa   ར་མོ་ཆེ།
Sera
  Lhasa outskirts སེ་ར་ཐེག་ཆེན་གླིང་།
Drepung
  Lhasa outskirts འབྲས་སྤུངས
Ganden
  40 km east of Lhasa
  དགའ་ལྡན་རྣམ་པར་རྒྱལ་བའི་གླིང་
Samye
  Samye བསམ་ཡས་གཏུག་ལྷ་གང་།
Trandruk
  five km south of Tsetong ཁྲ་འབྲུག་ལྷ་ཁང་།
Tashilhunpo
  Shigatse བཀྲ་ཤིས་ལྷུན་པོ།
Sakya
  Sakya ས་སྐྱ་དགོན།
Chamdo
  Chamdo, East Tibet
  ཆབ་མདོ་བྱམས་པ་གླིང་།
Toling
  Zanda, West Tibet མཐོ་གླིང་།
Kumbum (Taersi)
  26 km from Xining སྐུ་འབུམ།
Youning
  50 km from Xining དགོན་ལུང་བྱམས་པ་གླིང་།

Facts for the Visitor

VISAS & EMBASSIES

Visas for individual travel in China are easy to get. China will even issue visas to individuals from countries which do not have diplomatic relations with the People's Republic. However, citizens of South Africa can only visit China on an organised tour, and must make their application at least one month before their planned arrival in China.

Visas are readily available in Hong Kong, from Chinese embassies in most Western countries and from Chinese embassies in many other countries. If you can't wait until you get to Hong Kong or if you want to fly direct to China, then enquire first at the nearest Chinese embassy.

Chinese Embassies

Following are the addresses of Chinese embassies in major cities around the world.

Australia
    247 Federal Highway, Watson, Canberra, 2600 ACT
Austria
    A-1030 Vienna, Metterrichgasse 4
Belgium
    21 Blvd General Jacques, 1051 Brussels
Canada
    411-415 Andrews St, Ottawa, Ontario KIN 5H3
Denmark
    25 Oeregaardsalle, DK 2900 Hellerup, Copenhagen 2900
France
    11 Ave George V, Paris 75008
Germany
    5307 Wachtbergeriederbachen, Konrad-Adenauer Str, 104, Bonn
Italy
    56 Via Bruxelles, Roma 00198
Japan
    15-30 Minami-Azabu, 4-Chome, Minato-ku, Tokyo
Netherlands
    Adriaan Goehooplaan 7, Den Haag
New Zealand
    2-6 Glenmore St, Kelburn, Wellington
Spain
    Trafalgar 11, Madrid

Sweden
    Bragevagen 4, Stockholm
Switzerland
    Kalecheggweg 10, Berne
UK
    31 Portland Place, London WIN 3AG
USA
    2300 Connecticut Ave NW, Washington, DC 20008. Consulates: 3417 Montrose Blvd, Houston, Texas 77006; 104 South Michigan Ave, Suite 1200, Chicago, Illinois 60603; 1450 Laguna St, San Francisco, California 94115; 520 12th Ave, New York, New York 10036

In Hong Kong

In Hong Kong numerous travel agencies issue Chinese visas. Generally they offer a choice of a visa by itself, or a package deal including visa and transport to China. Some of the best agencies are:

Traveller Services – Room 704, Metropole Bldg, 57 Peking Rd, Tsimshatsui, Kowloon (☎ 3674127). Fast, reliable and cheap service.
Phoenix Services – Room B, 6th Floor, Milton Mansion, 96 Nathan Rd, Tsimshatsui, Kowloon (☎ 7227378). Many travellers have spoken very highly of this place.
Wallem Travel – 46th Floor, Hopewell Centre, 183 Queen's Rd East, Wanchai, Hong Kong Island (☎ 5286514). They specialise in travel to communist countries.
Visa Office of the Ministry of Foreign Affairs of the PRC – 5th Floor, Low Block, China Resources Bldg, 26 Harbour Rd, Wanchai, Hong Kong Island (☎ 8939812). Open Monday to Friday, 9 am to 12.30 pm and 2 to 5 pm, Saturday 9 am to 12.30 pm. This place has been dispensing the cheapest visas around; a three-month visa issued in two days for HK$90.

Visa applications require two passport-size photos. Your application must be written in English, and you're advised to have one entire blank page in your passport for the visa.

The visa application form asks you a number of silly questions – your travel itinerary, means of transport, how long you will stay, etc, but you can deviate from this as much as you want. You don't have to leave from the place you specify on your visa application form.

The cost of visas and the types of package deals you get in Hong Kong change quite frequently, so use this information as a rough guide only. The usual price for a three-month visa issued in three days is HK$140; issued in 24 hours, HK$180; issued the same day, HK$250.

If you want more flexibility to enter and exit China several times, multiple-entry visas are available from some agencies. This is particularly useful if you intend to follow complicated routes in and out of China via Nepal, Pakistan, Thailand or Myanmar (Burma). Multiple-entry visas will cost several times as much as single-entry visas.

Some agencies in Hong Kong are now able to obtain your visa on a separate paper which you present at the Chinese border. All that is required is your passport number, nationality, date of birth and full name. Certain ports of entry such as Shenzhen are experimenting with issuing five-day visas at the border. Chinese residents of Hong Kong, Macau and Taiwan can apply for a *hùi xiāng zhèng* which entitles them to multiple visa-free entry.

It should be possible to get a visa for stays longer than six months. All visas are valid from the date of issue, not from the date of entry, so it's useless to get a visa far in advance of your planned entry.

Visa Extensions

Visa extensions are handled by the Foreign Affairs Section of the local Public Security Bureaus (the police force). The Chinese government travel organisation, China International Travel Service, has nothing to do with extensions. Extensions cost Y25. The general rule is that you can get one extension of one month's duration, though at an agreeable Public Security Bureau you may be able to wangle more, for longer, with cogent reasons (illness, transport delays, etc).

PUBLIC SECURITY BUREAU (PSB)

The Public Security Bureau *(Gong An Ju)*

acts as China's police force. Foreigners are dealt with by the Foreign Affairs Section *(Wai Shi Ke)* which is responsible for Alien Travel Permits and visa extensions.

The PSB also introduces and enforces regulations concerning foreigners. So, for example, they bear responsibility for exclusion of foreigners from certain hotels. If this means you get stuck for a place to stay they can offer advice. Don't pester them with trivia or try to 'use' them to bully a point. Do turn to them for mediation in serious disputes with hotels, restaurants, taxi drivers, etc. This often works, if only as a 'face-saving' device since the PSB wields considerable power especially in remote areas.

You may also encounter PSB if you travel illegally through closed areas and are picked up. Occasionally you will be asked to write a self-criticism *(ZiWo PiPing)*. This details your abject contrition and should, if possible, include bootlicking apologies to your ancestors for besmirching the family name. Other punishments consist of hefty fines (always bargain down) or temporary confiscation of your passport until you have been bundled back to an open place or, in rare cases of repeat offenders, expulsion from the country.

DOCUMENTS

There are several bits of paper worth keeping or carrying on your travels in China.

The baggage declaration form is given to you at customs when you enter China and it lists all your personal valuables carried with you. Make sure you keep this form to be shown when you leave. If you lose it or some of your valuables, to avoid customs problems when you leave, visit your nearest Public Security Bureau (PSB) to report the loss and, most importantly, to obtain a loss report.

To keep track of your health details you should also carry an International Health Certificate. An AIDS certificate is now required if you are working in China on a long-term basis.

When you change money at the bank you are given a bank receipt at least one of which is necessary proof if you need to reconvert currency when leaving China.

Student cards from Taiwan and Hong Kong come in all types, both legal and illegal. The illegal kind still work in some places to obtain price reductions on transport or accommodation, but this sometimes works to the detriment of bona-fide foreign students. One French student had a ding-dong battle in Zhengzhou station with a smug booking clerk who threw her absolutely genuine card into the rubbish bin and told her it was a fake!

It's a good idea to keep a separate note of your travellers' cheque numbers, visa and passport details and plane ticket numbers.

ALIEN'S TRAVEL PERMITS (ATP) & OPEN PLACES

A few years ago only 130 places in China were open to foreign tourists. Then the number swept to 244 and at the time of writing was over 600. With the number of open places increasing so quickly the following list is only a rough guide of ideas for your own itinerary. As a rule of thumb, most of the places described in this book are open to foreigners with the mere requirement of a valid visa in their passport. A few places have been prised open before their time. To find out about newly opened areas it's best to check with the PSB in provincial capitals. Remote PSBs are often more helpful with visas, but tend to be the last to receive lists of new openings.

For a visit to closed places you will need to request an Alien's Travel Permit (Lüxing Zheng) from the Public Security Bureau in an open place. It is up to PSB whether they accept your application or not. However, in practice the choice of open places is now so extensive that the majority of travellers will have no need for this type of permit. With fluctuations in tension in certain Tibetan areas, Public Security may see fit to introduce new permit requirements. Foreign academics and researchers usually need to front up with the right credentials or letter of introduction (jie shao xin) and may then be given a free hand to pursue their lizards, donkeys or whatever in remote places.

Open Cities & Areas

Following is a list of cities, towns and places in Tibet and surrounding areas which are theoretically open to foreign travellers without special travel permits (*indicates provincial capital):

Gansu Province
Anxi County, Baiyin, Chengxian, Dangchang County, Diebu County, Dunhuang County, Jiayuguan, Jinchang, Jiuquan County, Lanzhou*, Linxia, Minqin County, Minxian, Pingjiang, Qingyang County, Tianshui County, Wenxian County, Wudu County, Wuwei, Xiahe (Labrang Monastery), Xifeng, Yongjing County, Yumen, Zhangye, Zhugqu County

Qinghai Province
Dulan County, Gangca County (Qinghai Lake: Bird Island/Niaodao), Golmud, Gonghe County, Guide County, Hualong Hui Autonomous County, Huangzhong County (and Taersi Monastery), Jianzha County, Ledu, Maduo County, Tongren County, Wulan County, Xining*, Xunhua Sala Autonomous County

Sichuan Province
Changning County, Chengdu*, Chongqing, Daxian, Daxian County, Deyang, Dukou, Fengdu County, Fengjie County, Fuling, Guangyuan, Guanxian County, Jiang'an County, Leshan, Liangping County, Lixian County, Luzhou, Maowen Qiang Autonomous County, Markam County, Meishan County, Mianyang, Nanchong, Nanping County, Neijiang, Songpan County, Suining, Wanxian, Wanxian County, Wenchuan County, Wushan County, Wuxi County, Xichang, Xingwen County, Xiuning, Ya'an, Yibin, Yunyang County, Zhongxian County, Zigong

Tibet Autonomous Region
Lhasa*, Nagqu, Nêdong County (Tsetong Town), Nyalam County, Shigatse County, Zhangmu (Nyalam)

Yunnan Province
Binchuan County, Chengjiang County, Chuxiong, Dali, Dayao County, Eryuan County, Gejiu, Jianchuan County, Jiangchuan County, Jianshui County, Jinghong County, Kaiyuan, Kunming*, Lijiang (Naxi Autonomous County), Lufeng County, Luxi County, Menghai County, Mile County, Nanhua County, Qujing, Simao County, Tonghai County, Weishan Yi and Hui Autonomous County, Wuding County, Yao-an County, Yongren County, Yongsheng County, Yuanmou County, Yuxi

Provincial Map of China

1 Xinjiang	14 Sichuan
2 Tibet	15 Hubei
3 Qinghai	16 Henan
4 Gansu	17 Anhui
5 Ningxia	18 Jiangsu
6 Inner Mongolia	19 Zhejiang
7 Heilongjiang	20 Fujian
8 Jilin	21 Jiangxi
9 Liaoning	22 Hunan
10 Hebei	23 Guangdong
11 Shandong	24 Guangxi
12 Shanxi	25 Guizhou
13 Shaanxi	26 Yunnan

Xinjiang Autonomous Region
   Aksu, Altay, Artux, Bole, Changji, Fukang County, Hami, Hotan, Huocheng County, Kashgar, Kashi, Karamay, Korla, Kuqa County, Kuytun, Shache County, Shushan County, Shihezi, Shufu County, Tacheng, Taxkorgan Tajik Autonomous County, Toksun County, Turfan County, Ürümqi*, Yecheng County, Yining

ITINERARIES

It is easy to try and do too much too fast in Tibet. Transport delays due to weather or mechanical breakdown are quite common. As a rule of thumb you should allow one day

in three for 'logistics', which include obtaining information and transport to or from places. Be prepared to spend half a day or more chasing transport. It will also take several days to become acclimatised to the altitude so be prepared to soft pedal when you first arrive. Political tension and military crackdowns can also stymie even the best laid plans.

Popular itineraries include the flights between Chengdu and Lhasa or Kathmandu and Lhasa followed by overland excursions around Lhasa and down the Nepal Highway. Another option is to combine the Nepal

Highway with a trip down the Karakoram Highway by performing a large semi-circular loop through the neighbouring provinces of Qinghai and Xinjiang. Depending on time available, it is possible to cover the fascinating territory of ethnic Tibet by travelling through Western Sichuan (Kham), Qinghai (Amdo) and Central Tibet. A trip of this kind could take several months. For a straightforward tour of Lhasa and the sights along the Nepal Highway you should allow three weeks to a month. In order to become properly acclimatised you should plan on a minimum stay of at least three weeks, preferably a month.

CUSTOMS

Customs procedures for China are generally smooth and quick. On arrival you must complete a baggage declaration form on which you should declare personal valuables such as watches, cameras, radios, calculators, jewellery, foreign currency and travellers' cheques, etc. Make sure you retain this form because you will have to present it together with your valuables at customs again on your departure. This is meant to deter you from selling on the black market or generously giving things away to locals.

If you do lose the form or anything you declared on it, make sure you go to the nearest PSB (Public Security Bureau) to obtain a loss report which you can then use as proof at customs when you exit.

Keep receipts for all substantial items you buy such as jewellery, paintings or antiques. This may also help determine duties payable when you have to face your own customs.

You are allowed to bring into China two cartons of cigarettes or the equivalent in tobacco products, two litres of alcoholic drink, 600 ml of perfume, 72 rolls of still film and 3000 feet of eight mm cine film.

Export of antiques over 120 years old will need special permission and customs may confiscate other antique items if they think they're from a dubious source.

MONEY
Currency

The currency used in China is Renminbi (RMB) which is denominated in *yuan* and designated in this book by a capital 'Y'. The yuan is further divided into *jiao* and *fen*. Ten fen make one jiao, and 10 jiao make up one yuan. Jiao and yuan are commonly referred to in spoken Chinese as *mao* and *kuai* respectively.

Tibetan 100 Sang banknote

China issues two kinds of money: Renminbi (RMB) and Foreign-Exchange Certificates (FEC).

Renminbi, the People's money used by millions of Chinese every day, circulates in notes of 1, 2 , 5, 10, and 50 yuan; 1, 2, and 5 jiao; 1, 2, and 5 fen. There are also coins for 1, 2, and 5 fen.

FEC is tourist money intended for use by tourists, Overseas Chinese, diplomats, etc for rail and air tickets, taxis, hotels and imported or luxury items. FEC, known in Chinese as *Wai Hui Juan* or simply abbreviated to *Wai Hui*, circulates in notes of 1, 5, 10, 50, and 100 yuan; and 1 and 5 jiao. Ever since its inception in 1980, there have been rumours that FEC will be abandoned or phased out, and the enthusiasm with which the Chinese enforce the regulations regarding its use varies greatly from place to place. One plan to phase out FEC in November 1986 was abandoned due to 'coordination' problems in the bank network.

In practice, some foreign visitors have travelled across China using only RMB, but to cover yourself you should carry a mixture of RMB and FEC. Although there is no basis, for example for the common scam of three-wheeler drivers demanding fares in FEC, some shops and hotels like to operate an interesting 'price differential'. You may be asked if you want to pay a given price in FEC or pay about 30% more in RMB. Some hotels simply will not accept payment in RMB no matter how hard you plead, cry or rant. Some train stations have separate booking offices for foreigners which insist on payment in FEC, and air tickets can only be bought in FEC.

On the other hand, in smaller towns and in the countryside where few foreigners go you may find ignorance of the FEC system, and you'll have to pay in RMB.

Travellers' Cheques & Credit Cards

All major currencies, travellers' cheques and credit cards are accepted by the Bank of China (Zhongguo Yinhang) and large tourist hotels in provincial capitals including Lhasa. When you change at the bank you will receive a money-exchange receipt which details the transaction. Hang on to the receipt because you can use it to reconvert your leftover Chinese currency when you leave.

Exchange Rates

A$1	=	Y4.16
C$1	=	Y4.78
DM1	=	Y3.37
HK$1	=	Y0.70
Y1000 (yen)	=	Y37
UK£1	=	Y9.1
US$1	=	Y5.2

Black Market

FEC is very much in demand with locals as a means of acquiring items unobtainable with RMB. As a result you may be approached to change your FEC for more than the equivalent in RMB; rates vary between 30% and 80% extra. This is illegal and you will be liable to a fine if caught, but this is one way to obtain RMB. Another legal way to obtain RMB is to ask specifically for it when changing money at the bank, although this obviously means that you miss out on the premium offered by the black market. It is not illegal for you to have RMB in your possession.

Some travellers changing on the black market have experienced short-changing (faked 'alert' or 'paper' replacement). Always agree first on the price, count what you are given and only then hand over your part. If real or 'engineered' danger appears in mid-transaction, don't be flustered into a hasty exchange only to find later you've lost out. Either hand back what you have been given or hang onto it and walk away coolly. The moneychangers will find you again – vested interest! Cash US dollars also attract interest in the market place.

Costs

Prices for foreigners in Tibet continue to rise, but it is still possible to budget for US$15 a day *if* you are allowed a choice. Group travel or organised tours can exceed US$100 per day. Transport, particularly air travel or vehicle hire, is a major cost and foreigners

People of Tibet (RS)

Top Left: Tibetan woman & child (RV)
Top Right: Old Tibetan man (RS)
  Bottom: Tibetan woman & child (RV)

Top Left: Tibetan woman with umbrella (RS)
Top Right: Tibetan nappy (RV)
  Bottom: Female temple repair squad at Samye (RS)

Top: Loaded Yaks on Tingri plains - en route to Everest (GW)
Bottom: Steps leading up to Potala Palace (RV)

are now charged double the local price for bus transport. Accommodation in the cheaper hotels in Lhasa is around Y10 per night in a dorm, but you may be forced to spend considerably more at the Lhasa Holiday Inn which does, however, reduce prices during the winter season. Food is inexpensive in street restaurants. For Western-style food in Lhasa you must shell out more, but it makes for a welcome change.

Outside Lhasa, unless you stay in the new major hotels, prices are reasonable for truck-stop accommodation and food. The less travelling you do in quick succession the easier it is on your wallet and nerves.

WHEN TO GO

Climate in Tibet sometimes gives the impression that all four seasons have been compressed into one day.

Winter brings intense dry cold and fierce winds although Lhasa sees little snow. During winter, when there are less tourists about, hotel rates are dropped and truckloads of colourful nomads arrive to visit Lhasa and its holy places. Snowfall up on the high passes can block overland transport for weeks on end.

In general, summer temperatures are pleasantly warm at midday and drop dramatically in the shade and at night. Summer in Lhasa sees periodic rainfall and frequent dust storms.

In autumn travel suffers major complications from flooding, melting snow and collapsing roads.

The best time to go is between May and September.

WHAT TO BRING

Tibet has only a handful of towns, and even in Lhasa you will be lucky to find anything more than essential items of food and clothing. Take as much as you can with you from home, Hong Kong, or neighbouring staging-points in China (such as Chengdu, Xining and Golmud).

Carrying Bags

If you are thinking of trekking or hitchhik-ing, a backpack is essential. One system that works well is to take a backpack, a day-pack and a food-bag. This means you can stash your backpack at the rear of the truck, bus (or yak) and still have essential items and valuables with you. Most of the hotels in Lhasa have luggage storage, so you can use them as a supply depot.

Clothing

Temperatures in Tibet can plummet with amazing speed from day to night and from sun to shade, so it's best to bring clothing you can wear in layers. Silk vests, T-shirts, socks, gloves and so on provide excellent insulation as inner layers.

Down jackets with an attached hood offer good protection against cold and can be used as a cushion or pillow on bus rides. To shield against the wind, a light anorak or gore-tex jacket is useful during the day when it can be worn over a thick sweater. Woollen long johns worn under corduroys also keep out the cold. A wide-brimmed sunhat (available in Lhasa) is good protection against the midday sun.

If you are hitching on the back of a truck, it gets cold – really cold over the high passes – so it's useful to have a woollen balaclava or headgear with earmuffs, a woollen scarf and gloves. Rain pants and a rain poncho keep out rain and snow and help retain body heat. They also keep some of the dirt out if you are on the back of a coal truck!

Medicines & Toiletries

Take along toilet paper (available in Chengdu – there are flat packs in Lhasa, but no rolls), multivitamin tablets, diarrhoea and headache medicines, disposable face-wipes and cough or cold medicines. To protect yourself at these altitudes it's essential to use lipsalve, suncream and sunglasses capable of dealing with high ultraviolet radiation. (See the section on health for more details on medicines.)

Food & Drink

Basically, anything that is brewed with hot water will be useful in Tibet. Instant coffee, drinking chocolate, tea(bags), soup cubes, drink powder and powdered milk can be a welcome addition to the diet after a few weeks in Tibet. Other food items worth considering are instant noodles, vegemite, nuts and raisins, chocolate and biscuits.

Accessories
A water bottle is essential. Other handy items include a Swiss army knife, torch (flashlight) for temples, candles, umbrella (collapsible), zip-lock plastic bags (both large and small), and cloth stuff-sacks. Some travellers take their own enamel mug, plate and chopsticks as preventative hygiene measures. Take large envelopes and sealing tape if you plan on sending bulky letters or parcels. If you bring a Walkman or a flash-unit, remember to load up on batteries. Stock up on film too – photographers in Lhasa who've forgotten to bring enough film can turn vicious in their hunt.

TOURIST OFFICES
Offices of Tibet
There is now a worldwide network of Offices of His Holiness The Dalai Lama which are also known as Offices of Tibet. Each office looks after the interests of Tibetans and generally promotes understanding of Tibet and Tibetans. This is also the place to look for information on the culture of Tibet, on its religion, history and way of life, and on current affairs regarding Tibet and Tibetans in exile. Following are the addresses and phone numbers of the offices:

India
     Mr Tashi Wangdi, Bureau of H H The Dalai Lama, 10 Ring Rd, Lajpat Nagar IV, New Delhi 110024 (☎ 641-4888, 641-2657; cable BUROFDALAI)
     Mr Sonam Topgyal, General Secretary, Information Office of H H The Dalai Lama, Gangchen Kyishong – 176215, Dharamsala, Himachal Pradesh (☎ 457)
     The Editor, Tibetan Review, c/o Tibetan SOS Youth Hostel, Sector 14 Extn, Rohini, Delhi – 110085

Japan
     Professor T Norbu, Rep of H H The Dalai Lama, Office of Tibet, Celebrity Plaza, 3F, Shinjuku 1-36-14, Shinjuku-ku, Tokyo, 160 (☎ 3570-6131, telex 2466998, cable LIAISON DALAI, TOKYO)

Nepal
     Mr Paljor Tsering, Rep of H H The Dalai Lama, Office of Tibet, Gadhen Khangsar, PO Box 310, Lazimpat, Kathmandu (☎ (4) 11660, telex 2368 TCTC)

The Netherlands
     Tibetan Affairs Co-ordination Office, Postbus 1276, 3500 BG Utrecht

Switzerland
     Mr Kelsang Gyaltsen, Rep of H H The Dalai Lama, Office of Tibet, Waffenplatzstr 10, CH-8002 Zurich (☎ (01) 201 3336, telex 845 815153, fax 41012022160)

UK
     Mrs Kalsang Takla, Rep of H H The Dalai Lama, Office of Tibet, Linburn House, 342 Kilburn High Rd, London NW6 2QJ (☎ (01) 328 8422, telex 892843 OFFLET G, fax 01-624 41 00)

USA
     Mr Rinchen Darlo, Rep of H H The Dalai Lama, Office of Tibet, 241 East 32nd St, New York, NY 10016 (☎ (212) 213 5010, telex 277638 TIBET UR)
     Mr Lodi Gyari, International Campaign for Tibet, Suite No 739, 1511 K St NW, Washington, DC 20005 (☎ (202) 628-4123, fax (202) 347-6825)

To keep up with the news on Tibet you can contact the Information Office in Dharamsala (see previous listings for address) which distributes free the bi-monthly *Tibetan Bulletin*. The monthly *Tibetan Review* is available from the same address by subscription. In Australia, the Tibet Information Service (145 The Boulevard, Ivanhoe 3079, Victoria) publishes an interesting and comprehensive monthly *News Digest*.

Information on political background and developments concerning Tibet is available from the Tibet Support Group (☎ (071) 240-2493) 1st Floor, 43 New Oxford St, London, UK. The Tibet Foundation (☎ (071) 379-0634, fax (071) 405-3814) 43 New Oxford St, London is a charity which provides impartial cultural and religious coverage of Tibet including newsletters, courses in the Tibetan language, and library and bookshop services. They're open Monday to Friday from 11 am to 6 pm.

All these information outlets operate on minimum budgets and rely on goodwill so you should remember to include payment of costs with your queries.

Overseas Representatives
China International Travel Service (CITS)
The Chinese fount of tourist information is the China International Travel Service (CITS). It is known in Chinese as *Guoji Lüxingshe*. The standard of their information on offer for Tibet is varied, to put it mildly, and sometimes you're lucky to get any at all. Following are the addresses and telephone numbers of CITS offices in Beijing, Hong Kong and the USA:

Beijing
　　6 Dong Chang'an Jie, Beijing 100740 (☎ 5121122; cable CITSH, 1954 Beijing; telex 22350, 22606 CITSH CN)
Hong Kong
　　6th Floor, Tower II, South Seas Centre, Tsimshatsui East, Kowloon (☎ 7215317, cable 2320 Hong Kong, telex 38449 CITC HX)
USA
　　60E, 42nd St, Suite 465, New York, New York 10165 (☎ 212-867-0271)

China Travel Service (CTS) Within China, CTS is concerned with tourists from Hong Kong, Macau and Taiwan, and with foreign nationals of Chinese descent (Overseas Chinese). Outside of China they will book tours for just about anybody.

Following are the addresses for the China Travel Service in Beijing and foreign countries:

Australia
　　Level 2, 724-728 George St, Sydney, NSW 2000 (☎ (02) 2112633, fax 2813595)
Canada
　　PO Box 17, Main Floor, 999 West Hastings St, Vancouver, BC V6C 2W2 (☎ (604) 6848787, fax 6843321)
China
　　8 Dongjiaomin Xiang, Dongchenchu, Beijing 100005 (☎ 5129933, fax 5129008, cable 2464 Beijing, telex 22487 CTSHO CN)

France
　　10 Rue De Rome, 75008, Paris (☎ (1) 45-22-92-72, fax 45-22-92-79)
Hong Kong
　　Central Branch, 2nd Floor, China Travel Bldg, 77 Queen's Road, Central (☎ 8533533, fax 5419777)
　　Kowloon Branch, 1st Floor, Alpha House, 27-33 Nathan Rd, Tsimshatsui (☎ 7211331, fax 7217757)
Japan
　　Nihombashi-Settsu Bldg, 2-2-4, Nihombashi, Chuo-Ku, Tokyo (☎ (03) 2735512, fax 2732667)
Macau
　　Ground Floor, Metropole Hotel, 63 Rua da Praia Grande
Philippines
　　489 San Fernando St, Binondo, Manila (☎ 40-74-75, fax 40-78-34)
Singapore
　　Ground Floor, SIA Bldg, 77 Robinson Rd, Singapore, (☎ 2240550, fax 2245009)
Thailand
　　460/2-3 Surawong Rd, Bangkok 10500 (☎ (2) 2332805, fax 2365511)
UK
　　24 Cambridge Circus, London WC2H 8HD (☎ (071) 8369911, fax 8363121)
USA
　　2nd Floor, 212 Sutter St, San Francisco, CA 94108 (☎ (415) 3986627, fax 3986669)
　　Los Angeles Branch, Suite 138, 2223E, Garvey Ave, Monterey Park, CA 91754 (☎ (818) 2888222, fax 2883464)

Complaint Hot Line
It probably doesn't do any good to complain, but it should at least make you feel better. China has recently set up English-language tourist complaint hot lines in nine locations, and it's possible that this service will be expanded. For what it's worth, the numbers are:

Beijing (☎ (01) 5130828)
Gansu Province (☎ (0931) 26860)
Guangdong Province (☎ (020) 677422)
Guilin (☎ (0773) 226533)
Jiangsu Province (☎ (025) 301221)
Shaanxi Province (☎ (029) 711480)
Shanghai (☎ (012) 4390630)
Tianjin (☎ (022) 318814, 318812)
Zhejiang Province (☎ (0571) 556631)

There is no complaint hot line for Tibetans in Lhasa, however; presumably those with complaints about the system in Tibet must phone from elsewhere.

SOME USEFUL ADDRESSES

Following are some organisations which can provide more information on what is going on in Tibet.

Appropriate Technology for Tibetans (ApTT) (☎ 081-4522820), 6 Rockhall Rd, London NW2 6DT, UK is a nonprofit environmental organisation which encourages sustainable land-use methods and appropriate technologies in a variety of projects to support Tibetan refugee rehabilitation settlements in India. The ApTT newsletter provides more detail on what is being done and what kind of help is needed.

Office of Tibet, Tibet Fund, Potala Publications, US Tibet Committee, Tibetan Association, Tibetan Women's Association, and Tibet House are now all at the same location in New York: 241 East 32nd St, New York, NY 10016. The phone number for Tibet House is (☎ (212) 213-5592). The joint phone number for all the other organisations is (☎ (212) 213-5010).

BUSINESS HOURS & FESTIVALS

Most shops are open between 9 am and 12.30 pm and then again from 2.30 pm until 5.30 pm. Many shops close on Sundays. Government offices are usually closed on Saturday afternoons and all day Sunday.

Virtually every month, at every full or new moon, there are local or national festivals in Tibet:

New Year Festival
The first day of the first month of the Tibetan calendar (usually February or early March) is celebrated all over Tibet. Monasteries, chortens and shrines are visited at dawn and offerings are made.

Great Prayer Festival
The Great Prayer (Tibetan: Monlam) Festival begins three days after the New Year Festival. This festival celebrates the victory of Buddha over his six opponents and used to last about three weeks in Lhasa.

Lesser Prayer Festival
This festival is held during the month following the Greater Prayer Festival.

Buddha's Anniversary Festival
Known as *Saka dawa*, the 15th day of the fourth month (approximately May) of the Tibetan calendar is celebrated as the anniversary of Buddha's birth, enlightenment and death. In Lhasa, the Jokhang Temple is packed with worshippers praying to Sakyamuni.

Incense Festival
This festival takes place on the 15th day of the fifth month (approximately late June). Apparently, on this day evil ghosts prowl around looking for a human spirit. However, if the spirit is really happy, the ghosts are unable to take possession. Tibetans dress up, wander around and party hard enough to repel the spirits.

Shoton (Xuedun) Festival
Literally the 'Yoghurt Banquet', this festival takes place between the end of the sixth and the beginning of the seventh month (approximately mid-August). In pre-1959 Tibet, this was also the opera season.

Washing Festival
This festival takes place during the beginning of the seventh month (approximately early September) and lasts about a week. Everybody in Lhasa goes to the river to wash themselves and their clothes. According to a legend, bathing like this can cure sickness of any description.

Ongkor Festival
Literally 'Looking Around the Fields', this festival takes place at the end of the seventh month (approximately late September) to ensure a good harvest. Tibetan opera, horse-racing and archery are common events. Reportedly, the town of Zétang puts on a spectacular show.

Tsong Khapa's Festival
This festival takes place on the 25th day of the 10th month (approximately late November) to celebrate the anniversary of the death of Tsong Khapa. Butter lamps are lit and left on windowsills and rooftops.

Banishing the Evil Spirits Festival
This festival (Tibetan: Guthok) occurs on the 29th day of the 12th month (approximately late January). Evil spirits are exorcised into ritual soup and left outside with burning straws.

POST & TELECOMMUNICATIONS
Postal Rates
International Mail The ordinary postal rates for international mail (other than to Hong Kong or Macau) are listed. There is a slightly reduced postage rate for letters and postcards to certain countries.

Letters sent by surface mail cost Y1.50 up to 20 grams, and Y3 above 20 grams and up to 50 grams. Air-mail letters are an additional

Y0.50 for every 10 grams or fraction thereof. Aerogrammes are Y1.90 to anywhere in the world.

Printed matter sent by surface mail is Y1 up to 20 grams, Y1.60 above 20 grams and up to 50 grams, Y2.80 above 50 grams and up to 100 grams, Y5.40 above 100 grams and up to 250 grams, Y10.20 above 250 grams and up to 500 grams, Y16.20 above 500 grams and up to one kg , Y27 above one kg and up to two kg, and for each additional kg or fraction thereof the charge is Y11.40. Air mail for printed matter is an additional Y0.40 for every additional 10 grams or fraction thereof.

Surface mail charges for small packets are Y3.60 up to 100 grams, Y7.20 above 100 grams and up to 250 grams, Y13 above 250 grams and up to 500 grams, Y21.60 above 500 grams and up to one kg . Air mail for small packets is an additional Y0.40 for every 10 grams or fraction thereof.

Rates for parcels vary depending on the country of destination. Charge for a one kg parcel sent surface mail from China to the UK is Y52, to the USA Y30.60, to Germany Y35.60. Charge for a one kg parcel sent air mail to the UK is Y82, to the USA Y77, to West Germany Y70.60.

Post offices are very picky about how you pack things; don't finalise your packing until the parcel has got its last customs clearance. If you have a receipt for the goods, then put it in the box when you're mailing it, since it may be opened again by customs further down the line.

Domestic Services Domestic mail within the same city costs half the price as domestic mail being sent elsewhere. Within a city, letters (20 grams and below) cost Y0.04, postcards Y0.02. Out of town, letters are Y0.08, postcards Y0.04. The fee for registration is Y0.12.

Postcards are Y1.10 by surface mail and Y1.60 by air mail to anywhere in the world.

Registration Fees The registration fee for letters, printed matter and packets is Y1.

Acknowledgement of receipt is Y0.80 per article.

Sending Mail

As well as the local post offices there are branch post offices in just about all the major tourist hotels where you can send letters, packets and parcels (the contents of packets and parcels are checked by the post office staff before mailing). In some places, you may only be able to post printed matter from these branch offices. Other parcels may require a customs form attached at the town's main post office, where their contents will be checked. Close surveillance of posted items is the norm, especially in Tibet, so be sure not to send anything that may arouse more than a passing interest.

The international postal service seems efficient, and air-mail letters and postcards will probably take around five to 10 days to reach their destinations. An International Express Mail Service now operates in many Chinese cities. If possible, write the country of destination in Chinese, as this should speed up the delivery.

Large envelopes are a bit hard to come by; try the department stores. If you expect to be sending quite a few packets then stock up when you come across such envelopes. A roll of strong, sticky tape is a useful item to bring along and serves many purposes. String, glue and sometimes cloth bags are supplied at the post offices, but don't count on it. The Friendship Stores will sometimes package and mail purchases for you, but only goods actually bought at the store.

Receiving Mail
It's worth noting that some foreigners in China have had their mail opened or parcels pilfered before receipt – and some have their outgoing mail opened and read. Officially, the People's Republic prohibits several items from being mailed to it, including books, magazines, notes and manuscripts.

Poste Restante There are poste restantes in just about every city and town, and they seem to work. Unfortunately, most post offices haven't discovered alphabetical order.

Hotels Some major tourist hotels will hold mail for their guests, but this doesn't always work. Many places will hold mail for several months if you write such an instruction on the outside of the letter.

Telephone
Many hotel rooms are equipped with phones from which local calls are free. Local calls can be made from public phones (there are some around – not many). There are also internal telex, telegram and long-distance phone services.

Direct dialling for international calls is gradually being introduced at top hotels in the major cities. You can also use the main telecommunications offices. Lines are a bit faint but usually OK and you generally don't have to wait more than half an hour before you're connected. Many large hotels now offer fax service to almost every country in the world that has direct dialling.

The usual procedure is to fill out a form with the relevant information concerning who you want to call or fax, and hand it to the attendant at the telephone desk.

Rates for station-to-station calls are Y18 per minute to most countries in the world. Hong Kong is slightly cheaper at Y12 per minute. There is a minimum charge of three minutes. Collect calls are cheaper than calls paid for in China. Time the call yourself – the operator will not break in to tell you that your minimum period of three minutes is approaching. After you hang up, the operator will ring back to tell you how much it cost. There is no call cancellation fee.

If you are expecting a call – either international or domestic – try to advise the caller beforehand of your hotel room number. The operators frequently have difficulty understanding Western names, and the hotel receptionist may not be able to locate you.

In major cities, the local directory assistance number is 114; long-distance (domestic) information is 113. However, operators only speak Chinese.

Fax, Telex & Telegram
Fax messages, telexes and telegrams can be sent from some of the major tourist hotels and from the central telegraph offices in some of the bigger cities.

International fax and telexes (other than those to Hong Kong or Macau) cost around Y18 per minute with a three-minute minimum charge. International telegram rates are usually around Y3.50 per word, and more for the express service. Rates to Hong Kong are less.

TIME
All time in China revolves around Beijing time so, officially, there is no time difference between Lhasa and Beijing. In effect there should be several hours difference.

The Chinese State Council has decreed that in the future clocks will be set back one hour at 2 am on the first Sunday of the second 10 days of April, and will be advanced one hour at 2 am on the first Sunday of the second 10 days of September.

When it's noon in Lhasa it is also noon in Hong Kong, 4 am in London, 2 pm in Melbourne and 8 pm the previous day in Los Angeles.

ELECTRICITY
Supply can be erratic, but when it's there, it's 220 volts, 50 cycles AC and plugs are generally of the two-pin American type. Since lighting both inside buildings and outside on the streets is unreliable, a torch is essential.

WEIGHTS & MEASURES
The metric system is widely used in China and Tibet. However, the traditional Chinese measures are often used for domestic transactions and you may come across them.

Metric	Chinese	Imperial
1 metre	3 chi	3.28 feet
1 km	2 li	0.62 miles
1 hectare	15 mu	2.47 acres
1 litre	1 gongsheng	0.22 gallons
1 kg	2 jin	2.20 pounds

BOOKS & MAPS
History & Politics
For political and historical coverage mention should be made of John Avedon's *In Exile From the Land of Snows* which provides an incisive modern day perspective on Tibetan culture. Standard works on Tibetan history are Tsepon Shakaba's *Tibet: A Political History*, David Snellgrove's *A Cultural History of Tibet* and Hugh Richardson's *Tibet & its History*. Sir Charles Bell wrote extensively and authoritatively on old Tibetan society in books such as *People of Tibet, Religion of Tibet, Tibet Past & Present,* and *Portrait of the Dalai Lama*. For the story of a Tibetan who rebelled against the Chinese, there is Jamyang Norbu's *Warriors of Tibet*.

Travel Classics
Amongst the travel classics is Heinrich Harrer's *Seven Years in Tibet* which has become standard reading on independent Tibet in the final years before the Chinese moved in. Harrer later wrote a highly critical sequel *Return to Tibet* after a visit in the early '80s. Alexandra David-Neill, an extraordinarily active explorer, wrote *Magic & Mystery in Tibet* which details her experiences with astounding aspects of Tibetan Buddhism. She was the first Western woman

to reach Lhasa and wrote about this visit in *My Journey to Lhasa*. A roundup of Tibet's foreign intruders is given in Peter Hopkirk's *Trespassers on the Roof of the World*.

Modern travelogues include Vikram Seth's humorous *From Heaven Lake: Travels through Sinkiang & Tibet*, Sorrel Wilby's Kailas to Lhasa trek in *Journey Across Tibet: A Young Woman's 1900 Mile Trek Across the Rooftop of the World* and Elaine Brook's *Land of the Snow Lion: An Adventure in Tibet*.

Travel Guides
Two guidebooks worth a mention are Keith Dowman's *The Power Places of Central Tibet: A Pilgrim's Guide* and Stephen Batchelor's *The Tibet Guide*.

If you are travelling in the regions surrounding Tibet there are Lonely Planet guides to *China, Nepal, India, Kashmir Ladakh & Zanskar, Karakoram Highway* and *Pakistan*. Lonely Planet also publishes individual trekking guides for the Nepal and Indian Himalaya, shoestring guides for travel across Asia, and a number of phrasebooks, including the *Tibet Phrasebook, Mandarin Chinese Phrasebook* and *Nepali Phrasebook*.

Buddhism
The Dalai Lama has written on Tibetan Buddhism in *The Buddhism of Tibet* and his autobiography in *My Land & My People*. Another well-constructed biography is *The*

Last Dalai Lama by Michael Harris Goodman.

Fiction

For racy reads with plenty of latitude for fiction try Lobsang Rampa's *The Third Eye* or Lionel Davidson's *The Rose of Tibet* which is a surprisingly detailed novel. The same applies to Gil Ziff's novel *Tibet* and to *Mipam: A Tibetan Love Story*, the first Tibetan novel written for foreigners, by Alexandra David-Neill's adopted son, Yongden. For the adventures of Tintin there's Herge's *Tintin in Tibet*.

Photography

One of the finest photographic records prior to the Chinese invasion of Tibet is found in Rosemary Tung's *A Portrait of Lost Tibet*.

Bookshops

Useful sources for these books are bookshops or publishers specialising in Tibet or Asia. In Hong Kong try Wanderlust at 30 Hollywood Rd and Swindons in Lock Rd. In the UK there is Wisdom Publications (☎ (081) 520-5588) 402 Hoe St, London E17 9AA, and Serindia Publications, 10 Parkfield, Putney, London SW15 6NH. In the USA, try Snow Lion Publications (☎ 1-800-950-0313) PO Box 6483, Ithaca, NY 14851; Wisdom Publications (☎ 1-800-272-4050) 361 Newbury St, Boston, MA 02115, and Potala Publications (☎ (212) 213-5011) 107 East 31st St, New York, NY 10016. There is also a Wisdom Publications (☎ (02) 922-6338) PO Box 1326, Chatswood, NSW 2067 in Australia. Some of these firms provide mail order services. In Kathmandu there are numerous bookstores which also sell second-hand books.

Maps

In the last few years several good maps of Tibet and China have been produced to meet the needs of tourists, travellers and trekkers.

Map of the People's Republic of China (Cartographic Publishing House (China) & Esselte Map Service (Sweden), 1985). The Swedes and the Chinese have jointly pro-

duced this beautiful map which covers China and Tibet. All names are given in pinyin with Chinese characters which can be useful for arranging transport with Chinese drivers. One drawback is the huge size of the thing – with careful pressure, you can tear off Ethnic Tibet at the middle seam.

The Mountains of Central Asia (The Royal Geographical Society & The Mt Everest Foundation, published by Macmillan, London, 1987). This is a handy map with clear presentation of topography, but the inclusion of a gazetteer has shot the price up to UK£14.95. More of a reference map than one to use out on the road since it lacks Tibetan script or Chinese characters.

South-Central Tibet (Stanfords International Maps, London, 1987). Useful map for Central Tibet which includes Tibetan transliteration and pinyin for major places.

Tibet Road Map (Editions Astrolabe, Paris, 1987). This French production extends beyond Central Tibet with eye-catching splashes of topographic colour.

Also on sale in Nepal is *Tibet & Adjacent Countries*, a reprint from 1919. An interesting read, if only to reconstitute the past prior to the Cultural Revolution or provide a name to a heap of modern-day rubble by the roadside.

Nelles Verlag in Germany produce a series of superbly detailed maps. For Tibet travellers, their most useful ones are *Himalaya* which covers most of Central Tibet; *India 1 – North* which covers most of the Indian border with Western Tibet; *India 5 – North East* which extends across the Indian borders into Eastern Tibet; and *Nepal* which takes in the Nepalese-Tibetan border region.

A large map which covers the whole of ethnic Tibet is available in Tibetan and an English version appeared in 1986. Although this is not a road map, it is useful for digging back into Tibetan places and spaces which have become obscured by Chinese nomenclature or political rearrangement. Read and wonder at the scope of Tibet. Contact your nearest Office of Tibet (see the preceding section on Tourism Information for full list of these offices) for details of purchase.

Map of Tibet (Wisdom Publications, London). At the time of writing this map was still being prepared.

In 1991, the National Geographic Society came out with a sumptuous map of Mt Everest complete with a mini history of first ascents between 1950 and 1990.

Now that foreigners have been allowed into Tibet and produced maps for ground-level tourist attack, there is less point in using the Defense Mapping Agency Aerospace Center's materials which are intended for aviators, but available to civilian purchasers from NOAA Distribution Branch (N/CG33), National Ocean Service, Riverdale, Md 20737, USA. If you still want to simulate the feel of flight, the relevant maps for coverage of ethnic Tibet are ONC-H-9; H-10;H-11;G-7; G-8; and G-9. H-9, which covers Central Tibet, will probably be of most interest. Large map specialists usually stock them.

More detailed mapping, usually only available through libraries in the USA, is produced by the Defense Mapping Agency Topographic Center, Maryland (☎ 301-2272000) as part of their JOG (Joint Operations Graphic) series. Mapping with similar depth of detail and restricted library access is produced by the Army Map Service (AMS) (202-8359681) Corps of Engineers, Washington, DC.

Probably the best coverage of the Lhasa-Kathmandu Highway and most of Central Tibet is provided by the *Latest Map of Kathmandu to Lhasa* (Himalaya Bookseller, Durbar Marg, GPO Box 528, Kathmandu, Nepal, 1987). This map also includes a Tibetan mini-glossary, a Lhasa city map and details of trekking routes.

For trekkers, the maps in Keith Dowman's *The Power Places of Central Tibet* and Gary McCue's *Trekking in Tibet* serve as a useful base.

Providing you can find your way around with Chinese characters, it's worth stopping at Xinhua (the Chinese bookstore monopoly) in major cities such as Lhasa, Xining, Chengdu, etc where you may find a job lot of city or even provincial maps. However, supply is totally erratic, staff often soporific and some mapping is classified as *nei bu* (restricted access) so not for the consumption of beady-eyed big-noses.

MEDIA

Newspapers

There are two daily newspapers in Lhasa, one in Tibetan and the other in Chinese. Both are called *Tibet Daily* although the Tibetan paper is mostly a translation of the Chinese one which offers a bland monotony of predictable nonevents.

Radio

In March 1991, the Voice of America (VOA) started broadcasting a Tibetan-language programme which sparked protests from the Chinese government and considerable interest from Tibetans. The Tibetan programme is broadcast daily on shortwave to Tibet and northern India from Tinang in the Philippines. The relevant frequencies are 15.43, 17.705 and 21.57 mHz; and transmission time is currently from 5.30 to 5.45 am (Indian Standard Time). Not content with mere protests, the Chinese have started jamming the VOA broadcasts and have set up their own Tibetan-language broadcasting service via satellite in order to spread the party's policies and 'resist political infiltration by foreign reactionary forces'. Sounds like the airwave debate is going to bring a little heat to the cold plateaux!

TV

Tibetans were first able to tune into TV in 1979 when the Tibetan TV Station began broadcasting colour videos of Beijing CCTV programmes, which were delivered by air usually a week after they had been seen elsewhere in China. Reportedly, only one colour TV then existed in Tibet as opposed to several thousand now. The Tibetan TV Station can now receive programmes direct through a satellite receiving station completed in Lhasa in September 1985. A second channel has started to broadcast news bulletins, plays, dubbed films, and programmes made by the station in Tibetan. This will perhaps offset the problems caused by broadcasting in Chinese to speakers of Tibetan only.

Film

Yin Hong, a film-maker with the Shanghai Popular Science Film Studio, has made several films on Tibet. His film *Tibet, Tibet* won first prize at an international film festival in France in 1985. Another recent film with a Tibetan background is *Horse Thief*.

FILM & PHOTOGRAPHY

Film is sometimes available at high prices in Lhasa or Chengdu but supplies are erratic so you are best off stocking up in advance in Hong Kong or Kathmandu. If you want to try the local product, there are various Chinese-made print films which can be processed in large cities or through major hotels. The nearest processing points for Kodachrome are in Japan and Australia.

Some of the best times to shoot are early and late in the day. Between 10 am and 2 pm the sun can be high and hot overhead producing a bluish haze which can be counteracted by using a skylight filter. A polarising filter is also very effective and essential for Tibet. A lens hood will reduce your problems with reflections and direct sunlight on the lens. Dust can be a real problem so take along plenty of cleaning materials and, of course, spare batteries for your camera.

Watch out for the sharp contrasts between sun and shade. If you can't get reasonably balanced overall light you may have to choose to correctly expose only one area or the other or use fill-in flash. Make sure you keep your camera somewhere safe. Theft is on the increase.

You are not allowed to take photos of airports, train terminals, harbour facilities (no problem in landlocked Tibet!) or military installations. In theory you are also not allowed to take photos out of the window of a plane but this rule could probably be stretched on those irresistible runs between Kathmandu and Lhasa or Chengdu and Lhasa.

In monasteries in Tibet there is sometimes complete prohibition of photos and at other times a fee (ranging between Y20 and Y150!) is required. This type of restriction may be to protect the interiors, guarantee postcard sales or simply to raise funds. During times of unrest, the PSB can crack down on foreign photographers and confiscate film.

Tibetans may ask you for a print if you take a photo of them. Often it is assumed that you are using Polaroid film so, if you aren't, you may have to explain with sign language and by flourishing a spare roll of film that it all has to be developed first. You can also do your subject a favour by agreeing to send a print to his or her address. Alternatively you could run the risk of being mobbed and offer a Dalai Lama picture in return for taking a photo.

Whatever you do, be tactful with your photos. Obviously, shoving a camera into someone's face is not going to create an atmosphere of trust. It's always polite to ask first and to respect 'no' as an answer. Some Tibetans are understandably wary of being identified should your photos become the subject of PSB interest. A gesture, a smile and a nod are usually sufficient.

Chinese security officials, especially those in Lhasa, are increasingly keen to secure mugshots of foreign visitors. Smile, and pull any face you like!

HEALTH

The information in this section on the medical mysteries of Tibet was kindly provided by Dr John Kendall of Travellers Medical & Vaccination Centre, Sydney, Australia.

Travel health depends on your pre-departure preparations, your day-to-day health care while travelling and how you handle any medical problem or emergency that does develop. While the list of potential dangers can seem quite frightening, with a little luck, some basic precautions and adequate information few travellers experience more than upset stomachs.

The marvels of Tibet do have a price – the physical rigours of travelling through the place. Anyone contemplating a visit to Tibet, no matter how brief, must prepare adequately or risk not only the trip, but also their health.

Tibet is very isolated and, especially if you're sick, at least as difficult to get out of as it is to get into. Transport is unreliable and being stranded due to mechanical breakdown is common. Access to modern medical care is nonexistent, and emergency transport either to Lhasa or out of Tibet is dictated by weather, cost, availability and official cooperation.

Travel Health Guides

There are a number of books on travel health:

Staying Healthy in Asia, Africa & Latin America, (Volunteers in Asia). Probably the best all-round guide to carry, as it's compact but very detailed and well organised.
Travellers' Health, Dr Richard Dawood, (Oxford University Press). Comprehensive, easy to read, authoritative and also highly recommended, although it's rather large to lug around.
Where There is No Doctor, David Werner, (Hesperian Foundation). A very detailed guide intended for someone, like a Peace Corps worker, going to work in an undeveloped country, rather than for the average traveller.
Travel with Children, Maureen Wheeler, (Lonely Planet Publications). Includes basic advice on travel health for younger children.

Pre-Departure Preparations

Health Insurance A travel insurance policy to cover theft, loss and medical problems is a wise idea. There are a wide variety of policies and your travel agent will have recommendations. The international student travel policies handled by STA or other student travel organisations are usually good value. Some policies offer lower and higher medical expenses options but the higher one is chiefly for countries like the USA which have extremely high medical costs. Check the small print:

1. Some policies specifically exclude 'dangerous activities' which can include scuba diving, motorcycling, even trekking. If such activities are on your agenda you don't want that sort of policy.
2. You may prefer a policy which pays doctors or hospitals direct rather than you having to pay on the spot and claim later. If you have to claim later make sure you keep all documentation. Some policies ask you to call back (reverse charges) to a centre in your home country where an immediate assessment of your problem is made.
3. Check if the policy covers ambulances or an emergency flight home. If you have to stretch out you will need two seats and somebody has to pay for them!

Medical Kit A small, straightforward medical kit is essential for travel in Tibet where modern medical care is nonexistent. A possible kit list includes:

scissors
tweezers/splinter probe
thermometer (one which can read low body temperature as well as high temperature)
good quality sewing needle
scalpel
sterile gauze swabs (large & small)
Band-Aids/elastoplast
roll of adhesive tape
sling (your scarf will double as a sling)
1 good quality 4-inch bandage
1 good quality 2-inch bandage
1 packet of steristrips
safety pins
Betadine (antiseptic)
Bactrim DS (sulphur drug) or Ampicillin (a penicillin derivative) for gut infections
Erythromycin for chest infections
Fasigyn or Flagyl for amoebic dysentery or giardia
antifungal cream (eg Daktarin or Canesten)
Soframycin eye/ear drops for conjunctivitis or outer ear infections
Imodium or Lomotil for diarrhoea
Aspirin/codeine tablets (eg Aspalgin)
Antihistamine (eg Phenergan) for allergic reactions or motion sickness
Diamox (Acetazolamide) – not for people

allergic to sulphur – for mild AMS
Rehydration salts for replacement of salts lost with severe diarrhoea
Iodine for purifying water

Ideally antibiotics should be administered only under medical supervision and should never be taken indiscriminately. Overuse of antibiotics can weaken your body's ability to deal with infections naturally and can reduce the drug's efficacy on a future occasion. Take only the recommended dose at the prescribed intervals and continue using the antibiotic for the prescribed period, even if the illness seems to be cured earlier. Antibiotics are quite specific to the infections they can treat, stop immediately if there are any serious reactions and don't use it at all if you are unsure if you have the correct one.

In many countries if a medicine is available at all it will generally be available over the counter and the price will be much cheaper than in the West. However, be careful of buying drugs in developing countries, particularly where the expiry date may have passed or correct storage conditions may not have been followed. It's possible that drugs which are no longer recommended, or have even been banned, in the West are still being dispensed in many Third World countries.

Health Preparations You, your past medical history and your current level of fitness are known factors. If you suffer from an on-going medical condition such as a heart condition, asthma, bronchitis or other lung condition, diabetes, stomach ulcer or have suffered a stroke then I'd suggest that you see a doctor, competent in travel medicine, before you even consider booking your ticket to Tibet. It is not the place to have an acute asthma attack or diabetic crisis.

As with all adventure travel, a high level of fitness will give your body greater physical reserve in case anything does happen. If you intend trekking, then it is a good idea to prepare yourself by walking up and down flights of stairs, four times a week with a pack on your back, from six weeks before

leaving. This will not only get your heart and lungs ready, but also your joints and muscles used to hard work. Remember though, nothing will be able to prepare you for the effects of high altitude.

The activities you have planned will make a difference to the preparation you need. For example, someone heading off with a determined gleam in their eyes, a pair of Alpine skis strapped to their back and a map of Mt Kailas in their hip pocket, will need more preparation than someone visiting Lhasa on a two-day tour.

Immunisations Vaccinations provide protection against diseases you might come into contact with along the way. For some countries no immunisations are necessary, but the further off the beaten track you go the more necessary it is to take precautions. These days vaccination as an entry requirement is usually only enforced when you are coming from an infected area – yellow fever and cholera are the two most likely requirements. Nevertheless, all vaccinations should be recorded on an International Health Certificate, which is available from your physician or government health department.

Plan ahead for getting your vaccinations: some of them require an initial shot followed by a booster, while some vaccinations should not be given together. Most travellers from Western countries will have been immunised against various diseases during childhood but your doctor may still recommend booster shots against measles or polio, diseases still prevalent in many developing countries. The period of protection offered by vaccinations differs widely and some are contraindicated if you are pregnant.

In some countries immunisations are available from airport or government health centres. Travel agents or airline offices will tell you where. The possible list of vaccinations includes:

Tetanus/Diptheria (a combined vaccine) All travellers should be immunised. The initial course (usually given in infancy) is three doses spread out over six months with a fourth, 12 months later. Booster shots are needed every 10 years.

Polio (oral sabin vaccine). All travellers should be immunised. The initial course (usually given in infancy) is three doses over six months, with a fourth dose given at age five years. A booster is required every 10 years.

Typhoid This vaccine does offer good protection and is recommended for all travellers in Tibet, especially if travelling overland through China or Nepal on your way to or from Tibet. The initial course is two shots, separated by two to four weeks. The booster dose is every three years (if you hate having shots, a tablet form is available).

Infectious Hepatitis Immune globulin is recommended for all travellers. A single shot given just prior to leaving for your trip. This will last three to six months and gives good protection against the Hepatitis A virus.

Cholera Not recommended. This vaccine does not give you good protection against cholera and is only recommended these days if you are visiting a country, such as Pakistan, that requires it as a condition of entry.

Rabies The last case of rabies in a Tibetan dog was apparently 24 years ago, and even then there was a question about whether the dog had entered Tibet from Nepal. So your risk of rabies in Tibet is small, if any. However, any traveller intending an extensive trip through Asia, of which Tibet is only one destination, should consider having the rabies pre-exposure vaccine. Remember that even if you've had this course of shots and then get bitten somewhere by a rabid dog, you'll need the second course of shots as well. However, you will not need the rabies immune globulin which is very expensive and difficult to get.

Meningitis Bacterial meningitis is very common in Nepal, but not in Tibet. If you intend visiting Nepal before or after Tibet, then you are strongly recommended to have the single meningitis shot, which will last one to two years.

Basic Rules

Care in what you eat and drink is the most

important health rule; stomach upsets are the most likely travel health problem but the majority of these upsets will be relatively minor. Don't become paranoid, trying the local food is part of the experience of travel after all.

Water Water should be considered contaminated anywhere in Tibet; someone will always be pissing upstream. In Lhasa, most places will give you boiled water to drink. The standard alternatives are tea, coffee or bottled drinks (including beer!). Outside the major towns, about the only drink you'll be offered is Yak butter tea. It takes some getting used to, but if you want to survive, drink as much as you're offered. It's actually very nutritious.

Water Purification The simplest way of purifying water is to boil it thoroughly. Technically this means boiling for 10 minutes, something which happens very rarely! Remember that at high altitude water boils at lower temperature, so germs are less likely to be killed.

Simple filtering will not remove all dangerous organisms, so if you cannot boil water it should be treated chemically. Chlorine tablets (Puritabs, Steritabs or other brand names) will kill many but not all pathogens. Iodine is very effective in purifying water and is available in tablet form (such as Potable Aqua), but follow the directions carefully and remember that too much iodine can be harmful.

If you can't find tablets, tincture of iodine (2%) or iodine crystals can be used. Two drops of tincture of iodine per litre or quart of clear water is the recommended dosage; the treated water should be left to stand for 30 minutes before drinking. Iodine crystals can also be used to purify water but this is a more complicated process, as you have to first prepare a saturated iodine solution. Iodine loses its effectiveness if exposed to air or damp so keep it in a tightly sealed container. Flavoured powder will disguise the taste of treated water and is a good idea if you are travelling with children.

Food Often you won't have a great deal of choice, it will be tsampa (tsampa is ground barley flour eaten mixed with tea, morning, noon and night!) or nothing. About the only rule you can stick to is making sure anything you eat is well cooked and served immediately. Don't use the wooden chopsticks provided with meals, because it is unlikely they have been washed properly and quite a few cases of hepatitis A originated this way. But do not despair completely, the markets in Lhasa have a lot of eggs, vegetables and fruits, but you should beware of the fly-blown meats and cheeses. Be your own chef and judge. Bon appétit!

Nutrition There is a real lack of good quality, nutritious food outside the major towns of Tibet. If your food is poor or limited in availability, if you're travelling hard and fast and therefore missing meals, or if you simply lose your appetite, you can soon start to lose weight and place your health at risk.

Make sure your diet is well balanced. Eggs, tofu, beans, lentils and nuts are all safe ways to get protein. Fruit you can peel (bananas, oranges or mandarins for example) is always safe and a good source of vitamins. Try to eat plenty of grains (rice) and bread. Remember that although food is generally safer if it is cooked well, overcooked food loses much of its nutritional value. If your diet isn't well balanced or if your food intake is insufficient, it's a good idea to take vitamin and iron pills.

Toilets Where would travel be without the never-ending supply of toilet stories? Tibet is no exception when it comes to Asian standards of hygiene. Although porcelain was invented by the Chinese, it has never managed to creep over the mountains into Tibet. Consequently toilets have remained 'pottery au naturel' or holes in the ground. These pits can have amazing effects on grown adults. I've seen people burst into tears, faint, shriek with laughter...thankfully, I've never seen anyone fall into one. I remember one dark windy night, a strange bat-like creature flapped up through the hole and scared the hell out of me. In fact a gust of wind had blown my toilet paper back up and out the hole. Disgusting really! And yes, there are flies on a hot summer day. Take a nose peg!

There are a few ways of minimising your risk of earning your own unique toilet story though. Always take a torch...once when I was sleeping by the fire in a very hospitable Tibetan family's kitchen, I felt mother nature's call. Not familiar with the maze of rooms that formed their cosy domicile, I found what I believed to be the adjoining livestock room and was just about to begin my micturition only to be greeted by screams of protest...I was actually in the main bedroom. Now I carry a torch everywhere with me.

Never go barefoot to the toilet...you can imagine for yourself the consequences you risk.

Watch out for dogs. It sounds (and is) disgusting, but the dogs are often at starvation point and so will fight for your offerings. Check around before relieving yourself.

Take enough toilet paper with you and always wash your hands after using the toilet.

Let me also stress that you should always resist the temptation to eat with your fingers. This is how illnesses like hepatitis A and dysentery are spread.

Everyday Health A normal body temperature is 98.6°F or 37°C; more than 2°C higher is a 'high' fever. A normal adult pulse rate is

60 to 80 per minute (children 80 to 100, babies 100 to 140). You should know how to take a temperature and a pulse rate. As a general rule the pulse increases about 20 beats per minute for each °C rise in fever.

Respiration (breathing) rate is also an indicator of illness. Count the number of breaths per minute: between 12 and 20 is normal for adults and older children (up to 30 for younger children, 40 for babies). People with a high fever or serious respiratory illness (like pneumonia) breathe more quickly than normal. More than 40 shallow breaths a minute usually means pneumonia.

Many health problems can be avoided by taking care of yourself. Wash your hands frequently – it's quite easy to contaminate your own food. Clean your teeth with purified water rather than straight from the tap. Avoid climatic extremes: keep out of the sun when it's hot, dress warmly when it's cold. Avoid potential diseases by dressing sensibly. You can get worm infections through walking barefoot. You can avoid insect bites by covering bare skin when insects are around, by screening windows or beds or by using insect repellents. Seek local advice: if you're told the water is unsafe don't go in. In situations where there is no information, discretion is the better part of valour.

Medical Problems & Treatment

Potential medical problems can be broken down into several areas. First there are the climatic and geographical considerations – problems caused by extremes of temperature, altitude or motion. Then there are diseases and illnesses caused by insanitation, insect bites or stings, and animal or human contact. Simple cuts, bites or scratches can also cause problems.

Self-diagnosis and treatment can be risky, so wherever possible seek qualified help. Although treatment dosages are given in this section, they are for emergency use only. Medical advice should be sought before administering any drugs.

An embassy or consulate can usually recommend a good place to go for such advice. So can five-star hotels, although they often recommend doctors with five-star prices. (This is when that medical insurance really comes in useful!) In some places standards of medical attention are so low that for some ailments the best advice is to get on a plane and go somewhere else.

Climatic & Geographical Considerations

The weather in Tibet is unpredictable and unforgiving. Fierce sun, blistering cold, raging dust storms and extreme changes in weather conditions can happen within hours. If you intend snooping around the more remote regions beyond the city limits of Lhasa then you must take with you sufficient warm clothing to survive a truck or bus breakdown at night on a mountain pass. Travellers have died from hypothermia in just this type of situation.

Dust storms are a problem, especially during the spring months between March and May when the temperatures rise in the valleys during the day, but remain low in the mountains, creating strong winds. This can present a real problem for anyone prone to respiratory tract conditions such as asthma or people who have chronic sinus problems.

The other seasons carry with them their own unique problems; the summer months can be very hot, and fierce sun combined with the thin air at high altitudes can really make a mess of fair skin.

All of Tibet, including Lhasa, is at high altitude; Lhasa itself is at 3685 metres above sea level. The Chinese once called the mountain regions of Tibet 'The Headache Mountains' because they knew that when they crossed the mountains to trade silk or salt many of them would suffer from headaches. Headache is in fact one of the early symptoms of AMS.

Sunburn A sunny day in Tibet is glorious. However, because the air is thinner and the snow-capped mountains are all around you acting as giant reflectors, you can get severely sunburnt in a very short period of time. You must protect your eyes with good quality sunglasses and also your skin with sun blockout. Look for creams/lotions with

PABA in them. Nothing seems more painful than eye-burn and 'lobster face', both results of sunburn.

Windburn The wind can blow up suddenly so you must have some form of windcheater with you at all times. Your face and hands will become very dry and chapped, so make sure you use protective sun cream and even moisturisers!

Cold To say that Tibet can be extremely cold is an understatement. Again, when travelling in Tibet, no matter what time of year, you must be prepared to cope with sudden, precipitous drops in temperature; take along thick woollen socks, thermal underwear, woollen pants, down jacket and down sleeping bag. If you can't afford all of the gear, you can actually outfit yourself pretty cheaply in China with second-hand clothes; especially useful are the army overcoats which are excellent value. Or if you are going via Nepal, you can pick up plenty of used trekking gear in Kathmandu. Remember, you need to be able to survive the unexpected, such as your bus/truck breaking down on top of a mountain pass or a sudden heavy snowfall.

Hypothermia occurs when the body loses heat faster than it can produce it and the core temperature of the body falls. It is surprisingly easy to progress from very cold to dangerously cold due to a combination of wind, wet clothing, fatigue and hunger, even if the air temperature is above freezing. It is

best to dress in layers; silk, wool and some of the new artificial fibres are all good insulating materials. A hat is important, as a lot of heat is lost through the head. A strong, waterproof outer layer is essential, as keeping dry is vital. Carry basic supplies, including food containing simple sugars to generate heat quickly and lots of fluid to drink.

Symptoms of hypothermia are exhaustion, numb skin (particularly toes and fingers), shivering, slurred speech, irrational or violent behaviour, lethargy, stumbling, dizzy spells, muscle cramps and violent bursts of energy. Irrationality may take the form of sufferers claiming they are warm and trying to take off their clothes.

To treat hypothermia, first get the patient out of the wind and/or rain, remove their clothing if its wet and replace it with dry, warm clothing. Give them hot liquids – not alcohol – and some high-kilojoule, easily digestible food. This should be enough for the early stages of hypothermia, but if it has gone further it may be necessary to place victims in warm sleeping bags and get in with them. Do not rub patients, place them near a fire or remove their wet clothes in the wind. If possible, place a sufferer in a warm (not hot) bath.

Altitude Sickness There is a great variation in different people's susceptibility to AMS. Some people get it at altitudes as low as 2450 metres; others feel fine at 6000 metres. In general, AMS is rare below 2450 metres.

Most people cover the altitude range 2450 to 4300 metres and so this is the range in which most cases of AMS occur. Remember that Lhasa is in this range and you will be at risk of AMS anywhere in Tibet.

People usually only reach altitudes of 4300 to 5500 metres in the Himalayan and Andes mountains. For example, trekking to Everest base camp or crossing any of the mountain passes leading into Tibet.

Only experienced mountaineers would usually be found at 5500 to 8800 metres. A prolonged stay at altitudes greater than 5500 metres (18,000 feet) results in a loss of physical conditioning rather than increasing fitness.

Anyone entering Tibet overland must be very aware of the risk of AMS, not only watching out for symptoms in themselves, but also in their companions. AMS can be rapidly fatal and hardly a year goes by without Western tourists dying in Tibet from this condition.

It is never possible to predict who will get AMS. Even experienced climbers who have been at high altitudes many times before may get AMS on returning to high altitudes. Everyone is at risk.

Acclimatisation Every school science teacher will gleefully tell you that water boils at a lower temperature at high altitude. Given a chance, they will also tell you the reason for this is the lower pressure of the surrounding air – in other words, the air is thinner. This also means there is less oxygen available to breathe at high altitude. To adapt to this reduced oxygen we breathe faster and deeper; our blood is pumped harder through our lungs; and our blood becomes thicker, with less water and more blood cells to carry oxygen. Other changes occur over a period of several weeks, these processes being known as acclimatisation.

The effects you will notice are:

* shortness of breath
* pounding of the heart
* tiring more easily

These are all normal adjustments.

Symptoms of AMS There are two types of AMS: benign and malignant. Benign AMS is the more common, milder form of AMS, but can herald the onset of the severe form. Symptoms include:

* headache
* loss of appetite
* dizziness
* sleeping difficulty
* cloudy head
* nausea & vomiting (especially in children)
* feeling unwell

Malignant AMS is very serious and can be rapidly *fatal*. It may occur without warning or it may be preceded with symptoms of benign AMS. The lungs and brain may be affected when fluid accumulates around them in conditions known as High Altitude Pulmonary Oedema and High Altitude Cerebral Oedema.

The symptoms of High Altitude Pulmonary Oedema are:

* extreme breathlessness
* cough
* white frothy sputum
* blue lips

The symptoms of High Altitude Cerebral Oedema are:

* severe headache
* drowsiness
* unsteady on feet
* disorientation
* abnormal behaviour
* progressively reduced level of consciousness leading to coma and death

The person with this form of altitude sickness may initially seem to be drunk or very antisocial. Make the effort to find out what is going on.

Treatment of AMS There is only one way to treat a person with AMS: get them down to a lower altitude immediately! Even if it is the middle of the night, you must go immediately. Every minute counts. Do not wait for more help.

If someone is unconscious and vomiting, then place them on their side so the vomit does not get into their lungs. If oxygen is available immediately, then give it, preferably at four to six litres per minute by a close fitting mask. Do *not* wait for it.

If someone is suffering from malignant AMS they must get out of Tibet as soon as possible. Do not try and go a long overland route, because inevitably you will have to go over a higher mountain pass to get out to lower altitude. If it is serious you must fly out.

In Tibet, the lowest altitude is still high altitude. A young man who was travelling from Nepal to Lhasa overland started acting strange in Shigatse. He had problems with his balance, was very sleepy and seemed withdrawn. When the bus finally arrived in Lhasa two days later, he was virtually comatose. Two days later he was dead.

Diamox (Acetazolamide) is not useful in preventing or treating serious malignant AMS. It may be useful in reducing the severity of the symptoms of benign AMS (for example, headaches), but do not take it routinely. If needed, take 250 mg every eight hours.

How to Minimise your Risk of AMS Ascend slowly. Rising to about 3000 metres usually presents no problem, but above 3000 metres your body needs time to acclimatise so anyone flying into Tibet must rest. Ascend only 300 metres per day and give yourself a full rest day every 1000 metres. Remember – climb high, sleep low!

Drink extra fluids. Trekking at high altitudes will dehydrate you because you sweat more and lose moisture in your breath because the air is cold and dry. Eat light, high carbohydrate meals because carbohydrate is more efficiently turned into energy.

Avoid tobacco as smoking produces carbon monoxide which reduces the amount of oxygen your blood can carry. Avoid alcohol as it increases urine output and will further dehydrate you. Do not take sedatives to help you sleep; you may be masking a symptom of AMS.

Do not trek alone.

Do not ignore the symptoms. If you are suffering from any symptoms of benign AMS don't go any higher until they have

disappeared and avoid heavy exertion. Light outdoor activity is better than bed rest. When you first enter Tibet, take it easy for the first few days. Don't go lumbering up to the Potala the moment you arrive in Lhasa! If you feel worse and the symptoms will not go away, then you must consider leaving Tibet quickly.

Motion Sickness Eating lightly before and during a trip will reduce the chances of motion sickness. If you are prone to motion sickness try to find a place that minimises disturbance – near the wing on aircraft, close to midships on boats, near the centre on buses. Fresh air usually helps, reading or cigarette smoke doesn't. Commercial anti-motion-sickness preparations, which can cause drowsiness, have to be taken before the trip commences; when you're feeling sick it's too late. Ginger is a natural preventative and is available in capsule form.

Diseases of Insanitation
Diarrhoea Unfortunately, most of the common causes of gut infections are found in Tibet including travellers' diarrhoea, dysentery (both bacterial and amoebic), giardia, etc. The good news is that they're less common than in places such as Nepal and India where the warmer weather is more suitable for bacteria to multiply rapidly. To be sage though, it is better to adopt the conservative approach which means care with whatever goes into your mouth!

Giardia This intestinal parasite is present in contaminated water. The symptoms are stomach cramps, nausea, a bloated stomach, watery, foul-smelling diarrhoea and frequent gas. Giardia can appear several weeks after you have been exposed to the parasite. The symptoms may disappear for a few days and then return; this can go on for several weeks. Metronidazole known as Flagyl is the recommended drug, but it should only be taken under medical supervision. Antibiotics are of no use.

Dysentery This serious illness is caused by contaminated food or water and is characterised by severe diarrhoea, often with blood or mucus in the stool. There are two kinds of dysentery. Bacillary dysentery is characterised by a high fever and rapid development; headache, vomiting and stomach pains are also symptoms. It generally does not last longer than a week, but it is highly contagious.

Amoebic dysentery is more gradual in developing, has no fever or vomiting but is a more serious illness. It is not a self-limiting disease: it will persist until treated and can recur and cause long term damage.

A stool test is necessary to diagnose which kind of dysentery you have, so you should seek medical help urgently. In case of an emergency, note that tetracycline is the prescribed treatment for bacillary dysentery, metronidazole for amoebic dysentery.

With tetracycline, the recommended adult dosage is one 250 mg capsule four times a day. Children aged between eight and 12 years should have half the adult dose; the dosage for younger children is a third the adult dose. It's important to remember that tetracycline should be given to young children only if it's absolutely necessary and only for a short period; pregnant women should not take it after the 4th month of pregnancy.

With metronidazole, the recommended adult dosage is one 750 mg to 800 mg capsule three times daily for five days. Children aged between eight and 12 years should have half the adult dose; the dosage for younger children is a third the adult dose.

Viral Gastroenteritis This is caused not by bacteria but, as the name suggests, by a virus. It is characterised by stomach cramps, diarrhoea, and sometimes by vomiting and/or a slight fever. All you can do is rest and drink lots of fluids.

Hepatitis Hepatitis A is the more common form of this disease and is spread by contaminated food or water. The first symptoms are fever, chills, headache, fatigue, feelings of weakness and aches and pains. This is followed by loss of appetite, nausea, vomiting, abdominal pain, dark urine, light-coloured faeces and jaundiced skin; the whites of the eyes may also turn yellow. In some cases there may just be a feeling of being unwell or tired, accompanied by loss of appetite, aches and pains and the jaundiced effect. You should seek medical advice, but in general there is not much you can do apart from resting, drinking lots of fluids, eating lightly and avoiding fatty foods. People who have had hepatitis must forego alcohol for six months after the illness, as hepatitis attacks the liver and it needs that amount of time to recover.

Hepatitis B, which used to be called serum hepatitis, is spread through sexual contact or through skin penetration – it could be transmitted via dirty needles or blood transfusions, for instance. Avoid having your ears pierced, tattoos done or injections where you have doubts about the sanitary conditions. The symptoms and treatment of type B are much the same as for type A, but gamma globulin as a prophylactic is effective against type A only.

Typhoid Typhoid fever is another gut infection that travels the fecal-oral route – ie, contaminated water and food are responsible. Vaccination against typhoid is not totally effective and it is one of the most dangerous infections, so medical help must be sought.

In its early stages typhoid resembles many other illnesses: sufferers may feel like they have a bad cold or flu on the way, as early symptoms are a headache, a sore throat, and a fever which rises a little each day until it is around 40°C or more. The victim's pulse is often slow relative to the degree of fever present and gets slower as the fever rises – unlike a normal fever where the pulse increases. There may also be vomiting, diarrhoea or constipation.

In the second week the high fever and slow pulse continue and a few pink spots may appear on the body; trembling, delirium, weakness, weight loss and dehydration are other symptoms. If there are no further complications, the fever and other symptoms will slowly go during the third week. However you must get medical help before this because pneumonia (acute infection of the lungs) or peritonitis (burst appendix) are common complications, and because typhoid is very infectious.

The fever should be treated by keeping the victim cool and dehydration should also be watched for. Chloramphenicol is the recommended antibiotic but there are fewer side affects with ampicillin. The adult dosage is two 250 mg capsules, four times a day. Children aged between eight and 12 years should have half the adult dose; younger children should have a third the adult dose.

Patients who are allergic to penicillin should not be given ampicillin.

Diseases Spread by People & Animals

Because of the high altitude and severe weather, mosquitoes cannot survive in Tibet, therefore all of the illnesses (malaria, dengue fever, Japanese encephalitis, etc) transmitted by mosquitoes are not found in Tibet.

Tetanus This potentially fatal disease is found in undeveloped tropical areas. It is difficult to treat but is preventable with immunisation. Tetanus occurs when a wound becomes infected by a germ which lives in the faeces of animals or people, so clean all cuts, punctures or animal bites. Tetanus is known as lockjaw, and the first symptom may be discomfort in swallowing, or stiffening of the jaw and neck; this is followed by painful convulsions of the jaw and whole body.

Rabies Rabies is found in many countries and is caused by a bite or scratch by an infected animal. Dogs are a noted carrier. Any bite, scratch or even lick from a mammal should be cleaned immediately and thoroughly. Scrub with soap and running water, and then clean with an alcohol solution. If there is any possibility that the animal is infected medical help should be sought immediately. Even if the animal is not rabid, all bites should be treated seriously as they can become infected or can result in tetanus. A rabies vaccination is now available and should be considered if you are in a high-risk category – eg, if you intend to explore caves (bat bites could be dangerous) or work with animals.

Meningococcal Meningitis Sub-Saharan Africa is considered the 'meningitis belt' and the meningitis season falls at the time most people would be attempting the overland trip across the Sahara – the northern winter before the rains come. Other areas which have recurring epidemics are Mongolia, Vietnam, Brazil, the Nile Valley and Nepal.

Trekkers to rural areas of Nepal should be particularly careful, as the disease is spread by close contact with people who carry it in their throats and noses, spread it through coughs and sneezes and may not be aware that they are carriers. Lodges in the hills where travellers spend the night are prime spots for the spread of infection.

This very serious disease attacks the brain and can be fatal. A scattered, blotchy rash, fever, severe headache, sensitivity to light and neck stiffness which prevents forward bending of the head are the first symptoms. Death can occur within a few hours, so immediate treatment is important.

Treatment is large doses of penicillin given intravenously, or, if that is not possible, intramuscularly (ie, in the buttocks). Vaccination offers good protection for over a year, but you should also check for reports of current epidemics. In Kathmandu you can get the vaccination from the International Clinic (☎ 410893) in Balawatar; it's across from the north end of the Soviet Embassy.

Tuberculosis Although this disease is widespread in many developing countries, it is not a serious risk to travellers. Young children are more susceptible than adults and vaccination is a sensible precaution for children under 12 travelling in endemic areas. TB is commonly spread by coughing or by unpasteurised dairy products from infected cows. Milk that has been boiled is safe to drink; the souring of milk to make yoghurt or cheese also kills the bacilli.

Diptheria Diptheria can be a skin infection or a more dangerous throat infection. It is spread by contaminated dust contacting the skin or by the inhalation of infected cough or sneeze droplets. Frequent washing and keeping the skin dry will help prevent skin infection. A vaccination is available to prevent the throat infection.

Sexually Transmitted Diseases Sexual contact with an infected sexual partner spreads these diseases. While abstinence is the only 100% preventative, using condoms is also effective. Gonorrhoea and syphilis are the most common of these diseases; sores, blisters or rashes around the genitals, discharges or pain when urinating are common symptoms. Symptoms may be less marked or not observed at all in women. Syphilis symptoms eventually disappear completely but the disease continues and can cause severe problems in later years. The treatment of gonorrhoea and syphilis is by antibiotics.

There are numerous other sexually transmitted diseases, for most of which effective treatment is available. However, there is no cure for herpes and there is also currently no cure for AIDS. The latter is common in parts of Africa and is becoming more widespread in Thailand and the Philippines. Using condoms is the most effective preventative.

AIDS can be spread through infected blood transfusions; most developing countries cannot afford to screen blood for transfusions. It can also be spread by dirty needles – vaccinations, acupuncture and tattooing can potentially be as dangerous as intravenous drug use if the equipment is not clean. If you do need an injection it may be a good idea to buy a new syringe from a pharmacy and ask the doctor to use it.

Cuts, Bites & Stings

Cuts & Scratches Treat any cut with an antiseptic solution and mercurochrome. Where possible avoid bandages and Band-aids, which can keep wounds wet.

Bites & Stings Bee and wasp stings are usually painful rather than dangerous. Calamine lotion will give relief or ice packs will reduce the pain and swelling.

Bedbugs & Lice Bedbugs live in various places, but particularly in dirty mattresses and bedding. Spots of blood on bedclothes or on the wall around the bed can be read as a suggestion to find another hotel. Bedbugs leave itchy bites in neat rows. Calamine lotion may help.

All lice cause itching and discomfort. They make themselves at home in your hair (head lice), your clothing (body lice) or in your pubic hair (crabs). You catch lice through direct contact with infected people or by sharing combs, clothing and the like. Powder or shampoo treatment will kill the lice and infected clothing should then be washed in very hot water.

Leeches & Ticks Leeches may be present in damp rainforest conditions; they attach themselves to your skin to suck your blood. Trekkers often get them on their legs or in their boots. Salt or a lighted cigarette end will make them fall off. Do not pull them off, as the bite is then more likely to become infected. An insect repellent may keep them away. Vaseline, alcohol or oil will persuade a tick to let go. You should always check your body if you have been walking through a tick-infested area, as they can spread typhus.

Women's Health

Gynaecological Problems Poor diet, lowered resistance due to the use of antibiotics for stomach upsets and even contraceptive pills can lead to vaginal infections when travelling in hot climates. Keeping the genital area clean, and wearing skirts or loose-fitting trousers and cotton underwear will help to prevent infections.

Yeast infections, characterised by a rash, itch and discharge, can be treated with a vinegar or even lemon-juice douche or with yoghurt. Nystatin suppositories are the usual medical prescription. Trichomonas is a more serious infection; symptoms are a discharge and a burning sensation when urinating. Male sexual partners must also be treated, and if a vinegar-water douche is not effective medical attention should be sought. Flagyl is the prescribed drug.

Pregnancy Most miscarriages occur during the first three months of pregnancy, so this is the most risky time to travel. The last three months should also be spent within reasonable distance of good medical care, as quite serious problems can develop at this time. Pregnant women should avoid all unnecessary medication, but vaccinations and malarial prophylactics should still be taken where possible. Additional care should be taken to prevent illness and particular attention should be paid to diet and nutrition.

Medical Facilities

There are very few places where you can get medical help. In Shigatse there is a Chinese hospital, but no-one could find an English-speaking doctor when I visited. In Lhasa there are two hospitals. One is Tibetan and relies on traditional Tibetan medicine. The other is Chinese and uses a combination of Western and Chinese medicine. Neither of them are able to deal with emergencies such as altitude sickness, which is often compounded by pneumonia.

If you do become ill let someone else know you are sick and ask for their help. Ask around at the traveller's hotels. Something

may possibly be operating similar to the Traveller's Co-op which used to be run out of the Banak Shol Hotel and had experience in assisting sick travellers or finding a travelling doctor.

The Lhasa Hotel is good at assisting sick travellers, provided you are a guest there. It may even be worthwhile checking in there, especially if you need to organise a flight out of Lhasa.

Always remember that if you are really sick, the best solution is to get out of Tibet by plane. Do not attempt the overland journey by bus because all routes out are long, arduous and involve climbing to higher altitudes over mountain passes. You must carry enough money to be able to get out of Tibet in a hurry! Plane fares are expensive, not to mention the exorbitant medical costs you will be lumbered with.

WOMEN TRAVELLERS

Sexual harassment is generally rare in Tibet and women in Tibetan society are treated much more as equals than those in Chinese society. It's not advisable to wear skimpy dress – given the rigours of the climate you'd also run the risk of frostbite! Wherever you are, it's worth noticing what local women are wearing and how they are behaving, and making a bit of an effort to fit in, as you would in any other foreign country. If you want to play safe, wear trousers or a below-the-knees skirt, with a shirt that covers your shoulders.

Some women have reported problems when staying at army camps where bored soldiers may have watched explicit videos and made erroneous assumptions about Western women.

DANGERS & ANNOYANCES
Theft

Both in Qinghai and Tibet, there has been a rise in theft from foreigners. In Xining, a nimble-fingered gang of pickpockets rides the buses. Sneak thieves operate on the train between Golmud and Xining. In Lhasa, the favourite venues for pickpocketing are the bus station, post office, Barkhor Market and hotels. Lhasa also has a chronic problem with bike theft.

Cable locks, sold in most cities in China, are useful for bikes and to secure gear on a train. Moneybelts are essential. If something is stolen, you should obtain a loss report from the nearest Public Security Bureau, though the PSB may refuse to include details of cash on the loss report.

Several foreigners trekking in the Everest base camp region reported thefts. Apparently local villagers or nomads who possess very little find the temptation of foreign goodies too great.

Dogs

Packs of dogs that congregate around the monasteries can be incredibly vicious. Don't go near them, and if they do get nasty pick up rocks, sticks, anything at all to ward them off until you can duck into a doorway and escape.

TOURS & TREKKING

Several companies have started to run Tibet tours from Kathmandu. When booking these tours you will be asked to sign a Risk, Release & Guarantee certificate and full payment usually has to be made 60 days in advance.

A 13-day journey overland from Kathmandu to Lhasa, with a few days in Lhasa itself, flying back to Kathmandu, will set you back around A\$2200, plus the cost of getting to Kathmandu and back. A four-week journey from Kathmandu into Tibet and then north through Amdo to Golmud and west over the Khunjerab Pass into Pakistan costs from around A\$2900, from Kathmandu. Among the firms running this kind of tour are the Australian-based companies World Expeditions and Peregrine Adventures.

You should also consider that the Chinese authorities reserve (and have certainly been known to exercise!) the right to:

- Change itineraries due to reasons beyond their control.
- Alter the length of the itinerary if necessary.
- Increase cost as a result of changes in the itinerary. Any such increase to be borne by the trip members and is liable to be collected direct.

Tours Organised by CITS

From Chengdu in Sichuan you can take a four-day tour to Lhasa through CITS – at Y1400 FEC per person (Y900 FEC per person for a group of 10) this covers transport and accommodation and seems to be the cheapest available from Sichuan. From Xining or Golmud in Qinghai there are cheaper CITS tours available which basically just cover transport costs.

Trekking Companies

Following are the addresses of trekking companies operating Tibet tours out of Kathmandu, Hong Kong, Australia, the UK and the USA:

Kathmandu
    Yeti Travel, PO Box 76 (☎ 221 754). Operate trips to Lhasa lasting between six and 12 days (prices range between US\$1240 and US\$2400). Adventure Travel Nepal, PO Box 242 (☎ 221 379)
    Nepal Travel Agency, PO Box 1501 (☎ 413 188). Operate tours to Kailas (from US\$2400 for 15 days); budget tours to Lhasa (from US\$380 for 9 days); and other itineraries which combine with Beijing or Hong Kong. They also expect to be handling bookings for the RNAC/CAAC flights between Kathmandu and Lhasa.
    Himalayan Rover Trek, PO Box 1081 (☎ 412 667). Operate 12-day budget tours (US\$480); Everest Base Camp treks (US\$90 per day) and tours to Kailas (20 days; US\$2400)
    Mountain Travel Nepal, PO Box 170, Kathmandu (☎ 414 508). Organise treks, tours, camping tours and expeditions to Lhasa, Everest, Xixabangma and Kailas. Prices range between US\$1680 and US\$6541 depending on number of participants and length of tour; tours are operated between May and November.
    Lama Excursions, PO Box 2485 (☎ 410 786)
    Ongdi Expeditions, PO Box 1273 (☎ 220 594)
Hong Kong
    China Tibet Qomolongma Travelways Ltd

(CTQT), Room 802, Crocodile House, 50 Connaught Rd C (☎ 5418896; telex 81506 CTQTL HX). Represents the Tourist Bureau of Tibet and serves as the general agent of CITS Lhasa. 'Crocodile House' conjures up interesting visions! They produce a glossy brochure with details of some 30 tours. These tours are divided between regular tours, which take in standard parts of China together with Tibet, and trekking tours which devote more time in Tibet to covering more exotic itineraries. The trekking tours include the Yunnan-Lhasa route, Sichuan-Lhasa routes (southern and northern roads), other destinations in Western Sichuan (Kham), routes to Kailas and Everest and Xixabangma. Prices seem to average about US$150 per day and most of the travel is by coach.

Australia
    Peregrine Adventures, 258 Lonsdale St, Melbourne 3000 (☎ (03) 663 8611)
    World Expeditions, 3rd Floor, 377 Sussex St, Sydney 2000 (☎ (02) 2643366)

UK
    Trans-Himalaya, 30 Hanover Rd, London NW10 (☎ (081) 459-7944). Operates specialist tours, many of which follow intricate routes across Eastern Tibet. Prices start at around £2000 for a 10-day trip.

USA
    Wilderness Travel (☎ 510-5480420 or toll-free 800-3682794), 801 Alston Way, Berkeley, California offer a 32-day 'Kailas Silk Road Expedition' which covers Hong Kong, Chengdu, Lhasa, Shigatse, the Kailas trek and finishes with a run down the Karakoram Highway to Islamabad. Prices start around US$4900 for land costs only.
    Mountain Travel-Sobek (☎ 510-5278100 or toll-free 800-2272384), 6420 Fairmount Ave, El Cerrito, California 94530 provide a Kailas Circuit tour (29 days, including four days of trekking); an overland tour from Kathmandu to Lhasa (16 days); and a specialist East Face Trek (33 days, including 12 days trekking). The Kailas Circuit tour is priced around US$6685; the Kathmandu-Lhasa overland tour starts around US$3495; and the East Face Trek costs around US$5990. All prices are for land costs only, and there are usually two departures annually for each tour. Rafters should note that this company plans to run raft tours from Shigatse using yak-hide coracles and Avon inflatables to negotiate the Yarlung Tsangpo (Brahmaputra).
    Boojum Expeditions (☎ 406-5870125), 14543 Kelly Canyon Rd, Bozeman, MT 59715 run horsepacking and mountainbiking trips to Eastern Tibet. The trips last from 16 to 22 days, and prices start around US$3,250 for land costs only.

HIGHLIGHTS

These highlights are limited to those which are easily (and legally) accessible!

Central Tibet
    Lhasa – Potala, Jokhang Temple, Drepung & Sera monasteries, Ganden Monastery, Samye Monastery
    Gyantse – Pango Chörten
    Shigatse – Tashilhunpo Monastery
    Sakya – Sakya Monastery
Qinghai Province
    Qinghai Lake, Taersi
Eastern Tibet
    Jiuzhaigou, Ya'an, Dêgê
Western Tibet
    Mt Kailas
Gannan
    Xiahe (Labrang Monastery)
Treks
    Everest trek, Kailas trek, Yarlung Valley to Ganden trek
Breakfast
    Dali – the karmic 'Dalai Lama's Breakfast' at the *Yin Yang Cafe*

ACCOMMODATION

For Tibetan nomads this poses no problem, since they trek around the highlands with their livestock and set up their tents wherever they wish. For foreigners, however, the range of places to stay is extremely limited (with the exception of Lhasa). In Lhasa and the few towns in Tibet you will usually be asked to fill out a registration form. Elsewhere, nobody really bothers with this formality – a point in your favour if you are travelling off the permitted track, since this is one way to attract the attention of the local PSB. A reader recently commented that hotel registers in Lhasa and elsewhere are a source of inspiration for the PSB on the movements of foreigners.

If there are no showers, ask for a basin and an extra thermos of hot water (*kai shui*). In recent years, there has been a tendency for the PSB to give foreigners no option but to use 'approved' accommodation with interesting, unannounced facilities such as concealed bugs to delight electronics fans. Extreme overpricing has also occurred.

Accommodation in Tibet falls into four

categories: guesthouses, hotels, truck stops and army camps.

Guesthouses & Hotels

Guesthouses (Chinese: ZhaoDaiSuo) are found in scarce numbers in large towns and provide minimum standard accommodation for visiting officials. They usually have showers, flush toilets, a restaurant, a small shop and perhaps laundry facilities.

Lhasa has several hotel projects aimed at providing western-style service for foreigners. The Lhasa Holiday Inn and the Tibet Guest House, complete with all mod cons specially for foreign tourists, have taken over from Guest Houses No 3 and No 1.

With the exception of Lhasa, hotels in Tibet are usually a cross between a hotel and a hostel (Chinese: Lüshe). They are usually found near bus stations and truck stops and offer a cheap bed, a scrawny dining room, outside toilet pits and little else. Expect to pay between Y2 and Y5 per person.

Truck stops

These provide drivers with petrol, a safe place to park, a bed to snatch a few hours of sleep plus a canteen serving simple dishes. For a four-bed room, prices vary between Y2 and Y3 per person. Truck stops are obviously the best place for hitchhikers to stay.

Army Camps

In some remote areas, army camps are the only place to stay. The commanding officers seem surprisingly unconcerned about taking in foreigners and try hard to please. Some camps try to charge extortionate prices but, depending on the rooms provided, prices usually vary between Y3 and Y6.

Caught Short in Tibet

Finally, a cautionary tale about a woman who was caught short in the freezing hours of early morning, in a room on the roof of a guesthouse, deep in the heart of Tibet. As the night was as cold as an iceberg, the need urgent and the toilet pit a long trek away, she decided to use the roof. Meanwhile, down in the room below, the Chinese cook was preparing to wash in a basin of hot water. Unfortunately, the roof of stamped earth was porous and the cook was dumbfounded by the deluge of what was quite clearly not rainwater. Within seconds, the enraged cook was demanding that the foreigner be thrown out, on the instant, by a sleepy, but secretly amused manager. Somehow the cook was placated and everyone went back to bed. By the morning, all trace of evidence had been absorbed by the roof.

FOOD & DRINK

Tibetan

Tibetan cuisine is not exactly the most varied in the world, but perhaps ingredients at this altitude are not easy to grow or catch. A couple of common Tibetan dishes are *momo* (a type of dumpling filled with meat) and *tukpa* (noodles with meat). The staple food of most Tibetans is *tsampa* (roasted barley flour), which they mix with yak-butter tea into doughy mouthfuls.

Outside of the main towns like Lhasa and Shigatse, there is very little food or drink around, unless you're fond of dried yak meat. Yak cheese, in its hard and dry state, can be eaten up to three years old, at which time it's bound to bust your teeth. It has to be chewed for several hours before it can be digested, and for this reason it is often given to Tibetan children as a kind of hard sweet.

Yak-butter tea is definitely an acquired taste. Some Tibetan women advised that it should not be drunk cold – otherwise those (rancid) globules of congealed fat may wreak havoc with your stomach. Given the choice, most travellers opt for a more familiar variety of tea (available in Lhasa and Shigatse) – sweet and milky. The Tibetans get their alcohol buzz by consuming large quantities of *chang*, which is a milky type of beer with a tangy taste, made from fermented barley.

Chinese

Since the Chinese are present in Tibet in large numbers, it is hardly surprising to find their cuisine as well. The most common types are Sichuan-style and Muslim-style. Sichuan cooking is hot and spicy, but tell the cook *bu yao lade* if you don't want the hot stuff. *Chao cai* (fried vegetables) and *hongchao yu* (fish in a spicy sauce) are two common dishes. Some northern Chinese dishes such as *jiaozi* (similar to ravioli), *baozi* (dumplings filled with meat) and *mantou* (plain dumplings) are also served. Muslim restaurants serve *lamian* (noodles with meat and vegetables) and lotus-seed tea. Most of the Chinese restaurants serve hardcore spirits such as *maotai* and beer trucked into Tibet from Lanzhou, Chengdu, Kunming and even Qingdao.

THINGS TO BUY

Whether you buy from a shop or a hawker, many of the goods on sale in Tibet have been imported from Nepal and you are most unlikely to find genuine antiques. The prices asked from foreigners have reached absurd heights. Whatever the starting price, be it in RMB or FEC, expect to halve it. Much of the 'turquoise' in the market is, in fact, a paste of ground turquoise and cement – some keen buyers bite the stones and reject them if the teeth leave white scratch marks. Also, bear in mind that Chinese Customs can confiscate antiques (anything made before 1959) if they

think you are carrying out 'too much'. This means that you would probably be better off looking in Nepal (Kathmandu) for Tibetan antiques whether genuine or fake.

Amongst smaller items on offer are prayer flags (Y1 each); stetson hats made in Tianjin at Y20 each; gaudy, embroidered hats with ear flaps at Y7.60 each and rolls of traditional striped cloth.

You may be offered skins of rare species, but don't buy unless you wish to encourage extinction.

Traditional Tibetan boots are an interesting buy. A ready-made pair costs around Y35 and made-to-measure from Y50 upwards. Traditional Tibetan tents can also be bought or even custom-made.

Many Tibetans will delve deep into the folds of their clothing and offer you religious objects or personal jewellery. You should be prepared to bargain or even barter. Items in demand are Dalai Lama pictures, pictures of deities and sometimes even your Western clothes.

Getting There & Away

The choice of entries and exits for Tibet has recently increased to include more international access to Lhasa. Most travellers use Lhasa as a focal point since it is the major transport hub in Tibet. Apart from the Kathmandu-Lhasa flight and the Nepal overland route, all other approaches to Tibet involve several legs of travel: first heave yourself into China and then continue to Tibet. Be warned that a heavy bureaucratic and/or military hand can block access for foreigners at the first hint of trouble in Tibet. At the time of writing, individual travel was occasionally allowed in theory, but foreigners who arrived in Tibet on their own found that life was made extremely difficult for them by the local Chinese authorities.

AIR

There are direct flights into Lhasa from Kathmandu, Chengdu, Beijing (via Chengdu, infrequent), Xi'an (via Golmud, very infrequent) and possibly Shanghai and/or Canton though these had not started at the time of writing.

In practice you will probably find Kathmandu and Hong Kong the two most useful international staging-points.

To/From China

The main route into Lhasa from China is from Chengdu in Sichuan, south-west China. The Chengdu-Lhasa flight takes about two hours and costs Y547 (US$150). There are several departures daily although the flights are notorious for delays (for details see the chapter on the Sichuan route). There is one weekly direct flight between Beijing and Lhasa (via Chengdu); direct flights between Lhasa and Shanghai or Canton are proposed but not effective at the time of writing. If you want to connect from Shanghai, Canton or other major cities in China you will probably have to link up separate flights. There are also flights between Lhasa and Xian which go via

Golmud, however, they have rarely been known to operate.

To/From Hong Kong

Hong Kong is the discount plane ticket capital of the region. Its bucket shops are at least as unreliable as those of other cities. Ask the advice of other travellers before buying a ticket.

There are charter flights between Hong Kong and Chengdu on Saturdays and possibly Wednesdays for HK$970 one way or HK$1380 return. The flight takes two hours.

To/From Nepal

Routes into Lhasa include the recently inaugurated Kathmandu-Lhasa connection which costs US$210 one way and departs on Wednesdays and Saturdays. This may be heavily booked with tour groups.

From Kathmandu, a one-way trip to Bangkok will be around US$280 and to Hong Kong US$375.

To/From Thailand & Myanmar

If you wish to enter or leave China via Thailand or Myanmar (Burma), there are flights between Bangkok and Kunming (Wednesdays, US$165 one way) and Rangoon (Yangon) and Kunming (every second Wednesday, US$225 one way). From Kunming you can then take rail, air or road connections to Chengdu.

To/From the USA

The *New York Times*, the *LA Times*, the *Chicago Tribune* and the *San Francisco Examiner* all produce weekly travel sections in which you'll find any number of travel agents' ads. Council Travel and STA Travel have offices in major cities nationwide.

The magazine *Travel Unlimited* (PO Box 1058, Allston, Mass 02134) publishes details of the cheapest air fares and courier possibilities for destinations all over the world from the USA.

Russian turbo-prop on 2 fen note

A one-way airfare from San Francisco to Hong Kong is likely to cost around US$350; from San Francisco to Kathmandu return is around US$1200.

To/From Canada
Travel CUTS has offices in all major cities. The *Toronto Globe & Mail* carries travel agents' ads. The magazine Great Expeditions (PO Box 8000-411, Abbotsford BC V2S 6H1) is useful.

To/From the UK
Trailfinders in west London produce a lavishly illustrated brochure which includes air fare details. STA also has branches in the UK. Look in the listings magazines *Time Out* and *City Limits* plus the Sunday papers and Exchange & Mart for ads. Also look out for the free magazines widely available in London – start by looking outside the main train stations.

Most British travel agents are registered with ABTA (Association of British Travel Agents). If you have paid for your flight to an ABTA-registered agent who then goes out of business, ABTA will guarantee a refund or an alternative. Unregistered bucket shops are riskier but also sometimes cheaper.

The Globetrotters Club (BCM Roving, London WC1N 3XX) publishes a newsletter called *Globe* which covers obscure destinations and can help in finding travelling companions.

A single airfare from London to Hong Kong is likely to cost from around UK£320; to Kathmandu it'll be from around UK£335.

To/From Europe
The newsletter *Farang* (La Rue 8 à 4261 Braives, Belgium) deals with exotic destinations; so does the magazine *Aventure du Bout du Monde* (116 rue de Javel, 75015 Paris).

To/From Australia & New Zealand
Australia and New Zealand don't have the same network of bucket shops that you'll find in the UK or the USA – instead, check the travel agents' ads in the Yellow Pages and ring around. STA has branches in major cities.

A Melbourne to Hong Kong airfare costs from around A$735 one way.

Round-the World & Circle Pacific Tickets
Round-the-World (RTW) tickets have become very popular in the last few years. The airline RTW tickets are often real bargains, and it can work out no more expensive or even cheaper than an ordinary return ticket. Prices start at around UK£850, A$1800 or US$1300. Many of them include Hong Kong, and Kathmandu occasionally appears.

The official airline RTW tickets are put together, usually by a combination of two airlines, and permit you to fly anywhere you want on their route systems so long as you do not backtrack. Other restrictions are that you (usually) must book the first sector in advance and cancellation penalties then apply. There may be restrictions on how many stops you are permitted and usually the tickets are valid from 90 days up to a year. An alternative type of RTW ticket is one put together by a travel agent using a combination of discounted tickets.

Circle Pacific fares are similar; they use a combination of airlines to circle the Pacific – combining Australia, New Zealand, North America and Asia. As with RTW tickets there are advance purchase restrictions and limits to how many stopovers you can take. These fares are likely to be around 15% cheaper than Round-the-World tickets.

A Round-the-World ticket going from London to New York, San Francisco, overland to Vancouver, Honolulu, Cairns, Sydney, Bangkok, Hong Kong, overland to Beijing and back to London costs around UK£1350. From New York to Paris, overland to Cairo, Nairobi, Bombay, Delhi, Kathmandu, Bangkok, Hong Kong, Taipei, Anchorage, and back to New York costs US$2000. A Circle Pacific fare from Melbourne to Hong Kong, Vancouver, Los Angeles, Honolulu, Nadi, Auckland and back to Melbourne is A$2550.

Arriving in Tibet by Air

The airport nearest to Lhasa is 96 km away at Gonggar. Travellers are met by CAAC buses, and the trip into Lhasa costs Y7. Baggage is delivered separately to the CAAC office in Lhasa, where you collect it at least three hours after arrival.

Buying a Plane Ticket

The plane ticket will probably be the single most expensive item in your budget, and buying it can be an intimidating business. There is likely to be a multitude of airlines and travel agents hoping to separate you from your money, and it is always worth putting aside a few hours to research the current state of the market. Start early: some of the cheapest tickets have to be bought

months in advance, and some popular flights sell out early. Talk to other recent travellers – they may be able to stop you making some of the same old mistakes. Look at the ads in newspapers and magazines (not forgetting the press of the ethnic group whose country you plan to visit), and watch for special offers. Then ring around travel agents and bucket shops for bargains. (Airlines can supply information on routes and timetables, however, except at times of inter-airline war they do not supply the cheapest tickets.) Find out the fare, the route, the duration of the journey and any restrictions on the ticket. Then sit back and decide which is best for you. Remember – a few hours work now on air routes and tickets could save you enough money to live on for several days once you reach your destination.

You may discover that those impossibly cheap flights are 'fully booked, but we have another one that costs a bit more...' Or the flight is on an airline notorious for its poor safety standards and leaves you in the world's least favourite airport in mid-journey for 14 hours. Or they claim only to have the last two seats available for that country for the whole of July, which they will hold for you for a maximum of two hours. Don't panic – keep ringing around.

If you are travelling from the UK or the USA, you will probably find that the cheapest flights are being advertised by obscure bucket shops whose names haven't yet reached the telephone directory. Many such firms are honest and solvent, but there are a few rogues who will take your money and disappear, to reopen elsewhere a month or two later under a new name. Don't give a bucket shop all the money until you have the ticket in your hand. If they insist on cash in advance, go somewhere else. And once you have the ticket, ring the airline to confirm that you are actually booked onto the flight.

You may decide to pay more than the rock-bottom fare by opting for the safety of a better-known travel agent. Firms such as STA, who have offices worldwide, Council Travel in the USA or Travel CUTS in Canada are unlikely to disappear overnight, leaving you clutching a receipt for a nonexistent ticket, but they do offer good prices to most destinations.

Once you have your ticket, write its number down, together with the flight number and other details, and keep the information somewhere separate. If the ticket is lost or stolen, this will help you get a replacement.

Taking a Bike

Bicycles can travel by air. You *can* take them to pieces and put them in a bike bag or box, but it's much easier simply to wheel your bike to the check in desk, where it should be treated as one of your two pieces of baggage. You may have to remove the pedals and turn the handlebars sideways so that it takes up less space in the aircraft's hold; check all this with the airline well in advance, preferably before you pay for your ticket.

Getting the bike into Tibet may present major problems. See under Offbeat Options in the Getting Around chapter for more information.

LAND

Overland road travel provides five options: highways between Tibet and Nepal, Qinghai, Sichuan, Xinjiang and Yunnan. All of these routes are described in detail in later chapters of this book. At the time of writing the Nepal and Qinghai routes are the only two which are officially open. The overland routes may be impassable for weeks at a time in winter, and flooding is common in late autumn.

For details of vehicle hire, hitchhiking, public transport etc, see the Getting Around chapter.

Nepal-Tibet Highway

Officially called the Friendship Highway, the Nepal route connects Lhasa with Nepal and runs from Lhasa to Khasa (Zhangmu) via Gyantse and Shigatse. This is a journey of about three days by bus, or longer if you hire a vehicle and stop to see the sights on the way. There are three important monaster-

ies on the way, and if the weather's good you'll get a fine view of Mt Everest from the Tibetan village of Tingri (Lao Tingri). From Khasa, it's 11 km to the Nepalese border post at Kodari, which has transport connections to Kathmandu. As it is possible to fly between Kathmandu and Lhasa, it is not necessary to travel by road in both directions.

On the Tibetan side of the border the road is washed away most years and may be impassable to motor vehicles. You may have to scramble over several km of rubble on foot. See the 'Nepal Route' chapter for more detail.

Qinghai-Tibet Highway

The Qinghai route follows the recently asphalted road connecting Xining with Lhasa via Golmud; it crosses the desolate, barren and virtually uninhabited Tibetan plateau. Modern Japanese buses do the run between Lhasa and Golmud in 30 hours, but present policy does not allow tickets to be sold to foreigners. Trucks take two to three days, but drivers are forbidden to give lifts to foreigners. At the time of writing a CITS tour seems to be the only option.

This is the world's highest road; take food, drink and very warm clothing. Golmud is connected by rail with Xining (25 hours), Lanzhou and the rest of China.

See the 'Amdo & the Qinghai Routes' chapter for more details.

Sichuan-Tibet Highway

The Sichuan land routes are officially closed to foreigners. It is possible to get a permit (and a bus) from Chengdu as far as Kangding; beyond that point trucks are the major form of transport, and drivers caught giving lifts to foreigners could lose their licences or be heavily fined.

On the northern route, most foreigners who get as far as Dêgê are sent back and fined. If you're coming in the other direction, nobody minds. If you do get as far as Chamdo, you are likely to have to hitch another lift – this is the major truck depot on the way. The road beyond Chamdo, past Bamda, is particularly dangerous – there

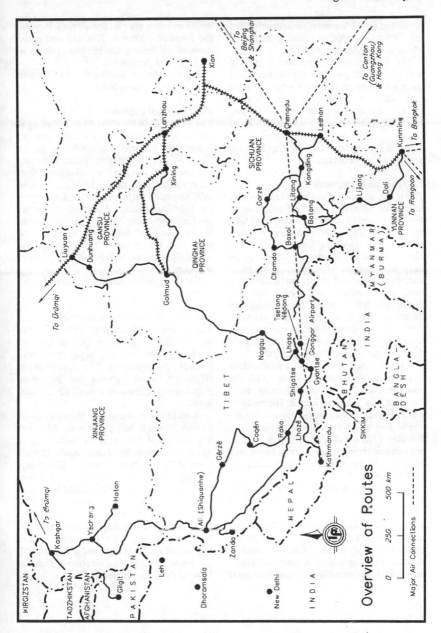

Overview of Routes

0   250   500 km

Major Air Connections - - - - -

have been many deaths on the section called the '72 Switchbacks', and later at Tangmai, which is notorious for mudslides.

The southern route branches off beyond Kangding and goes through Litang and Batang to Markam (which is where you are most likely to be turned back). Beyond Markam, the road goes on through Zogang to join the northern route between Baxoi and Bamda.

See the chapter 'Kham & the Sichuan Routes' for more details.

Xinjiang-Tibet Highway

This is one of the roughest roads in the world, and is not officially open to foreigners. A direct run from Lhasa to Kashgar would take around nine days. Some travellers have succeeded in hitchhiking unofficially from Lhasa to Kashgar, taking anything from 16 days to a couple of months. Foreigners attempting to travel in the other direction have been fined and turned back (often at Yecheng, before the road starts climbing into the mountains). In this case, CITS anxieties about your safety have a solid basis in fact: foreigners have died on this route, from accidents, exposure or altitude sickness.

Kashgar itself was closed to individual travellers at the time of writing, with the possible exception of those coming from Pakistan via the Karakoram Highway – which is currently closed to travellers who would like to go west from Xinjiang into Pakistan. (The Karakoram Highway is open, politics and snowfalls permitting, between 1 May and 30 November or 31 October for tour groups.)

The Xinjiang route goes from Lhasa to Lhazê, then turns off north beyond Raka to Coqên, and on to Ali (Shiquanhe). (A detour south at this point to the ruins at Zanda is a must.) The road then goes north, through the disputed territory of Aksai Chin – an area so desolate that the Indian authorities didn't notice the Chinese building a road through it

until two years after its completion. Beyond the disputed border is Xinjiang and some more rough driving through Mazar down to Yecheng and the desert.

For more details, see the chapter 'Western Tibet & the Xinjiang Routes'.

Yunnan-Tibet Highway

The early part of the route from Kunming is on the tourist trail; it is not until you get towards the Yunnan-Tibet border that you're likely to run into trouble. From Kunming you can travel west by bus to Xiaguan , then north to Dali and towards Lijiang. The road to Tibet passes the Lijiang turn-off, then goes through Zhongdian, Dêqên and across the border into Yanjing. See the chapter 'Yunnan Route' for more details. At Markam, the route joins the Sichuan-Tibet Highway. You are likely to be turned back at Zhongdian or Markam.

For more details see the 'Yunnan Route' chapter.

The Great Asian Overland Revival

This is now an off-beat possibility if you use the Karakoram Highway (see chapter on Xinjiang route and the separate Lonely Planet publication *The Karakoram Highway*), Nepal Highway (see chapter on Nepal route) or Trans-Siberian Railway routings.

Assuming you can master the visa technicalities through India, Pakistan, Iran and beyond, the Asian overland route is open again. For more detail you could consult Lonely Planet's *West Asia on a Shoestring*. Taking the Trans-Siberian Railway via Mongolia or Manchuria and the USSR is a grand outward or homeward mode of transport – full details in my modestly recommended tome *Trans-Siberian Rail Guide* (Bradt Publications, 1991). For an extraordinary account of an Asian overland trip in 1984-5 try Nick Danziger's *Danziger's Travels: Beyond Forbidden Frontiers*.

Top: Canoes on Yarlung Zangbo River, near Chushul (RS)
Bottom Left: Yak-hide boat, Samye ferry crossing (RS)
Bottom Right: Yadong bus passing Mt Chomolhari (RS)

Top: Near Lhasa (RV)
Bottom: Painted sculpture south of Lhasa (RV)

Getting Around

In the past, yak trains took a leisurely average of 10 months to complete the trip from Lhasa to Chengdu and back again. Pilgrims would prostrate themselves – and some still do – for thousands of km taking many months, even years, to complete pilgrimages. Today there is a much wider choice of transport but the soft options are in limited supply and you pay the price for luxury. The rough options are the most interesting, perhaps because they retain a whiff of danger and are utterly unpredictable.

HELICOPTER
In 1984, China purchased 24 F-70-CT helicopters (a variation of the Sikorsky Blackhawk) from the USA for military use in Tibet. These choppers are specially adapted for high altitude flying and can be used for troop transport. According to CITS in Lhasa, there are plans to use helicopters (perhaps these are the ones) for tourism. It looks like the vultures and hawks circling around sky burial sites may soon be sharing thermals with airborne tourists.

RENTED VEHICLES
One increasingly popular way to get around is to take control of your transport by renting it. The most frequently used centre for these deals is Lhasa although you can also negotiate in Xining and Chengdu via CITS or privateers.

Destinations or itineraries can be arranged as far as cash, the drivers and the vehicles will carry you. Public Security sometimes throws a fit at the more outlandish destinations.

Trips around Lhasa are common as are more complicated itineraries to and from the Nepalese border. Some people have even negotiated rentals along the Xinjiang route to Mt Kailas or from Xining along the Qinghai route to Lhasa.

The types of vehicles available include Toyota Landcruisers, Beijing jeeps, minibuses and buses. Toyota Landcruisers are the most expensive option but offer more – or relatively more – comfort than the Beijing jeeps or buses.

As a rough guide only, for a six-day trip to the Nepalese border in a Toyota Landcruiser (maximum seven passengers) expect to pay Y1300 per person; a similar trip in a deluxe minibus (maximum 10 passengers) costs Y1000 per person; a five-day trip to the border in a modern bus (maximum 25 passengers) costs around Y500 per person. Hiring a Landcruiser will cost around Y6 per km, minibus Y6.20 per km, bus Y7 per km.

Before organising your own group rental, check the notice boards at the hotels for 'seat available' ads. Most of the hotels in Lhasa seem to be getting into the vehicle rental business – ask the manager. Lhasa also has a couple of taxi services.

Be careful about paying deposits; it's best to write out a contract which contains exact details of your itinerary (dates, places, time required), name of driver, licence-plate number, desire to stop for photography and no price increase for technical or climatic problems. PSB may possibly help with translation.

Several readers have complained about transport managers inventing astronomical prices or drivers completely ignoring requests to keep to the agreed itinerary.

Remember too, breakdowns, flooded rivers, incompatible companions and unenthusiastic drivers can all occur in the rental game.

BUS
Bus travel in Tibet is rough and erratic. When you are on the bus, the Tibetans do their best to ensure a safe journey by chanting prayers in the valleys and whooping at the top of high passes. The buses are antiquated, have poor brakes, cracked windows and next to no suspension. Avoid sitting at the back unless

your skull and your backside are cast-iron. If you have to leave your luggage on the roof, make sure it is properly tied down and secure against dust, rain and snow. A flexible bicycle lock helps keep your gear on the bus and deters thieves. Large plastic bags are useful to pack your gear inside the backpack. As you can't normally climb onto the roof to extract items from your pack en route, it's essential to have a smaller bag (containing food, water, warm clothing, toilet bag, photo gear and valuables) with you inside the bus. Bus drivers will often go for hours without food or rest, so when they do stop, make the most of it.

TRUCKS & TRUCKING

Of all the forms of transport in Tibet, trucking is the one most travellers rave about. Sadly, there has been an official crackdown on truck drivers taking foreigners and if they do, they now risk fines and confiscation of their licence. This has put severe restrictions on hitchhiking as a means of getting around, but some persevering souls have still managed to find a lift. Despite its attractions, hitchhiking in Tibet has a very real element of danger; trucks regularly part company with the road and disappear over precipices. A number of foreigners have been killed or injured in smashes or frozen to death on the back of a truck.

When all goes right, to ride over the high passes of the roof of the world, tucked in tight behind the cab, clutching its roof, watching an endless road disappear into a horizon of snowcaps and barren plateau is a rare experience – hitchhiker's heaven.

Beer from Kunming, building materials from Xining, videos from Chengdu – just about everything is trucked into Tibet. If you're lucky, you'll be in the back amongst the crates and boxes, or if you're luckier you'll be up in the cab with one knee jammed in the glove-box and the other crippled by the gear lever.

Kinds of Trucks

There are three main types of truck used in Tibet. The Jiefang looks like a dinosaur, is usually painted green, has a long snout and can carry up to eight tons. A brand new Jiefang costs around Y15,000 and an updated model has now appeared on the roads. These are the slowest trucks on the road and the cab gets very cramped with two passengers.

The Dongfeng is a newer and more popular truck, often painted light brown, with a rounded front and a carrying capacity of 10 tons. The price for a new Dongfeng is around Y20,000. This is a faster truck with space in the cab for two passengers. As the old Jiefang is phased out, this is becoming

Jiefang truck on 1 fen note

中國人民銀行

X Ⅱ Ⅱ

壹分

一九五三年

the most common type of truck on the road in Tibet.

The Isuzu WuShiLing is a modern, Japanese-style truck with a sleek, rounded front and load capacity of 18 tons. A new Isuzu will set you back Y25,000. This is the fastest type of truck and the cab has plenty of room for two passengers. Other types of truck, such as Mercedes and Roman, have been imported and are in use in Qinghai and Tibet.

Most trucks have a stencilled sign on the front bumper which states in units of 10,000 km how far the driver has driven. For the mileage of the vehicles, most drivers can only hazard a guess. Road conditions are atrocious in the winter and can also deteriorate rapidly at other times of the year. On the routes in and out of Tibet be prepared for landslides, rockfalls, mudslides, flooding, snowstorms and broken bridges. Bad weather, poor maintenance of vehicles, fatigue and drink cause frequent accidents and dramatic wreckage can often be seen littering the mountainsides. Drivers have a disconcerting love of coasting down from the high passes at top speed. Ailing carburettors, flat tyres and overheated engines are a common source of delay. After blowing a gasket on our truck I spent three hours with the driver carefully cutting a new gasket out of cardboard provided by a passing Tibetan!

Licence Plates

Many trucks have large logos painted in Chinese, Uigur or Tibetan on the cab doors which give an indication of their destinations, but the best clue is the licence plate. Each licence plate consists of the Chinese characters for its province of origin followed by a number.

The Chinese characters for some of the more common plates are:

Tibet	西藏
Gansu	甘肃
Qinghai	青海
Xinjiang	新疆
Sichuan	四川

Truck Drivers

Truck drivers usually belong to one of three ethnic groups: Han Chinese, Muslim Chinese and Tibetan. The Han and Muslim Chinese are mostly from Sichuan, Qinghai, Xinjiang and Gansu provinces. They have a hard and monotonous life. If you speak some Chinese (or Tibetan for Tibetan drivers) – see phrases in this book or use a phrasebook – they will almost always go out of their way to help or please. Many drivers told me that they liked picking up foreigners, but they found it a strain to spend days (for some routes it could be weeks) on the road with no way of talking to their passengers. Some drivers will even let you take the wheel.

China produces over 1000 billion cigarettes a year for its estimated 300 million smokers and these truck drivers must be among the heaviest smokers in China. Even if you don't smoke, take along cigarettes for the driver. No conversation is started, no deal clinched without the communion of tobacco. Etiquette demands that you offer cigarettes, beer, food or whatever at least three times. If you know the driver is refusing out of politeness, you can poke a cigarette into his top pocket. If you are a nonsmoker and want to stay that way your willpower will be sorely tried – just keep repeating *bu hui*, which means you don't smoke. Other ways to keep the driver amused include showing your family photos and playing Chinese chess at truck stops. Many drivers will pay for your meals, but you should at least make a show of refusing, and pay for the occasional beer.

For some truck rides you pay for an official ticket at the truck depot. For others, you make a private deal with the driver. It's best to reject demands for payment in FEC and hand over the cash only when you've arrived.

In parts of Tibet, traffic is rare and lifts even rarer (some hitchhikers have waited for days), so you can't afford to be choosy if the driver is only going part of the way to your destination. A good policy is to first name a point on your route that is close, then when you're on the truck, check out its destination. The driver will usually take you all the way if the destinations are identical or drop you off when he leaves your route.

Supplies

Make sure you are properly prepared with food, water and clothing for trucking. Keep a small bag with you containing warm clothes, valuables and photo gear, food and water. If you are in the back of the truck, useful items are gloves, waterproof trousers, rain poncho, down jacket, down sleeping bag, sunglasses, wide-brimmed hat, sun-cream and lipcream.

Getting a Ride

Truck depots used to arrange rides and issue official tickets, although PSB offices have cracked down on this. With persistent asking it may still be possible to arrange a private deal with drivers at truck depots, gas stations, truckstops/hotels and friendly checkpoints.

If all else fails, just grab your courage, station yourself visibly on the roadside, and show passing vehicles you are not yet another inert rock in the landscape by waving them down with a regal gesture. You might also like to try the system used by Tibetan ladies which is to put both hands in 'thumbs up' position vertically on top of each other and pump them up and down as if churning yak butter. The effect is heightened by shouting and dancing up and down at the same time. Extremists lie down or stand in the middle of the road but this is not recommended unless you are interested in sky burial.

Locals often show an avid interest in your progress or lack of it. After watching Landcruisers and minibuses packed with foreigners swirl past in clouds of dust, they are delighted to find a foreigner who has actually fallen to earth. Be prepared for wonderful, impromptu Tibetan lessons, long drinking sessions and hilarious group attempts to snare a ride. Tibetans are a rare breed.

TRAIN

Tibet is the only province in China without a railway system. For years the Chinese have been considering the idea of a Qinghai-Tibet railway, but the only section completed so far is the one between Xining and Golmud. The proposed rail route from Golmud to Lhasa will (eventually?) continue from Golmud through Nachitai, TuoTuoHe, Amdo, Nagqu, Damxung and Maizhokunggar before terminating at Lhasa. If the project succeeds, it will be the highest railway in the world and a formidable technical achievement. The route would pass through the Qaidam Basin (consisting mostly of deserts, salt lakes and areas of saline soil), cross the high ranges of the Kunlun and Tanggula mountains and pass over the Golmud, Tongtian and Lhasa rivers. Long stretches of the route would not only enter permafrost areas but also be exposed to the danger of massive earthquakes around Nagqu and Damxung. Now that the Qinghai-Tibet Highway has been widened and asphalted it appears that the railway idea has been derailed until the year 2000 or never.

OFFBEAT OPTIONS

Hitchhiking

The major problem with hitchhiking now is the crackdown on truckers carrying foreigners.

Outside of Lhasa group tours or groups of travellers who have rented a vehicle may stop for you on the road, but they might also ask you to pay your share. You may well find yourself hitchhiking on tractors, walking-tractors, horse-carts, dump-trucks and road-graders. Many tractors and walking-tractors cover huge distances – I followed one convoy all the way from Xining to Yushu. Dump-trucks are definitely a novel way to travel. One sighted near Gyantse was bouncing along with an entire Tibetan family singing, drinking and eating in the dumper part. Thumbs up! Keep on trucking....

Bicycle

Long-distance bikers, sighted in droves between 1986 and 1988, are now made unwelcome by Chinese border officials, who impose fines or even confiscate bikes of Tibet-bound foreigners. In mid-1985 a Canadian and an Australian came across the

Nepal-Tibet border at Gyirong over the high passes with mountain-bikes strapped to yaks. In Shigatse they were collared by the PSB, fined, dumped on the back of a truck and sent back to the Nepalese border. On the way, their truck broke down, so the intrepid duo grabbed their bikes and split north again! On reaching Lhasa, the police arrested them at their hotel. The bikes were confiscated and they were deported to Nepal. Here's the punch-line: the bikes remained in Lhasa and were rented out to tourists at Y15 a day.

Lhasa has several places for bike rental. Models are of the black clunker variety – Phoenix, Forever, or else lesser breeds of Chinese lineage with no gears, heavy frames, unpredictable braking devices. Bicycling is a quick and convenient way to cover Lhasa in the absence of a logical local bus system. Watch out for theft, and don't overdo the pedal power at this altitude.

For an interesting read about biking in Tibet you can try *The Adventures of Rossinante* (Oxford Illustrated Press) by Bernard Magnouloux. Tiger Tops (PO Box 242, Kathmandu, Nepal) intend to run bike trips between Kathmandu and Lhasa.

Boat

There are plans afoot to provide tourists with boating trips in Tibet on the Mekong, Salween and Brahmaputra rivers but CITS has not yet disclosed details. At the moment it is possible to hire yak-hide boats opposite Jarmalinka Island in Lhasa for a short paddle. The ferry ride to reach Samye is another scenic boat trip lasting about an hour. In Lhasa some travellers were already excitedly talking about bringing kayaks and inflatable boats next time to have a crack at some of the wildest waters in the world.

An American river guide brought along his collapsible kayak and paddled along the Brahmaputra. Hitching occasional rides with his kayak on trucks, he made it down to Mt Kailas and proceeded to paddle around Lake Manasarovar. He returned to Lhasa and whilst he was taking a nap on Jarmalinka (Thieves Island) his kayak was stolen.

Several months later, some foreigners strolling by the river noticed a Chinese busy ferrying his bike across the river on top of a kayak!

Glacier Sliding

When Huc and Gabet travelled across Tibet during the last century they came across a novel form of glacier transport:

'Here we are, at the glacier of the Mountain of Spirits,' said Li Guoan. 'We shall have a bit of a laugh now'...They made the animals go first, the oxen , and then the horses. A magnificent long-haired ox opened the march; he advanced gravely to the edge of the plateau; then, after stretching out his neck, smelling for a moment at the ice, and blowing through his large nostrils some thick clouds of vapour, he manfully put his two front feet on the glacier, and whizzed off as if he had been discharged from a cannon. He went down the glacier with his legs extended, but as stiff and motionless as if they had been made of marble. Arrived at the bottom, he turned over, and then ran on, bounding and bellowing over the snow...

The men, in their turn, embarked with no less intrepidity and success than the animals, although in an altogether different manner. We seated ourselves carefully on the edge of the glacier, we stuck our heels close together on the ice, as firmly as possible, then using the handles of our whips by way of helm, we sailed over those frozen waters with the velocity of a locomotive. A sailor would have pronounced us to be going twelve knots an hour. In our many travels we had never before experienced a mode of conveyance at once so commodious, so expeditious, and above all, so refreshing.

Trekking

Trekking options are described in the Trekking chapter.

Lhasa ལྷ་ས་

Lhasa, once the national capital of Tibet, is at an altitude of 3683 metres in the Tibetan Himalaya beside the Lhasa (Kyi Chu) River. For centuries it remained isolated from the outside world – a tantalising morsel for travellers, missionaries and explorers. In the heyday of the Asian trail, many an overlander made a pilgrimage to the Nepalese border with Tibet to gaze wistfully and dream of Lhasa. Today, this city, described by Emanuel Freyre in 1716 as being the 'size of three parishes', has grown to 12 times that size and the Potala, no longer separated from the city by a stretch of greenery extending over 1½ km, is hemmed in by the ugly paraphernalia of Chinese-style city planning. The population is estimated at 150,000, with the Han Chinese making up by far the highest percentage and, it is rumoured, the growing numbers of group tours may soon account for a creditable slice.

At first sight, Lhasa appears to be a Chinese cake with the Potala as icing on top. But time spent around the Jokhang and Barkhor Bazaar should show that a distinctively Tibetan lifestyle still survives in Lhasa, despite all its outward Chinese trappings.

History

Lhasa became a centre of national power when King Songtsen Gampo moved his capital there from the Yarlung Valley during the 6th century AD. After the assassination of King Langdarma in 842, Lhasa lost political influence but later became the religious centre of Tibet. From the 17th century onwards, Lhasa again became the seat of government until the Chinese occupation in 1951 which was followed by the final imposition of direct Chinese administration after the uprising in 1959.

In 1965 the Tibetan Autonomous Region was founded and Lhasa designated its capital. In September 1985, Lhasa was chosen as the stage for celebrations of the 20th anniversary of this autonomy but the contrived and unconvincing show was marred by restrictions on Tibetans and foreigners.

In October 1987, February 1988 and December 1988 there were violent demonstrations against Chinese rule. In March 1989, violent clashes resulted in hundreds of Tibetan casualties and were only stopped when Beijing imposed martial law. The decree was lifted in May 1990, but the situation remains tense.

On 23 May 1991, Beijing splashed out a cool Y1.5 million to commemorate the 40th anniversary of communist rule in Tibet. By all accounts it was an action-packed day: orchestrated crowds and organised smiles; tank parades; secret police and soldiers keeping the festivities properly channelled; and a top-ranking Chinese government delegation even felt spirited enough for a temporary twirl with local dancers. Despite Chinese assurances that all was calm in Lhasa, all Beijing-based foreign journalists were banned from travelling to Tibet.

Warning

Foreign contacts with Tibetans are closely monitored – audio and visual surveillance extends from the street to the hotel. However tempting or frustrating the scenario might be, think very carefully about the nature of your discussions in public. Foreigners often do not stay long enough to see the repercussions of careless talk with the locals. Plainclothes police (known in Chinese as *bian yi*) and concealed soldiers are abundant in Lhasa.

Climate

The best time to visit Lhasa is between May and September. Once you are used to the altitude, it's an invigorating climate: low humidity, moderate rainfall and an average of eight hours of sunshine daily. In the summer, dust is a problem. In the winter, there is surprisingly little snow but be prepared for icicles on the ceiling if your room is unheated.

Month	Average°C	Max°C	Min°C
Jan	0.3	12.2	-14.4
Feb	1.6	15.5	-11.6
Mar	5.5	18.3	-8.3
Apr	9.1	21.6	-4.4
May	13.0	25.0	-0.5
Jun	17.0	27.8	4.4
Jul	16.4	27.2	6.1
Aug	15.6	25.5	5.5
Sep	14.3	23.9	3.9
Oct	9.2	21.6	-5.0
Nov	3.9	16.6	-9.4
Dec	0.0	13.9	-13.3

Orientation
Traditionally, pilgrims who entered Lhasa performed three circuits in a clockwise direction. The greater the number of circuits, the greater the merit acquired.

The Lingkhor (with an outer circuit of about eight km in length) went west, parallel to the road now called YanHe DongLu, and then branched off northwards in a long loop behind Chagpori (the 'iron mountain' on which the medicine college once stood) and continued behind the Potala before running eastwards, parallel to the road now called JianShe Lu. Pilgrims following the circuit then took the route that branched off southwards, parallel to the road now called LinKuo Lu, until they reached their point of departure. Much of the Lingkhor has been obliterated by barracks, offices and apartment blocks, but I did see prostrators following the first part of the route from Lhasa Bridge and then continuing along YanHe DongLu, so it is still travelled, if only in part.

The Barkhor (with an inner circuit of about 800 metres in length) runs round the outer walls of the Jokhang and is still very much in use. The final circuit performed by pilgrims is that made within the Jokhang temple. In March 1991, the entire Barkhor was turned to rubble by the Chinese authorities, perhaps as an attempt to stifle the attractions of this circuit for political protest.

Although the Potala dominates the skyline, it is the Jokhang, the 'Cathedral of Buddhism', which remains the centre of Tibetan life in Lhasa. Roads fan out from the Barkhor like a spider's web, linking up with LinKuo Lu and JieFang Lu, which run north to south, and with XingFu Lu, RenMin Lu and YanHe Lu, which run east to west.

Lhasa is speedily growing in size and losing its Tibetan identity with the same rapidity. In time for the 20th anniversary celebration, a large square with food and goods shops, was laid out in front of the Jokhang. The city can be divided into three types of neighbourhood: Tibetan, Muslim, and Chinese. The area around the Jokhang and the area which was once the village of Chö at the foot of the Potala are still traditionally Tibetan in style.

The area east of the Jokhang, with a short radius around the mosque, has retained a strong Muslim atmosphere. The rest is Chinese. In the west, an ugly industrial zone sprawls from Doilungdêqên past the Norbulinka to the Potala. In the north, the residential blocks of New TuanJic village vie with factories in a burst of concrete growth.

Information
General information is sometimes provided by members of the staff at the Lhasa Holiday Inn, otherwise head for the Tibetan hotels in the city centre. Most of the hotels used by foreigners have notice boards airing 1001 wishes: Tiniba is urgently sought to combat giardia, bus tickets are offered to the Nepalese border...

CITS CITS has an office at the Lhasa Holiday Inn (Room Nos 1219 and 1238) and another branch at the No 3 Guesthouse (Di San Zhaodai Suo). Although CITS is expected to be the leading light for tours and vehicle hire, it continues to receive criticism for inefficiency, price-gouging and lack of interest in correcting errors.

Public Security Bureau The Public Security Bureau is behind the Potala. Hours are Monday to Saturday from 10 am to 1 pm and from 4 to 6.30 pm; it is closed on Sunday

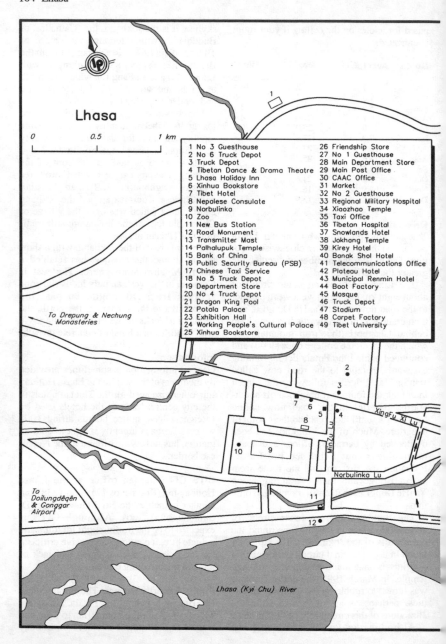

Lhasa

0   0.5   1 km

1 No 3 Guesthouse
2 No 6 Truck Depot
3 Truck Depot
4 Tibetan Dance & Drama Theatre
5 Lhasa Holiday Inn
6 Xinhua Bookstore
7 Tibet Hotel
8 Nepalese Consulate
9 Norbulinka
10 Zoo
11 New Bus Station
12 Road Monument
13 Transmitter Mast
14 Palhalupuk Temple
15 Bank of China
16 Public Security Bureau (PSB)
17 Chinese Taxi Service
18 No 5 Truck Depot
19 Department Store
20 No 4 Truck Depot
21 Dragon King Pool
22 Potala Palace
23 Exhibition Hall
24 Working People's Cultural Palace
25 Xinhua Bookstore

26 Friendship Store
27 No 1 Guesthouse
28 Main Department Store
29 Main Post Office
30 CAAC Office
31 Market
32 No 2 Guesthouse
33 Regional Military Hospital
34 Xiaozhao Temple
35 Taxi Office
36 Tibetan Hospital
37 Snowlands Hotel
38 Jokhang Temple
39 Kirey Hotel
40 Banak Shol Hotel
41 Telecommunications Office
42 Plateau Hotel
43 Municipal Renmin Hotel
44 Boot Factory
45 Mosque
46 Truck Depot
47 Stadium
48 Carpet Factory
49 Tibet University

To Drepung & Nechung
Monasteries

To
Doilungdêqên
& Gonggar
Airport

XingFu Xi Lu

MinZu Lu

Norbulinka Lu

Lhasa (Kyi Chu) River

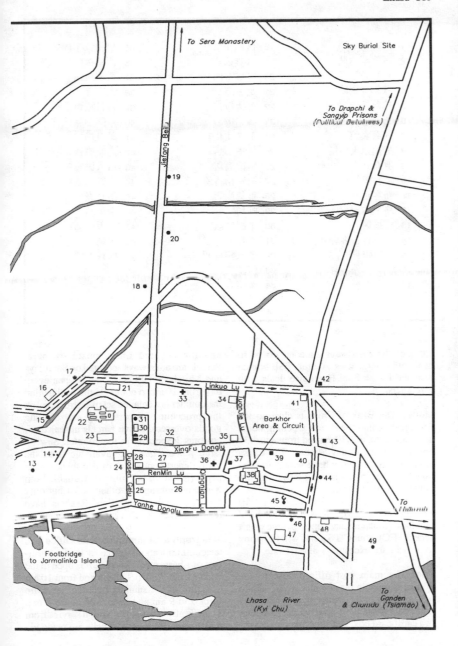

To Sera Monastery

Sky Burial Site

To Drapchi &
Sangyip Prisons
(Political Detainees)

Jiefang Beilu

• 19

• 20

18 •

17 •

16

Linkuo Lu

• 42

21

33

34

41

Tuanjie Lu

15

22

• 31

Barkhor
Area & Circuit

30

• 43

23

29

32

35

14

XingFu Donglu

13

Duosen Gelu

28

27

36

37

39

40

24

• 44

25

26

RenMin Lu

38

45

Yanhe Donglu

46

48

To

47

49

Footbridge
to Jarmalinka Island

Lhasa River
(Kyi Chu)

To Ganden
& Chamdo (Tsiamdo)

1	区三所	18	区汽车五队	35	出租汽车局
2	区汽车六队	19	百货商店	36	西藏医院
3	货车站	20	区汽车四队	37	雪域旅馆
4	歌舞戏剧院	21	龙土潭	38	大昭寺
5	拉萨饭店	22	布达拉宫	39	吉日旅馆
6	书店	23	展览馆	40	八郎学旅社
7	西藏宾馆	24	工人文化宫	41	邮电局
8	尼泊尔大使馆	25	新华书店	42	高原旅社
9	罗布林卡	26	友谊商店	43	市人民宾馆
10	动物园	27	第一招待所	44	皮鞋制造厂
11	新客运站	28	百货商店	45	清真寺
12	路上的纪念碑	29	邮局	46	卡车站
13	广播区	30	中国民航	47	露天运动场
14	巴拉鲁普客寺	31	市场	48	地毯厂
15	中国银行	32	第二招待所	49	西藏大学
16	公安局外事科	33	医院		
17	出租汽车	34	小昭寺		

although there is always someone around to deal with emergencies. Another PSB branch near the Banak Shol Hotel also deals with foreigners.

Money The Bank of China is close to the PSB, just behind the Potala. Opening hours are from 10 am to 1.30 pm and from 4 to 6.30 pm. It's closed all day Sunday. The Lhasa Holiday Inn also has a bank with staff who may be snooty about serving those who are not staying at the hotel.

There is virtually no black market left for FEC in Lhasa. If you need RMB for local purchases (outside Lhasa, most people won't accept FEC), your CITS guide will be happy to provide for exchange – at a 1:1 rate.

Post The main post office, close to the Potala, is open in the summer from 9 am to 6.30 pm and in the winter from 10 am to 5 pm. Poste Restante is here – letters are kept in a cardboard box. Get your first-day covers

and the coveted Lhasa postmark here. Parcels are not always accepted on Saturdays and Mondays. GPO customs is open every day from 10 am to noon. On the wall behind the counter is a detailed set of instructions on the procedure for wrapping and sending goods overseas. Leave parcels unsealed for customs inspection at the counter. Sew up large parcels in cloth (available from the main department store) or use thick brown paper (*Niupi zhi* in Chinese), available from Xinhua Bookstore or other stores but only seal them after inspection. Readers have reported 'security checks' on most items.

Telegraph & Communications Office The telecommunications office is in the northeast of Lhasa, on Linkuo Lu. It is open in the winter from 7.30 to 9.30 am and from 10 am to 6 pm. In the summer opening hours are from 7 to 9 am and from 9.30 am to 6 pm. There is also meant to be a night service from 6 to 11 pm. International calls are made via or courtesy of Beijing with varying degrees of success...or attention.

Nepalese Consulate The Nepalese Consulate General (☎ 22880) is at 13 Norbulinka Lu. Hours are Monday to Saturday, from 10 am to 1.30 pm and from 4 to 7.30 pm. An exit stamp from PSB is no longer required. Visa fees vary according to the applicant's nationality; it costs Y170 for British subjects and Y50 for everyone else except the Chinese, who pay just Y10. Just bring along the cash with your passport and two photos, and the visa should be ready in a day. The one-month visa is valid for entry within three months.

CAAC The CAAC office (☎ 22417) is at 88 Jiefang Lu. The admirable sign: 'Lhasa Reception Centre For The Unorganised Tourists' has now vanished because presumably, all tourists in Tibet are now 'organised'!

Xinhua Bookstore The Xinhua Bookstore is at the western end of RenMin Lu. Opening hours are from 9 am to 6 pm in summer and from 9.30 am to 5.30 pm in winter. Maps are on sale here, either in Chinese or Tibetan. Potala tea towels, postcards and, sometimes, cassettes of Tibetan music are also on sale but there are no books in foreign languages on Tibet or Lhasa. Another branch of Xinhua has opened beside the Lhasa Holiday Inn.

Maps You can find maps of Lhasa in either Chinese or Tibetan (none in English) from Xinhua Shudian (Xinhua Bookstore) (see the preceeding section on the Xinhua Bookstore). Maps in English are sold by the gift shop in the Lhasa Holiday Inn. An outline map of Tibet is available from room No 1219.

Hospitals Several hospitals in Lhasa treat foreigners. The Tibetan Autonomous Region People's Hospital and the Regional Military Hospital have been recommended. The Lhasa Holiday Inn may be able to refer you to a doctor in the hotel. The Tibetan Hospital

(☎ 24211), close to the Jokhang, specialises in traditional Tibetan medicine. One of the doctors speaks English. According to foreigners treated there, the herbal remedies for ailments such as diarrhoea are most effective. The hospital also has a room with various medical *thangkas* on display which are quite interesting.

Friendship Store The Friendship Store is on RenMin Lu, about halfway along, nearly opposite the No 1 Guesthouse. It is roughly open from 9.30 am to 4.30 pm daily. See the Things to Buy section that follows in this chapter.

The Potala ཕོ་ད་ལ་

The Potala Palace, perched high above Lhasa on the Marpori (red mountain), is a place of spiritual pilgrimage and a mammoth tribute to Tibetan architectural skills. The name Potala derives from the Sanskrit 'Potalaka', the abode of the Bodhisattva Avalokitesvara.

In the 7th century King Songtsen Gampo first built a small meditation pavilion on this site, followed later by a palace. During the 9th century these buildings were destroyed after lightning set them on fire. On the orders of the Fifth Dalai Lama construction was started in 1645, but he died before the Red Palace was started. However, before dying he asked his prime minister (regent) to keep his death secret lest construction work be discontinued. The prime minister found a monk who resembled the deceased and thus

was able to conceal the death until all 13 storeys had been completed. From the time of the Fifth Dalai Lama onwards, the Potala became the official winter residence of the successive Dalai Lamas.

During the 1959 uprising, the PLA shelled the Potala. It is rumoured that the wholesale destruction of the Potala during the Cultural Revolution was averted by Zhou Enlai, who pledged his own troops for its protection. In June 1984 an electrical fault caused a massive fire which destroyed the Hall of the Buddha Maitreya. Large water tanks and extensive plumbing were then installed as part of a fire-control plan. The authorities are now planning an assault on what may prove to be the deadliest threat yet – wood-boring insects!

Built of wood, earth and stone, the Potala has 13 storeys rising over 117 metres high. The whole structure is a maze of rooms – over 1000 of them – with 10,000 shrines and some 200,000 statues. The walls, varying in thickness between two and five metres, were strengthened against earthquakes by pouring molten copper inside them. No steel frame was used, and no nails were used in the woodwork.

Seen from the front, the Potala consists of the Red Palace in the centre flanked, on both sides, by the White Palace. The White Palace was completed in 1653; construction of the Red Palace started in 1690 and was completed in 1694.

The **Red Palace** contains assembly halls, shrines, 35 chapels, four meditation halls and seven mausoleums. These mausoleums contain the remains of all the Dalai Lamas from the fifth to the 13th, (with the exception of the sixth) with their salt-dried bodies placed in individual chortens which are covered with stupendous amounts of gold plating and inlaid with diamonds, pearls, turquoise, agate and coral. The Fifth Dalai Lama's chorten is covered with 3700 kg of gold! His chorten is 20 metres high, rising through three storeys. Nearby is the tomb of the 13th Dalai Lama, which is 22 metres high, made of solid silver, and covered with gold leaf and precious stones. For details of

the Dalai Lamas refer to the Religion section in Facts about the Region.

The western section of the Potala used to house a community of over 150 monks, while the eastern section contained government offices, a school for monk officials, and the meeting halls of the National Assembly. The Potala also served as a storehouse for thousands of ancient scrolls, volumes of illuminated scriptures, armour and armaments from ancient times, gifts and treasures. The myriad storehouses and cellars in the base of the building contained government stocks of provisions for officials, monasteries, and the army. The torture chambers, reserved for high-ranking offenders, were once standard fare on the tour-group menu, but appear to be out of bounds again.

At the base of the Potala is a collection of buildings, which once formed a separate village, called Sho (Chö). It contained government offices, the Tibetan Army Headquarters and a printing works once famous for its wood blocks of the *Kanjur*. The area has now lost much of its character because of infringing Han architecture, and there are plans to turn the whole area into ugly blocks of flats.

The Roof The roof of the Potala houses what was once the Dalai Lama's quarters. There is a reception hall and a set of rooms which comprised the Dalai Lama's private quarters.

It is difficult if you are not on an official tour to gain access to more than the reception hall on the roof, which has stupendous views of Lhasa, and ornate decorations. The monks are not keen on allowing foreigners access. One American gleefully scrambled up through a side door. When he tried to come down again, a grim-faced monk locked the door and told him he would only be allowed down on a payment of Y10.

Opening Hours & Taboos The Potala is open Monday and Thursday from 9 am to noon. Check times before going – the religious significance of the palace means that it is subject to rapid closure if the mood gets rough in Lhasa. The Potala telephone number is 22896 if you care to test your language skills to the limit. Rooms are constantly being closed and reopened, so it pays to make several visits, and it's best to steer clear of the place until you're acclimatised to the altitude as the steps up can be heavy going (tour groups are often driven up a road at the back). It seems that groups can visit on almost any day, so you might be able to tag along. If you go on your own, it's worthwhile just to follow the pilgrims as they present offerings, recite prayers and prostrate themselves in a long procession up and down stairs, through countless halls, past frescoes, images, shrines and relics.

Visitors enter the Potala through the East Gate, which is reached by climbing a long series of stone steps that were designed wide and low enough for horse riders, or for palanquin bearers. Inside the East Gate there is a ticket office on your left; tickets cost Y25. Once through the East Gate, you enter the Deyangshar (East Terrace) where Cham dances and religious rituals were once held. A small shop on the right sells postcards and a brochure in Chinese about the Potala. Remember to take a torch as most rooms are dimly lit, a water bottle and, perhaps, some Dalai Lama pics. Always walk in a clockwise direction around shrines and sacred images, otherwise you will offend the monks and the pilgrims. Most visitors exit from the north side of the Potala, down steps and along a path which leads to the Dragon King Pool (LongWangZe).

Surprisingly, some monks in the Potala speak a little English and show a keen interest in worldly affairs which may be rigorously monitored by CITS guides and security officials. Photography is officially forbidden in the Potala and the same applies to smoking and shouting. However, it is possible to take photos if you pay the horrendously high fees which can vary between Y10 and Y50 *per photo*. You may find Dalai Lama pics are a cheaper alternative for gaining permission to take photos.

As part of a drive to make the Potala more palatable to tourists, the Tibet Tourist Corporation plans to reduce the butter lamps, install bright lighting and provide modern toilets. These measures may please tourists who, inevitably, consider the Potala as something lifeless, a desiccated museum. But, from the Tibetan point of view, no amount of tinkering with the Potala can disguise the eerie absence of the force within – the Dalai Lama.

The Dragon King Pool

This pool is said to have appeared when workers dug out clods of earth behind the Potala to make cement for the walls during reconstruction work in 1645. Later, the Dragon King Temple (Lukhang) was erected on an island in the lake. According to one legend, an evil dragon which required a male human sacrifice once a year used to live here. After many years of sacrifices, one boy chosen for sacrifice decided to fight the dragon. The fight lasted seven days and seven nights before the dragon was killed. To celebrate this victory, Tibetans come here every year on April 15 for a festival. The pool is inside a pleasant park which is a favourite picnic spot for Tibetans.

Opposite what is now the entrance to CAAC, at the foot of the Marpori, is a small temple with prayer wheels outside. An old Tibetan lady is often found nearby, carefully carving inscriptions on small stones. For a few *mao* she will carve a stone for you.

Chagpori

Chagpori (iron mountain) is opposite the Potala and can be easily identified by the radio mast on the top. This was the site of a famous college of medicine that was razed during the Cultural Revolution, but is now being rebuilt. Inside the hill are meant to be vast meat-storage lockers with sufficient frozen carcasses to feed the Chinese army garrison for many weeks. Lower down the hill, partially set into a cave, is the small Palhalupuk Temple with prayer wheels and friendly monks. There are excellent views from here and plenty of fine spots from which to photograph the Potala. The climb up this hill is best done after you have acclimatised to the altitude for a few days.

Exhibition Hall

At the foot of the Potala is the Exhibition Hall, open from 3 to 4 pm Monday, Thursday, and Sunday only. The rooms are devoted to fauna & flora; historical exhibits; monastic life, complete with groaning tape; handicrafts; ethnic exhibits and daily life; and modern local art. The historical exhibition has some interesting photos, captioned in Chinese, but draws predictable conclusions about China and Tibet. It's fun to observe the reaction of nomads on a pilgrimage to Lhasa when they see the display of nomad life. Most of them get a giggle out of seeing their home in a museum – complete with stuffed dog.

Norbulinka (Summer Palace) དོར་བུ་གླིང་ཁ་

Construction of the Norbulinka (precious jewel park) was started by the Seventh Dalai Lama in 1755. This is a large complex of small palaces and chapels within a walled garden, about four km west of the Potala. The earliest building in the park is the Gesang Pozhang Palace built by the Seventh Dalai Lama. In 1954 the present Dalai Lama started construction of the New Palace, which was completed by 1956. The PLA inflicted heavy casualties and immense damage during the uprising in 1959 when the Norbulinka was shelled the day after the Dalai Lama had slipped away in disguise on his flight to India. During the Cultural Revolution further damage was done. Until recently, many of the frescoes on the walls were still daubed with crude slogans and pictures of Mao.

The New Palace (the main building of the Norbulinka open to the public) is tiny compared to the Potala, but it contains fascinating murals in excellent condition. A guide who speaks some English will first take you round the South Hall and North Hall. The tour then continues through the Dalai Lama's meditation room, bedroom (notice the Russian radio), sitting room

(complete with Philips radiogram), bathroom (plumbing by courtesy of a British company), reception room and throne room (which has a superb mandala and fresco depicting the Dalai Lama with foreign heads of state). The New Palace (☎ 22644) is open from 9 to 11.30 am and from 3.30 to 5 pm; closed on Sundays. Admission costs Y2 for foreigners and Y0.30 for locals. Photography is not allowed. Take your shoes off at the entrance and leave them with the exotic pile left by pilgrims.

The gardens are a favourite picnic spot. Performances of Tibetan dances and opera are held here during the Shoton (Xuedun) Festival, which falls on the last day of the sixth lunar month (end of July). Behind the New Palace is a depressing zoo where sad-eyed lynxes, deer, Himalayan brown bears, monkeys and seagulls endure baiting with cigarettes and dream of feeding time when they receive – what else in Tibet – *tsampa*! In one of the courtyards behind the New Palace is the orange, rusting hulk of a 1931 Dodge. Nearby, is the almost indistinguishable wreckage of two 1927 Baby Austins: one blue, the other red and yellow. These were presented to the 13th Dalai Lama, carried by yaks over the Himalaya in pieces and then reassembled. After the death of the 13th Dalai Lama, these cars, the only ones in Lhasa, remained unused until the 1950s, when the present Dalai Lama succeeded in putting them into working order with the help of a Tibetan trained as a driver in India.

Jokhang Temple གཙུག་ལག་ཁང་

The Jokhang is the religious and geographical centre of Lhasa. From morning to night an astounding display of chanting, prostrating pilgrims revolves around Barkhor Bazaar and the Jokhang. Hundreds of faces, ornaments, clothes and colours swirl round in a gigantic whirlpool of religious fervour.

The temple was founded in 650 by Songtsen Gampo on the site of what was once a great underground lake in which visions of the future could be seen. Legend recounts that the lake was filled in by a sure-footed goat which carried soil on its back and walked across the lake on wooden planks. According to one version (favoured by the Chinese), Songtsen Gampo built this temple to house the statue of Sakyamuni presented to him by Princess Wen Cheng. Other sources indicate that the temple already existed before the arrival of the Princess. Tsong Khapa introduced the Mönlam Chenmo (Great Prayer Festival) in 1409 and designated the Jokhang as the principal venue for religious celebrations of the Yellow Hat sect which he founded.

The square in front of the Jokhang has been 'modernised'. The incongruous result looks like a cross between a Western shopping mall and a Chinese square. Perhaps as a result of the construction work, my attempts to find the famous willow tree planted by Princess Wen Cheng were unsuccessful. Two stone buildings opposite the Jokhang entrance house two stone *stele* (tablets).

The flagstones at the entrance to the Jokhang have been polished smooth by thousands of pilgrims. Pilgrims crowd around, constantly praying and prostrating. Follow the pilgrims inside, past rows of prayer wheels and then continue (clockwise) on a grand tour of the main hall which is surrounded by chapels dedicated to Avalokitesvara, Amitabha, etc. Within the central hall is the famous sitting statue of the 12-year-old Sakyamuni (one of only three made during his lifetime) which was a gift from Princess Wen Cheng to her husband, Songtsen Gampo. There is a vague rumour that zealous Red Guards erroneously smashed the statue of Wen Cheng herself, and that what you're now looking at is a duplicate (?).

The Jokhang (☎ 23129) is worth visiting as often as possible. Strictly speaking, it is only open in the morning until 11 am (closed on Sunday), but many of the monks are pleased to see foreigners and will sometimes take you on an impromptu tour in the afternoon. Take a torch and Dalai Lama pics, which could help relax the rules against photography. Whatever you do, be considerate of the pilgrims and respect the sacred nature of these places.

Barkhor
This is Lhasa's inner pilgrim circuit, shaped roughly like an octagon, which runs round the Jokhang. The circuit is lined with markets, shops, stalls and street vendors providing every conceivable item a Tibetan could need. The best place to start your circuit is right outside the Jokhang, but remember to walk in a clockwise direction and mind you don't step on the prostrators. Apart from numerous alleys (too tiny to describe, but great to explore – just keep heading for the Jokhang and you'll eventually hit the circuit), there are two other ways to enter: one is via a street running past the mosque, the other is via a street running south off XingFu DongLu, just before the Banak Shol Hotel. If you enter off XingFu DongLu, you'll cross Yak Alley which is a gory sight with tables of meat and yak carcasses on the ground and packs of dogs. There's a small open-air market here as well as stalls selling *chang* (Tibetan barley beer).

Just past Yak Alley you reach a large square with a monument used for burning incense. One corner of this square is reserved for carpets which are not necessarily Tibetan and rarely of good quality. However, the carpet lads from Xinjiang know about the merits of foreign currency. Tibetans, especially the tough-looking Khampas, will be keen to sell or barter earrings, purses, tinder boxes, coral, turquoise, old coins, daggers and ornaments. Bargaining is a 'must' since prices are usually steep, and it's worth remembering that the export of antiques (ie

anything that is pre-1959) is prohibited by law. Not all the turquoise on sale is genuine. Some is just a paste of cement and turquoise. Keen buyers bite the stones and reject them if their teeth leave scratch marks!

Prayer-flag sellers have bunches of flags. Jars of yoghurt are usually available in the early morning; it's best to have your own jar (use an empty fruit jar) otherwise you may be refused or have to pay a small deposit. If you feel thirsty or hungry, try one of the Muslim teahouses for *lamian* (noodles with meat and vegetables) and lotus-seed tea with rock crystal sugar. Some of the traders are Nepalese, speak excellent English and are willing to chat or help, even if you don't buy any Nepalese glucose biscuits or Indian snuff. Some stalls sell skins of rare animals. The quality is dubious and, anyway, who wants to encourage the extinction of rare species. Other stalls sell ceremonial scarves *(khata)*; felt stetsons made in Tianjin; gaudy,

embroidered hats with ear-flaps; and rolls of attractive, striped cloth. Street vendors sell bunches of juniper for incense, and incense holders (made out of soldered tin cans).

Pilgrims who have travelled vast distances and lack the money to return, sit against walls selling clothes and jewellery or reciting prayers. Another strange sight on the circuit is a troupe of scantily clad prostrators (foreigners have nicknamed them the Olympic Prostrating Team) performing dramatic rituals. In the evening, monks hold recitation sessions with prayer books, ritual drums and bells.

This is one place in Lhasa where Tibetans rule, in numbers and in spirit – any Han Chinese who venture here keep a low profile. Knife fights are not uncommon. The riots of 1987, 1988 and 1989 were particularly fierce around the Barkhor and there is heavy surveillance by plainclothes police. In March 1991, the Chinese government launched a

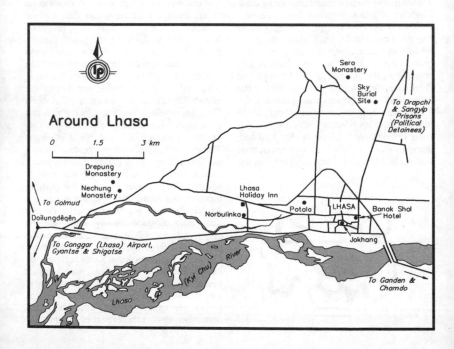

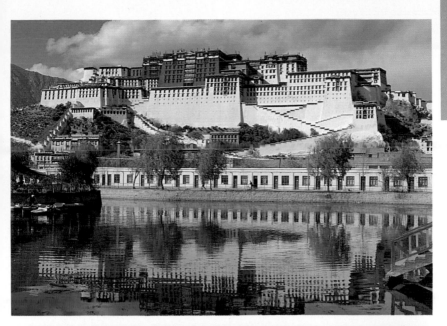

Top: Potala Palace - Lhasa (RV)
Bottom: Jokhang Temple - Lhasa (GW)

Top: Jokhang Temple - Lhasa (RV)
Bottom: Stall in the Barkhor (RV)

plan to bulldoze parts of the Barkhor for 'improvement', but most Tibetans consider this plan a great affront to their religion and a blatant attempt to raze Lhasa's focal point for dissent. In recent years, almost all Tibetan demonstrations have originated around the Barkhor.

Ramoche Temple

This temple is in the north of town, just off TuanJie Lu, and is still under renovation. In 1985, prior to renovation, Ramoche contained pictures and statues of Mao Zedong. Built in the 7th century by Princess Wen Cheng, this temple contains a small chapel, a main hall, and the main shrine which has an image of Akshobya Vajra (Buddha of the East). This image is reputed to have been broken apart during the Cultural Revolution: the lower half was found on a Lhasa rubbish heap, the upper half was discovered in a pile of religious artefacts in Beijing.

Jarmalinka Island

A pleasant place on the Lhasa (Kyi Chu) River with superb views of the Potala is Jarmalinka Island, connected to YanHe XiLu by a bridge which is festooned with prayer flags. You pay the bridge keeper a fee of Y0.10 to cross. If you arrive early in the morning, you can sometimes hire yak-hide boats for about Y1 per person for a return trip across the river. Water burials take place a short distance downstream. Jarmalinka Island is a popular picnic spot for Tibetans on Sundays. During the Washing Festival, which usually lasts for seven days during September, the whole area is crowded with bathing Tibetans. A recent foreign visitor to the island reported her surprise at meeting Chinese prostitutes and transvestites there!

Theatre

The ungainly looking building opposite the Lhasa Holiday Inn is the Tibetan Dance and Drama Theatre. With any luck, the shows here will be genuinely Tibetan, not a clumsy Chinese approximation.

Drepung Monastery
འབྲས་སྤུངས་དགོན་པ་

This Gelukpa monastery, once the largest in the world, was founded by Jamyang Choje Tashi Pelden, a disciple of Tsong Khapa, in 1416. The name Drepung means 'rice heap', perhaps a reference to its general appearance, but in fact named after a Tantric temple in India. It stands at the foot of a mountain about six km west of Lhasa, with fine views across the Lhasa Valley. The buildings were extended in the first half of the 17th century during the time of the Fifth Dalai Lama. This was a monastic university – one of the 'three seats of state'. The other two were Ganden and Sera monasteries.

Various paths lead up from the road past store rooms and monks' quarters which once housed 10,000 monks. Monks were usually housed according to the area they came from. Thus there were quarters for monks from Sichuan, Qinghai (Tsinghai), Chamdo (Tsiamdo), Siberia, Ladakh, and Mongolia. Four colleges (dratsang) here taught different aspects of Buddhism.

The **Ganden Potang** (Ganden Palace) was built by the Second Dalai Lama and was used as a residence for the Third, Fourth and Fifth Dalai Lamas. After the Fifth Dalai Lama moved to the Potala, this palace was maintained as a residence for the ruling Dalai Lama.

The **Tsokchen** (Main Assembly Hall) was reconstructed after it fell to bits in 1735. The central hall contains a large statue of Manjusri, an image of Sakyamuni and 16 Arhats together with sculptures of the Fifth and 13th Dalai Lamas. A small chapel contains the image of the Buddhas of the three periods (Kashyapa, Sakyamuni and Maitreya). There are various chortens at the rear and eight Boddhisattvas line the walls. On the upper floor there are images of Maitreya (including a giant statue of Maitreya at the age of 12), Tsong Khapa, a chorten containing relics of the Second Dalai Lama and relics of the Third and Fourth Dalai Lamas.

To the right there is a Dolma Lhakang (Tara Chapel) with three different aspects of Tara. Near the roof are three more chapels

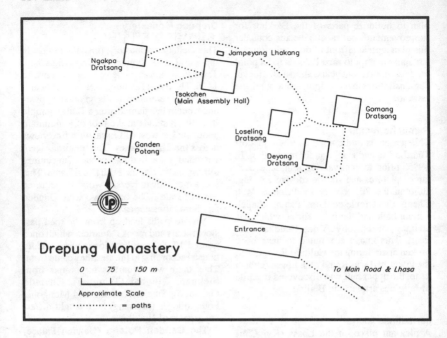

Ngakpa
Dratsang

Jampeyang Lhakang

Tsokchen
(Main Assembly Hall)

Gomang
Dratsang

Loseling
Dratsang

Ganden
Potang

Deyang
Dratsang

Entrance

Drepung Monastery

0   75   150 m

Approximate Scale

············· = paths

To Main Road & Lhasa

containing images of Maitreya, Sakyamuni and the Fifth Dalai Lama respectively plus many other images of Tibetan gurus. In the Maitreya chapel is a white conch with an anticlockwise spiral, believed to have been discovered by Tsong Khapa.

The **Jampeyang Lhakang** (Manjusri Chapel) is behind the Main Assembly Hall and contains an image of Manjusri carved on a boulder.

The **Ngakpa Dratsang** (Tantric College) is mainly dedicated to Yamantaka. In a chapel at the rear of the college is the most famous image, reputedly moulded by Tsong Khapa around the relics of the translator Ra Lotsawa. There are also statues of Tsong Khapa, the Fifth Dalai Lama and of the wrathful protectors. In the main hall is a large library together with images of Indian and Tibetan masters plus some statues of Tsong Khapa.

The **Loseling Dratsang** was the College

of Logic. In the main hall is a throne used by the Dalai Lamas, the images of the Fifth, Seventh and Eighth Dalai Lamas, a mandala of Yamantaka as well as more statues of the 13th Dalai Lama and Tsong Khapa. In the side chapels are images of the 16 Arhats, Maitreya, Sakyamuni and many little Buddhas. The Gonkhang (protector chapel) with the figures of Yamantaka and other Tantric divinities is upstairs.

The main hall of the **Gomang Dratsang** contains images of Mahakala, Tsong Khapa, 1000-armed Avalokitesvara, Maitreya and Amitayus. The first chapel contains the trio of Amitayus, Tara and Vijaya. The second chapel contains a central image of Akshobhya with Sakyamuni, Maitreya and Chenrezig. Mahakala and Yamantaka are represented in the Gonkhang upstairs (women are not allowed to enter).

In the central hall of the **Deyang Dratsang** are images of Tsong Khapa, Tara and the Fifth Dalai Lama. Maitreya and Tsong Khapa are represented in the side chapel. The Gonkhang is upstairs.

During the uprising in 1959, many monks from Drepung abandoned their vows and took up arms against the Chinese. Spent cartridges can still be found away from the paths. The few monks left here are not eager to admit foreigners to the temples, but you can ramble round, taking a look at whatever happens to be open. The kitchens are gigantic. You can also walk up to see carvings and paintings on the mountainside or just sit and absorb the atmosphere in ghostly silence. CITS has information on a walk you can go on behind Drepung. It takes about six hours to reach the top of the mountain, from where you can reportedly see as far as the mountains of Bhutan. The walk was supposedly a favourite of the Dalai Lama. It takes 2½ hours to come down.

Drepung has one population that is thriving – dogs. Most monasteries have resident packs of dogs which are believed to be reincarnations of past monks who failed to return in a higher form. Apparently the dogs are still interested in religion and lope around seeking admission to their former monastery.

Just below Drepung lies **Nechung Monastery**, which was once the seat of the State Oracle of Tibet. The main temple has well preserved frescoes and thangkas. The Nechung Chogyal (State Oracle) has been relocated at Gangchen Kyishong in Dharamsala, India.

Drepung is a two-hour walk or one-hour bike ride from Snowlands Hotel. Opening hours are Monday to Saturday from 9 am to 4 pm; it is closed on Sunday. Entrance fee is Y3. Bus No 1 departs at 9 and 11 am from outside the Banak Shol Hotel, but it may be quicker and easier to hitch a ride on a truck, walking tractor or whatever. There are organised trips from the Lhasa Holiday Inn and transport can also be arranged from the Tibetan hotels in the centre of town.

Please keep in mind the information under 'Warning' at the beginning of this chapter. Rebellious monks from all the monasteries around Lhasa have been imprisoned/tortured/executed in recent years and, as a result, there is intense surveillance of foreign contacts.

Sera Monastery སེ་ར་དགོན་པ་

This Gelukpa monastery (about three km north of Lhasa) was founded by Shakya Yeshe, a disciple of Tsong Khapa, in 1419. Further extensions were made in the early 18th century. Sera means 'Enclosure of Roses, but also 'Beneficent Hail' – a name said to derive from the fact that Sera was in continual competition with Drepung, and that the 'hail' of Sera scattered the 'rice' of Drepung. Sera was a monastic university which was smaller than Drepung, but similar in the layout of its buildings. Only 100 monks remain out of a population that once exceeded 5000.

Sera was at one time famous for its fighting monks, who spent years perfecting the martial arts. Here, as at Drepung, many monks renounced their vows to take up arms during the uprising in 1959. Restoration work is still in progress to repair immense damage inflicted during the Cultural Revolution. It's best just to wander around and see which of the temples are open.

In the main hall of **Sera Me**, the shrine is dedicated to Sakyamuni, who is flanked by Maitreya and Manjusri. On the shrine are also statues of Tara. At the rear of the hall are five chapels dedicated (from left to right) to Yamantaka, Tsong Khapa, the Buddhas of the three periods with statues of the 16 Arhats, Sakyamuni (Miwang Jowo) with Boddhisattvas, and Tsong Khapa (again) with gurus of the Yellow Hat sect. On the upper floor is a chapel dedicated to Sakyamuni and at the rear is a Dolma Lhakang (Tara Chapel) with a number of images of Tara, Amitayus and Vijaya.

In the main hall of **Ngakpa Dratsang** (Tantric College) are statues of the founder and principal masters of Sera Monastery. At the back of the building are two chapels: the first has Sakyamuni and the Arhats, the second is the Gonkhang dedicated to

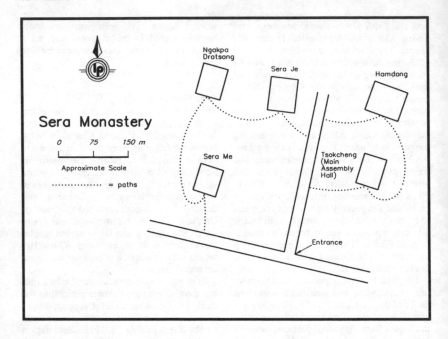

Yamantaka. The chapel upstairs is dedicated to Buddha Amitabha.

The main hall of **Sera Je** has a statue of the 13th Dalai Lama, chortens with relics of eminent lamas of Sera and an image of Tsong Khapa. The minor chapels are dedicated to the Buddhas of the three periods and Tamdrin (Hayagriva, the Horse-Headed). The latter is probably the most venerated shrine in Sera. The chapels at the rear are those of Maitreya, Tsong Khapa and Manjusri. Upstairs is a chapel dedicated to Tamdrin with statues of Guru Rinpoche (Padmasambhava) and the Fifth Dalai Lama, plus a chapel for Avalokitesvara. To the right of Sera Je is a courtyard used by the monks to practise their debating skills under the watchful eye of the abbot.

In the main hall of **Hamdong** are images of Sakymuni, Amitayus, Tara and Vijaya. The chapels contain statues of Maitreya and of the Buddhas of the three periods. There is also a Gonkhang.

In the main hall of the **Tsokchen** (Main Assembly Hall) are the images of Maitreya, the founder of Sera, and of the Fifth and 13th Dalai Lamas. The smaller chapels are dedicated to Sakyamuni and the Arhats, to Maitreya and the eight Boddhisattvas, and to Tsong Khapa. The Gonkhang is dedicated to Yamantaka, the protector of the Yellow Hat sect. Upstairs is a Demchog (Samvara) chapel followed by one containing a large image of Maitreya and, lastly, one dedicated to Sakyamuni.

If you hike up the mountain behind the monastery, you'll find rock paintings, carvings and a panorama of Lhasa.

The opening hours are from 9 am to noon and from 3 pm to 6 pm, and the entrance fee is Y3.

Bus No 10 runs to Sera Monastery at 9 am from opposite the Banak Shol Hotel. It's probably easier to walk (one hour from the Snowlands Hotel), bike (half an hour from the Snowlands Hotel) or hitchhike straight up JieFang BeiLu. There are organised trips from the Lhasa Holiday Inn.

Some travellers hiked past Sera Monastery, further north up the valley to another temple, a nunnery and hermit caves. About three km east of Sera are two prisons: Drapchi and Sangyip. Political detainees are said to be in residence there and you can learn the grisly details of their existence – detention; torture; execution – from Amnesty International publications.

Sky Burial

In September 1985 the sky burial site (about 15 minutes east of Sera Monastery, at the foot of the mountain) was officially closed to tourists. Unless this decision is reversed, you would be unwise to visit as you would incur the wrath of the Chinese authorities and the Tibetan burial squad. Enterprising tourism officials are now toying with the idea of erecting coin-operated telescopes to give a vulture's-eye view of this ritual.

Of the five types of burial practised in Tibet (sky burial, water burial, earth burial, fire burial and embalming), sky burial is the most common. Bodies are laid out in the open, and are carefully skinned and dissected. The bones are crushed and mixed with tsampa. At the end of this procedure, huge flocks of vultures, hawks and ravens descend and polish everything off with great zest. Although it might be thought a strange way to leave this earth, sky burial is a necessity in a country like Tibet, where fuel is scarce and the ground is usually far too rocky to be dug. Tibetans believe that the sky burial offers the deceased the chance to gain merit by offering their corpse for the benefit of sentient beings.

Unfortunately, this site became a magnet for large numbers of tourists who sat around looking – except for their photo gear – remarkably like the vultures perched in rows on the mountain behind. At first, the Tibetans performing the burials welcomed the tourists who, for the most part, did not abuse the privilege. Later, the families of the deceased objected to photographs being taken and warned the burial team that payment for burial would only be made if the photography was stopped. As the driver of the corpse truck said to me: 'How would you like it if swarms of people came to photograph your dead mother?'

It was then only a matter of time before serious confrontations took place. An Australian tried to hide up the mountain and take photos with a telephoto lens. While hopping around on the skyline, he scared the birds away – an exceptionally evil omen. The irate burial squad gave chase, brandishing knives and showering him with rocks. A three-day ban on tourists followed, but the scene did not improve. Hong Kong citizens and Han Chinese were chased off by the burial squad, who tried to club them with bloody bones. Then a new approach was tried. Photo bags were collected at the beginning of the ceremony and then handed back at the end when photos were allowed. This didn't work either. As the crowds of camera-toting sightseers grew larger and more inquisitive, not a day passed without Landcruisers, PLA soldiers or surreptitious photographers being bombarded with rocks, chased with knives or threatened with meaty leg bones ripped straight off the corpse. Closure of the site was the result.

Now, presumably early in the morning each day, on the flat rock near Sera, sky burials are performed as usual. There are no tourists, no photos – just the corpse, the relatives, the burial squad...and the vultures.

Places to Stay

Tour groups are assigned to specific hotels. At present the Chinese authorities' favourites are the Lhasa Holiday Inn, Sunlight Hotel and Tibet Hotel – all of which are in 'safe' locations, are easily sealed off, monitored, and reportedly equipped with eavesdropping room service. Individual tourists may or may not be able to avoid this dictatorial allocation and head for the hotels run by local Tibetans in the heart of Lhasa. Although these Tibetan hotels are friendly places, their existence generally hinges on a willingness to allow surveillance. Consequently, all the following accommodation categories may be subject to occasional 'closure' depending on the political situation.

Most of the hotels in the bottom-end category are clustered in the Barkhor area and are managed by Tibetans.

Places to Stay – bottom end

Snowlands (☎ 23687), close to the Jokhang Temple, is a friendly place with a few doubles, but mostly four-bed or five-bed rooms (Y10 FEC per bed). The hotel is constructed on three floors around a courtyard, so life is communal. Most people go to other hotels for showers. A bathhouse is under construction, but for now water comes from a pump in the yard. There are plenty of thermoses of hot water (kai shui) and bowls for washing. It's impossible not to like the Tibetan women who run the place with laughter and water fights. The odoriferous toilets are a standing joke – put a clothes-peg over your nose, enter, take aim, fire and exit as fast as your legs permit!

The restaurant downstairs serves Sichuan-style food. Bikes are available for hire at Y10 per day or Y1 per hour. Check your bike *before* departure. Although the bikes arrived new (in knock-down form), their assembly wasn't exactly perfect and I had a close shave when the brakes failed at a busy crossroads. The shop next door sells stationery, sweets, Nepalese biscuits and excellent sets of thangka posters at Y10. A room next to reception is used for storing baggage. Reception will help to organise a taxi. There's an impromptu notice board on the 2nd floor for seats on hired buses, hitchhiking partners and so on.

The *Banak Shol Hotel* (☎ 23829) is on Xingfu Donglu near the Barkhor. This has also achieved star ratings as a travellers' hang-out in Lhasa and has a friendly atmosphere and staff. It has quite a warren of rooms, ladders and toilets in the ramparts. Doubles cost Y22 and a bed in a dorm costs Y10. Walls are thin and one traveller said he was kept up all night by the couple next door bemoaning the breathtaking problems of

high-altitude copulation. There are showers downstairs in the courtyard.

The hotel is run by a Tibetan cooperative which also markets tsampa and runs the restaurant/teahouse downstairs. The restaurant now has a dining room for foreigners which is a favourite meeting place. You choose your ingredients from bowls in the kitchen, put them on a plate and have them cooked. Depending on the food selected, a serving costs Y2. Sweet, milky tea costs Y0.25. Bikes are for hire here at Y10 per day or Y1 per hour. Luggage storage costs Y0.50 per piece per day. Postcards are on sale at reception where the staff can also help you to organise a taxi or a tour.

The *Kirey Hotel*, close to the Banak Shol, charges Y10 for dorm beds. Doubles start at Y15 per person. It lacks atmosphere but has great showers for which you pay a small charge if you're not staying there.

The *Plateau Hotel* is opposite the telecommunications office on the edge of town. Doubles cost Y12 per person, triples cost Y9 per person, and four-bed rooms cost Y8 per person. The solar-heated showers work sporadically. Ask at the desk about bike or vehicle hire.

The *Yak Hotel* (formerly known by the ponderous name of Beijing East Road Tribal Hostelry) is diagonally opposite the Kirey Hotel, on Xingfu Donglu. Beds cost Y15 FEC.

Across the street from the No 1 Guesthouse is the *Public Bathhouse*, also known as the 'People Wash Shop', which is usually open from 9 am to 7.30 pm, including Sundays. This bathhouse also has rooms for Y10 a night.

There are also certain places which offer really cheap beds (maybe Y3 per person). Constant harassment by the PSB (who hate to see foreigners paying less than double the local rate) means that these hotels indulge in a creative game of opening and closing – now you see the foreigner, now you don't!

Places to Stay – middle

The one redeeming feature of the *No 1 Guesthouse* (☎ 22184) is its position in the centre of town. The atmosphere is strongly Chinese without a trace of Tibet. It costs Y10 FEC per bed. Reception has a sign asking for FECs for all payments. Baggage can be stored in a room opposite reception. Bikes are available for hire and reception also arranges taxis and Landcruisers for tours.

Solar-heated showers are available daily from 4 to 6 pm (except on Sundays) on the 3rd floor of a building at the rear of the compound. You don't have to stay here to use them. Buy shower tickets (*xizao piao*) for Y1.50 FEC at reception. In the winter, higher room prices include a heating supplement and, reportedly, the shower closes down. The restaurant serves plain Chinese food. Buy meal tickets (*fan piao*) for Y2 at reception. The *No 2 Guesthouse* (☎ 22185) is 100 metres east of the Potala on XingFu DongLu. It's for Chinese guests (local or overseas) but some foreigners have stayed – for Y30 a double.

Places to Stay – top end
The *Lhasa Holiday Inn* (☎ 2221, 23222) is the lap of Lhasa luxury and boasts 500 rooms. A total of US$8 million in foreign currency reserves was used to purchase the latest in foreign plumbing gadgetry. Nearly 2000 workers and technicians from Jiangsu Province toiled to complete this three-building complex in the nick of time for the autonomy celebrations in September 1985. Every single item required for construction was lugged overland from China.

Doubles start at Y195 per room and triples cost Y170 per room. The rates in winter (1 November to 1 March) may be dropped by 30%. The facilities include Chinese and Western restaurants, a coffee shop, souvenir shops, a bank and a wrestling arena (to practise the clinches with CITS?). A free shuttle service using minibuses operates between the hotel and the Barkhor. The transport desk arranges day trips to the Drepung, Sera or Ganden monasteries (prices range between Y20 and Y100 per person); there's also a daily bus from the hotel to the airport (leaves at 6.30 am and costs Y30 per person). If you want to hire a taxi, Landcruiser, minibus or

bus, enquire at the transport desk about the amazingly autonomous prices fixed by the Tibet Autonomous Price Bureau. CITS can be found here in room No 1219.

The *Tibet Hotel* (Xizang Binguan) is a few metres up the road from the Lhasa Holiday Inn. Built in mock Tibetan style, it was already showing signs of dilapidation within a few months of opening. It's intended for foreign tour groups and Chinese officials on junkets. Doubles start at Y176 in the high season and Y120 in the low season, or you could try the tackily decorated Tibet suite for US$60. The forecourt is frequented by browsing yaks which nonchalantly obstruct the entrance ramp – they're about the only appealing characteristic of the place.

Places to Eat
The restaurant scene in Lhasa tends to flourish and fade as rapidly as tourist numbers increase or dwindle according to the political situation. The restaurants mentioned here may be subject to rapid closure if the politics get heavy.

Since most of the food in Lhasa is trucked in from China, it's not surprising that meals are relatively expensive. All of the restaurants serve Western, Sichuan or Muslim dishes. There are no restaurants specialising in Tibetan food, which is restricted to a few dishes like *momo* (dumplings) and *tukpa* (noodles with meat). Nobody seems to mind if you bring your own bottles of beer, plastic containers of chang or cans of food (tinned fruit is pleasant as a dessert).

Inside the Kirey Hotel is the *Kailas Restaurant* which serves good breakfasts. The menu includes spring rolls, pancakes, chapattis, French toast and dishes for vegetarians.

Just west of the Banak Shol Hotel is the *Plateau Restaurant* (Top of the World) which has a wide menu and friendly service.

The *Liu Sichuan Family Restaurant* is near the taxi office that is close to the Snowlands Hotel. It serves good breakfasts and sweet buns.

The *Yak Hotel Restaurant* also does good breakfasts and has fast service.

The *Unity Restaurant* is further west down the street from the Yak Hotel. It is a Tibetan 'chang' hall serving chang from a teapot for 20 fen a cup. Spicy food is also sold here to a predominantly Tibetan clientele.

The *Lhasa Holiday Inn* has a Chinese restaurant which is reasonable value if you eat as a small group; expect to pay about Y10 per head for about five dishes. The coffee shop (open from 8 am to 10 pm) serves Western food such as hamburgers, French fries and Lhasa club sandwiches. Prices are relatively high, but breakfast includes endless refills of strong filter coffee.

The *No 1 Guesthouse* has a restaurant serving standard fare suited to the taste of Lhasa's Chinese expats.

Recent travellers have also recommended the freshness (a rarity in Lhasa) of the vegetable dishes at the 'Dining Room' on RenMin Lu, and the more expensive tofu (soybean curd) dishes at the Sichuan Restaurant on Qingnian Lu. Opposite the Yak Hotel, the Beijing Coffee Shop reportedly provides instant coffee and 'something else, only for men'.

Try Barkhor Bazaar and the area around the mosque (look for blue flags with red Chinese characters) for Muslim teahouses and restaurants where you can have noodles, lotus-seed tea or even mint tea. Street stalls and small places tucked down alleys are always interesting spots to meet the locals over a bowl of noodles and a container or two of chang. Finally, those who want to forage for themselves will find a choice of fruit and vegetables in the market close to the CAAC office.

Entertainment

Nightlife in Lhasa is low-key and impromptu. Videos are the latest rage and films (mostly kung-fu) are usually advertised on boards outside houses on the streets near the Banak Shol and Snowlands hotels. There's a cinema close to the Banak Shol Hotel and another opposite the Tibetan Hospital. Discos and dances take place on Saturday and Sunday nights at various locations around the Barkhor area. Ask at the Banak Shol or Snowlands hotels for the precise time and location of the weekly bop.

The night of a full moon sees packs of dogs and restless travellers roaming around Lhasa. Others spend the evening sampling chang at stalls and stumbling round the Barkhor in slow and erratic circles. Street lighting is just a glimmer, so watch out for fast-moving Khampas on bikes. Keep an eye open for packs of dogs in the shadows: if someone treads on a dog it will probably shoot off like a rocket and sink its fangs into the nearest person – not always the perpetrator!

Tibetans love picnics. At weekends and on public holidays, they head out for the nearest park, lake or river armed with plastic containers of chang, thermoses of butter tea, tsampa, biscuits and a makeshift tent to enjoy themselves singing and dancing. I lost count of the number of times I was beckoned to join a group for nonstop hospitality and laughter.

Photo studios in Lhasa offer cheap amusement too. You can have your picture taken sitting behind a cardboard cutout of an MiG fighter, a Shanghai sedan or even the Potala. Try the photo stalls in front of the Potala or the studios on JieFang Lu and RenMin Lu. Film development costs Y1.5 plus Y0.30 per print (black and white with frilly edges).

Things to Buy

Lhasa does not have the facilities of large Chinese cities, so don't expect to be able to buy vital items of food, clothing or medicine or photo equipment. Bring everything with you. If you plan to make Lhasa a base for long trips, use your hotel baggage room as a supply depot.

The Friendship Store is a large building on RenMin Lu, about 100 metres past the No 1 Guesthouse, in the direction of the Jokhang. Opening hours vary, but the core time is from 9.30 am to 4.30 pm, including Sundays. The selection is sparse, stocks are often sold out, and prices are relatively high. The 1st floor has cosmetics, stationery and canned foods. The FangFang lip salve sold here in small pink sticks is good to stop your lips cracking and you can get gauze face masks to protect you against the dust. Packs of instant noodles, tins of pineapple slices, chocolate bars and peanut nougat are useful for trips out of Lhasa. The 2nd floor has clothing. The 3rd floor is the pricey part for foreigners and sells T-shirts (Yak, Everest, and Potala), sweets, canned drinks, jam, peanuts, Nepalese glucose biscuits, foreign smokes, slides and postcards. To the right of the entrance to the Friendship Store is another shop which has a selection of fruit, fish and meat in tins.

There are several bakeries in Lhasa. One is in Barkhor Bazaar, another is diagonally across the street from the Friendship Store and yet another is next to the Snowlands Hotel. The main department store in Lhasa is on RenMin Lu, opposite the XinHua Bookstore. Water bottles are sold here for Y1.90. The carpet factory in the east of town, on YanHe DongLu, sells unexceptional carpets. Some are not Tibetan but Chinese in style. Tibetan dragons have four claws, whereas Chinese dragons have five. There are at least two boot factories in Lhasa, both near the mosque. Leather boots take a week to make and, depending on the style, cost between Y30 and Y50. Colourful Tibetan

boots with curled toes can be bought made-to-measure or in Barkhor Bazaar. Some visitors also buy local cloth and ask a tailor to make a *chuba* (a wonderfully warm, wraparound, Tibetan coat). Total cost for cloth and tailoring is about Y80.

Barkhor Bazaar is the main hunting ground for shoppers. Tibetan handicrafts include rolls of striped cloth, daggers, religious ornaments, tinder boxes, tsampa bowls, bracelets, carpets, boots, rosaries, purses, rings, prayer flags and prayer wheels. Old coins, turquoise, amber Tibetan stone-eye (stones with circular patterns) and coral are also offered here. Local food items sold here include puffed rice, wheat, barley, tsampa, yak butter, corn, dried apples and pears, and nuts. Bargain for everything or, even better, try bartering with Dalai Lama pics, foreign coins, badges or clothing.

Getting There
It's worth emphasising that all transport options may be subject to immediate closure – at the drop of a baton – should the political situation become abnormally unstable.

Air Although there are supposed to be flights from Xian via Golmud to Lhasa, this service doesn't seem to operate. Most travellers arrive from Chengdu or Kathmandu, where flights are more frequent. Official policy encourages the use of air routes and discourages land routes.

Chengdu-Lhasa planes (one or two daily) leave Chengdu around 6.45 to 7.30 am, and get to Gonggar Airport around 9.30 am if there are no delays. Being tested on the run to carry goods to Tibet, are Chinese-made Yun-8s, which are produced in Xian, and copied from Western jets. Tickets cost Y656 FEC. Flights have also started to Beijing for Y1149 and to Canton for Y1080.

The recently inaugurated Kathmandu-Lhasa connection costs US$210 one-way and departs on Wednesday and Saturday. Recent reports indicate that only Saturday flights are operating. The flight lasts one hour and, on a clear day, the snowcap views are unbelievable.

Gonggar Airport Lhasa's airport is not in Lhasa, but 96 km away at Gonggar. On arrival at the airport, there will be buses waiting to take you on the 90-minute ride to Lhasa. CAAC buses to and from the airport are no longer free. The CAAC service to and from Gonggar Airport costs Y7. Don't wait around at the airport for your baggage. It will be delivered separately, at least three hours later, to the CAAC office in Lhasa where you collect it. On arrival, be prepared for intensive perusal of your visa. If at all possible you should appear to belong to a group – even if you don't!

Mercifully, asphalting of the road to the airport was completed in June 1985 as a special project for the autonomy celebration in September. If this had not been done, some of the first impressions made on visiting dignitaries would have been dents in their heads after being bounced into the roof of the bus. Prior to asphalting, unsuspecting tourists fresh off the plane, who were eager to be enchanted by Tibet, were treated to a long and atrociously bumpy ride. Numerous foreign heads were launched against the bus roof. One lanky German cracked his neck and spent the rest of his painful time in Lhasa walking with a stoop!

Truck The major routes for travelling by truck into Lhasa are as follows:

Sichuan-Tibet Highway (Chengdu-Chamdo (Tsiamdo)-Lhasa)
Yunnan-Tibet Highway (Kunming-Dali-Markam-Lhasa)
Qinghai-Tibet Highway (Xining-Golmud-Lhasa)
Xinjiang-Tibet Highway (Kashgar-Ali (Shiquanhe)-Lhasa)
Nepal-Tibet Highway (Khasa (Zhangmu)-Shigatse-Lhasa)

For details of these routes see the relevant chapters in this book. Strictly speaking, foreigners are only officially tolerated on the Nepal-Tibet Highway and the Qinghai-Tibet Highway. Official pressure, however, has

now made truck travel virtually impossible for foreigners.

Bus Buses run on the Qinghai-Tibet and Qinghai-Sichuan highways. At present, the official policy is to pressure foreigners away from bus travel and into expensive group packages with hired vehicles.

Golmud-Lhasa costs about Y198 FEC on a Japanese bus or Y158 RMB on a Chinese bus. The trip takes about 30 hours. For more details, see the Qinghai Routes chapter.

Fiat Fantasy
Yup, some strange things happen out there on the Golmud route. A Scandinavian was bouncing along on the back of the Golmud bus, headed for Lhasa, trying to keep his toes warm (the route is freezing cold) and trying not to throw up from the effects of altitude sickness. He decided to risk raising his bilious eyes, and there, in the dead centre of absolutely nowhere, was a mirage enveloped in a cloud of dust – a Fiat racing car bombing past the bus. Realising that he must have contracted some rare form of altitude sickness that included hallucinations, he wisely dropped his head again only to hear the shattering sound of another Fiat speeding by. Feverishly fumbling for his camera to try to prove possession of his mental faculties, he was too late to capture the third and final mechanical monster roaring past.

Getting Away
Again, all transport options are subject to spontaneous closure during periods of political unrest.

Air There are flights to Chengdu (Y656) and Kathmandu (US$210). There are also flights to Beijing for Y1149 and to Canton for Y1080. Tickets are sold at the CAAC office. Since Gonggar Airport is 96 km out of Lhasa, and flights leave in the morning, passengers are usually required to stay overnight at the airport. The airport bus leaves from the CAAC office between 4 and 5 pm and costs Y10 FEC. On arrival at the airport hotel, a ramshackle collection of barracks, there is a long bout of queuing for bed tickets, bath tickets, food tickets...the paper never ends. Last-minute packing comes to an abrupt halt at 10.30 pm, when the generator packs up for the night. There's no need to set your alarm as hotel staff and loudspeakers will turf you out of bed at 6.30 am. The electricity supply is totally at the discretion of hotel staff.

Rented Vehicle For vehicle rental to the Nepalese border, see the Lhasa to Kathmandu section of the Nepal Route chapter.

Truck Until recently it was quite easy to get a truck out of Lhasa, but the authorities have now advised depots not to take foreign guests. Checkpoints inside and outside Lhasa check whether you have an official ticket and will fine the driver if he has done a private deal. Unless you are prepared to spend a lot of time hunting for rides or waiting for a blue moon, you are most unlikely to be successful.

However, some trucks leave in the middle of the night when officialdom is tucked up in bed, and once you are out of Lhasa, there are fewer complications. Tsetong (Zêtang), Shigatse and Gyantse, to name a few, all have depots with trucks doing long-distance runs. If you walk out very early over the Lhasa River Bridge (for the Sichuan Highway) or pass the checkpoint at Doilungdêqên (for the Qinghai Highway or Shigatse), you may have some luck.

There are plenty of truck depots or departure points dotted around Lhasa. Some depots specialise, whereas others serve several destinations. The following list is a rough guide only:

To Golmud To go to Golmud, go to the No 1, 2, 4 and 5 truck depots; the truck depot in front of Potala; the truck depot at junction of XingFu XiLu and MinZu Lu; or the truck depot on YanHe DongLu just before the carpet factory. Some Golmud trucks leave from Tsetong (No 1 truck depot) and there are plenty from Shigatse which go via Yangbachen (Yangbajing). Some Lhasa trucks leave in the afternoon, spend the night at Yangbachen and then do a straight run to Golmud.

To Sichuan Most of the trucks only run as far as Chamdo. From there you find another ride to Chengdu. The No 6 truck depot has trucks going in this direction. In Tsetong (Zêtang), the No 2 truck depot has trucks running the Chamdo route.

To Xinjiang There are very few trucks to Xinjiang direct from Lhasa. Look for large new Isuzu trucks with Uigur (looks like Arabic) writing on the cab doors. Try the truck depot at the junction of XingFu XiLu and MinZu Lu or the area around the mosque. There is a hotel just past the mosque with a courtyard that is used as a truck stop by Muslim drivers. Trucks also travel to Xinjiang from Shigatse.

To the Shannan Area, Shigatse & Gyantse To go to any of these places, try the No 2 Guesthouse – go through the entrance gate and turn left into the small parking area. Trucks for these destinations also leave from the truck depot just before the carpet factory, on YanHe DongLu.

Bus Bus stations in Lhasa operate buses to destinations within Tibet and to Sichuan and Qinghai provinces. The official bus station – an architectural monstrosity – is the new one near the Norbulinka, but the old one, 100 metres east of the post office, still serves as a pick-up point and outlet for ticket sales. A reader recently reported that bus tickets are now being sold from an office on RenminLu, in the centre of Lhasa. However, some buses depart from the new bus station without visiting the old one beforehand, so you may have to trek across town early to be on time check with the ticket clerk.

To buy tickets, get to the ticket office before 9 am. All foreigners now pay at least double the local price and this is increasingly being asked for in FEC. There are also constant changes in prices and the FEC market. The following is a rough timetable for selected destinations (check with the ticket clerk for additional buses or changes in departure days):

Destination	Departure	Ordinary/ Deluxe	km
Tsetong (Zêtang) (four hours)	daily	Y30/36	195
Gyantse (five hours)	daily	Y45/56	250
Shigatse (12 hours)	daily	Y55/66	355
Khasa (Zhangmu) (three days) only	Saturday	Y128/155	880
Golmud (two days)	daily	Y152/198	1127

Tickets are sold the day before departure.

Some foreigners have rented an entire bus (usually a vintage bone-shaker carrying a maximum of 25 passengers) with a driver for trips to the Nepalese border via Gyantse, Shigatse, Sakya, Lhazê and Xêgar (Xin Tingri). Rental charges vary, but previous deals have been calculated at Y0.025 per km, Y1 per hour and Y1 per day per seat. This totals about Y2500 RMB for six days.

Apparently, the ticket office also sells tickets for truck passengers (which are slightly cheaper than those for the bus) but the staff threatens to keel over and expire at the idea of selling these tickets to foreigners.

The airport bus is intended for CAAC passengers, but you might wriggle on and spend the night at the airport hotel before continuing to Samye or Tsetong the next morning. Perhaps you are seeing off or meeting a friend...The pilgrim bus to Ganden which leaves daily at 7.30 am from Barkhor Bazaar (opposite the carpet corner) is also a possible means of getting out for some serious hitchhiking on the Sichuan route. Get off the bus on the main road before it turns off to the left and starts to climb up to Ganden.

Getting Around
Bus Buses materialise at stops so infrequently that they are not a dependable means of transport in Lhasa.

Taxis & Rented Vehicles Taxis are expensive and in short supply. There are two taxi services in town. The ChengGuanQu ChuZu QiChe GongCi is about a five-minute walk from the Snowlands Hotel. This company has a notoriously battered vehicle pool including Shanghai and Warszawa limousines, Beijing jeeps (*Beijing Jipu* in Chinese), minibuses (*Mianbao Che* in Chinese), and an antique Austin Gypsy. A Shanghai ride to Drepung Monastery costs Y32 return (Y16 one-way) plus Y20 per hour for waiting time. Prices vary, but the basic rate per km for a minibus is Y1.80 and Y1.20 for a Beijing jeep. It's best to book vehicles in advance. Another taxi service (Chinese Taxi Service) operates from offices behind the Potala, about 50 metres east of the PSB.

Virtually all the hotels, from the Lhasa Holiday Inn to the Yak Hotel, are able to arrange vehicle hire. Use their notice boards if you want to join or set up trips around Lhasa or further afield.

Additional charges are made for the number of passengers and the number of days travelled. There are no rules but it used to be possible to try for a discount for a group of over five people. A separate per diem is often charged for the driver and you are usually charged for the return section of a trip even if you only go one-way, for example, exiting from Lhasa along the Nepal route to Khasa. For more information about vehicle hire options and prices, refer to the Lhasa to Kathmandu section in the Nepal Route chapter.

Bicycle This is really the best way to move, but take it very slowly until you have become accustomed to the altitude. Most of the hotels hire out bikes. Average rental per day is Y10 or Y1 per hour. As a deposit you will have to leave a passport or Y200 FEC or Y250 RMB.

Go early to have a good choice of bikes. Check your bike thoroughly before you leave, otherwise you are likely to end up in a tangle of metal with Chinese and Tibetan cyclists at the first crossroads. If left in the sun, overinflated tyres are quick to explode at this altitude.

Bike theft has reached epidemic proportions in Lhasa, so if you are out at night, wheel your bike inside the restaurant, hotel, or wherever you can keep an eye on it and, preferably, use a lock of your own as well as the fitted lock. I had a meal in a restaurant opposite the Banak Shol Hotel with a friend who had locked and parked his bike outside, about four metres behind our table. Within half an hour the lock had been picked and the bike stolen, and the next day my friend had to forfeit his Y50 deposit.

On Sundays there is a bike market outside the main mosque – maybe this is where some of the stolen ones resurface. A bike in reasonable condition should cost about Y70. Make sure you get the licence and check its number with the number on the bike. When you leave Lhasa you can resell it to a foreigner or a local. You can make a big saving on rental charges if you're staying for a reasonable length of time. An Australian duo managed to buy a motorbike with a sidecar here. Unfortunately, the gears broke at Damxung and they were forced to sell at a loss.

Hitchhiking This is an excellent way to travel a long distance across town or even further. A smile, a determined signal and you are off on a walking tractor, riding on the back of a truck, riding pillion on a bike (hop off discreetly if police are around as it's illegal) or bouncing along with a tractor and trailer.

Yarlung Valley Monasteries & Sites

GANDEN MONASTERY
དགའ་ལྡན་དགོན་པ་

Tsong Khapa founded this, the first Gelukpa monastery, in 1409 on one of the most spectacular sites in Tibet, about 40 km east of Lhasa near Dagzê. Here too, work has begun to restore the damage wreaked during the Cultural Revolution. So extensive is the damage, one might easily think Ganden had been subjected to saturation aerial bombardment. The four main temples now house about 200 monks who are the remnants of a population that once exceeded 4000. The views from Ganden (4300 metres), down into the Kyichu Valley and across to the distant snowcaps, are quite exceptional. When I went, I hiked around the mountain tops and saw several sky burials.

Admission costs Y3. There is no official accommodation, although you might be able to arrange some with the monks or use one of the ruined buildings (if you can stand the cold). Take food and water.

Getting There & Away
To reach Ganden you can take a pilgrim bus, pilgrim truck or hitchhike. If you hitchhike, you should be out early on the road, just past the bridge outside Lhasa. From Dagzê it's a long climb up the mountain (at least two hours). Pilgrim trucks for Ganden leave at about 6.30 am from the nomad encampments in the north of Lhasa and from the square outside the Jokhang Temple – days and times of departures are flexible and they are now very reluctant to take foreigners. Trucks usually return around 3 pm. To hire a Landcruiser for the day will cost about Y170 FEC. The best option is to take the pilgrim bus which leaves daily at 6.30 am from Barkhor Bazaar. Buy your ticket at 4 pm the day before from a tin shack on the Barkhor about a quarter of the way round in anticlockwise direction. Be there early and sit on the left; it costs Y7 return. The bus takes two hours and returns around 2 pm. If you want to stay longer at Ganden, you can climb down the mountain and hitchhike back.

MINDOLING MONASTERY
Mindoling, one of the most important Nyingmapa (Red Hat Sect) monasteries, was founded in 1676 by Terdak Lingpa. The four main temples, one of which houses a fine statue of Sakyamuni, are being restored. The monastery is approximately mid-way between Zhanang and Samye ferry. Ask the bus driver for Mindoling Gompa and be fully prepared with food, water and clothing as it is a long trek away from the road. Alternatively, you can hire a vehicle for several days to visit Mindoling as part of a round trip to the sights of the Yarlung Valley – expect to pay about Y600 FEC for a Landcruiser.

SAMYE MONASTERY
Samye was built between 763 and 775 by Padmasambhava (also known by Tibetans as Lopon Rinpoche), during the reign of King Trisong Detsen. It is said that Samye was modelled on the university of Otantapuri in India and planned as a representation of the universe. The main temple in the centre corresponded to Mt Rirab (the centre of the cosmos), while four pagodas (white, black, green and red) represented the four worlds to the north, south, east and west. Smaller temples represented the islands between the worlds and two temples to the north and south of the main temple represented the moon and sun respectively. The main temple, dedicated to Chenrezig, once had three storeys which each had a different architectural style. The lower storey is Tibetan, the middle storey is Chinese and the top storey, now missing, was Indian. The stele outside the entrance has an inscription which was made by King Trisong Detsen in 779 to proclaim Buddhism as the religion of Tibet.

Once reputed to be a forest of 108 temples, Samye is still one of the most imposing

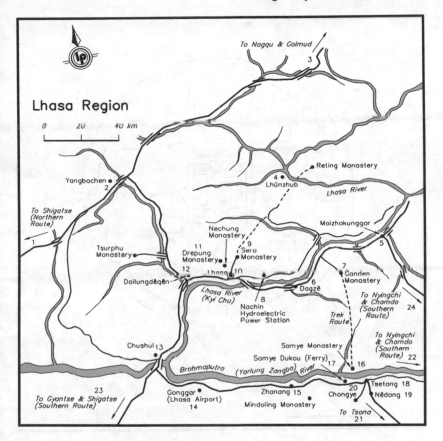

1 至日客则	13 曲水
2 羊八井	14 贡嘎
3 至那曲，格尔木	15 扎囊
1 林周	16 桑耶寺
5 墨竹工卡	17 渡口
6 达孜	18 泽当
7 甘丹寺	19 乃东
8 纳金电话	20 穷结
9 色拉寺	21 至错那
10 拉萨	22 至林芝，昌都
11 哲蚌寺	23 至江孜，日客则
12 堆龙德庆	24 至林芝，昌都

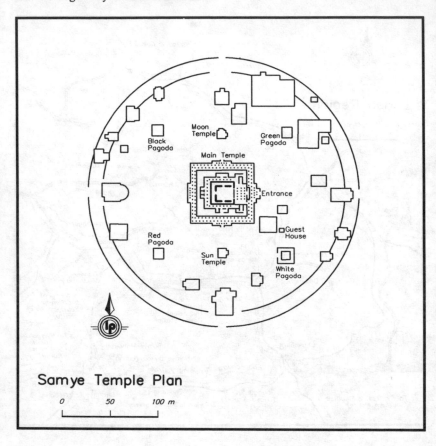

Samye Temple Plan

0   50   100 m

sights in Tibet. Reconstruction is now in progress to repair damage done during the Cultural Revolution and some temples still function as granaries – you literally have to wade through the grain to look at the frescoes.

The chief monk is not always willing to open up the upper storey of the main temple to individual visitors and you may be told that each photo taken inside the temple will cost Y10. In contrast, the Tibetans renovating other temples are very friendly and will usually let you wander around and give you butter tea. South of the main temple in

Samye is another large temple, Kamsum Sanggak Ling – this temple is still full of grain but it contains superb frescoes and a stunning mandala on the 5th floor.

In the valley to the north behind Samye is **Chimpuk**, a cave retreat, which can be reached on foot in about four hours. The view of Samye from the top of Mt Hepori to the east (follow the pilgrim tracks up to the chortens) is spectacular.

The Only Place to Stay

The only accommodation at Samye is in a small courtyard near the entrance to the main temple. The old lady in charge does not welcome visitors. Providing you do not impose on her for anything more than a roof over your head, she will grudgingly give you a bare, four-bed room (Y2 per bed). If she asks for a letter of introduction...well, your passport is near enough. No light (take candles) or food is available here. Hot water may be forthcoming if you're lucky.

Guru Padmasambhava

Getting There & Away

Getting to Samye is quite an experience and is not advisable for those averse to the fun of rough travel. There are sometimes pilgrim buses from Lhasa to Samye which leave in the afternoon, stop overnight near the ferry and then wait to pick you up from the ferry next day in the late afternoon. You can also take the bus from Lhasa in the direction of Tsetong (Zêtang) and ask to get off at the ferry (Samye Dukou) which is between km markers 89 and 90, the distance marked from Chushul (Qüxü) Bridge. Another possibility is to take the airport bus from Lhasa to the airport, stay overnight at the airport hotel and then get out early to hitchhike.

You can hire a Landcruiser from Lhasa or as part of a tour of the Yarlung Valley sights (about Y600 FEC) and include a day at Samye. The Landcruiser will drop you off in the morning and pick you up again at a time to coincide with the ferry.

The ferry is a makeshift affair, using small boats with outboard motors, which takes you across the Brahmaputra (Yarlung Zangbo) River. In theory, there are crossings at 9 am, noon, 3 and 6 pm but engines break down, important cadres keep the boats waiting for hours and, sometimes, boats get stuck on sandbanks in mid-stream. The crossing fee appears to be Y0.50 for locals and Y1 for foreigners and Chinese cadres. Be prepared to wade to get into the boat.

The trip – what a trip – takes about an hour and you can lie back on sacks of flour gazing at the sky and the mountains or watch their reflections in the water. On the other side you may have to wade ashore. Everybody has fun. The Tibetan women laugh themselves silly if you give them a piggyback to the shore. Onward travel to Samye (there is no road, just a track) takes about 45 minutes, costs Y1 and is provided by a horse-cart or a tractor and trailer. The cart is a peaceful ride but tends to get stuck in sand. The tractor also gets stuck occasionally but it is quicker, unless a tyre blows in which case you have a long walk ahead.

In 1991, the use of the ferry described above was officially discouraged by officials who required tourists to use the 'foreigners' ferry' which departs from a landing spot about 12 km (Km marker 112) west of Tsetong...and reportedly charges a hefty Y25 per passenger.

South of the main temple in Samye is another large temple, Kamsum Sanggak Ling – about 10 minutes on foot. A tractor or horse-cart usually leaves from here at 10 am to catch the noon ferry back to the other side where you can hitchhike back to Lhasa or continue to Tsetong (Zêtang), about 30 km. A combination of blown tyres and broken engines left me waiting on the riverside for five hours. Apart from getting my feet badly sunburnt, I had a great time with a whole squadron of girls and grannies from Nêdong drinking butter tea, munching *tsampa*, getting drunk on chang and paddling with the local dogs.

For trekkers, Samye to Lhasa is about a three or four-day trek. There is another popular trekking route between Ganden and Samye via Yamalung which takes two to three days.

TSETONG (ZÊTANG) & NÊDONG
ཚེད་ནང་

These two towns are about 195 km from Lhasa in the Yarlung Valley which is considered the cradle of Tibetan culture. Tsetong, the capital of Shannan prefecture, has merged with Nêdong into a sprawl of Tibetan and Chinese buildings. There are various sights to see around these two places and they can be used as a base for trips to Chongye (Qonggyai), Samye, Tsona (Cona) and further towards Chamdo.

Tsetong Market
In Tsetong itself, the market is worth a visit since all sorts of Tibetans trek in from outlying areas.

First Field in Tibet
Behind the hospital is the First Field in Tibet. According to legend, this field was planted by Chenrezig's monkey incarnation, Trehu. Tibetan farmers make an annual pilgrimage here before the planting season, to take back a handful of earth which they sprinkle on their own fields to increase fertility.

Monkey Cave
This cave is one of three in the mountainside (Gangpo Ri) east of the town. Allow three hours for the stiff climb and follow the piles of stones left by pilgrims or ask a local to guide you.

For Tibetans this cave has great importance as it is connected with the legend of their origin.

The Origin of Tibet
According to this legend, before humans came to Tibet, it was a land peopled by spirits. Then Chenrezig and his consort Dolma decided to send incarnations. Chenrezig's incarnation was a chaste monkey, Trehu Changchub Sempa. Dolma's incarnation was Tagsenmo, a beautiful ogress with a taste for cannibalism. Trehu was quite content to sit and meditate in his cave. But, one day, when he heard Senmo weeping he felt pity and went to investigate. Senmo explained that she was lonely and needed Trehu as a husband. Trehu was not keen on the idea but Chenrezig advised him that

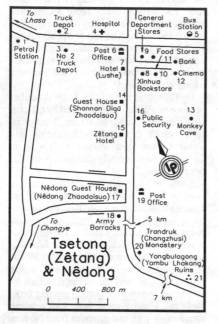

1	加油站	11	银行
2	运输一队	12	电影院
3	运输二队	13	猴子洞
4	医院	14	山南地区招待所
5	运客站	15	泽当宾馆
6	邮局	16	公安局
7	旅社	17	乃东招待所
8	新华书店	18	兵营
9	百货商店	19	乃东邮局
10	食品店，市场	20	昌珠寺
		21	雍布拉冈

it was time for Tibet to have children so he should live with Senmo. Senmo and Trehu then married and had six children. According to one form of the legend, the children grew up to found the six different types of people found in Tibet today. In Tibetan, Tsetong means 'playground', a reference to the place where the six children played.

Trandruk (Changzhusi) Monastery

This monastery is about five km south of Tsetong. It was founded during the reign of Songtsen Gampo. According to legend, many years ago this area was a vast expanse of water, inhabited by a deadly dragon. Songtsen Gampo decided to reclaim the land beneath the water, in order to found a city. He enlisted the help of two magicians who asked a roc (a mythical bird) to slay the dragon. The roc then beat the dragon over the head with its wings and killed it. Seven days later the waters dried up and a grateful Songtsen Gampo built the monastery.

In the 14th and 18th centuries the monastery was enlarged. At present all the buildings are under repair. The main temple, three-storeys high, has a large Sutra Chanting Hall in the centre of the ground floor. A small temple at the rear of the walled compound has some interesting *thangkas*.

Yambu Lhakang (Yongbulagong)
ཡུམ་བུ་ལྷ་ཁང་

According to legend, this was the first building in Tibet, constructed as a palace for the first king, Nyatri Tsanpo. Yongbulagong is on a mountain top about seven km past Trandruk Monastery. If you hitchhike, get out on the road early as traffic is infrequent. You may also be able to rent a bike or vehicle from the Tsetong Hotel. This tiny palace, recently reconstructed, is an imposing sight. It now functions as a chapel and is tended by a small group of monks.

Places to Stay

The *Zêtang Hotel* (Zedang Fandian) is the plushest pad in town. Reportedly built under the supervision of the White Swan Hotel in Canton, it is, however, a complete shambles. At present it looks remarkably like a two-funnelled ship stranded behind steel railings

Yongbulagong before destruction

– a fine example of the incongruity of modern Chinese architecture in Tibet.

Doubles cost Y70. For students there's a discount price of Y25. Theoretically there should be hot water (solar-heated) at 7.30 pm, but when I was there, hot water seldom appeared, the toilets leaked and there were no towels or room-cleaning service.

The restaurant serves set meals which are mediocre. Bikes are sometimes hired out by staff. Landcruisers or minibuses may be available at Y2.40 per km, depending on the moody staff.

The *Zêtang Guest House* has started turning away foreigners and directing them to the Zêtang Hotel. It has no character but clean rooms. It's Y10 FEC for a bed in a four-bed room. The manager is meticulous about checking your credentials. Buy meal tickets at reception; breakfast from 8 to 8.30 am, lunch from noon to 12.30 pm, dinner from 7 to 7.30 pm. The shop in the foyer is well stocked with beer, sweets, etc (opening hours are 1 to 3.30 pm and 7 to 8 pm).

There is a large truck park in front which is a good place to find lifts to Lhasa, Golmud, Gyantse, Nyingchi, etc. Ask at the office next to the gate if they can connect you with a driver. It may also be possible to hire a Landcruiser here for a visit to Samye, Chongye or Mindoling.

Watch out for flooding! One night when I was there, a massive thunderstorm followed by a catastrophic downpour left the truck park under a metre of water. The desperate management smashed a hole through the outside wall to pull the plug on their problem. As a result, the Tibetan construction workers who had been living next door in makeshift tents literally floated off down the road.

There are various hotels near the market which are primarily intended for construction workers from China. You get a bed for Y2 in a no frills 10-bed dormitory. *Nêdong Guest House* is a Tibetan-style building opposite Nêdong post office. This place is essentially a restaurant and now usually turns foreigners away to the Tsetong Hotel. The friendly Tibetan family in charge may fix a bed with a mattress in a room upstairs for Y1.50 – once they get over the shock that you actually want to stay there. Admittedly it is very basic and fly-blown, but it has what the Chinese concrete hutches lack – character.

In the evening, giggling Tibetan girls from the construction sites drop in for a cup of tea while horsemen (tough looking dudes from the Wild East) hitch their horses to the doorpost and order plates of *tukpa* (meat and noodles). Meanwhile, across the street, hordes of Tibetans cluster round a TV to watch a video about the Gestapo! Where am I?

Getting There & Away
From Lhasa main bus station there are buses to Tsetong or you can hitchhike on trucks. Some travellers were able to hire a Landcruiser from Lhasa for a four-day trip (about Y600 FEC) to Samye, Tsetong and Chongye. Not a bad idea, since transport in this area can be a real pain if you are dependent on local buses and trucks.

Buses to Lhasa leave most days at 8.30 am from the traffic circle. Buy your tickets the day before from a small tin shack close to the traffic circle, opposite the market road. I only took the bus as far as Samye ferry, but the decrepit old banger took four hours and as many breakdowns to cover 30 km! If you want to hitchhike to Lhasa, try asking drivers at the Zêtang Guest House or at the petrol station about three km out of town on the road to Lhasa. The No 1 Truck Depot has trucks to Lhasa and Golmud. The No 2 Truck Depot has trucks to Nyingchi and Chamdo.

CHONGYE
Chongye, about 28 km south-west of Tsetong, was the ancient capital of the Tubo Dynasty. When King Songtsen Gampo moved the capital to Lhasa, Chongye lost influence as a centre for government, culture and trade. Apart from a ruined palace (Chingwa Tagtse) with Tibet's much smaller equivalent of the Great Wall, the main attractions here are the tombs of the Tibetan kings.

The Tombs of the Tibetan Kings
ནས་རྒྱལ་བར་སོ་

The Tibetans did not give their kings a sky burial but chose internment in tombs instead. Experts differ in their explanations: some believe this was due to the cultural influence of the Tang Dynasty in China, others consider this was a result of Buddhist influence. Both of these explanations have been undermined by an archaeological survey of Tibet, started in 1984, which has discovered over 1000 graves in 20 groups near Nêdong. Since these graves belong to a neolithic culture which flourished over 3000 years ago, it appears that burial in the ground was a common practice long before the Tibetan kings were interred in tombs.

Historical records speak of 13 tombs at Chongye, but only nine have been found. The easiest tomb to identify (if you can find a guide, then so much the better) is that of Songtsen Gampo which has a small temple on top containing, amongst others, images of Songtsen Gampo, Princess Wen Cheng (Tibetan: Munshang Kongjo) and Princess Bhrikuti.

Getting There & Away
To reach Chongye, you can hitchhike out on the road (however, traffic is very sparse), organise a Landcruiser from the Zêtang Hotel or ask truck drivers at Tsetong Market. For hardier souls, there are enterprising bike menders hiring out bikes near the central traffic circle. Allow three hours by bike one way. It may be possible to stay in Chongye but take food and water.

REMOTE DESTINATIONS

Tsona (Cona)

Tsona lies in a mountain valley close to the Bhutanese border, about 211 km south of Tsetong. Travellers reported that the lush scenery is similar to that around Yadong. There is a bus for Tsona leaving most days. Buy your ticket – if the clerk allows – the day before from the ticket office at the traffic circle. You could also try hitching a ride with the trucks parked near the market or station yourself on the road from Nêdong to Qungdogyang. Be prepared for a long wait – traffic is infrequent on this road.

Reting

Reting, about 150 km north-east of Lhasa (near Lhünzhub), was a famous monastery of the Kadampa sect and was founded in 1056 by Dronton. To reach Reting you might be able to hire a jeep, take the bus to Lhünzhub (and then trek the rest) or trek the whole way.

Tsurphu

Tsurphu (Tulung Churbu Gompa) lies about 70 km north-west of Lhasa, just off the main Lhasa-Yangbachen (Yangbajing) road. Turn left at km marker 1897 and continue 28 km up the side valley. It was a famous monastery of the Kagyupa sect founded in 1189 by the first Karmapa, Dusum Kyempa. To reach Tsurphu you might be able to hire a jeep, hitchhike along the main road towards Yangbajing then trek the rest, or trek the lot.

Gyantse & Chumbi Valley

GYANTSE རྒྱལ་རྩེ་

Gyantse lies beside the Nyan Chu River between Lhasa and Shigatse. It is Tibet's fourth largest town but has retained its Tibetan character. In former times, Gyantse used its location on the main trade routes to India to develop itself into a hub for the wool trade.

In 1904 the Younghusband Expedition encountered strong resistance from the Dzong (fort) which dominates Gyantse.

By the 1950s the wool trade had dwindled and today Gyantse retains few handicraft industries, with most employment now being in agriculture.

Kumbum (Pango Chörten)

This beautifully designed stupa is the main attraction of Gyantse. It was built in 1440 by Rapten Kunsang. On the ground floor there are four chapels divided by 16 smaller chapels. Above this level are three more tiers of chapels surmounted by a dome. The shaft above this is painted with all-seeing eyes on all four sides. Over this rise a series of 13 gilded rings and a metal parasol which is topped off with a number of gold ornaments. The monks may not allow you to complete the pilgrim circuit to the top, but the lower tiers contain excellent murals. Take a torch. Admission is Y3.

Palkhor Choide Monastery

The monastery next to the Kumbum stupa was founded in 1418 by Rapten Kunsang. At one stage it consisted of 16 colleges repre-

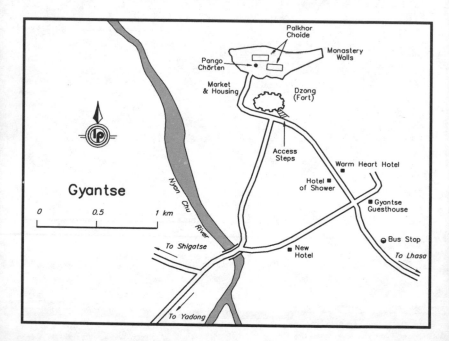

senting an eclectic mixture of sects. Now there are only four buildings remaining.

The Dzong (Fort)

Perched high above Gyantse is the Dzong which was attacked by the British in 1904. The entrance is usually locked, but you may be able to get the key (for a fee of Y2) from a small house at the foot of the steps leading up the hill; it's close to the tiny bridge on the main road. One of the rooms in the fort is papered with *Times of India* newspapers from 1942! There are great views from the top of the Dzong.

Places to Stay & Eat

The *Warm Heart Hotel* just north of the crossroads has beds for Y3 in a six-bed room.

Opposite this hotel is the *Hotel of Shower* which charges Y5 for a bed in a triple. The shower consists of a tap in the courtyard about four feet off the ground – the sight of lathering foreigners is a great hit with passing nomad pilgrims. This Tibetan-run hotel also has a restaurant which serves meat momos and cups of chang.

The *Gyantse Guesthouse* (Gyantse Xian Zhaodai Suo) is a green building to the east of the crossroads. Beds are Y5 each. Close to the Kumbum is *The Hotel* with beds for Y2 and a restaurant selling vegetable soup and dumplings.

The bus stop has rough accommodation at Y5 per bed in a six-bed room.

South of the crossroads there is a new hotel under construction.

Getting There & Away

Bus connections to Lhasa usually consist of buses from Shigatse or elsewhere which are passing through. They are often packed solid and you'll be lucky to find a seat for the five-hour ride. The fare is Y60 on a Japanese bus. Wait for the buses at the crossroads; if buses stay overnight at the bus station in Gyantse, talk to the drivers and they might let you on the bus in the morning.

The same problems apply for travel to Shigatse (two hours, Y10) or the Nepal border.

Transport to Yadong is scarce, and a checkpoint en route turns back foreigners.

YADONG ROUTE & CHUMBI VALLEY

The route from Gyantse to Yadong is not only scenic but also has many historical associations. Yadong lies in the Chumbi Valley and it was along this route that the British expedition under Colonel Francis Younghusband advanced from India into Tibet, to briefly occupy Lhasa. Under the terms of the agreement reached in 1904, foreign traders were granted the right to use this route as far as Gyantse. The Dalai Lama stayed in Yadong in 1950 to avoid the invading Chinese and again in 1956 when he visited India for Buddhist celebrations.

The checkpoint en route to Yadong is turning back foreigners, but if you feel like giving it a try, visit the truck stops in Gyantse and ask for a ride to Yadong. Walk out to the road junction just outside Gyantse early in the morning if you want to thumb a ride. A fully laden truck takes a day, an empty truck about nine hours. There is occasionally a bus from Shigatse.

Gyantse to Yadong

About two km out of Gyantse the road divides into two: left to Yadong, right to Shigatse. On the way to Kangmar you pass a ruined Dzong and Gompa, a hydroelectric power station and rock paintings.

Gala is approached across a huge, barren plain. The checkpoint at Gala is a small office in front of two mud walls which jut into the road, leaving an opening just large enough for trucks to squeeze through. The officials religiously record details of anybody, Chinese or foreigner, who passes.

Access to Yadong, which is in a border area, is strictly controlled. Permission seems to be granted purely on a pot-luck basis. Some foreigners are refused point-blank, others receive permission just to take a peep round the corner at Bam Tso. Others show papers, speak a bit of Chinese and are waved through. If you are refused, you can either hitchhike across to Dinggyê or catch a truck back to Gyantse.

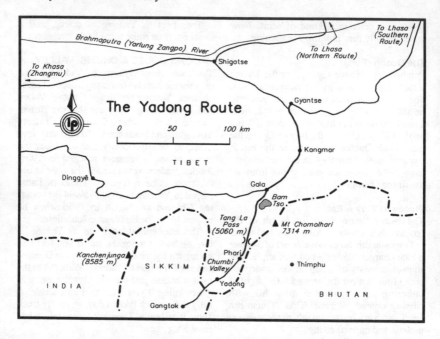

The Yadong Route

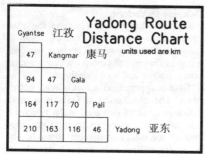

Gyantse	江孜	**Yadong Route Distance Chart**		
47	Kangmar	康马	units used are km	
94	47	Gala		
164	117	70	Pali	
210	163	116	46	Yadong 亚东

After Gala, the road follows the shore of **Bam Tso** which, contrary to what it appears to be on the map, is a huge, dry, salt lake. However, disappointment is short-lived. On the left, **Mt Chomolhari** (7314 metres) approaches closer and closer, soaring above the plain, while to the right, a whole series of peaks dominated by **Kanchenjunga** (8585

metres), comes briefly into view behind distant rolling hills. After crossing the **Tang La Pass** (5060 metres), just before reaching Phari (Pali), you reach **Phari Gompa** which was once inhabited by hundreds of monks but now, reportedly, only has 30. Although currently under restoration, an army unit is still stationed there.

The tiny settlement of **Phari (Pali)** presents a strange sight. The road cleaves it like an apple into two distinct architectural segments: Tibetan stone and mud buildings on one side, Chinese prefabs on the other.

As the road leaves the desolate plain and starts to descend into Yadong, vegetation slowly starts to reappear, becoming lusher and lusher. Most of the trucks on this route run empty down to Yadong and return with timber. There is a timber checkpoint (permits are required for the timber) about an hour after Phari. The houses lower down the valley resemble Swiss chalets and, in contrast to the barren plain, the rest of the route to Yadong is a riot of flowers, fields, streams and forests.

YADONG

Yadong is right next to Sikkim and Bhutan. One traveller obtained a visa at the Bhutanese border, but had to leave his camera behind. Bhutanese and Sikkimese traders amble in and out of town shouldering huge bags of goods. Most of them simply appear out of or disappear into surrounding forests where they climb mountain trails to avoid border posts. Apparently, some traders are also looking for a different commodity: marriageable women. The borders seem porous. One Tibetan I met had left for India via Bhutan, spent four years in New Delhi, Dharamsala and elsewhere before returning to Tibet via Nepal.

According to a newspaper report, 'wild men' or 'snowmen' also roam the forests, so keep your eyes peeled. Locals were keen to report another mysterious occurrence called the 'Thumbs-up American'. This was a rare hitchhiker who had arrived on the back of a truck. He spoke no Chinese other than the word for America and restricted communication to his vertically raised right thumb.

The forests around Yadong provide splendid hiking, with mountain strawberries, hemp, irises, azaleas and rhododendrons in abundance, but watch out for voracious midges. Accept at once if a driver offers to take you to a logging camp near the border – it's a great trip.

Places to Stay & Eat

The best hostel in Yadong is the one close to the bridge. Most of the trucks stop here, so it is easy to arrange a ride. A bed in a five-bed room costs Y2.50. The rooms are on the 2nd floor. The toilets are outside, just in front of the bridge. You can eat in the kitchen or join

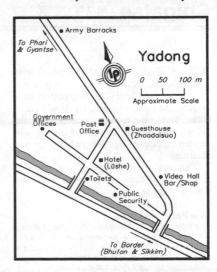

everyone else in the restaurant. The food here was some of the best I had in Tibet: momo, mutton with potatoes, chapattis, vegetables in batter and gallons of hot, milky tea. Ask the manager if you want to have a shower. The shower is in a building across the bridge, under a waterfall.

Getting There & Away

There is, reportedly, a bus from Lhasa to Yadong on Tuesdays and from Yadong to Lhasa on Thursdays. It is unlikely that you will be sold a ticket at the bus station in Lhasa. An easier way to return is on one of the many trucks heading back to Gyantse with timber. I had a bumpy, but magic ride, travelling through the night, stretched out on the timber in the back of the truck, gazing up at an unbelievable number of stars.

Shigatse གཞིས་ཀ་རྩེ་

With a population of 40,000, Shigatse (3841 metres) is the second-largest town in Tibet. It has a long history of importance as a trading and political centre for West-Central Tibet. Today the town is dominated by the ruins of an old fort beneath which sprawl modern, unappealing Chinese buildings and facilities.

The main attraction of the town is Tashilhunpo Monastery, the seat of the Panchen Lama.

The Panchen Lama

The Fifth Dalai Lama declared his teacher, Lobzang Chokyi Gyaltsen, a manifestation of Buddha Amitabha and conferred on him the title of 'Panchen' (Great Scholar). This title was applied retroactively to the three previous abbots of Tashilhunpo.

From the 17th century onwards, the older of the Panchen Lama and the Dalai Lama served as tutor to the younger. The political rivalry that occurred sporadically between the Dalai Lamas and the Panchen Lamas was exploited by the Chinese.

The Sixth Panchen Lama was visited in 1774 by the Scotsman George Bogle, who rounded off his official mission by befriending the Panchen Lama and marrying a Tibetan relative of the Panchen Lama.

The Ninth Panchen Lama disagreed with the Thirteenth Dalai Lama and finally fled into exile in China where he died.

His successor was born in 1938 in Amdo (Qinghai) (Tsinghai). It is unclear whether his incarnation was officially recognised and he remained in the hands of the Chinese from early childhood. From 1959 onwards the Panchen Lama was employed by the Chinese as a spokesman on Tibet. During the 1960s he rebelled against this role and openly supported the Dalai Lama. He disappeared for several years and was rumoured to have died under torture or in prison. Reportedly, his 'cauliflower' ear was a result of beatings received. In 1978, he resurfaced and resided in Beijing where he held honorary posts.

He made only occasional visits to Tibet and died during one such visit to Shigatse in 1989. Well...one day he appeared in good health at the inauguration of a memorial building; the next day, the 51-year-old leader was reported by Chinese authorities to have died from a heart attack. By strange coincidence, the Panchen Lama's parents both suffered heart attacks either on the day before or after his death, and his senior tutor succumbed to a heart attack the day after his death. A British pathologist was asked at the time to comment on this strange occurrence: he considered that heart attacks simply don't happen in epidemics.

Tashilhunpo Monastery བཀྲ་ཤིས་ལྷུན་པོ་དགོན་པ་

The monastery was constructed in 1447 by the First Dalai Lama, Gendun Drub. At the peak of its activity, Tashilhunpo had over 4000 monks, but there are only some 600 today.

The Maitreya Hall, to the west of the entrance, was built in 1914 and houses a huge statue of Buddha Maitreya. Over 26 metres high, the statue is plated with 279 kg of gold.

The building close by, topped with a golden roof, is the Tomb of the Fourth Panchen Lama and was built in 1662. The embalmed body is contained in a large silver stupa.

To the east of the complex is the main chanting hall, which is connected to numerous chapels containing shrines, statues and thangkas. At the rear of the inner courtyard is the throne of the Panchen Lama.

At the foot of the mountain behind the monastery is a large tower from which huge thangkas are unfurled during religious ceremonies.

There is a pilgrim circuit which runs round the walls of the monastery. Follow it clockwise to the thangka tower where the path splits, leading down either to the monastery or over to the ruined fort. The views from this circuit over Shigatse are spectacular, but beware of the dogs lurking beside the path.

Tashilhunpo Monastery is open from 9 am to noon and from 2 pm to 5 pm; closed on Sundays. Admission is Y5. Photography is generally prohibited.

Places to Stay & Eat

The *Shigatse Binguan (Shigatse Hotel)*, on the outskirts of town, is a Chinese-style hotel built for tour groups. Doubles for Y70 are poor value, but if you are on a sanctioned

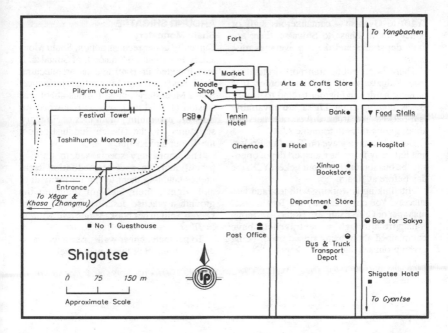

Shigatse

0   75   150 m

Approximate Scale

---

tour, you'll have no choice. CITS is also located here and there is a good food store.

Attached to the bus station is a hostel which charges Y8 per bed. It's nothing special, but is useful if you want to be close to transport. Across the road from the bus station is another hostel.

The Tibetan-run *Tensin Hotel* is popular for its roof terrace and location opposite the market in the Tibetan part of town. It charges Y10 per person in a double or Y6 in a four-bed room. For Y35 you could also try the Dalai Lama Suite, which comes complete with thangkas, furniture and plates filled with cookies and candies. The manager may, after a wait of several days, be able to organise transport for excursions to Sakya, Rongbuk, Shalu, etc. A day's vehicle hire to Sakya is Y300. The trip to Rongbuk for four people costs Y950.

The *Chengguan Di Yi Zhaodai Suo (No 1 Guest House)*, opposite the entrance to Tashilhunpo Monastery, is a basic place also run by Tibetans. It's popular with pilgrims and bedbugs. A bed costs Y6.

Shigatse has plenty of free-enterprise restaurants on the streets which serve good Chinese food. Shigatse is also a good place to stock up on supplies – try the department store just round the corner from the bus station.

Getting There & Away
Bus & Truck Shigatse is an important transport centre with connections to the Nepalese border, western Tibet, Lhasa and Golmud. There are two routes between Lhasa and Shigatse. The northern route runs via Yangbachen (Yangbajing) over three passes and crosses the Brahmaputra by ferry at Datsukhar. The more commonly taken southern route runs via Gyantse over two passes.

Buses to Lhasa, a 12-hour trip, cost Y55 and leave daily from the bus station. The bus station sometimes refuses to sell tickets

(Y10) to Gyantse – cantankerous staff or policy? From Lhasa to Shigatse, there are daily departures and the trip averages nine hours.

There is no public transport originating from Shigatse to the Nepalese border. It is proving harder and harder to find transport. Buses coming from Lhasa are invariably jam-packed and truck drivers are nervous about giving rides to foreigners.

Buses to Sakya leave on Tuesday, Friday, and Saturday from the transport depot opposite the bus station. Buy your ticket (Y28) the day before at 10 am.

Hitchhiking is working with less and less success. You could also try the Tensin hotel manager or CITS (Shigatse Hotel) to arrange transport although some travellers have complained about being ripped off or being given promises that weren't kept.

AROUND SHIGATSE
Shalu Monastery
Currently under reconstruction, Shalu Monastery lies about 20 km south of Shigatse. It was founded in 1040 and its architectural style has a strong Mongolian influence. Shalu Monastery's most famous abbot was Buston (1290-1364), who is renowned for his work assembling thousands of Buddhist scriptures into the Tibetan Buddhist canon, the Tenjur and Kanjur.

This monastery specialised in training practitioners in special meditation techniques enabling them to run for many days and nights, their feet not touching the ground, a practise described by Alexandra David-Neill in her book, *Magic and Mystery in Tibet*.

To get there, either walk or arrange transport from CITS or the Tensin Hotel.

Sakya

The monastery of Sakya was founded in 1073 by Khon Konchok Gyalpo, whose family traced its lineage back to the mythical descent to earth of three brothers or 'gods of clear light'. Under his son, Kunga Nyingpo, Sakya became a centre for the Sakyapa religious order.

During the 13th century, Sakya Pandita (1182-1253), also known as Kunga Gyaltsen, was invited to the court of the Mongolian emperor with whom he then formed close ties. After the death of Sakya Pandita, his nephew Phakpa (1235-80) became the personal spiritual teacher to Kublai Khan and the Sakyapa received the patronage of the Mongolian emperor until the decline of the Mongols in the mid-14th century. From then onwards the influence of the Sakyapa waned and the Gelukpa (Yellow Hats) came to power.

The head of the Sakyapa, known as Sakya Trizin (throne holder), is elected alternately from one of two families. The post is thus hereditary, although there is a tradition that seven incarnations of Manjusri, the Buddha of Wisdom, have occurred in the Sakyapa lineage.

The present head of the Sakyapa lives in Dehra Dun in north India. The head of the other family lives in Seattle but he is not the throne holder.

Sakya Monastery ས་སྐྱ་དགོན་པ་

Originally Sakya consisted of a Northern and a Southern monastery. During the Cultural Revolution, the Northern Monastery was

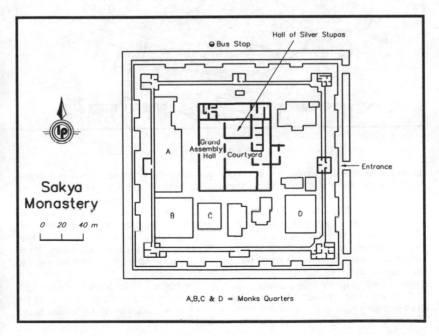

Sakya Monastery

0   20   40 m

A,B,C & D = Monks Quarters

ཀ། འཇམ་དབྱངས།   ལ་སྐྱ་པཎྜི་ཏ་པན་མོ།

Sakya Pandita

reduced to the rubble which can now be seen on the hillside above the river, behind the village.

The Southern Monastery looks grim and oppressive, more like a dungeon or a fortress than a monastery. It was constructed during the 13th century by Phakpa. The monks are not always keen to open rooms for viewing and are particularly zealous about enforcing a ban on photography within the halls.

There are generally four parts open. The most imposing room is the Grand Assembly Hall which is directly in front of you when you enter the courtyard. Rows of massive pillars made from tree trunks fill the hall and between them is carpeted seating for several hundred monks. Lining the walls are some impressive Buddhas, including some containing relics sacred to the Sakyapa. Surrounding the statues are vases, cups, ritual vessels, books, etc, which belonged to Sakya leaders.

The Hall of Silver Stupas, to your right when you enter the courtyard, contains the silver-coated pagodas of 11 former Sakya leaders.

Opening hours for the monastery are uncertain, but are probably from 9 am to 4 pm. Entrance fee is Y5.

Places to Stay & Eat

The place most people stay at is the *Sakya Guest House*, which is where the bus drops off or picks up passengers on the Shigatse run. A bed in a dorm costs Y5.

You are best off bringing your own food to Sakya. Stock up in Shigatse. The Guest House sometimes has meagre rations or you could try the teahouse and restaurant to the east of the monastery on the street running parallel to the monastery entrance.

Getting There & Away

If you don't have your own transport, there is a bus running between Shigatse and Sakya twice a week. The bus leaves Shigatse on Tuesday and Friday, returning from Sakya on Wednesday and Saturday. The trip takes about six hours and costs Y28. You may also be able to rent a vehicle from the Tensin Hotel in Shigatse.

Trekking in Tibet

Although tour groups already follow impressive trekking itineraries across Tibet and individual trekkers have also managed to complete a wide range of trips, trekking in Tibet is still in its infancy with next to no infrastructure.

Bearing in mind the lack of support systems, you are well advised not to go on your own. Travel in a small group or pairs to ensure that someone can help in an emergency. Before you go, make sure that you have solid mountaineering experience, preferably at high altitude, and that you understand the medical problems you may encouter, since medical assistance is virtually nonexistent outside Lhasa.

On some treks, such as the Everest trek, guides and pack animals may be available for hire. During the harvest season (August and September) villagers are understandably reluctant to spare their time or animals for trekkers.

A yak can handle up to 80 kg (equivalent to three packs) and travels at a sedate pace of three km per hour. Hiring a yak for a day will cost Y10 to Y20 and the rate for a yak handler or guide will cost about the same. Inevitably, these prices will increase once more travellers start to trek. Unless you can yak fluently in Tibetan, you will find Lonely Planet's *Tibet phrasebook* useful when negotiating arrangements.

You should assume the need for self-sufficiency for all food, fuel, clothing, medical and accommodation requirements. You can stock up with bare essentials of food in Lhasa, but Kathmandu has a much better range of specific trekking foods. Vitamin tablets, freeze-dried and water-soluble foods and high-energy supplements would all be useful. Some luxury items like chocolate will liven up your diet. A water bottle is essential. Make sure you have a medical kit with you and that you are fully aware of the nature of altitude sickness (see the Health section in the Facts for the Visitor chapter). A tent provides shelter when you can't sleep in villages. There is a small company producing Tibetan-style tents in Lhasa. Dress warmly in several layers against wind, rain and snow and use thermal underwear. Down sleeping bags and jackets are good protection, as are a pair of dark goggles or sunglasses against the sunlight in these high altitudes.

The best time to trek is from spring (late April to July) although it's possible to go as late as September. Some flooding occurs during autumn (October and November) but rainfall is relatively light.

At present there is a lack of detailed information, so the following is only a very rough guide to a selection of treks. A booklet entitled *Tibet: A Trekking Guide to Southern Tibet* by Bob Gibbons & Sian Pritchard-Jones provides details on Everest and Gosainthain treks. A wider range of ideas aimed at the pilgrim spirit is found in *The Power Places of Central Tibet: The Pilgrim's Guide* by Keith Dowman. *The Tibet Handbook* (Odyssey, 1992) also details routes trekked by the author, Victor Chan. *Trekking in Tibet: A Traveler's Guide* (The Mountaineers, 1991) by Gary McCue concentrates in great detail on a selection of treks and day hikes in Central Tibet and includes coverage of the Mt Kailas circuit. Depending on the time available and your degree of preparedness, you could also mount your own treks to other destinations.

For further information on trekking in Tibet contact the Chinese Mountaineering Association (CMA), (telex 20089 CMA BJ CN), 9 Tiyuguan Rd, Beijing, People's Republic of China, or the Tibet Mountaineering Association (TMA), (telex 68029 TMA CN), No 7, East Lingkor Rd, Lhasa, Tibet, People's Republic of China. For the names and addresses of tour and trekking companies operating tours into Tibet, refer to the Tours & Trekking section in the Facts for the Visitor chapter.

Mt Kailas (JL)

Top: Trekking to Advanced Base Camp - Everest (GW)
Bottom: Base Camp - Everest North Face (GW)

THE EVEREST BASE CAMP TREK

There are two routes to Rongbuk: one from Tingri (Lao Tingri) and the other from Xêgar (Xin Tingri). The Xêgar route is easier to follow since there is a 4WD track followed by expeditions on their way to Everest Base Camp. If you dislike walking along this track, you can avoid it most of the time and follow other paths through the valleys.

From Xêgar to Rongbuk is a four-day trek (plus two days for the return trip). You can do it in three days if you take a lift on the first day. You can also take it easy and do it in six days, allowing yourself plenty of time to stay in the villages en route.

For the first day you can arrange a lift for the seven km from the hotel to the Chinese checkpoint; or you can start your first day by sleeping at the checkpoint. If you walk, it takes about 2½ hours. Since all vehicles stop at the checkpoint, it's a good place to get a lift for the 11 km to the bridge at km marker 494. Just past this bridge, off to the left, is the start of the track to Everest Base Camp, which is about 90 km away. A tractor may sometimes give a lift on this stretch of road for Y12 for four people.

From the road it's a 1½ hour walk along the path to the village of Shö. You can stay in one of the Tibetan houses there for Y5 per person, which seems to be the going rate in the area.

From Shö at 4300 metres its an exhausting three or four-hour climb up to the Pang La Pass at 5200 metres. You may be exceptionally lucky and manage to get a ride with a passing vehicle, but most of them are not interested in stopping. The trail drops down for four or five hours via the small village of Holum to Peroochi at 4350 metres in the next valley. Peroochi has a 'lodge' which charges Y5 per person. Simple food and tea is available as are flasks of hot water for Y2. Donkeys and yaks may be available for hire here, but be prepared to bargain. A donkey (for two people) costs around Y10 per person per day; a yak costs around Y20 per person per day.

At Peroochi take the right-hand fork in the trail over a wooden bridge to reach Pasum,

the next village, at 4450 metres. This takes two to three hours. Pasum also has a lodge with beds for Y5 per person.

From Pasum the trail continues on an even climb until shortly before Chosong, when you follow the track up and over the mountain to reach a footbridge over the river. It takes about 4½ hours between Pasum and Chosong. You can stay in Chosong for Y5 per person.

From here its another 2½ hour walk to the 'tent', a business enterprise, complete with radio cassette player, started by Nepalese who may or may not still be in business when you arrive. The sign outside offers food and a place to sleep (Y5). You also have a selection of tins left behind by other travellers.

From the tent to Rongbuk is another two-hour walk. The monastery has been partly restored and there's a building with very dark and damp rooms (Y5 per person). Very little food is available, so bring your own. Hot water costs Y2 per flask. The monks come around to sell exotica such as Japanese crackers or Californian prunes and to see if you have similarly intriguing leftovers.

From Rongbuk to base camp is another 2½ hour trek. For those who want a far stiffer and more dangerous climb, it's another six hours from there to the advanced base camp. If you stay at the first base camp and expeditions are also present, check with them about which streams are being used for washing and drinking. It is unwise and unfair to expect expeditions to provide shelter or food.

If you are lucky and don't mind being tossed about like a pancake, you may find a truck for the return ride to Xêgar.

Keep an eye on your belongings at all times. Several foreigners have reported thefts, and one trekker even lost her entire backpack! Apparently local villagers or nomads who possess very little find the temptation of foreign goodies too much. For background details on Mt Everest, see the Nepal Route chapter. For an approximate orientation guide, see the Mt Everest Area map.

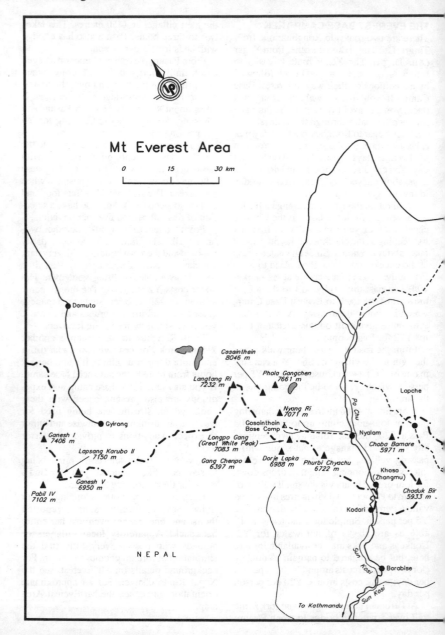

Mt Everest Area

0   15   30 km

MT GOSAINTHAIN (XIXABANGMA)

At 8046 metres, this is one of the world's highest peaks. Of the three approaches (south, north and east), the trek to South Base Camp from Nyalam appears most feasible during early summer (late April to June) and early winter (October to December). The trail from Nyalam runs west, starting from the small monastery in the Tibetan section of the town, and follows the Nyan Chu River valley. The route continues past a glacial lake. It should take two to three days to reach South Base Camp.

MT KAILAS

This peak in Western Tibet is a centre of pilgrimage. Completion of the *parikarama* (circuit) takes two to three days. See the Xinjiang Routes chapter for details.

A Japanese photographer tried twice to reach Mt Kailas from Lhasa on horseback. The first time was in the winter when he bought a horse for Y300 and resold it for Y250 after abandoning the attempt because of bad weather. The second time was in the summer when he bought a horse for Y450 and sold it for Y300 after successfully completing the trip.

K2

See the Xinjiang Routes chapter for a brief rundown on the six-day trek to base camp.

GANDEN – SAMYE

Ganden and Samye are linked by a two to three-day trek via Yamalung Cave and Ngamgo village. This has proved popular with those combining a visit to Ganden with a trip to the Yarlung Valley.

NAM TSO

Nam Tso is the second-largest salt lake in China and the largest in Tibet. It is also a renowned bird sanctuary. From Damxung to the lake is about 40 km along a rocky track. There is a pass (5132 metres) over the Nyaiqên Tanglha Mountains approximately midway. Since Damxung is on the Qinghai (Tsinghai) route, you could arrange a lift as far as there.

The Nepal Route

The road connecting Lhasa with Nepal is officially called the Friendship Highway and runs from Lhasa to Kathmandu via Gyantse, Shigatse and Khasa (Zhangmu) (the Chinese border post). The Chinese section was constructed by 1966 and the Chinese completed the Nepalese section in the '70s.

It's a spectacular trip which includes three of the major monasteries in Tibet (Palkhor Choide in Gyantse, Tashilhunpo in Shigatse, and Sakya – all covered in separate chapters). En route you can sometimes glimpse Mt Everest from the Tibetan village of Tingri (Lao Tingri) or stop off for some trekking in the region (see the Trekking in Tibet chapter).

With the introduction of a flight between Lhasa and Kathmandu, it's now possible to enter and exit Tibet via Nepal without having to go overland each way. However, bearing acclimatisation to high altitude in mind, it makes more sense to exit Tibet on the overland route.

Accommodation on the trip is mostly basic and overpriced like the food, which can also be scarce. Whichever direction you intend to travel in, take food and warm clothing with you.

To enter Nepal you will need a visa which is obtainable from the consulate near the Norbulinka. For opening hours and further information, refer to the information section in the Lhasa chapter. It is also possible to get a visa at the Nepal border, but check at the consulate near the Norbulinka first.

OVERLAND TRANSPORT FROM LHASA TO KATHMANDU

Local buses to Khasa leave early in the morning on Tuesday and Saturday only. The fare is Y128 and the trip takes around three days.

Trucks are not officially allowed to take foreigners any more and as a result hitchhiking has become increasingly difficult.

To hire vehicles (bus, minibus, jeep, Landcruiser) check the notice boards at the hotels first to see if you can join a pre-existing deal and thus save yourself the exertion of setting up transport from scratch. Most of the hotels, including the Lhasa Holiday Inn, Banak Shol, Kirey, Yak and Plateau, have been in the vehicle-hire business, but this could change rapidly if politics or security officials intervene. There are also several taxi services, including one next to the Yak Hotel and another behind the Potala, close to the PSB.

Be careful about paying deposits when hiring vehicles; it's best to write out a contract which includes exact details of your itinerary (dates, places, time required), the name of the driver, the licence-plate number, the option to stop if you want to take photos, and no price increase for technical or climatic problems. PSB may help with translations. Several readers have complained about transport managers inventing astronomical prices or drivers completely ignoring requests to keep to the agreed itinerary.

For a six-day trip to the Nepalese border in a deluxe minibus (maximum 10 passengers), expect to pay Y1000 per person, a 200% increase since the days of nongroup travel. A similar trip in a Landcruiser (maximum seven passengers) costs Y1300 per person. Hiring a Landcruiser will cost around Y6 per km, a minibus Y6.2 per km, and a bus Y7 per km.

Route Description

There are two routes from Lhasa to Shigatse: the northern route runs via Yanghachen; the southern route via Gyantse is the one more commonly travelled.

About 20 km after leaving Lhasa on the southern route, you'll see a seated Buddha carved in rock on your right. Shortly afterwards you reach a small monastery on the right. This is Drölma Lhakang (Nethang) where Atisha resided until his death in 1054.

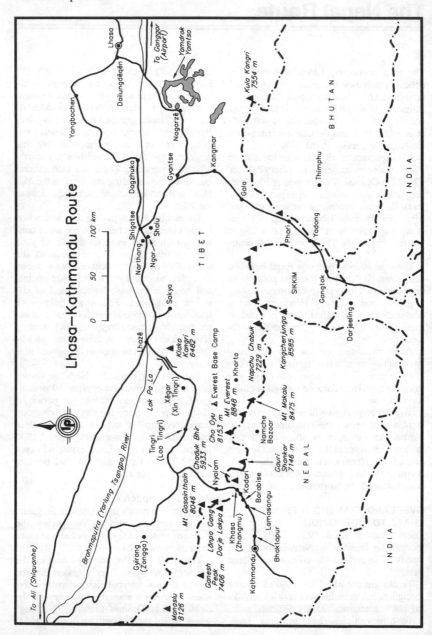

Nepal Route Distance Chart
units used are km

Lhasa 拉萨											
250	Gyantse 江孜										
340	90	Shigatse 日喀则									
490	240	150	Sakya 萨迦								
540	290	200	50	Lhazê 拉孜							
630	380	290	140	90	Xêgar						
700	450	360	210	160	70	Tingri					
850	600	510	360	310	220	150	Nyalam (Zhalangmu) 聂拉木				
880	630	540	390	340	250	180	30	Khasa (Zhangmu)			
889	639	549	399	349	259	189	39	9	Friendship Bridge		
891	641	551	401	351	261	191	41	11	2	Kodari	
1002	752	662	512	462	372	302	152	122	113	111	Kathmandu

The monastery contains several well-preserved images and stupas.

After crossing the bridge over the Yarlung Tsangpo, the road snakes up to the Khamba La Pass (4900 metres). From the pass there are fine views over Yamdrok Yamtso, one of Tibet's largest lakes. Shaped like a scorpion, it is an intense blue. The road descends from the pass to **Nagarzê**. To the east of Nagarzê are the remains of Samding Monastery, which was once headed by Tibet's only female incarnation, Dorje Phagmo (the Thunderbolt Sow). In 1716, the Mongols invaded this area and attacked the monastery only to find it occupied by pigs. When the Mongols gave up their attack, they were astonished to find the pigs transformed into the abbess and her attendant monks and nuns. In recognition of this feat, the Mongols showered the monastery with gifts. A spicy tale of fiction loosely based on this monastery is *Rose of Tibet* by Lionel Davidson. The present incarnation has renounced religion, lives in Lhasa and has declared herself loyal to the Chinese.

From the lake, the road climbs over the Karo La Pass (5045 metres). It was here in 1904 that the Tibetans made a stand against the Younghusband expedition. Relying in vain on their amulets for protection, the Tibetans quickly lost 700 soldiers and were puzzled when the British field hospital made efforts to treat the wounded.

The road descends to a wide plain before reaching **Gyantse** (3800 metres) (see the Gyantse chapter) and, several hours later, **Shigatse** (3900 metres) (see the Shigatse chapter).

From Shigatse to the turn-off for **Sakya** (see the Sakya chapter) is 128 km. En route you cross the Tso La Pass (4500 metres). Sakya is another 26 km down the side road from Tso La Pass. From the turn-off on to **Lhazê** (at km marker 400) is 22 km. Shortly after Lhazê the road divides to run west to Western Tibet and Xinjiang, and south-west to the Nepal border.

The route proceeds from Lhazê (4080 metres) over the Gyatso La Pass (5252 metres), km marker 363, to Xêgar (Xin Tingri).

Xêgar (4420 metres), also known as New Tingri (Xin Tingri), is a Chinese settlement about seven km off the main road. The large and expensive hotel there charges Y15 per bed. There is also a restaurant. On the hillside above the village are the ruins of an old fort and the once famous 'Shining Crystal' Monastery. From the ruins there are fine views across the valley to the mountains.

A couple of km down the road past the Xêgar turn-off is a checkpoint where passports may be checked. Eleven km past the checkpoint, at km marker 494, is the turn-off to Rongbuk Monastery (for more information see the Everest Base Camp Trek section in the Trekking in Tibet chapter).

The next stop, at km marker 542, is the old trading post of **Tingri** (4342 metres), also known as Old Tingri (Lao Tingri), which has an army camp where it is sometimes possible to stay the night (Y20). From Tingri, weather permitting, there are spectacular views of Mt Everest and the Himalaya.

Mt Everest

At 8848 metres, this is the world's highest mountain, which was first measured in 1852 during a survey of India. The surveyors named it after Sir George Everest, who was the Surveyor-General of India, although it does have the much older Tibetan name of Chomolongma (Goddess Mother of the World).

At the beginning of this century, John Noel reconnoitred the Everest region. In the 1920s several expeditions were mounted, including one in 1924 during which George Mallory and Andrew Irvine disappeared. When asked by a reporter why he climbed Mt Everest, it was Mallory who gave the terse reply, 'Because it is there'. Their disappearance has long been a source of controversy. Whether they reached the summit will never be known.

Several expeditions attempted the climb before WW II, but all were unsuccessful.

With the closure of Tibet by the Chinese in 1951, the British approached Mt Everest through Nepal. On 29 May 1953, the summit was climbed by the New Zealander Edmund Hillary and Sherpa Tenzing Norgay.

Since then at least 220 people have climbed Mt Everest. It has been climbed on more than half a dozen different routes and variants, with and even without oxygen. The famous Italian climber Reinhold Messner has climbed the mountain solo without oxygen and without Sherpa support. Teams have ascended from opposite sides and met on the summit. One member of a Norwegian expedition flew a kite on the top. Film footage has been shot all the way to the summit and there have been several live TV broadcasts from there too.

Finally, one loony has skied down Mt Everest from the South Col, while various others have hang-glided from its slopes.

Everest by Walt Unsworth (London, Oxford University Press, 1989) provides coverage of almost all the vital statistics of climbs on the mountain; and the 1991 edition of the National Geographic Society's map, entitled *Mt Everest*, includes a mini history of first ascents from 1950 to 1990.

For details on the Everest Base Camp trek, see the Trekking in Tibet chapter.

The road climbs before crossing La Lung La Pass over arid, barren landscape and then reaches **Nyalam** (Zhalangmu). About 12 km before Nyalam, at Zhonggang (km marker 682), is the famous cave where Milarepa spent many years of his life. The small Pelgye Ling Monastery there has been restored by Nepalese artisans. The dangers of the road at Nyalam (km marker 694) earned it its name which translates as Path to Hell. The descent from Nyalam (3750 metres) to Zhangmu (2300 metres) is an extraordinary plunge into lusher and lusher greenery fed by the monsoon.

The border town of **Zhangmu** (Khasa in Nepalese) at km marker 725, is ranged vertically along several hairpin bends. It's an active trading centre for Chinese, Tibetan and Nepalese goods. The bank is open in the morning and late afternoon, but closed on Sunday. Exchange procedures in Khasa are erratic. FEC can be changed into foreign currency (US dollars) and a small black market functions changing rupees for FEC or RMB.

The border post for passport and customs control is just below the Zhangmu Hotel, where service is poor and beds cost Y25.

Khasa
(Zhangmu)

Not to Scale

Frequent flooding in the past few years has washed out the road from Khasa down to the **Friendship Bridge**. Until repairs have been made, you will have to scramble nine km, crossing landslides and dodging rock falls. Sherpas will also act as porters for about Y10 or Rs 30, but get the price straight (preferably written down!) before hiring them.

Nepalese border formalities are performed two km further on at **Kodari** (1873 metres). Chinese customs officers are likely to confiscate Dalai Lama pictures, Tibetan flags, and so on if they find them in your luggage. From **Tatopani**, two km further, there is truck transport to Kathmandu or you can be dropped off in the larger town of **Barabise** to catch a bus. From Barabise to Kathmandu takes about five hours. Nepal is two hours behind Tibet.

Once in Kathmandu, the area for budget travellers is Thamel, which has an abundance of restaurants, hotels and bookstores. Tibetan handicrafts and artefacts available in Nepal are often more varied and of better quality than similar items produced in Tibet. See the Lonely Planet guide *Nepal – a travel survival kit* for more detail.

KATHMANDU TO LHASA

It's not clear at present whether the introduction of a flight between Lhasa and Kathmandu will lead only to tour groups being allowed to travel overland from Nepal into Tibet.

Previously, Chinese visas were obtained in Kathmandu in one of three ways. First, by telexing full details to the Beijing CITS office (Comprehensive Service Department, CITS Head Office, Beijing – telex 22350 CITSH CN) either through the central telegraph office in Kathmandu or more expensively at many travel agencies. In the past, authorisation to issue visas was usually given, provided you could show the embassy official a bank receipt from the Bank of Nepal to prove payment of visa fee in US dollars into an account in Beijing. The total cost of this rigmarole was about US$30. Check the current status with the embassy (Baluwatar – ☎ 4-12589).

Second, couriers would fly passports back and forth after obtaining visas in Hong Kong. This was a short-lived phenomenon and is unlikely to be revived.

Third, visas would be issued automatically for a short tour to Tibet (at an average cost of US$350). The seven-day Chinese visa could be extended when you hopped off your tour, for example, on the third day. There are numerous travel agents in Kathmandu offering these tours (for details see the Tours and Trekking section in the Facts for the Visitor chapter).

At present, the overland route looks likely to be closed, and the only travellers likely to obtain visas are those taking the Kathmandu-Lhasa flights as a package tour. One Italian reader proved to be a lucky exception.

In 1991 Susanna applied for a visa at a Chinese embassy in Italy and mumbled her way through the embassy's request to see her flight ticket into China. The visa was granted, and Susanna flew to Kathmandu, where she showed the CAAC office her visa and was allowed to book her flight to Lhasa. At the same time, she sagely booked an outward flight from Lhasa to Chengdu (as a sign of her intention to leave Tibet).

After arriving safely at Lhasa's airport, she

encountered a hostile reaction from PSB and CITS officials when it was noticed that she was not part of a group. With a little ingenuity, and help from a genuine tour group, this obstacle was overcome. Possession of the Lhasa-Chengdu air ticket also weighed in her favour and allowed her to proceed to Lhasa for an interesting, but heavily monitored week, staying in Tibetan hotels in the Barkhor area as an independent tourist. On her return to Kathmandu, Susanna managed to persuade the CAAC office to refund the unused Lhasa-Chengdu ticket in US dollars.

Transport from Kathmandu to Khasa includes taxis, buses and trucks.

Once the road has been repaired, taxis may resume running across the Friendship Bridge even up to the Chinese customs post for Rs 700 to Rs 800 (up to four people).

A Tibetan refugee bus runs once or twice a month from Kathmandu to the Sino-Nepalese border. Call the Tibetan Refugee Office for details (Kathmandu ☎ 41 1660) between 10 am and noon and 2 to 5 pm except Saturday. The ticket price averages Rs 50 to Rs 70, but depends on the number of people travelling.

Public buses run at various hours in the morning to Barabise from the rear of the main bus stand in Kathmandu. At Barabise it's usually possible to take a truck or taxi to Kodari. One bus leaves Kathmandu at 6 am direct to the Friendship Bridge and from there it's an uphill climb.

Kham & the Sichuan Routes

Prior to the '50s the eastern district of Tibet existed under the name of Kham. During the '50s the Chinese broke up Kham into constituent parts which were allotted to the adjoining Chinese provinces of Sichuan, Qinghai, Gansu and Yunnan. However, travelling today in Western Sichuan it is easy to see that the region is still essentially Tibetan. The main Tibetan areas in Sichuan are now designated as Aba (Ngawa) Tibetan Autonomous Prefecture, Garzê Tibetan Autonomous Prefecture and Muli Tibetan Autonomous County.

The scenery in these areas counts as some of the most imposing in the world. Vast mountain ranges are crisscrossed by some of Asia's mightiest rivers such as the Mekong, the Salween and the Yangtze. Forests give way above to grasslands whilst below they blend into subtropical greenery – the contrasts and extremes of landscape are spectacular. However, massive deforestation is an unpleasant aspect which will soon be apparent to travellers in Eastern Tibet. There have been few attempts at replanting and official Chinese reports have estimated that between 1959 and the early '80s, US$54 billion of trees were felled in Tibet. The land area deforested in Tibet within the same time span has been estimated at 130,000 sq km. The majority of the felled trees were in Eastern Tibet. According to some sources, for example, the Aba region (Tibetan: Ngaba) has lost 68% of its forest cover since the '40s.

The Sichuan-Tibet Highway, begun in 1950 and finished in 1954, is one of the world's highest, roughest, most dangerous and most beautiful roads. The highway has been split into northern and southern routes. The northern route runs via Kangding, Garzê and Dêgê before crossing the boundary into Tibet. The southern route runs via Kangding, Litang and Batang before entering Tibet.

The Public Security Bureau in Chengdu directs all foreigners to take the plane to Lhasa; the land route between Chengdu and Lhasa is closed to foreigners for safety reasons. Some palefaces have succeeded and arrived intact in Lhasa. Less fortunate were some Americans and Australians on the back of a truck which overturned close to Dêgê; one member of the group lost half an arm and another member sustained multiple injuries to her back. It took several days for medical help to arrive and even longer before the injured could be brought back to Chengdu.

At present, the bus service on the Sichuan-Tibet highway only seems to function well as far as Kangding. The Exit/Entry Administration Office of Chengdu's PSB hands out permits to Kangding, Garzê (Garzi) Autonomous Prefecture fairly regularly. Once upon a time there was a legendary crate, the Chengdu-to-Lhasa bus, which suffered countless breakdowns and took weeks to arrive. In 1985, a monumental mudslip on the southern route took out the road for dozens of km and the service has been discontinued.

Trucks are the only transport travelling consistently long hauls on this highway. The major truck depots are in Chengdu, Chamdo (Tsiamdo) and Lhasa. Trucks usually run from Lhasa or from Chengdu only as far as Chamdo, where you have to find another lift. The police have now clamped down on truckers giving lifts to foreigners; there is rumoured to be a sign in Chinese near Dêgê which warns drivers not to take foreigners. Certainly at Dêgê itself, there is a checkpoint on the bridge where guards turn back foreigners. If a driver is caught, he could lose his licence or receive a massive fine. Foreigners caught arriving from Chengdu are often fined and always sent back. If you're arriving from Tibet nobody gives a damn.

In sum, the odds are stacked much higher against you when travelling into, rather than out of, Tibet. Whatever you do, bear in mind the risk and equip yourself properly with food and warm clothing.

CHENGDU

Chengdu is the capital of Sichuan Province. It is a thriving industrial centre, but the back streets still have traditional architecture and peaceful teahouses.

Information

CITS The office (☎ 28731) in the Jin Jiang Hotel occasionally shows signs of life, at which times it is sometimes possible to extract nuts-and-bolts information.

CITS also organises all-inclusive tours to Lhasa at astronomical prices. There are constant changes in the degree of compulsion to take one of these tours – hopefully there will soon be a reversion to the old system whereby you could book just the flight without costly tour paraphernalia.

The cheapest option to get you into Lhasa on a tour, which disbands once you are in Lhasa, is to take a package which includes a one-way flight and four days' accommodation at the Lhasa Holiday Inn. This costs Y1400 FEC per person (Y900 FEC per person for a group of 10). The most expensive tours provide a return flight and six days' accommodation for about Y3000 FEC; cheaper versions provide a return ticket and three days' accommodation for Y1637 FEC.

Other travel offices in the Jin Jiang Hotel which may offer Tibet tours are: Holiday Inn/Asia Pacific, 5th Floor, East Wing (☎ 24481 ext 594), and Sichuan China Travel Service (CTS), Room 394, 3rd Floor, East Wing (☎ 22630, 24481 ext 394)

Contrary to what you may be told here, there are much cheaper tours to Lhasa from Qinghai Province (Xining CITS or preferably Golmud CITS) which basically just cover transport costs.

Public Security This office (☎ 6577) has two staff members who speak English. They are unable or unwilling to do much more than extend a visa and are, reportedly, most unhelpful in the event of theft, loss reports etc. They're on Xinhua Donglu, east of the intersection with Renmin Zhonglu.

For permits to visit 'closed' areas in Sichuan, you must apply to the Exit-Entry Administration branch of the Sichuan PSB on Wenmiaohou Jie, which is off Jiangxi Jie to the west of the Jin Jiang Hotel. Certain members of the staff speak excellent English. This office is open Monday and Wednesday 8.30 to 11 am and 3 to 5 pm, and Saturday 8.30 to 11 am.

Money All of the hotels mentioned in Places to Stay have foreign exchange counters. The Jin Jiang Hotel has a branch of the Bank of China on the ground floor. On the streets in the vicinity of the Jin Jiang and Traffic hotels you'll be pestered by hordes of moneychangers – the black market rate in Chengdu is usually a bit above average.

Post The main post office is on the corner of Huaxinzhen Jie and Shuwa Beijie. Poste restante mail is kept behind the window marked 'International Post' – names of addressees for poste restante parcels are marked on a chalkboard.

Poste restante service at the GPO is generally efficient. Nonetheless, since it's across town from the Jin River tourist area, many tourists have their mail addressed to the Jin Jiang Hotel. In my experience this hotel is not an especially good place to receive mail if you're not staying there. If you do attempt to pick up mail at the Jin Jiang, be sure to check both the reception desk and the hotel's post office.

Consulates The US Consulate General has an office in Chengdu in the Jin Jiang Hotel (☎ 51912, 52791, 24481 ext 138).

Airline Offices The CAAC branch here is called China Southwest Airlines. The main office is diagonally opposite the Jin Jiang Hotel. This office is linked with the national CAAC reservation network and is a good place to purchase tickets between China destinations other than Chengdu.

The smaller Sichuan Provincial Airlines has its office on Renmin Donglu near the Shuncheng Jie intersection (just east of the Telecommunications Building).

Maps City bus maps can be found at train stations, the Jin Jiang Hotel and Xinhua Bookstores. Three different maps in Chinese provide excellent detail for Sichuan Province, Chengdu city and its surrounding areas. The English 'Tourist Map of Chengdu', available at the Jin Jiang Hotel's gift shop, is very useful for city excursions.

Warning There have been several reports of foreigners becoming targets for rip-offs and theft in Chengdu.

To avoid getting ripped off by taxis, pedicab drivers, restaurants, always get the price at the start of proceedings. Pickpockets are common around bus stations, train stations and post offices, and watch out for gangs who razor your bags on buses. It's a good idea to use a money belt. If you want to play it safe with train tickets, make a note of the ticket numbers. If the tickets are stolen you'll be given replacements, providing you can supply the numbers of the old ones.

Should things get out of hand, use the phone (☎ 6577) to locate an English-speaker at the Gong An Ju, Wai Shi Ke (Public Security Bureau, Foreign Affairs Section); they might be of use.

Chengdu Climate Chart

Month	Average °C	Max °C	Min °C
Jan	6.7	18	-4
Feb	8.1	21	-3
Mar	12.7	30	-1
Apr	17.7	32	3
May	22.3	36	9
Jun	24.1	36	15
Jul	26.5	36	17
Aug	25.8	38	16
Sept	22.0	35	12
Oct	17.6	30	6
Nov	12.5	24	1
Dec	7.7	21	-3

Places to Stay – bottom end

The *Jiaotong (Traffic) Hotel* (☎ 52814), next to Xinnanmen Bus Station, is the backpacker's palace. It's clean, comfortable, fairly quiet and close to a number of good dining spots. A bed in a triple is Y14 with immaculate showers and toilet down the hall. A double with communal bath is Y28 but there are only four of them and they're usually booked out. A double with private bath is Y50 person; a bed in a four-bed dorm costs Y4. The staff at reception are friendly and there's a notice board with travel info next to the counter. Another useful service here is a baggage room where you can leave heavy backpacks for a few days while you head off to Emeishan, Jiuzhaigou or wherever. To get here from the northern train station, take a trolley bus No 1 till it terminates at the Xinnanmen Bus Station.

Even cheaper is the *Binjiang Hotel* (☎ 24451) on Binjiang Lu, across the river from the Jiaotong toward Renmin Lu. This big, noisy hotel is not as pleasant as the Jiaotong overall, but some travellers claim they prefer it (hooked on the TV blare, no doubt). Per-person rates in the six-bed dorms are Y9, in a four-bed Y11, triple (with private bath) Y14. Doubles with bath are available for Y25 or Y43 with air-con. Students and overseas Chinese can obtain a discount from these rates, but in the winter the hotel charges an additional Y1 heating charge. This is one of those hotels where every room seems to have its TV on at full volume most of the time.

At the very bottom of the cheapies is the *Black Coffee Hotel*, a few minutes' walk east of the Binjiang Hotel. This is one of China's most unusual hostelries, a bomb-shelter which has been converted into an underground hotel. It's a bit dank and airless, but at least it's fairly quiet. Doubles cost Y14 per person; a bed in a four-bed room costs Y5. Scattered throughout the musty maze of rooms are a disco, bar, restaurant, and small sitting rooms where local Chinese bring their dates for furtive fumbling.

Another budget possibility is CAAC's *Blue Sky Hotel* next door to the China Southwest Airlines office on Renmin Nanlu. Doubles are Y45, triples Y16 per person. The staff seems terribly disorganised here, however, and the rooms are nothing special.

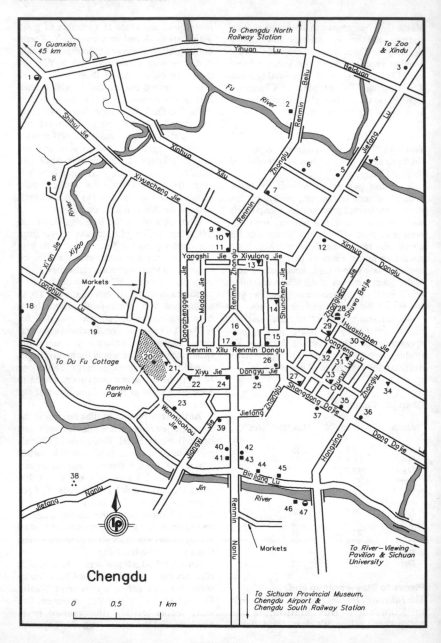

Chengdu

To Chengdu North Railway Station

To Guanxian 45 km

To Zoo & Xindu

Yihuan Lu

Beilu

Jietang Lu

Fu River

Shibui Jie

Renmin

Zhonglu

Xinhua Xilu

Xiwecheng Jie

Xi'an Jie

Xijiao River

Renmin

Xinhua

Donglu

Tonghui Lu

Markets

Yangshi Jie

Xiyulong Jie

Zhonglu

Shuncheng Jie

Zhonglieci Jie

Shuwo Beijie

To Du Fu Cottage

Dongchenggen Jie

Madao Jie

Renmin

Huaxinzhen Jie

Dongfeng

Renmin Park

Renmin Xilu

Renmin Donglu

Chunxi Lu

Zhonglu

Xiyu Jie

Dongyu Jie

Wenmiaohou Jie

Jiangxi Jie

Jiefong

Zhonglu

Shangdong Dajie

Hongxing

Dong Dajie

Jiefang Nanlu

Bin Jiang Lu

Jin River

Renmin Nanlu

Markets

To River–Viewing Pavilion & Sichuan University

To Sichuan Provincial Museum, Chengdu Airport & Chengdu South Railway Station

0   0.5   1 km

■ PLACES TO STAY

2 Tibet Hotel
41 Jin Jiang Hotel/CITS
43 Minshan Hotel
44 Binjiang Hotel
45 Black Coffee Hotel
46 Jiaotong (Traffic) Hotel

▼ PLACES TO EAT

4 Teahouse
10 Rong Le Yuan Restaurant
13 Chen Mapo (Granny's Beancurd) Snackshop
14 Xiao Yuan Teahouse & Bar
21 Renmin Teahouse
22 Wang Pang Duck Restaurant
27 Chengdu Restaurant
29 Zhong Shuijiao Ravioli Restaurant
30 Shi Mei Xuan Restaurant
31 Lai Tangyuan Rice-Ball Restaurant
33 Yaohua Restaurant
34 Snackshops (Sweets)

OTHER

1 Ximen Bus Station (Buses for Guanxian)
3 Bamboo Weaving Factory
5 Sichuan Embroidery Factory
6 Wenshu Monastery
7 Chengdu Theatre
8 Tomb of Wang Jian
9 Drum & Cymbal Shop
11 Foreign Languages Bookstore
12 Public Security Bureau
15 Telecommunications Building
16 Sichuan Exhibition Hall
17 Mao Statue
18 Cultural Park & Qingyang Palace
19 Lacquerware Factory
20 Monument to the Martyrs of the Railway Protecting Movement 1911
23 Public Security Bureau (Exit/Entry Administration)
24 Xinhua Bookstore
25 Advance Rail Ticket Office
26 Renmin Market
28 GPO
32 Bank of China
35 Bicycle Hire Shop
36 Bicycle Hire Shop
37 Friendship Store
38 Temple of Wuhou
39 Bicycle Hire Shop
40 Bicycle Hire Shop
42 China Southwest Airlines/Blue Sky Hotel
47 Chengdu Bus Terminal (Xinnanmen Bus Station)

■ PLACES TO STAY

2 西藏饭店
41 锦江宾馆
43 岷山饭店
44 滨江饭店
45 黑咖啡饭店
46 交通饭店

▼ PLACES TO EAT

4 解放北路茶馆
10 荣乐饭店
13 陈麻婆豆腐
14 晓园茶馆
21 人民茶馆
22 王胖鸭店
27 成都餐厅
29 钟水饺饭店
30 市美轩餐厅
31 赖汤元饭店
33 耀华饭店
34 小吃（东风路）

OTHER

1 西门汽车站
3 竹编工艺厂
5 蜀绣厂
6 文殊院
7 成都剧院
8 王建墓
9 鼓店
11 外书店
12 公安局外事科
15 电讯大楼
16 四川省展览馆
17 毛泽东像
18 文化公园
19 漆器厂
20 烈士纪念碑
23 省公安局厅出入境理处
24 新华书店
25 火车售票处
26 人民市场
28 邮总局
32 中国银行
35 出租自行车店
36 出租自行车店
37 友谊商店
38 武侯祠
39 出租自行车店
40 出租自行车店
42 中国西南航
47 新南门汽车站

Places to Stay – middle

The *Tibet Hotel* (☎ 33401) at 10 Renmin Beilu is about five blocks south of the northern train station. Rooms are clean and service is efficient. A small outdoor cafe on the Renmin Beilu side of the hotel is a pleasant spot for a cup of coffee and a book. All rooms are air-con; triples cost Y54 and doubles are Y88 to Y110. A few dorm beds are available for Y12 but they're often full.

Places to Stay – top end

The *Jin Jiang Hotel* (☎ 24481) at 180 Renmin Nanlu has just undergone a partial facelift. The acres of reflective surfaces in this 1000-room hotel now require the full-time ministrations of polishers and, presumably, are also the justification for rocketing room prices.

For those wishing to splurge, there's a deluxe suite for Y1500 or the simple version for Y160. Standard singles and doubles cost Y173.

There are several restaurants on the ground, 1st, and 9th floors. The Jin Jiang Garden Restaurant on the 9th floor has a sign: 'sloppy dressers is not welcome'. The Western breakfast costs Y12 for skimpy portions. The outdoor terrace with a view across the city haze is a pleasant place for a drink. Watch out for blatant short-changing by surly staff – a quick word with the manager helps iron this out.

On the same floor, the billiards room and disco should now be operating again after renovation. Expect to pay around Y10 FEC to enter the disco. The ballroom disco held on Saturdays (possibly more frequently now) on the ground floor is for Chinese only – no dogs or foreigners.

In the lobby there's a taxi counter which can also arrange minibuses or Landcruisers for trips further afield. The open-plan coffee shop is useful as a meeting point or rest-stop – pick up your copy of *China Daily* from the reception desk.

To find the CITS office, walk through the lobby and past the bank, and it's just before the rear exit on your left.

The bank is on the ground floor; go through the lobby in the direction of the rear exit. Efficient staff change most currencies and you can use credit cards to draw up to Y500 daily. Unorthodox moneychanging takes place outside the hotel gates. You can try the Friendship Store in the city centre for a less obtrusive change.

The telephone office, next to the bank, operates until 11 pm. Overseas connections are erratic, as one operator is helpful, the other stroppy. The World Trade Centre Club has an office next to the telephone office.

Opposite the bank and the telephone office are two shops. One sells export quality food and drink; the other sells handicrafts and tourist paraphernalia. Between the two you should be able to stock up on Kodachrome, Johnny Walker, Nescafé and other items close to your heart.

The corridor to the right as you enter the lobby once housed a post office, telex rooms, and a photo-processing and photocopying centre and a shop right at the end but it's now being renovated.

To hire a bike, turn left at the main gate and continue down the street for 30 metres where you'll find a bicycle hire shop on your left inside the wall. If you park your bike in the Jin Jiang's bike parking lot just before the bike hire shop, take a look at the signs in English and Chinese. For the same amount of time, foreigners pay Y0.30 while Chinese pay Y0.03. Of course it's peanuts, but when I casually asked the attendant if there was any special reason for the price difference, she said the Chinese sign was not intended for me – I was meant to read the foreigners' sign!

Within Chengdu the Jin Jiang Hotel, known as the Jin Jiang Binguan, is a well-used focal point when asking directions.

Opposite the Jin Jiang on Renmin Nanlu is the newer, 21-storey *Minshan Hotel* (☎ 583333), which does a brisk tour group business. Modern doubles start at Y232. The Minshan has a couple of bars, a teahouse and three restaurants.

Places to Eat

Chengdu has a great variety of restaurants.

Top: Pango Chorten, Gyantse (RS)
Bottom: Monks at Rongbuk Monastery (GW)

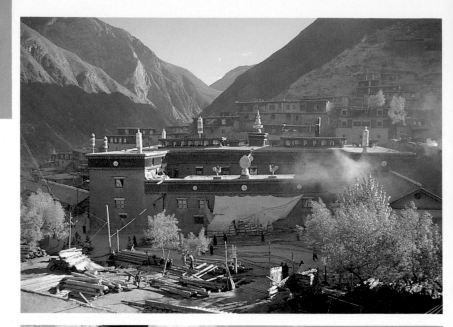

Top: Dêgê Printing Monastery, Tibet-Sichuan border (RS)
Bottom: Yamdrok Yamtso (GW)

In the vicinity of the Jin Jiang and Jiaotong hotels there are several. Two well-known restaurants are the *Chengdu* and *Rong Le Yuan*. There are lots of snack-restaurants specialising in foods such as *mapo doufu* (Pockmarked Grandma's Beancurd) or sweet dumplings.

For something different you could try the *Tongrentang Dinetotherapy Restaurant* (☎ 24519) at 111 Shengli Lu, which is run by a Chinese medicine practitioner. All dishes are prepared according to traditional Chinese diet therapy. On the ground floor a blackboard lists inexpensive daily specials such as snow pear soup, ox penis soup, ginseng flour dumplings and cardamom on steamed bread. Arrive early for lunch; dinner has to be reserved in advance. On the 1st floor you can put in an order a day in advance for excellent dinner banquets costing from Y10 per person.

Getting There & Away

Transport connections in Chengdu are more comprehensive than in other parts of the south-west.

Air China Southwestern Airlines has plenty of air connections out of Chengdu, including Beijing (Y570), Canton (Y430), Changsha (Y340), Chongqing (Y100), Guilin (Y313), Guiyang (Y170), Kunming (Y220), Lanzhou (Y302), Lhasa (Y629), Nanjing (Y522), Shanghai (Y500), Wuhan (Y336) and Xi'an (Y208).

The smaller Sichuan Provincial Airlines has cheaper regional fares but flies hand-me-down planes from CAAC, for example, the Soviet-made YUN-7. Sample fares: Chongqing (Y87), Dazu (Y82), Kunming (Y199) and Xi'an (Y181).

Direct charter flights have been introduced between Chengdu and Hong Kong. Flights depart Hong Kong and Chengdu weekly on Saturdays and possibly now on Wednesdays; economy tickets are HK$970 one way or HK$1380 return.

Bus The main bus station is Xinnanmen Che Zhan (Xinnanmen Bus Station), conveniently next to the Jiaotong Traffic Hotel. It handles departures for Emei, Baoguo, Leshan, Dazu, Zigong, Ya'an and Kangding.

The Ximen Che Zhan (Ximen Bus Station), in the north-west of the city, runs buses to Guanxian (irrigation project and vicinity) and to places on the Jiuzhaigou route such as Nanping, Songpan and Barkam. The best way to get there from the Jin Jiang or Traffic hotels is to take bus No 35 west to the terminus at Qingyang Gong Bus Station and then change to bus No 5 – ask to get off at Ximen Che Zhan.

Train The most commonly used train station is Chengdu North (main) Train Station. Ticket offices in Chengdu may try to sell foreigners soft-sleepers and deny that hard-sleepers are available. The advance train ticket office, a smaller building on Dongyu Jie, is for Chinese-price tickets only. It's best to go early in the day.

CITS has also been known to dish out Chinese-priced tickets (especially for soft-sleepers) to foreigners. Perhaps this is because they're mixed in with CTS. Their top speed for obtaining tickets seems to be four days.

There are also plenty of black-market train tickets for sale on the streets – either in front of the train station or wherever foreigners congregate. Expect to pay a markup of 50% or more for a black-market hard-sleeper ticket (still cheaper than the tourist price – and you can pay in RMB instead of FEC).

From Chengdu there are direct trains to Emei (three hours, Y7 hard-seat, Chinese price), Kunming (25 hours, Y150 hard-sleeper, tourist price), Chongqing (11 hours, Y80 hard-sleeper, Y40 hard-seat, tourist price) and Xi'an (about 20 hours, around Y110 hard-sleeper, tourist price).

For the routing to Kunming via Lijiang and Dali, travel to Jinjiang (railhead for Dukou) on the Chengdu-Kunming line and then take buses. For some reason, the time-tables don't include train No 91 which leaves Chengdu at 7.53 pm and arrives in Jinjiang at 10.40 am – Y70 hard-sleeper, tourist price.

CHENGDU TO KANGDING

The first stop of importance is **Ya'an** which is now open to foreigners. Ya'an was once a major trading centre for brick tea and furs. It has a lively, border town atmosphere.

The road continues to **Luding** famous for its 250-year-old suspension bridge across the Daduhe River. On the Long March, when the Communists were being pursued by the Nationalists, a regiment of Communists managed to hold this bridge long enough to allow the rest of their army to cross.

Kangding (Dartsedo in Tibetan) (4115 metres) was once a trading gateway to Tibet with Chinese merchants buying silver, herbs, musk or furs whilst Tibetan traders used hundreds of porters to ferry brick tea into Tibet. Huc and Gabet passed through Tachienlu (Kangding) in the 19th century:

Tachienlu signifies the forge of arrows, and this name was given to the town because, in the year 234 of our era, General Wu Hou, while leading his army against the southern countries, sent one of his lieutenants to establish there a forge of arrows. This district has by turns belonged to the Thibetians and to the Chinese...says the 'Chinese Itinerary'...Chinese and Thibetians dwell there together. It is thence that the officers and troops which are sent to Thibet quit China. Through it passes also a large quantity of tea coming from China and destined to supply the provinces of Thibet; it is at Tachienlu that is held the principal tea fair. Although the inhabitants of this canton are very addicted to the worship of Buddha, they seek to get a little profit...

The town has a predominantly Han population. It is well-stocked with stores and markets and makes a convenient stopping-point. On the fourth day of the fourth lunar month there is a major festival with horse-racing, dancing, etc.

There are three or four lamaseries in town in various stages of reconstruction. The most active is **Nanwusi** in the western part of the town on the north bank of the Zheduo River. **Kangding Da Lamasi** is the most picturesque, sitting on a mountain 500 metres above the north side of town; the five pavilions and surrounding trails afford good views of Kangding and nearby snow peaks.

Foreigners are usually directed to the *Ganzijun Fenqu No 2 Hotel*, a truck stop with rooms for Y10.

One recently opened area near Kangding is the **Hailuogou Glacier Park** – a must for

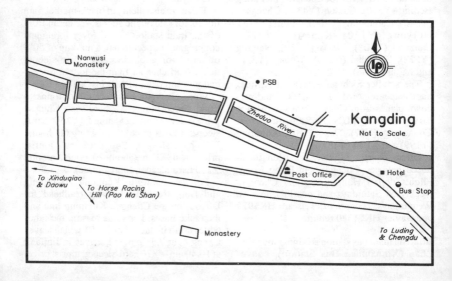

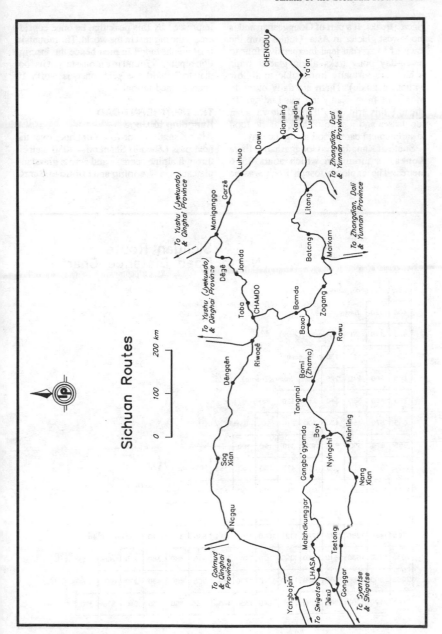

Sichuan Routes

To Yushu (Jyekundo) & Qinghai Province

To Zhongdian, Dali & Yunnan Province

To Zhongdian, Dali & Yunnan Province

To Yushu (Jyekundo) & Qinghai Province

To Yushu (Jyekundo) & Qinghai Province

To Golmud & Qinghai Province

To Shigatse

To Gyantse & Shigatse

CHENGDU
Ya'an
Qionglai
Kangding
Luding
Dawu
Luhuo
Garzê
Manigango
Dêgê
Jomda
Toba
CHAMDO
Litang
Batang
Markam
Bomda
Baxoi
Zogang
Rawu
Riwoqê
Dêngqên
Bomi (Zhamo)
Tangmai
Bayi
Nyingchi
Mainling
Nang Xian
Sog Xian
Nagqu
Gongbo'gyamda
Maizhokunggar
Tsetang
LHASA
Yangbajain
Qüxü
Gonggar

0   100   200 km

glacier freaks. It's part of Gonggashan and is the lowest glacier in Asia. Guides from the town of Moxixian lead inexpensive four to seven-day pony treks along glacier trails (which are virtually impossible to follow without a guide). There are daily buses to Moxixian from Kangding via Luding. To attempt this trip, you'll need down gear, sunglasses and a store of high-calorie food to supplement camp food along the way.

South of Kangding is Gonggashan (Minya Konka), a mountain which soars 7556 metres. The explorer Joseph Rock was so impressed by this peak that he once considered it the highest in the world. The mountain is often shrouded in mist hence the inscription reputedly found in a monastery at its foot that to behold the peak once is worth 10 years of meditation.

THE NORTHERN ROAD
Kangding to Dêgê

After Kangding, the road continues over the next pass (Zheduo Shankou – 4050 metres) through alpine scenery and across grassland plateaux via **Qianning** and **Luhuo** to **Garzê**.

Sichuan Route
North Road Distance Chart
units used are km

Lhasa 拉萨															
285	Gongbo'gyamda														
405	120	Bayi													
425	140	20	Nyingchi (Linzhi) 林芝												
555	270	150	130	Tangmai											
645	360	240	220	90	Bomi (Zhamo) 波密										
765	480	360	340	210	120	Rawu									
855	570	450	430	300	210	90	Baxoi 八宿								
955	670	550	530	400	310	190	100	Bamda							
1120	835	715	695	565	475	355	265	165	Chamdo 昌都						
1455	1170	1050	1030	900	810	690	600	500	335	Dêgê 德格					
1655	1370	1250	1230	1100	1010	890	800	700	535	200	Garzê 甘孜				
1765	1480	1360	1340	1210	1120	1000	910	810	645	310	110	Luhuo 炉霍			
2035	1750	1630	1610	1480	1390	1270	1180	1080	915	580	380	270	Kangding 康定		
2085	1800	1680	1660	1530	1440	1320	1230	1130	965	630	430	320	50	Luding 泸定	
2405	2120	2000	1980	1850	1760	1640	1550	1450	1285	950	750	640	370	320	Chengdu 成都

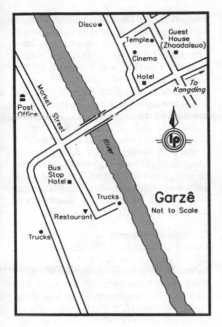

Garzê
Not to Scale

Garzê is a delightful Tibetan village with a monastery.

The **Ganzisi** lamasery just north of the town's Tibetan quarter is worth a visit for views of the Ganzi Valley, although it's not a particularly spectacular structure.

The *Ganzixian Hotel* has beds for Y10, a decent dining room, friendly staff and plenty of hot water.

At intervals along the route I saw the bizarre sight of prostrators, presumably on their way to Lhasa. The plant-hunter F Kingdon Ward came across one of these people at the turn of the century:

I now saw for the first time one of those extraordinary people of whom I had often read, who proceed by measuring their length on the ground over the entire distance, thus acquiring a vast amount of merit. He was a ragged-looking man, dirty and ill-kempt, as well he might be, with a leather apron over his long cloak, and his hands thrust through the straps of flat wooden clogs, like Japanese sandals. Standing up with his arms by his side, he clapped the clogs

together in front of him once, twice, then slowly raised them above his head, and clapping them together a third time, stretched himself at full length on the ground with his arms straight out in front of him. Mumbling a prayer he again clapped, made a mark on the ground at the full stretch of his arms, and rose to his feet. Then he solemnly walked forward three steps to the mark he had made, and repeated the performance; and so the weary journey went on.

At the village of **Maniganggo** the road splits, one fork leading into Qinghai Province, the other ascending to the Cho La pass at 4600 metres.

Dêgê

The next stop is Dêgê, famous for its printing-works monastery which has a huge collection of Tibetan scriptures. Curiously, devout pilgrims wait here under a waste pipe for ink to be drained off from cleaning the printing blocks. The inky water is considered sacred and swallowed or rubbed into the skin. The printers work in pairs: one inks the block, the other rolls the paper across it.

The bridge on the road outside Dêgê is a favourite point for the army of police to turn back aspiring Tibet travellers.

One crafty Brazilian smuggled himself across under a pile of boxes of tea. However, an Aussie couple had the strangest experience when the walking tractor on which they were travelling was stopped and ceremoniously sprayed with disinfectant. After that they were allowed to proceed.

From Dêgê, the road proceeds over the Jinjiang river (known further downstream as the Yangtze), past the army camp of **Jomda** and over a pass at 4350 metres to Chamdo.

Chamdo

Huc and Gabet recorded their impressions in the 19th century:

Tsiamdo (Chamdo) presents the appearance of an ancient town in decay; its large houses, constructed with frightful irregularity, are scattered confusedly over a large tract, leaving on all sides unoccupied ground or heaps of rubbish...Possibly musk, skins of wild beasts, rhubarb, turquoises, and gold-dust, provide the population with the means of a petty commerce, and thus with the necessaries of life...You admire there a large and magnificent Lamasery...inhabited by 2000 Lamas. The sumptuous decorations that ornament this temple make it regarded as one of the finest and most wealthy in Thibet. The Lamasery of Tsiamdo has for its ecclesiastical superior a Houtouktou (Living Buddha) Lama, who is at the same time temporal sovereign of the whole province of Kham.

Chamdo is the administrative centre of the Prefecture of Chamdo. Prior to the '50s it was the regional centre for Kham and had a thriving monastic community. Most of the present population are Han Chinese engaged in trade, trucking or logging. The locals in this area are the Khambas, Eastern Tibetans easily identifiable by the red plaited braid in their hair. These fierce tribespeople have often fought to remain free from the Chinese. In 1950 Chamdo was captured by the Chinese, but many Khambas turned to guerrilla warfare until their base in Mustang, Nepal was destroyed in the '70s by Nepalese and PLA forces.

The only sight in Chamdo is the Jampa Ling Monastery which dates back to the 15th century. Although Tsong Khapa visited Chamdo in 1373 and suggested a monastery be built, it was not until 1473 that one of his disciples started the construction of the monastery, which later housed a community of 2500 monks, with five main temples.

Chamdo to Nyingchi

I found transport from Chamdo with a truck full of entrepreneurs. Apart from selling chocolate, champagne and cigarettes to army bases, these businessmen also brought with them a video recorder complete with Hong Kong-made kungfu movies. Each night we would set up a video show at an army barracks in return for food and lodging. They seemed to be operating on the edge of legality, and this impression was confirmed a year later when I attempted to visit them in their home town in Sichuan only to find out that they had all been arrested for economic crimes.

After crossing a pass at about 4600 metres, the route continues across desolate plateaux to the army post of **Bamda**. Shortly after Bamda, the Southern Road joins up from Zogang. Between Bamda and Baxoi is a dangerous section of road called the '72 Switchbacks'. This dizzying series of hairpin bends drops down to a river. After passing through the alpine lake region of **Rawu**, the road loses altitude down to the jungle atmosphere of **Bomi** and **Tangmai**. The section of road at Tangmai is notorious for mudslides and has reputedly claimed the lives of over 70 drivers in the last 30 years. Be prepared for last-minute warnings about road blasting – our truck just managed to skid to a halt before being rocked by a nearby explosion.

Chamdo

To Chengdu

Truck Depot

Sky Burial Area

Truck Depot

Army Barracks

Jampa Ling Monastery

PSB

No 1 Guesthouse

Hospital

Bookstores

Post Office

Bank

Bank

Market

Cinema

Truck Depot

Hotel

0   75   150 m

Approximate Scale

To Bamda & Lhasa

Roads in these regions are dangerous, and you can't expect more than minimum standards of vehicle, driver or road maintenance. Shock-horror stories circulating in recent years about Jiuzhaigou included a minibusload of Hong Kongers which reported sighting a UFO; another bus-load plunged over a precipice with the loss of all 20 passengers. An outbreak of plague in the area caught two more Hong Kongers, who were immediately cremated.

Transport is not plentiful and unless you catch a bus at its originating point, be prepared when boarding en route for some tough competition for any seats. To maximise your chances of a seat on a bus out of Jiuzhaigou, it's best to book your ticket three days in advance at the entrance to the reserve. Hitching has worked.

Huanglong Si
This valley with terraced ponds and waterfalls is about 56 km from Songpan, off the main road to Jiuzhaigou. Admission costs Y1.5 FEC. The most spectacular terraced ponds are behind the Huanglong Si (Yellow Dragon Temple), about a two-hour walk from the main road. Huanglong Si is almost always included on the itinerary for a Jiuzhaigou tour, but some people find it disappointing and think an extra day at Jiuzhaigou is preferable. An annual Miao Hui (Temple Fair) held here around the middle of the sixth lunar month (roughly mid-August) attracts large numbers of traders from the Qiang minority.

Places to Stay
In Songpan, the *Songpan Zhaodaisuo* has doubles, triples and five-bed rooms; prices average Y5 per bed.

In Jiuzhaigou, the state run *Zhaodaisuo* hotel and the privately run *Sushe Hostel* compete happily for FEC. At places like the *Yangtong Zhaodaisuo*, *Nuorilang Zhaodaisuo* and *Rizi Zhaodaisuo*, prices range between Y28 and Y40 a double.

The hostels charge an average of Y3 per person for a room with no frills. The *Xiniu Haishi Sushe* has been recommended.

Nobody has a decent word for food in this region. Chengdu would be a good place to stock up.

Getting There & Away
Tours During the summer, various companies in Chengdu operate tours to Jiuzhaigou. Some include side-trips in the general region. The most welcome customers are Hong Kongers, who tend to travel in miniature armies and can easily book out a whole bus. Most of the trips are advertised for a certain day, but the bus will only go if full. If you are unlucky you may spend days waiting. Find out exactly how many days the trip lasts and which places are to be visited. If you're not sure about the tour company, avoid paying in advance. If there's a booking list, have a look and see how many people have registered. You can register first and pay before departure.

A standard tour includes Huanglongsi and Jiuzhaigou, lasts seven days and costs an average of Y170 to Y250 per person. There are longer tours which include visits to the Tibetan grassland areas of Barkam and Zoigê. Prices vary according to the colour of your skin, availability of FEC and scruples of the companies involved. An agency next to Chengdu's northern train station was offering four-day Jiuzhaigou tours for only Y140 per person – according to a couple of travellers who took the tour, it was good value.

In Songpan, you can also arrange pony treks to nearby Munigou, where there is a waterfall, hot springs and temple – and few tourists. The cost is Y20 per person per day, plus nominal rental on tents and bedding.

The following places in Chengdu have been known to offer tours: Ximen Bus Station, travel agencies in the Jiaotong (Traffic) Hotel, the Jin Jiang Hotel, the Sichuan Province Tourism Bureau (opposite the Jin Jiang Hotel on Renmin Nanlu) and CITS. These latter two are the most expensive.

A word of warning: several tour operators in Chengdu have been blacklisted by Hong Kong travellers for lousy service, rip-offs and rudeness. Ask around among travellers to pinpoint a reliable agency.

Bus Until helicopters and jets send shock waves over Jiuzhaigou, the local bus remains the best means of transport. It can be taken in one dose or as part of a bus/train combination. Several intriguing routes follow.

The bus going directly north from Chengdu (Ximen Bus Station) to Songpan takes 12 hours and costs Y20 on an ordinary bus, Y34 for a deluxe coach. From Songpan to Jiuzhaigou is another 2.5 hours, Y11. Tour buses direct to Jiuzhaigou charge an extortionate Y134 to travel the 438-km route.

Another option is to travel north on the Chengdu-Baoji train line as far as Zhaohua, where you should immediately book your bus ticket (Y14), stay overnight, and take the bus to Nanping next day at 6.20 am. The trip takes 12 hours along a notoriously dangerous road which briefly enters Gansu Province. In Nanping, another overnight is required before taking the 7.30 am bus to Jiuzhaigou; the trip takes three hours and there is no bus on Wednesdays.

A third option is to take a train or bus to either Mianyang or Jiangyou, both north of Chengdu. Then take a bus to Pingwu, where you can change for a bus to Jiuzhaigou. This road is reportedly superior to the one between Zhaohua and Nanping.

Other possibilities include dropping down from Gannan and cutting across from Qinghai.

Warning Beginning in 1990, the ticket office in Chengdu was requiring that foreigners present a PICC (People Insurance Company of China) card certifying that they're carrying a PICC insurance policy for bus travel in northern Sichuan (the same applies for most of Gansu Province further north). This policy apparently follows from a lawsuit brought upon the Chinese government by the family of a Japanese tourist who was killed in a bus crash in the Jiuzhaigou area. The card costs Y20 and is available from the PICC office on Renmin Donglu in Chengdu. The bus station won't accept any other type of travel insurance. It's a good idea to have this card with you at all times while travelling in northern Sichuan – any bus driver could ask to see it.

The Yunnan Route

The Yunnan-Tibet Highway offers an alternative to entering Tibet via the Sichuan-Tibet Highway but it is conspicuously 'off the paperwork trails'. Not surprisingly, only a few foreigners who attempt this route actually complete it. Various checkpoints (Zhongdian and Markam, to name a couple) are now on the alert and diligently turn back those without permits. Hitching on trucks is preferable to public transport. Security officials will usually send you back to your starting point, although they prefer to return you to Yunnan rather than Tibet. If you are in the middle of the route and are questioned while overnighting, you might say you have come from your destination. The best policy once you've got beyond Dali is to keep moving, arrive late, leave early. If you have no luck in town, walk out of town to hitch. Make sure you take food and warm clothing.

KUNMING TO DALI
There are minibuses and buses (mostly soft-seat) travelling by day or night to Xiaguan; from Xiaguan to Dali is then a short minibus ride for Y0.40. The journey takes a minimum of 10 hours, sometimes 14. Tickets cost between Y24 and Y37; the more expensive tickets are for luxury buses and may even include meals. It's up to you whether you want to do the trip by day or by night – the driving is just as crazy.

Tickets to Xiaguan (some departures direct to Dali) are sold at the main bus station, west bus station and Kunhu Hotel, and by tour operators.

XIAGUAN
Xiaguan lies at the southern tip of Erhai Lake about 400 km west of Kunming. It was once an important staging-post on the Burma Road and is still a key centre for transport in north-west Yunnan. Xiaguan is the capital of Dali Prefecture and was previously known as Dali; if your destination is Dali, you can avoid misunderstanding by asking for *Dali Gu Cheng* (Dali Old City).

Things to See
Xiaguan has developed into an industrial city specialising in tea processing, cigarette making and the production of textiles and chemicals. There is little to keep you here other than transport connections.

The Yunnan Route

0   50   100 km

Erhai Lake Park (Er Hai Gong Yuan) has good views of the lake and mountains. You can reach the park by boat. A larger boat runs round the lake; get details at Xinqiao Matou, the pier beside the new bridge.

Places to Stay

The official tourist abode is *Erhai Binguan (Erhai Guesthouse)*, which has doubles for Y40 and dorm beds for Y8. Outside the bus station a sign pointing in the right direction informs foreigners that they should only stay at the hotel. Other hotels with lower prices (Y12 for a double) can be found if you walk in the opposite direction and ask around.

Getting There & Away

There are frequent buses running between Xiaguan and Kunming. You have the choice of hard or soft-seat on a day or night bus. Depending on your bus, tickets cost between Y24 and Y36.

Minibuses provide a shuttle service for the 15 km between Xiaguan and Dali. The fare varies between Y0.50 and Y1, depending on the vehicle.

Xiaguan also has bus connections for Lijiang, Binchuan (Mt Jizu), Weishan and Yongping.

AROUND XIAGUAN

There are several places around Xiaguan which are already on the Chinese tour circuit so perhaps even a big-nose can investigate them on a day trip or overnight basis. They involve just a little trial and error, with no satisfaction guaranteed.

Jizu Shan (Mt Jizu) is one of China's sacred mountains and attracts Buddhist pilgrims, including Tibetans. Kasyapa, one of Sakyamuni's 10 disciples, is said to have booted out the mountain's resident deity and settled down here in 833 BC. The mountain is called Jizu Shan (Chicken-Foot Mountain) because the three slopes resemble the claws of a chicken. The Cultural Revolution damaged many of the temples, which have been gradually renovated from 1979 onwards. Over 150,000 tourists and pilgrims clamber up the mountain every year to watch the dawn. Tianzhufeng, the main peak, is a cool 3240 metres high, so you will need some warm clothing.

To reach Jizu Shan from Xiaguan you

Yunnan Route Distance Chart

units used are km

Kunming 昆明									
398	Xiaguan 下关								
412	14	Dali 大理							
524	126	112	Jianchuan 剑川						
553	155	141	29	Baihanchang					
705	307	293	181	152	Zhongdian 中旬				
989	491	477	365	336	184	Dêqên 德钦			
1092	594	580	468	439	287	103	Gejiehe 隔界河		
1100	602	588	476	447	295	111	8	Yanjing 盐井	
1212	714	700	588	559	407	223	120	112	Markam 芒康

should first take a bus to Binchuan, which is 70 km east of Xiaguan. Then take another bus from Binchuan for the 33-km ride to Shazhi, a village at the foot of Jizu Shan. During peak tourist season there may be a direct bus between Xiaguan and Shazhi.

Weishan is famous for the Taoist temples on nearby Wei Bao Shan (Mt Weibao). There are reportedly some fine Taoist murals here. It's 61 km due south of Xiaguan so it could be done as a day trip. You might have to convince the ticket clerk at Xiaguan bus station that you are not taking this route to Xishuangbanna.

Yongping is 55 km south-west of Xiaguan on the old Burma Road. The Jinguang Si (Jinguang Temple) is the attraction here.

DALI

Dali perches on the western edge of Erhai Lake, with the Cangshan mountain range rising as an abrupt backdrop. The area is inhabited by the Bai, who number about 1.1 million in Yunnan.

In ancient times Dali was the centre of the Bai Nanzhao Kingdom which remained a powerful force until the Mongols invaded in

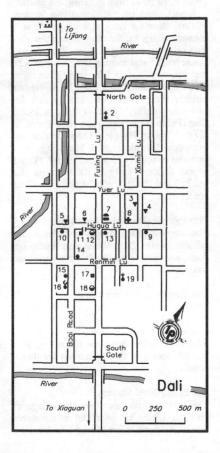

1	Three Pagodas
2	Protestant Church
3	Garden Restaurant
4	Garden Teahouse
5	Teahouse Restaurant
6	Yin Yang Cafe
7	Post Office
8	Hospital
9	Cinema
10	Public Security Bureau
11	No 2 Guesthouse
12	Bus Ticket Office (Kunming)
13	Bank of China
14	Men's Bathhouse
15	Cinema
16	Mosque
17	No 1 Guesthouse
18	Bus Stop (Lijiang)
19	Catholic Church

1	三塔	13	中国银行
2	新教堂	14	男浴室
3	花园饭馆	15	电影院
4	花园茶馆	16	清真寺
5	茶馆饭店	17	第一招待所
6	阴阳咖啡馆	18	汽车站（丽江）
7	邮局	19	土教堂
8	医院		
9	电影院		
10	公安局外事科		
11	第二招待所		
12	汽车售票处（昆明）		

the 13th century and were later followed by the Chinese.

As part of a major drive now being made to gain income from tourism, Chinese indulge their fantasies by acclaiming this region as China's Switzerland; foreigners blow rings of sweet-smelling smoke and hazily discuss a 'new Kathmandu'. Dali is unlikely to match the sophistication of such places, but it's already a haven for foreigners who want to slow the pace, and tune out for a while.

Information & Orientation

Dali is a midget-sized city which has preserved some cobbled streets and traditional stone architecture within its old walls. Unless you are in a mad hurry (in which case use a bike), you can get your bearings just by taking a walk for an hour or so. It takes about half an hour to walk from the southern gate across town to the northern gate. Maps of Dali are available at the reception desks of the two hotels.

Many of the sites around Dali couldn't be considered stunning on their own merits, but they do provide a daily destination towards which you can happily dawdle even if you don't arrive.

Public Security is at the northern end of the block behind the No 2 Guesthouse. Previous goodwill has been overtaxed by some travellers, so this is no longer the place to get a third visa extension.

Money The Bank of China is opposite the post office.

Post The post office is in Fuxing Lu opposite the Bank of China.

Zong Sheng San Ta (Three Pagodas)

Standing on the hillside behind Dali, the pagodas look pretty, particularly when seen reflected in the nearby lake. However, you can't climb them, and the surrounding temple complex is a wreck.

Guanyin Tang (Goddess of Mercy Temple)

The temple is built over a large boulder said to have been placed there by the Goddess of Mercy to block an invading enemy's advance. It is five km south of Dali.

Erhai Lake

The lake is a 40-minute walk from town or a 10-minute downhill zip on a bike. You can watch the large junks or the smaller boats with their queue of captive cormorants waiting on the edge of the boat for their turn to do the fishing. A ring placed round their necks stops them from guzzling the catch.

From Caicun, the lakeside village due east of Dali, there's a ferry at 4 pm to Wase, a pleasant village on the other side of the lake. You can stay overnight at the *Wase Guesthouse* for Y5 and catch a ferry back at 5.30 am. Plenty of locals take their bikes over. Since ferries crisscross the lake at various points, there could be some scope for extended touring. Close to Wase is Putuo Dao (Putuo Island) with the Xiao Putuo Si (Lesser Putuo Temple). Other ferries run between Longkan and Haidong, and between Xiaguan and Jinsuo Island. Ferries appear to leave early in the morning (for market) and return around 4 pm; timetables are flexible.

Zhonghe Si (Zhonghe Temple)

The temple is a long, steep hike up the mountainside behind Dali. When you finally get there, you may be received with a cup of tea and a smile.

Gantong Si (Gantong Temple)

This temple is close to the town of Guanyin, which is about six km from Dali in the direction of Xiaguan. In Guanyin you should follow the path uphill for three km. Ask friendly locals in the tea bushes for directions.

Qin Bi Xi (Qinbi Stream)

This scenic picnic spot near the village of Qiliqiao is three km from Dali in the direction of Xiaguan. After hiking four km up a

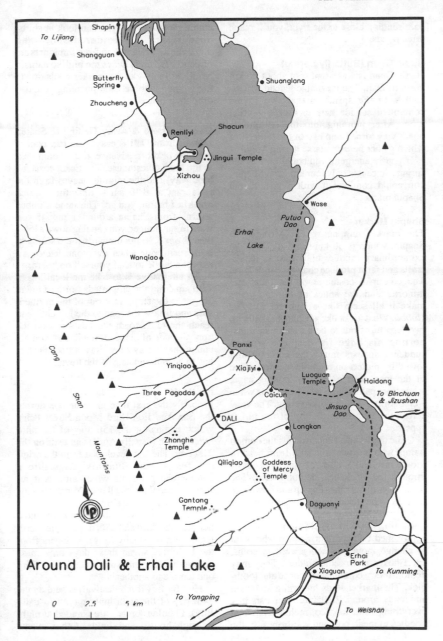

To Lijiang
Shapin
Shangguan
Butterfly
Spring
Zhoucheng
Renliyi
Shacun
Jingui Temple
Xizhou
Shuanglang
Wase
Putuo Dao
Erhai
Lake
Wanqiao
Cang
Shan
Panxi
Yinqiao
Xiajiyi
Three Pagodas
Caicun
Luoguan
Temple
Haidong
To Binchuan
& Jizushan
DALI
Longkan
Jinsuo Dao
Zhonghe
Temple
Qiliqiao
Goddess
of Mercy
Temple
Mountains
Gantong
Temple
Daquanyi
Erhai Park
Xiaguan
To Kunming
To Weishan
To Yongping

Around Dali & Erhai Lake

0   2.5   5 km

path running close to the river, you'll reach three ponds.

Hudie Quan (Butterfly Spring)
Hudie Quan is a pleasant spot about 26 km north of Dali. The inevitable legend associated with the spring is that two lovers committed suicide here to escape a cruel king. After jumping into the bottomless pond, they turned into two of the butterflies which gather here en masse during May.

If you're energetic you could bike to the spring. Since it is only four km from Shapin, you could combine it with a visit to the Shapin market.

Shapin Market
The market happens every Monday at Shapin, which is 30 km north of Dali. An extraordinary mixture of livestock, handicrafts and farm produce changes hands here. The colourful costumes of the local Bai minority and the antics of the fair-goers make it all seem like a film set for *The Hobbit*. What looks like a fishing basket with two legs turns out to be a fisherman transporting his huge fish-traps; a woman suddenly appears round the corner being towed by piglets on multiple leashes; some of the men wear a feathery-looking cape, made from palm fibres, which expands when wet to form a waterproof covering. The view across the lake from the top of the hill is superb.

Quite the weirdest apparition is the demon tramp, who is covered in soot from head to foot. Only the whites of his eyes show through the blackened, demonic face. The black soles of his shoes flap up and down like flippers as he strides down the street staring at everyone and laughing.

In the market itself, you will be approached by persistent women who want to change money or sell jewellery, coins, snuff boxes and needle-holders. They may demonstrate a combined ear, nose and toothpick. The market starts humming at 10 am and ends around 2.30 pm. You can buy everything from tobacco, melon seeds and noodles to meat, pots and wardrobes. In the ethnic clothing line, you can look at shirts, headdresses, embroidered shoes and moneybelts. Prices asked from foreigners are often in FEC and always too high so bargain hard and long – as the market cools down, the women who've been pursuing you also drop their prices.

Getting There & Away Getting to Shapin Market from Dali is easy. You can book a minibus ticket in advance at the booth next to the No 2 Guesthouse. The ticket costs Y7 (one way) and the minibus leaves from the restaurant at 8.30 am – time for a quick breakfast before you go. The same minibus returns from Shapin around 1 pm; if you want to stay longer, you can flag down a local bus. From 2.30 pm onwards there seems to be a rush hour when everyone leaves, so expect a tussle to haul yourself on board.

An alternative is to take the local bus at 7.30 am from the crossroads north of town. To get to the stop, walk out of the northern gate and follow the road to the left until you reach the main road; the bus stops on the opposite side of the road. It will cost you Y2 and probably fray a few nerves since the bus has to accommodate half the town.

Festivals
Probably the best time to be here is during the San Yue Jie (Third Moon Street Fair), which begins on the 15th day of the third lunar month (usually April) and ends on the 21st day. The fair developed from the original festival of Buddhist rites into a commercial gathering which attracts thousands of people from all over Yunnan to buy, sell, dance, race and sing.

Rao Shan Lin (Walkabout Festival) is held between the 23rd and 25th days of the fourth lunar month (usually May). Villagers from the Dali area spend these days on a mass outing, dancing and singing their way from one temple to another.

Huo Ba Jie (Torch Festival) is held on the 24th day of the sixth lunar month (usually July). Flaming torches are paraded at night through homes and fields. Other events include firework displays and dragon-boat racing.

Places to Stay

Just about everyone who makes it to Dali heads for the *No 2 Guesthouse (Dali City Hotel No 2)* on Huguo Lu in the centre of town. The staff is friendly, there's hot water in the evening and rates are low. A bed in the five to eight-bed dorms is Y5; in a three-bed it's Y6 per person. Doubles without bath are Y12 and doubles with bath are Y24.

The only other place in town is the *No 1 Guesthouse (Dali Hotel)* off Fuxing Lu, which is slightly more upscale at Y6 for dorms, Y40 to Y60 for doubles. This is where the odd tour group puts up and the staff are somewhat churlish.

Next to the gates of each hotel are small agencies where you can purchase bus tickets to Lijiang or Kunming.

Places to Wash

On Renmin Lu, the next street south of Huguo Lu (behind the No 2 Guesthouse), is a bathhouse where men can have a hot bath and a massage for a few yuan (rates are posted). The best masseur is O Jing Bao, a deaf man who knows all the right pressure points. His wife has a massage house for women directly opposite the No 2 Guesthouse gate.

Places to Eat

There are plenty of restaurants in Dali serving Western or Chinese dishes. Restaurants seem to open and close rapidly here – do your own exploring or ask other foreigners in town for the latest gourmet opinions. Prices are generally lower at the less frequented restaurants, which can be just as good as the trendy hang-outs where prices tend to rise with their fame.

Several small, family-run restaurants along Huguo Lu near the No 2 Guesthouse cater to foreigners with muesli, yoghurt, pancakes, pizza, sandwiches and other world traveller standards. Long-termers include *Jim's Peace Cafe*, the *Yin Yang Cafe* (also called the *Tibetan Cafe* – with the karmic

'Dalai Lama's Breakfast'), the *Coca-Cola Restaurant*, *Happy Restaurant* and the lovely *Teahouse Restaurant*.

If something more local in flavour is required, try the rambling, leafy *Garden Teahouse* or the very Chinese *Garden Restaurant* on Xinmin Lu.

Things to Buy

Dali is famous for its marble. You may not want to load up your backpack with marble slabs, but local entrepreneurs produce everything from ashtrays to model pagodas.

Several tailor shops along Fuxing Lu and Huguo Lu are willing and able to produce clothing from local batik cloth at low cost and high speed. They also sell ready-made clothing based on local designs but adapted to Western sizing.

Most of the 'silver' jewellery sold in Dali is actually brass. It looks nice but you shouldn't pay more than, say, Y4 for a bracelet.

Getting There & Away

Public buses to Lijiang leave at 7.20 am from Dali Hotel (No 1 Guesthouse) on Fuxing Lu. Tickets cost Y11 and the trip takes 6½ hours. You can also purchase tickets for private minibuses to Lijiang at the office next to No 2 Guesthouse; these are Y12 and as much as an hour faster than the large public buses. The scenery on the Dali-Lijiang road is stupendous in parts.

Polish-made buses to Kunming leave from opposite the post office on Fuxing Lu at 6.30 am. The trip takes 11 hours and tickets cost Y27. Deluxe night buses to Kunming leave at 6 pm and cost Y37 (including a midnight meal along the way). Tickets for either bus should be purchased in advance at the ticket office (corner of Fuxing Lu and Huguo Lu), which is open 7.30 am to 8 pm

Minibuses to Xiaguan leave frequently (when full) during the day from the minibus station on the main street. The price varies between Y0.50 and Y1, depending on the vehicle.

Getting Around

Bikes are the best way to get around. Prices

average Y3 per day, though cheaper rates are available.

The No 2 Guesthouse rents out bikes, but requires your passport as a deposit. The Rising Sun Bike Rental, in front of the guesthouse, has maps of the area and doesn't require a passport as a deposit. A couple of restaurants on Huguo Lu also rent bikes.

DALI TO LIJIANG

Most travellers take a direct route between Dali and Lijiang. However, a couple of places visited by Chinese tourists might make interesting detours for foreigners. Transport could be a case of pot-luck with buses or hitching.

Jianchuan

This town is 92 km north of Dali on the Dali-Lijiang road. Approaching from the direction of Dali, you'll come to the small village of Diannan about eight km before Jianchuan. At Diannan, a small road branches south-west from the main road and passes through the village of Shaxi (23 km from the junction). Close to this village are the Shi Bao Shan Shiku (Shibao Shan Grottoes). There are three temple groups: Shizhong (Stone Bell), Shiziguan (Lion Pass) and Shadeng Cun (Shadeng Village).

Heqing

About 46 km south of Lijiang, Heqing is on the road which joins the main Dali-Lijiang road just above Lake Erhai at Dengchuan. In the centre of town is the Yun He Lou, a wooden structure built during the Ming Dynasty.

LIJIANG

North of Dali, bordering Tibet, is the town of Lijiang with its spectacular mountain backdrop.

Lijiang is the base of the Naxi (also spelt Nakhi) minority, who number about 245,000 in Yunnan and Sichuan.

The Matriarchal Naxi

The Naxi are descended from Tibetan nomads and lived until recently in a matriarchal society. Women still seem to run the show, certainly in the old part of Lijiang.

The Naxi matriarchs maintained their hold over the men with flexible arrangements for love affairs. The *azhu* (friend) system allowed a couple to become lovers without setting up joint residence. Both partners would continue to live in their respective homes; the boyfriend would spend the nights at his girlfriend's house but return to live and work at his mother's house during the day. Any children born to the couple belonged to the woman, who was responsible for bringing them up. The father provided support, but once the relationship was over, so was the support. Children lived with their mothers; no special effort was made to recognise paternity. Women inherited all property, and disputes were adjudicated by female elders. The matriarchal system appears to have survived around Yongning, north of Lijiang.

Naxi women wear blue blouses and trousers covered by blue or black aprons. The T-shaped, traditional cape not only stops the basket always worn on the back from chafing, but also symbolises the heavens. Day and night are represented by the light and dark halves of the cape; seven embroidered circles symbolise the stars. The sun and moon used to be depicted with two larger circles, but these have gone out of fashion.

The Naxi created a written language over 1000 years ago using an extraordinary system of pictographs. The most famous Naxi text is the Dongba classic in 500 volumes. The Tibetan origins of the Naxi are confirmed by references in Naxi literature to Lake Manasarovar and Mt Kailas, both in Western Tibet.

There are strong matriarchal influences in the Naxi language. Nouns enlarge their meaning when the word for 'female' is added; conversely, the addition of the word for 'male' will decrease the meaning. For example, 'stone' plus 'female' conveys the idea of a boulder; 'stone' plus 'male' conveys the idea of a pebble.

Naxi Glossary

The transliteration used for the Naxi language is pretty mind-boggling, but you might like to try the following tongue gymnastics:

Where are you going?	*zeh gkv bbeu?*
Lijiang	*ggubbv*
Going to Lijiang.	*ggubbv bbeu*
You understand Nakhi?	*nakhi kou chi kv?*
Drink wine!	*zhi teh!*

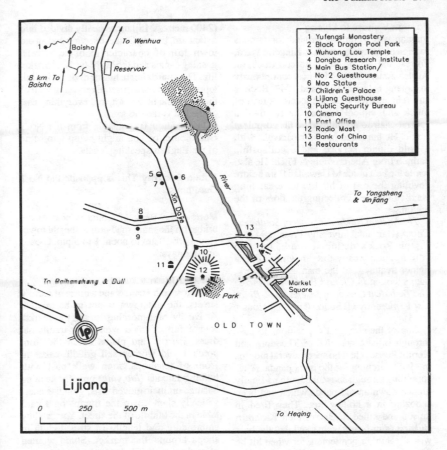

1	雨风寺
2	黑龙潭公园
3	五凰楼
4	东巴研究所
5	汽车总站/第二招待所
6	毛泽东像
7	儿童宫
8	丽江宾馆
9	公安局外事科
10	电影院
11	邮局
12	广播楼
13	中国银行
14	饭馆

Foreign Visitors in Lijiang

Yunnan was a hunting ground for famous foreign plant-hunters such as Kingdon Ward, Forrest and Joseph Rock. Joseph Rock, an Austro-American, lived almost continuously in Lijiang between 1922 and 1949. Rock is still remembered by some locals. A man of quick and violent temper, he required a special chair to accommodate his corpulent frame. He burdened his large caravans with a gold dinner service and a collapsible bathtub from Abercrombie & Fitch. He also wrote the best guide to Hawaiian flora before devoting the rest of his life to researching Naxi culture and collecting the flora of the region.

The Ancient Nakhi Kingdom of Southwest China (Harvard University Press, 1947) is Joseph Rock's definitive work; the two volumes are heavy-duty reading. For a lighter treatment of the man and his work, take a look at *In China's Border Provinces: The Turbulent Career of Joseph Rock, Botanist-Explorer* by J B Sutton (Hastings House, 1974).

One of the strangest expeditions to pass through Lijiang was that of Theodore and Kermit Roosevelt, who spent several months in 1935 searching for the giant panda. After stumbling through snow, the brothers finally hunted down an old panda which had been snoozing in a hollow tree. They fired in unison and killed it. One of their Kashmiri *shikaris* (gun-bearer) remarked that the bear was a 'sahib', a gentleman, for when hit he did not cry out as a bear would have. It was the first giant panda killed by a White man, and the Roosevelts were exultant.

In retrospect, this seems a dubious distinction: latest reports from China indicate that there are less than 700 giant pandas left in the wild and that they are heading for extinction by the end of the century.

Information & Orientation

Lijiang is a small town in a beautiful valley. The main attractions are in the surrounding area, so use a bike to get out of town to the mountains, where you can hike around. You may need time to acclimatise to the height (2400 metres). Lijiang is neatly divided into a standard, boring Chinese section and an old town full of character, cobbled streets, gushing canals and the hurly-burly of market life. The approximate line of division is a hill topped with a radio mast. Everything west of the hill is the new town, and everything east of the hill is the old town.

Information is available from the No 1 Guesthouse, or you might bump into some of the English-speaking locals.

Public Security This is opposite the No 1 Guesthouse.

Money The Bank of China is next to the bridge on the main road beside the old town. Hours are 10 am to noon, 1 to 5 pm. Closed on Mondays.

The Old Town

Crisscrossed by canals and a maze of narrow streets, the old town is not to be missed. Arrive by mid-morning to see the market square full of Naxi women in traditional dress. Parrots and plants adorn the front porches, old women sell griddle cakes in front of teashops, men walk past with hunting falcons (*lao ying*) proudly keeping balance on their gloved fists, grannies energetically slam down the trumps on a card table in the middle of the street. You can buy embroidery and lengths of striped cloth in shops around the market. Some women offered intricate Tibetan locks for Y8.

Above the old town is a beautiful park which can be reached on the path leading past the radio antenna. Sit on the slope in the early morning and watch the mist clearing as the old town comes to life.

Heilong Tan Gongyuan (Black Dragon Pool Park)

The park is on the northern edge of town. Apart from strolling around the pool, you can visit the Dongba Research Institute, which is part of a renovated complex on the hillside. At the far side of the pond are renovated buildings used for an art exhibition, a pavilion with its own bridge across the water and the Ming Dynasty Wuhuang Lou Temple.

Museum of Naxi Culture

Mr Xuan Ke, a Naxi scholar who spent 20 years in labour camps following the suppression of the Hundred Flowers movement, has turned his Lijiang family home into a small repository for Naxi and Lijiang cultural items. Besides clothing and musical instruments (including an original Persian lute that has been used in Naxi music for centuries), his home displays Dr Joseph Rock's large, handmade furniture and has a small library of out-of-print books on Lijiang. Dr Rock was a close family friend.

Xuan Ke speaks English and is always willing to discuss his original ideas about world culture (eg that music and dance originated as rites of exorcism). His home is in the old town, opposite the No 40 Restaurant.

Baisha

The star attraction of Baisha will probably hail you in the street. Dr He looks like the stereotype of a Taoist physician and there's a sign outside his door: 'The Clinic of Chinese Herbs in Jade-Dragon Mountains of Lijiang'. The doctor speaks English and is keen to catch up on foreign contacts. Over a cup of healthy tea, you can discuss herbal medicine and sign his visitors' book. He can give you directions for **Dabaoji Palace**, which has some interesting frescoes. The temple dedicated to Saddok, the patron god of Lijiang, is currently being renovated.

On the hillside, about five km past Baisha, is **Yufeng Si** monastery. The last three km of the track require a steep climb. If you decide to leave your bike at the foot of the hill, don't leave it too close to the village below – the local kids like to let the air out of the tyres!

The monastery has a magnificent view across the valley to Lijiang. The Cultural Revolution ejected the monks and destroyed the original religious objects. A large statue of Sakyamuni was heaved out of the main temple and smashed in front of the horrified monks. The temples are all silent shells and quiet courtyards filled with orchids, hydran-

geas and camellias. Above the temple is a building containing the famous camellia tree which produces hundreds of flowers between February and April. This tree is a favourite with the occasional group of noisy Han tourists. A stone-faced old monk patiently explains its 500-year history; he risked his life during the Cultural Revolution to water the tree secretly at night.

Soaring 5500 metres above Lijiang is **Mt Satseto**, also known as Yulong Shan (Jade Dragon Mt). In 1963, the peak was climbed for the first time by a research team from Beijing. You can reach the snow line on one of the adjoining peaks if you continue along the base of the hillside, but ignore the track to Yufengsi. On the other side of the next obvious valley, a well-worn path leads uphill to a lake.

Getting There & Away If you're going to Baisha by bike, follow Lijiang's main street past the Mao statue and keep to the left. About two km out of town you'll see a reservoir on your right. Turn left off the main road and follow the trail for another eight km. You can also hire a three-wheeled taxi in Lijiang to drive you to all the sights in and around Baisha for about Y25 per vehicle (figuring a half-day trip – you'll have to spend more for longer outings).

Festivals

The 13th day of the third moon (late March or early April) is the traditional day to hold a Fertility Festival.

July brings Huopao Jie (Jumping Over Fire Festival), also celebrated as the Torch Festival by the Bai in the Dali region. The origin of this festival is traced back to the Nanzhao Kingdom.

Origin of the Torch Festival

The King of Nanzhao, intent on securing more power, invited all the kings from the surrounding area to a feast. Amongst those invited was the King of Eryuan. The Queen of Eryuan suspected the motives for such a feast and did all she could to dissuade her husband from going. He insisted he was honour bound to accept the invitation and went to the feast.

When the kings had become properly drunk, the

King of Nanzhao withdrew from the scene, ordered his servants to lock the doors of the banquet hall and then set it alight. All the kings were burnt to a cinder. The Queen of Eryuan had had premonitions of treachery and had given her husband engraved metal rings to wear around his wrists and ankles. On the basis of these rings she was able to identify the remains of her husband, who was then buried with full honours.

The King of Nanzhao kept sending marriage proposals to the bereaved queen. Finally, she realised she had no option so she accepted on condition that she could dispose of her husband's ceremonial robes first. A huge fire was prepared for the robes; as the flames rose higher and higher to consume them, the queen leapt into the heart of the fire.

Places to Stay

The very basic *No 2 Guesthouse* next to the bus terminal offers doubles for Y6 per person with shared bath or Y24 per person with private bath. Hard dorm beds are Y3 per person. Evenings can be a bit noisy as there's a Chinese disco on the premises that operates nightly, but by midnight all is usually quiet.

The *Lijiang Guesthouse (No 1 Hotel)* has more comfortable four-bed dorms for Y5 per bed. A double without bath costs Y24, double with bath Y48. The hotel has two blocks; the one at the back is deluxe. The Hotel Service Bureau is on your left when you come out of the lobby. This is the place to ask about hiring a vehicle, and you might like to look at the excellent map on their wall. Next door to the Service Bureau is the shower room – ask at the reception desk for the precise opening time. To the right of the showers, a few doors down, is the bike depot.

Places to Eat

Like Dali, Lijiang has a legion of small, family-operated restaurants catering to the fantasies of China backpackers. Kitchens are tiny and waits are long (if one of the ubiquitous Dutch tour groups is in town, forget it), but the food is usually interesting. There are always several 'Naxi' items on the menu, including the famous 'Naxi omelette' and 'Naxi sandwich' (goat cheese, tomato and fried egg between two pieces of local *baba* flatbread). Try locally produced *yinjiu*, a lychee-based wine with a 500-year history – tastes like a decent semisweet sherry.

Diagonally opposite the bus terminal, next to the Mao statue, is *Peter's*, a small restaurant operated by a former Yunnan opera diva. Down in the old town, next to the canal, are the similar *Old Town House* (operated by a Bai family), *Mimi's* (Chinese family) and *No 40 Restaurant* (Naxi family). All serve Naxi, Western and Chinese dishes, but according to local wisdom No 40 has the most authentic Naxi food. On the opposite side of the canal, a young Naxi woman had just opened the friendly *Kele*.

The *Lijiang Guesthouse* dining room is not a taste-bud experience. On the same street near the intersection with Xin Dajie is the *Xuefengyuan Restaurant*, which offers a respite from all the foreigner places. The speciality of the house is various forms of *baba*, the Lijiang national dish – thick flatbreads of wheat, served plain or stuffed with meats, vegetable or sweets. Morning is the best time to check out the baba selection. The restaurant also serves other Naxi dishes and a variety of Chinese standards. In the old town, you can buy baba from street vendors. Close to the cinema is a place which serves only baba, noodles and *doujiang*, the standard soybean drink – a very inexpensive and filling breakfast. There are several smaller restaurants just before the entrance to the Black Dragon Lake Park. Xin Dajie has several pastry shops.

Entertainment

One of the few things to do in the evening in Lijiang is to attend performances of the Naxi orchestra, usually given at the Lijiang Hotel. What's distinctive about the group is not only that all 16 to 18 members are Naxis, but that they play a type of Daoist temple music that has been lost elsewhere in China. The pieces they perform are supposedly faithful renditions of music from the Han, Song and Tang dynasties, played on original instruments (in most of China such instruments didn't survive the Communist revolution). This is a very rare chance to hear Chinese music as it must have sounded in classical China. Xuan Ke usually acts as a spokesman for the group at performances, explaining each musical piece and describing the instruments.

Getting There & Away
Bus Buses run daily between Lijiang and Dali. The trip takes about six hours and the fare is Y12 by minibus, Y11 by ordinary bus. Buses to Dali and Xiaguan leave at 7 and 11 am from the bus station next to the No 2 Guesthouse opposite the Mao statue. This appears to be the main bus station. A couple of other places serve as bus depots or sell tickets.

There is a bus connection between Lijiang and Jinjiang, a town on the Kunming-Chengdu railway. The trip takes nine hours and the ticket costs Y18. The bus leaves at 6.30 am from the bus station in front of the Mao statue, where train tickets from Jinjiang to Kunming or Chengdu can be booked in advance as well. The bus arrives in Jinjiang in time to connect with the train departing for Chengdu at 7 pm. During the rainy season, July to September, the Lijiang-Jinjiang road is often washed out and Chengdu-bound travellers have no alternative but to return to Kunming to catch a train or plane onward.

Getting Around
The modern part of town is a tedious place to walk around. The old town, however, is best seen on foot. The No 1 and No 2 guesthouses hire out bikes for Y0.60 per hour or Y5 per day. Bikes are good for anything within a radius of 15 km, but after that you'd be better off hiring a vehicle. The Lijiang Guesthouse hires out Beijing jeeps at Y0.60 per km and Y2 for each hour of waiting time.

Lijiang is also famous for its easily trained horses, which are usually white or chestnut with distinctive white stripes on the back. It might be possible to arrange an excursion on horseback.

AROUND LIJIANG
Monasteries
Lijiang originally had five monasteries, which all belonged to the Karmapa (Red Hat sect) of Tibetan Buddhism introduced to Lijiang in the 16th century by Lama Chuchin

Chone. This lama founded the Chinyunsi monastery close to Lashiba Lake.

About 16 km south of Lijiang is **Shangri Moupo**, a mountain considered sacred by the Tibetans. Halfway up the mountain there was once a large monastery, **Yunfengsi**, which was a popular destination for pilgrims. The present condition of the monastery might be worth investigating. Behind the mountain is a large white cliff where shamanistic rites were once performed by *dtombas* (Naxi shamans).

Shigu (Stone Drum)
The marble drum is housed in a small pavilion overlooking a bend in the Yangtze, 70 km west of Lijiang. In April 1936 the Red Army crossed the river at Shigu on the Long March. During the Cultural Revolution, Red Guards split the drum in defiance of an old prophecy that calamity would befall the country when the drum split. The parts have since been patched together again.

To reach Shigu, you can either hire a jeep from Lijiang or try your luck with local transport. You should try to catch a local bus going in the direction of Judian and make it clear that you want to get off at Shigu. Another useful place to pick up a lift to Shigu is Baihanchang, an important road junction about 24 km before Shigu. If you want to make the sortie, be patient and prepared with warm clothes, food and water.

Hutiaoxia (Tiger Leap Gorge)
At this 15-km gorge the Yangtze (here called Jinshajiang) drops nearly 300 metres in a series of 34 rapids. No kayak or raft team has ever successfully navigated the rapids, though a 1986 Chinese expedition using inner-tube barrel made it with the loss of two lives. A narrow path clings to vertical cliffs at a height over 3700 metres and attracts daredevil trekkers from around the world – take it easy if you're susceptible to vertigo. At some places the gorge is only 30 metres wide. Warm clothes, food, water and sturdy footwear are recommended. Some trekkers also carry a sleeping bag since the guesthouse beds are often short of blankets. A few

hardy trekkers camp out on the trail along the way.

To reach Hutiaoxia, 94 km from Lijiang, take the 7 am bus from outside the shop just north of the Mao statue (Y12); the bus arrives at Daju, near the northern mouth of the gorge, at about noon. The *Tiger Leaping Hotel* has dorms for Y2 a bed.

To start the 30-km trek, cross the bridge towards the cliff and follow a track to the left until you come to the river (a 90-minute walk – or an hour for brisk walkers). A gang of local extortionists at the river will ask Y20 per person to operate the ferry the short distance across the river but with some arguing back and forth will usually settle for Y10 per person (the traveller notebooks in Lijiang are full of maledictions hurled at these ferrymen). The first part of the hike takes about 4½ hours, at which point most hikers call it a day and spend the night at one of two small guesthouses in the village of He Tao Yuan.

The second day's trek to the other end of the gorge takes about seven hours, after which it's another 90 minutes or so to the next village with accommodation, Qiaotou (Xiaqiaotou).

Those who want to see the gorge without actually making the somewhat dangerous trek can follow a trail from Daju to an observation point (and camping area) on the south bank of the Jinsha River.

Zhongdian

Located 104 km north of Qiaotou, Zhongdian is not officially open to foreigners yet, but there's a CITS brochure in English about the area. PSB are fining any Tibet-bound foreigners found on this closed route.

The nearby lake region of Baishuitang is said to approach the splendour of Jiuzhaigou in northern Sichuan.

Luguhu

This remote lake overlaps the Yunnan-Sichuan border and is a centre for several Tibetan, Yi and Mosu (a Naxi subgroup) villages. The Mosu still practice matriarchy. Several islands on the lake can be visited by dugout canoe, which can be rented for Y3 to Y4 per day. Twelve km west of the lake is **Yongningsi**, a lamasery with at least 20 lamas in residence.

The *Luguhu Guesthouse* at the west end of the lake has basic rooms for Y4 to Y7 per bed. A new, larger hotel was under construction in mid-1990. Food at Luguhu seems to be limited most of the year to potatoes and squash.

From Lijiang it's a nine-hour bus trip to Ninglang, the Luguhu County seat, and then a four-hour hitch or three-day hike to Luguhu. In Ninglang a government guesthouse has rooms for Y20. Luguhu can also be reached from Xichang (via Muli) in Sichuan Province.

DALI TO MARKAM

The route from Dali skirts Erhai Lake, runs northwards to **Jianchuan** and on to **Baihanchang** where it is joined by a road from Lijiang. After Baihanchang you continue past Mt Yulongxue (5596 metres), across the Jinsha (Yangtze) River to **Zhongdian**, a small town where the Tibetans dress in a distinctive red turban. From Zhongdian there is also a road branching off to **Litang** (426 km) on the Sichuan-Tibet Highway. Leaving Zhongdian the road recrosses the Jinsha River and heads over Hengduan Shan to **Dêqên** which is still in Yunnan. From Dêqên the route goes over a pass at Gejiehe and drops down into **Yanjing** (Salt Well) which is in Tibet. After Yanjing the road briefly follows the Lancang (Mekong) River before veering off to **Markam**, a small town on the Sichuan-Tibet Highway. For onward travel refer to the South Road via Litang section in the Sichuan Routes chapter.

1	兰 州	14	至 敦 煌
2	乐 都 (瞿 昙 寺)	15	安 多
3	西 宁 市	16	那 曲
4	五 峰 寺 (互 助)	17	玉 树
5	塔 尔 寺 (湟 中)	18	石 渠
6	湟 源	19	马 尼 干 戈
7	倒 淌 河	20	阿 坝
8	青 海 湖	21	花 石 峡
9	鸟 岛	22	玛 多
10	黑 马 河	23	共 和
11	茶 卡	24	监 夏
12	德 令 哈	25	夏 词
13	格 尔 木		

(*Cordyceps or Aweto*), Xining wool, hides, carpets, furs and jewellery. The horses from this area are the subject of a Tibetan saying: 'the best religion from U-Tsang (Central Tibet), the best men from Kham (Eastern Tibet) and the best horses from Amdo (Northern Tibet)'. Huge petroleum resources are now being tapped in the Qaidam basin. Coal, iron ore and other minerals are also extracted near Xining which has a thriving industrial base concentrating on dairy products and textiles.

FESTIVALS
First Lunar Month
2nd day
Lei Tui Hui (Gathering At Thunder Terrace)
1992 (5 February)
Huzhu Tu Autonomous County
10th-11th days
Sunning Buddha, Sorcery Dances
1992 (13-14 February)
Longwu Monastery, Tongren County
14th day
Religious Celebration
1992 (17 February)
Youning Monastery, Huzhu Tu Autonomous County

14th-15th days
Great Prayer Meeting, Butter Lamp Festival
1992 (17-18 February)
Taersi Lamasery
14th-15th days
Turning Buddha Ritual
1992 (17-18 February)
Longwu Monastery, Tongren County

Second Lunar Month
2nd day
Sorcery Dances
1992 (5 March)
Villages in Huzhu Tu Autonomous County
2nd day
Flower Fair
1992 (5 March)
Weiyuan Town, Huzhu Tu Autonomous County

Third Lunar Month
3rd day
Sorcery Dances
1992 (5 April)
Villages in Huzhu Tu Autonomous County

Fourth Lunar Month
8th day
Bathing Buddha
1992 (10 May)
All monasteries

8th day
  Sorcery Dances
  1992 (10 May)
  Villages in Huzhu Tu Autonomous County
8th day
  Spring Flower Festival
  1992 (10 May)
  Qutan Monastery, Ledu County
14th-15th days
  Sunning Buddha & Sorcery Dances
  1992 (16-17 May)
  Taersi Lamasery

Fifth Lunar Month
5th day
  Dang Lei Yu (Warding off Thunder & Rain)
  1992 (5 June)
  Tongren
15th day
  Turning Sutras
  1992 (15 June)
  Taersi Lamasery

Sixth Lunar Month
6th day
  LaoYe Shan Flower Fair
  1992 (5 July)
  Datong County
7th-8th days
  Sunning Buddha & Sorcery Dances
  1992 (6-7 July)
  Taersi Lamasery
11th day
  Dan Ma Hui Folk Song Fair
  1992 (10 July)
  Weiyuan, Huzhu Tu Autonomous County
13th day
  Folk Song Fair
  1992 (12 July)
  Songshuwan, Huzhu Tu Autonomous County
21st day
  La Ye Hui (Nightlong Singing)
  1992 (20 July)
  Guide County
17th-25th days
  Liu Yue Hui (June Festival)
  1992 (16-24 July)
  Tongren County
28th day
  Folk Song Fair
  1992 (27 July)
  Tuguan, Huzhu Tu Autonomous County

Seventh Lunar Month
12th day
  Nadun Hui (Farmer's Fair)
  1992 (10 August)
  Sanchuan, Minghe County

15th day
  Flower Fair
  1992 (13 August)
  Ledu County

Eighth Lunar Month
10th-20th days
  Mongolian Nadamu
  1992 (6-16 September)
  Ulan, Haixi Prefecture

Ninth Lunar Month
22nd-23rd days
  Sorcery Dances, Religious Celebrations
  1992 (17-18 October)
  Taersi Lamasery

Tenth Lunar Month
25th day
  Nirvan Memorial Ritual for Tsong Khapa
  1992 (19 November)
  Taersi Lamasery

GETTING THERE & AWAY
The Xining-Golmud railway was opened recently for civilian use. Roads have been expanded since the initial burst of road construction by the PLA during the 1950s. The major routes are from Xining to Tibet (via Golmud); Xining to Sichuan (via Maniganggo or Aba); Xining to Xinjiang; and Xining to Lanzhou. Truck transport has increased at a tremendous rate – Golmud now has a nickname, 'the city of vehicles'. Air communications are limited to flights from Xining to Golmud, Xi'an, Lanzhou and Beijing.

Qinghai-Tibet Highway

The Qinghai-Tibet Highway is the world's highest road, passing through the Qaidam Basin, and the Kunlun, Tanggula and Nyainqên Tanglha (Nyechentangla in Tibetan) mountain ranges at altitudes between 4000 and 5000 metres. The People's Liberation Army (PLA) completed the Qinghai section in 1952 and the Tibet section from 1953-4. The route is a long succession of desolate runs through uninhabited high

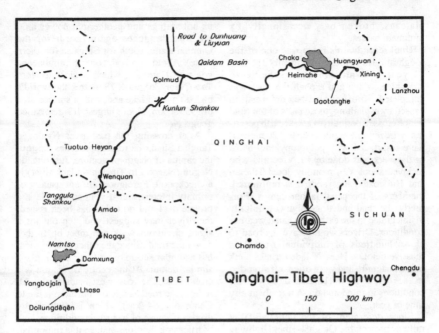

Qinghai–Tibet Highway

| 0 | 150 | 300 km |

Lhasa 拉萨									
78	Yangbajain 羊八井								
317	239	Nagqu 那曲							
453	375	136	Amdo 安多						
542	464	225	89	Tanggula Shankou 唐古拉山口					
1021	943	704	568	479	Kunlun Shankou 昆仑山口				
1127	1049	810	674	585	106	Golmud 格尔木			
1611	1533	1294	1158	1069	590	484	Chaka 茶卡		
1691	1613	1374	1238	1149	670	564	80	Heimahe 黑马河	
1910	1832	1593	1457	1368	889	783	299	219	Xining 西宁

**Qinghai Route
Distance Chart**
units used are km

Most travellers take the train between Xining and Golmud but the road route has been included here for those interested in variety or a direct connection with the Qinghai–Sichuan Highway.

plateaux, broken only occasionally by mountain passes.

Until recently, this route was one of the roughest rides in the world. In July 1985 an 11-year, 770-million-yuan scheme to straighten, widen and asphalt the road was completed. To offset road-bed deformation caused by asphalting, those parts of the road which crossed permafrost areas (earth perennially frozen to a depth of up to 120 metres) were resurfaced with polypropylene. Most of the work was done by PLA recruits who received about Y14 monthly, local Tibetan and Hui road gangs and, it is murmured, members of the penal labour camps. Formerly, the sand and stone highway quickly disintegrated in the extremely harsh weather conditions. Drivers would leave the road to churn hundreds of individual tracks on massive detours. Heavily-laden trucks sank into a quagmire and were often left stranded in a sea of mud for weeks. Bear these weather conditions in mind and dress warmly at any time of year.

Since deferment of the Qinghai-Tibet railway project, the Qinghai-Tibet Highway has become the most important transport artery and the fastest road route into Tibet with a huge volume of truck traffic. Average time for a fully laden truck from Golmud to Lhasa is two to three days. From Lhasa to Golmud, when trucks are usually empty, the run averages two days. For details of transport on this route from Lhasa, refer to the Getting Away section in the Lhasa chapter. If you're going from Golmud to Lhasa, bus and truck information is in the Staging-point Golmud section of this chapter.

LHASA TO GOLMUD

Immediately after leaving Lhasa you reach **Doilungdêqên** where the road branches north for the Qinghai route and south for Lhasa airport (Gonggar) and Shigatse (southern route). At Doilungdêqên there is a small hotel, army barracks, petrol stations and, of course, a checkpoint. If you are hitch-hiking from here, try moving a short distance further on.

At **Yangbachen** (Yangbajing), noted for its hot springs and geothermal power unit, the road branches again: north for the Qinghai route, south for Shigatse (northern route). About two hours out of Yangbachen you pass Damxung which is close to **Nam Tso** (Nam Co), at 4678 metres the world's highest named lake and, with a surface area of 1959 sq km, Tibet's largest. It is also called Tengri Nor.

After crossing the pass over Nyainqên Tanglha Shan, the road approaches **Nagqu**, the capital of Nagqu prefecture. Just outside Nagqu (Nagchu in Tibetan – black river) is a checkpoint. Foreigners are not usually of primary interest, but if your truck ride is a private deal and no ticket has been issued, the driver may suggest you step out for a short, circuitous walk and meet up further down the road. Since the other side of town has a similar set-up, your truck may make a similar detour. At the centre of Nagqu is a crossroads. The road west leads to the Ali region; the road east is the northern route to Chamdo (764 km) which is disliked by drivers because of bad road conditions, lack of truckstop facilities and, so it is rumoured, attacks by marauding bandits. This is the road used when there are blockages, for example landslides at Tangmai, on the usual southern route between Chamdo and Lhasa.

The route continues through **Amdo**, a scruffy, semi-Chinese town where another road branches west to Ali (Shiquanhe) (1336 km) on the Xinjiang route. After Amdo you cross the Tanggula mountains at **Tanggula Shankou** (5180 metres), a pass which is snowbound virtually all the year round.

A short distance to the west lies Mt Geladaintong (6621 metres) where the Tuotuo River rises as the source of the Yangtze: the world's third longest river, with a total length of 6380 km. Just north of Tanggula Shankou (Pass) is **Wenquan**, which at 5100 metres is the world's highest town. It was built by the Chinese in 1955. At Tuotuo Heyan the road crosses the Tuotuo and continues in a flat run over the steppes. You may be lucky and see large herds of Tibetan gazelles down from the hills grazing by the roadside, before you reach the pass

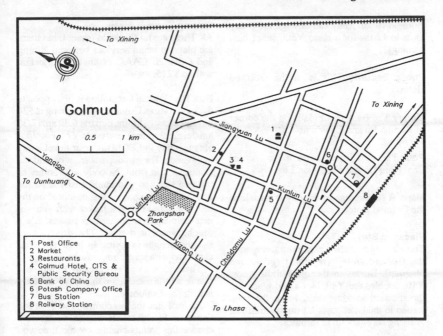

Golmud

1 Post Office
2 Market
3 Restaurants
4 Golmud Hotel, CITS &
   Public Security Bureau
5 Bank of China
6 Potash Company Office
7 Bus Station
8 Railway Station

1 邮局
2 市场
3 餐厅
4 格尔木宾馆
5 中国银行
6 青海钾肥厂总工办
7 长途汽车站
8 火车站

over the Kunlun mountains at **Kunlun Shankou** (4837 metres). The rest of the route is downhill to **Golmud**.

About an hour before Golmud there is a checkpoint for skins and furs and little interest is shown in passengers. Drivers caught smuggling face fines of up to Y300. After running through dramatic scenery with eroded gorges and rock caves (a Sakyamuni

statue found in one of these long-deserted caves in 1918 is now in a museum in the USA) you descend into the flat Qaidam Basin. About three km out of Golmud there is another checkpoint. This *is* for passengers, and drivers who are carrying passengers on a private deal will be fined. Understandably, some drivers disagree with this – so hang on to your fillings if they take evasive action and turn a dried riverbed into a racetrack detour.

GOLMUD
Golmud (3200 metres) is a newly developed town with a population of about 90,000, and functions as a military garrison and gigantic supply station for Chinese operations in Tibet. Its ugly sprawl has no attractions worth noting, so most travellers speed through, spending only the time it takes to arrange onward transport.

Information
CITS The office (☎ 2001 ext 254) is in the

Golmud Hotel. They can arrange three-day tours to Lhasa for a mere Y300 (after bargaining).

Public Security This is in the Golmud Hotel.

Money The Bank of China is on the corner of Kunlun Lu and Chaidamu Lu.

Post The post office is on the corner of Chaidamu Lu and Jiangyuan Lu.

Maps A simple map of the city is on sale at the Golmud Hotel.

Places to Stay

There's only one place accepting foreigners, the *Golmud Hotel* (☎ 2001) (*gé ěr mù bīngǔan*). Dorms in the old building cost Y10, doubles are Y40. Not a bad place but the showers seldom work. From the train station to the hotel costs Y1 on the minibus. Walking takes about 35 minutes.

Places to Eat

Just outside the gate of the Golmud Hotel is the *Golmud Hotel Restaurant*. The food is good and very cheap, but the English menu is almost impossible to read. Right next door is *The Best Cafe*, also good, friendly and has a decent English menu.

Things to Buy

If you are Lhasa-bound and haven't already stocked up on food, clothing and medicines, remember, Golmud is your last chance. Try the department stores and Friendship Store across the street from the Municipal Guesthouse for chocolate, canned food, cigarettes (Golmud has an extraordinary range of imported foreign cigarettes, such as Dunhill, Capstan and Marlboro), medicines (there are plenty of Chinese medicines available for coughs, diarrhoea and skin complaints) and warm clothing (hats, thick overcoats and sweaters). The market has plenty of fresh fruit and vegetables.

Getting There & Away

Air There are no flights at present, but there are plans to begin services between Xining and Golmud. CAAC estimates the airfare will be Y215.

Bus The Golmud bus station is just opposite the train station. Golmud to Dunhuang is 524 km and takes 13 hours, departs 6.30 am (7.30 am during summer), and costs Y24. Foreigners must pay in FEC! Buy your ticket a day in advance. The bus departs from behind the station, not in front. Nobody will bother to tell you this and you could easily miss the bus this way. Luggage must be stored on the roof. Be sure to keep a jacket with you – it gets cold in those mountain passes. It's a rough, washboard road. The drivers take sadistic delight in trying to blow out your eardrums with screeching music.

There are also daily buses to Xining, but it makes little sense to go this way – the train is faster and smoother.

As for Tibet, the bus company will not sell tickets to foreigners. However, on the rare chance that things change by the time you read this, buses depart daily for Lhasa from the same terminal where you get the bus to Dunhuang. It's essential to take food, drink and warm clothing to survive the long, icy night. There is also a deluxe Japanese bus going to Lhasa – this is the preferred way to make the journey. These buses depart from the Xizang Lhasa Yunshu Gongsi which is on the road heading out of town towards Lhasa. Again, they will not sell tickets to foreigners. Should you manage to get a ticket from a Chinese friend, it will do you little good (unless you look Chinese) because the bus must pass through several police checkpoints.

Trying to sneak into Lhasa is not advised. Many travellers have tried – most have been caught and fined.

Train From Xining, there are two trains, one express and one local. The local runs daily, the express every other day. Xining to Golmud costs Y130 in hard-sleeper, Y66 for a hard-seat. Be careful of luggage thefts at

Top: Defensive Yak, Qinghai Lake (RS)
Bottom Left: View of Yadong Valley, close to Sikkim border (RS)
Bottom Right: Jiegusi Monastery, Yushu, Qinghai (RS)

Top: Full moon at sunset over Lake Manasarovar (JL)
Bottom: Lake Manasarovar and the channel to Lake Rakastal (JL)

night – it's best to chain your bag to the luggage racks.

AROUND GOLMUD
Qinghai Potash Plant
(qīnghǎi jiáfēichǎng)

Potash is Golmud's reason for existence. Most of the town works at the plant – it's not exactly a scenic area, but it's different. Only three such plants exist in the world – this one was built with US technical assistance. Potash is harvested from three reservoirs six metres deep and three sq km in size. Tours of the plant are given free of charge. The plant is 60 km from Golmud. To arrange a visit, drop in at the potash company office in Golmud – the tall modern steeple building near the train station. The place you need to find is called the General Engineering Office *(zǒnggōngbàn)*. As you approach the plant, the scenery becomes incredibly desolate – not a blade of grass grows in this salty soil.

XINING

Xining (2275 metres), the only large city in Qinghai, is the capital of Qinghai Province with a population of 570,000 and an area of 350 sq km.

Nowadays, it serves as a stopover for foreigners following the route between Qinghai and Tibet. Perched on the edge of the high plateau, you can pause to consider the direction of your plunge.

The centre of life in Xining is the main street, running from Xining Daxia Hotel due west to the large traffic circle at Ximen (East Gate).

Public Sentencing

The square near the station is frequently used as a setting for macabre rallies where criminals are publicly sentenced before massive crowds. Heavily armed, white-gloved soldiers stand on the back of trucks holding shaven-headed criminals – some tearful, others defiant – by the scruff of their necks to face a crowd that relishes entertainment. Officials sit with microphones behind a long table on the entrance steps and deliver the sentences which are echoed back and forth across the square. The spectacle ends when the trucks roar off in a long convoy, sirens blaring, to the execution site where a shot in the back of the head finishes the day. By late afternoon posters have appeared all over town with newly printed details of the criminals, their crimes and the final flourish of a crimson tick.

Information

CITS This office (☎ 45901 ext 1109) is in the front building of the Xining Guesthouse *(xīnìng bīngǔan)*. The Qinghai Tourist Corporation *(qīnghǎi lǚyóu zhōng gōngsī)* in Qinghai Hotel, can issue travel permits more readily than CITS and seem to be more knowledgeable. It costs about Y400 FEC per person for one-way tours to Lhasa although you'd probably manage a cheaper arrangement from Golmud.

Tours are also arranged to places on and around Qinghai Lake. Depending on the size of your group (minimum eight passengers, otherwise no tour) and the itinerary, you'll pay between Y45 and Y92 per person – excluding the cost of food and accommodation.

Public Security This is now on Bei Dajie, It's open from 9 am to noon and 2.30 to 6 pm. The staff speak excellent English (there's even a French speaker), readily provide extensions and know the the rules of the permit game which they observe thoroughly.

Money The Bank of China is also on the main street, a short distance from the mosque. It is open from 9 am to noon and 2.30 to 6 pm, closed on Wednesday morning and all day Saturday and Sunday. Moneychangers also roam the streets and occasionally visit the cloth market, which is down a side street, diagonally opposite the Bank of China.

CAAC Their office (☎ 43696) is presently on Kunlun Lu, but they have plans to move to Bayi Lu on the east side of town. See map for the present and proposed future locations of CAAC.

Maps At the time of my last visit, the Xinhua Bookstore and CITS did *not* have maps of the city. I finally found excellent maps at a

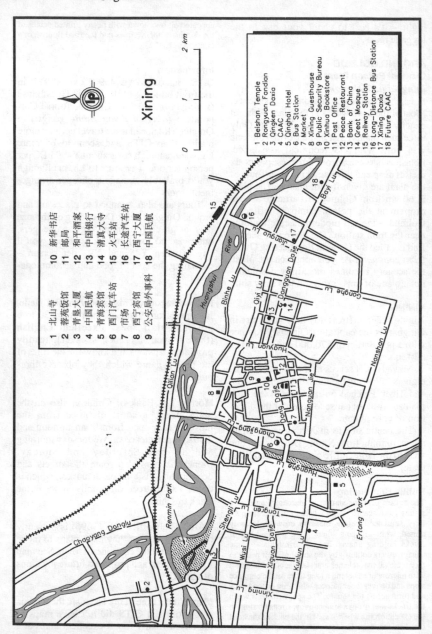

Xining

1	北山寺	10	新华书店
2	蓉苑饭馆	11	邮局
3	青垦大厦	12	和平酒家
4	中国民航	13	中国银行
5	青海宾馆	14	清真大寺
6	西门汽车站	15	火车站
7	市场	16	长途汽车站
8	西宁宾馆	17	西宁大厦
9	公安局外事科	18	中国民航

1 Beishan Temple
2 Rongyuan Fandian
3 Qingken Daxia
4 CAAC
5 Qinghai Hotel
6 Bus Station
7 Market
8 Xining Guesthouse
9 Public Security Bureau
10 Xinhua Bookstore
11 Post Office
12 Peace Restaurant
13 Bank of China
14 Great Mosque
15 Railway Station
16 Long-Distance Bus Station
17 Xining Daxia
18 Future CAAC

small unnamed bookstall half a block to the west of the Xinhua Bookstore (see map in this book).

Dangers & Annoyances Theft is *very* common in Xining. Be especially careful of the pickpockets on city buses (No 9 is notorious).

Xining Climate Chart

Month	Average °C	Max °C	Min °C
Jan	-7.7	0.9	-13.8
Feb	-4.6	3.5	-10.6
Mar	1.8	9.3	-3.6
Apr	8.3	16.3	1.8
May	12.3	19.8	6.2
Jun	15.3	22.7	9.1
Jul	17.2	24.3	11.3
Aug	16.8	23.9	11.4
Sep	12.2	18.5	7.8
Oct	6.7	13.9	1.5
Nov	-0.3	7.1	-5.8
Dec	-6.2	2.1	-12.1

Things to See

Xining is without stunning sights within the city proper. Most travellers use it as a staging-point. Still, there is a charm to the frontier-post atmosphere of this city and you might be content to stroll the streets, rewarded by the occasional sight of Tibetans, Tu, Mongolians, Salar or Kazakhs.

Dongguan Mosque is on the main street. Built in the Ming Dynasty (1368-1644) in the style of a Chinese palace, this is one of the largest mosques in north-western China. On Fridays the mosque is packed with worshippers.

The **Beishan Monastery** lies north of Xining on a mountain top with superb views.

Hutai (Tiger Terrace) is in the western part of the city. Bus No 9 stops close to it.

The **People's Park** has a dilapidated zoo and a boating lake. Bus No 1 stops at the entrance.

Places to Stay

The *Xining Guesthouse* (☎ 23901) is in a large, tranquil compound with a pleasant garden at the back. To get there take bus No 9 from the train station and get off at the fifth stop. This is the largest hotel in Xining with 300 rooms and over 1000 beds. At the gate there is a taxi office. The rear building contains reception, accommodation, Chinese and Western restaurants (breakfast, 7.30 to 8 am; lunch, 12 to 12.30 pm; dinner, 6.30 to 7 pm), shops, telephone service, etc. The front building houses CITS, an interpreting bureau and other offices. A bed in a four-bed room costs Y11 to Y65 FEC. Ask at the desk for the details of the Xining Guesthouse disco. To reach the city centre, walk uphill around the crescent-shaped park in front of the hotel and ride bus No 3 for one stop.

The *Xining Daxia* (☎ 77991) has 220 rooms and 560 beds. Take bus No 1 from the station and get off at the second stop. There is less comfort here but a bed in a four-bed room costs Y6 FEC. Left-luggage facilities are on the ground floor. Hot showers can be elusive.

The *Station Hotel* is on the right of the station square when you leave the station building.

The *Qinghai Hotel* (☎ 44365) (*qīnghǎi bīnguǎn*) was still under construction at the time of writing this, but it was almost finished and should be open by the time you read this. It's meant to be a high-class international hotel for tour groups. CITS estimates that prices will start at Y100 for a double. The location is almost nine km from the train station – not too good unless you want to commute by taxi.

Places to Eat

For a change from the bland fare and hushed surroundings of hotel restaurants, walk along the main street and plunge into any of the market areas. You can buy kebabs with flat bread, Muslim noodles (*lamian*), dumplings and seafood soup. A tasty local dish is 'mutton eaten with the hands' (*Shou Zhua Yang Rou*). In the morning look for fresh yoghurt and a sweet barley dish called *tianpei* – if you happen to have measles, this is supposed to be a good cure.

The *Swan Restaurant* is 10 minutes from the Xining Binguan. Walk up Beidajie St toward the main street until you see a sign on your left pointing down a side street. The menu here, officially titled: 'Menu of China: Western Style of Swan Room', offers translated exotica. Item No 22, 'A Photograph of the Whole Family', has been reduced from Y2.80 to Y2.50, or perhaps you'd prefer 'Dregs of Pork Fat and Chinese Cabbage'.

On the north side of Ximen (West Gate) roundabout there is an excellent dumpling (*jiaozi*) restaurant. The *Heping Restaurant*, a couple of blocks east of the main department store is also worth visiting. In the early evening there is plenty of activity and a wide variety of food stalls in the station area.

Things to Buy

If you are heading for Tibet, stock up in Xining. The main department store has a great variety of goods. As is now the case in many Chinese cities, the Friendship Store is disappointing. Leather goods (shoes, boots, bags) and exotic medicines (musk, Chinese caterpillar fungus and pilose antler) are special buys. For last minute purchases, there's a large department store at the left of the station square.

Getting There & Away

Air There are flights from Xining to Beijing (Y597), Lanzhou (Y56) and Taiyuan (Y422). The airport is being expanded and there are plans to add flights soon to Golmud and Xi'an. Lanzhou has useful connections such as Lanzhou-Xi'an-Guangzhou (Y700; three flights per week).

Train Trains run direct from Xining to Golmud, Baoji, Xi'an, Lanzhou, Zhengzhou, Qingdao, Beijing and Shanghai. There is a special ticket window (No 2) for foreigners at the station. There have been several reports of theft on the train, particularly at night.

Golmud to Xining

Train No	Dep	Arr
508 (slow)	1819	1932 (next day)
304 (direct)	1146	0900 (next day)

Xining to Golmud

Train No	Dep	Arr
507 (slow)	0740	0810 (next day)
303 (direct)	1746	1446 (next day)

From Xining

Destination	Train No	Dep
Beijing	122	1233
Lanzhou	302	0805
Qingdao	104	1824
Shanghai	178	1648
Xi'an	276	1412

Distances by Train from Xining

Beijing	2098 km
Chengdu	1172 km
Golmud	781 km
Guangzhou	3021 km
Lanzhou	216 km
Shanghai	2403 km
Xi'an	892 km
Zhengzhou	1403 km

Bus The long-distance bus station – walk straight ahead out of the station for 50 metres and it's on your left – is now willing to sell tickets to foreigners. There are daily departures in the morning for Qinghai Lake and Golmud (Y59; 1½ days). Buses to Taersi leave frequently from Ximen Bus Station, near the Ximen roundabout.

Those interested in hitching could take a city bus to the end of the line and start there. Buses to Huangyuan (51 km west of Xining on the Golmud road) leave at 7 am from the north side of the roundabout on Shengli Lu.

Getting Around

Three-wheelers and taxis are available at the station. Xining Guesthouse has a taxi office and a special shuttle bus for the station which is probably only for group tours. Bus No 1 runs from the train station, past Xining Daxia, all the way down the main street and then continues to the People's Park. Bus No

9 is useful since it leaves from the station and passes Xining Guesthouse (get off at the fifth stop). Watch out for pickpockets on the buses.

AROUND XINING
Taersi Lamasery

Taersi, or Kumbum (Tibetan – one hundred thousand images), was built in 1577 and is one of the six great lamaseries of the Gelukpa (Yellow Hat sect). Tsong Khapa, founder of the Gelukpa, was born here. The present Dalai Lama was born nearby in 1935.

In the 17th and 18th centuries Taersi was a teeming religious centre with over 3000 monks. Between 1967 and 1979 the lamasery was closed and the remaining monks were imprisoned or banished. Chueshu, a 'living Buddha' from Kumbum was sent to prison for 21 years in 1958 but has since returned. Today, the buildings are being renovated but the number of monks in residence is less than 500. Temple festivities take place on days determined by the lunar calendar in January, February, April, June and September.

Six temples are open. The main temples are: the Grand Temple; the Lesser Temple; the Great Hall of Meditation; the Flower Temple and the Nine-Chamber Temple. The eight stupas at the entrance to the monastery complex are called the *ruyi* stupas. The creation of butter sculptures with extraordinary detail is a speciality of this monastery.

Tickets must be bought at a small window beneath a large map of the monastery area opposite the eight stupas. It is possible to stay at the monastery in converted monks' quarters close to the eight stupas. Rooms at ground level tend to be damp. The friendly staff charge Y10 per bed. Giant portions of excellent food are served in the dining room.

Taersi is a 45-minute bus ride (26 km) from Xining. Buses leave from Ximen Bus Station in Xining at frequent intervals between 7 am and 6.30 pm. Minibuses do the trip quicker for Y5. On one trip I watched a furious conductress jump off the bus in pursuit of a farmer attempting to slip off without paying. The irate lady threatened to

beat him over the head with his pickaxe, newly acquired at the market. Perhaps it was the fear of damage to his shiny pickaxe which made the man pay on the instant. The bus drops you, not at the monastery, but in the main square of Huangzhong. This is where you catch the bus back to Xining.

To reach the monastery, walk up the hill for about one km. On the way you pass rows of stalls selling trinkets, antiques, yoghurt and assorted tourist trappings. At the eight stupas, turn right into the monastery complex. Photographers around the stupas specialise in hiring out pseudo-Tibetan clothing to giggling Han Chinese for an 'ethnic' snapshot.

Pilgrims to Taersi follow a circuit clockwise around the wooded hills above the monastery buildings. You may not have the time or energy to prostrate for about six km but it is a peaceful walk. At the end of the circuit, close to the eight stupas, is a large *chorten* with hundreds of carved prayer stones. The surrounding hills are great for hiking.

Qinghai Lake

With an area of over 4000 sq km, this is the largest salt-water lake in China. Bird Island (Niao Dao), at the western edge of the lake, is famed as a paradise for ornithologists. Thousands of birds, including such rare species as the black-necked stork, congregate here during late spring and early summer. To protect the birds, unescorted tours of the island are not allowed. CITS in Xining can arrange tours to the island and include other destinations if required.

If you want to visit the northern part of the lake on your own (it's not officially encouraged), try taking the Golmud train and hop off about three hours later at Ketu, which is an hour's walk from the lake.

The southern shore of the lake is more interesting, and accessible by bus or CITS tour. The small settlement of Heimahe, further west along this shore, is accessible if you take the southern bus route between Xining and Golmud. It's possible to stay at Heimahe and use it as a base for long hikes

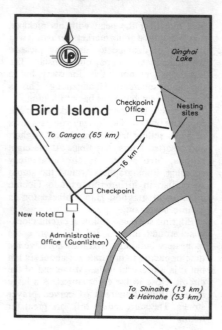

Chaka is a famous salt lake (Yanhu) with open-face salt mines.

Ledu (Qutansi Monastery)
Ledu is 63 km east of Xining. Buses run direct from Xining, or you could take a train.

Tu Autonomous County
Two monasteries (Youning Monastery and Wufeng Monastery) have been renovated in the Tu Autonomous County about 50 km north of Xining. The construction of Youning Monastery was ordered in 1602 by the 4th Dalai Lama. One hundred lamas of the Tu nationality are now in residence (the Tu nationality has close links with the Tibetans).

Laoye Shan
This is a scenic mountain area 40 km north of Xining. Buses run from Xining.

LINXIA
Linxia, once an important town on the Silk Road route between Lanzhou and Yangguan, is now a regional centre for the Hui and Dongxiang minorities.

The Dongxiang minority speak their own Altaic language and fascinate scholars, who believe them to be descendants of Central Asians who migrated to Linxia during the 13th century. Some may have been forcibly transferred to China after Kublai Khan's conquest of Afghanistan, Iraq, Syria and Egypt. You'll see blue eyes, high cheekbones and large noses.

The Yugur minority, numbering only 8000, lives around the town of Jishishan near the Yellow River about 75 km from Linxia. The Yugur speak a language partly derived from Uigur and are followers of Tibetan Buddhism.

Novel River Transport
Not far from Jishishan, at Dahejia or San'erjia, there is reportedly an amazing form of river transport with which to cross the provincial boundary between Qinghai and Gansu. It's all done with a cowhide. The prospective 'passenger' gets inside the *pi fa* (cowhide), which is then inflated by the ferryman who ties the opening up tight. He dumps the cowhide with

along the lake shore. To reach Niao Dao (Bird Island), take the road branching north from Heimahe – a bus goes in this direction as far as Shinaihe (40 km). From there it's a hike or a hitch for the 13 km to the Niao Dao hotel. Here you must register and pay Y5 admission before being shepherded to the island (16 km). The island is a breeding ground for thousands of wild geese, gulls, cormorants, extremely rare black-necked cranes and many other bird species. Note, you will *only* see birds in any quantity during the mating and breeding season between March and early June – worth remembering if you are considering a CITS tour.

In most of the small settlements around Qinghai Lake (such as Heimahe or Niao Dao) you can find a bed for between Y3 and Y6 a night. Food is simple; take supplies and warm clothing.

If you are continuing to Golmud, the only noteworthy stop is Chaka (just over two hours from Heimahe). About four km from the passenger into the river, leaps on top and attempts to steer the contraption as it shoots across the river in six minutes flat – no, make that inflated! According to the ferryman there is enough air inside the cowhide to last for 15 minutes.

Things to See

Linxia is a fascinating slice of Arabia with the full Muslim trimmings. Apart from numerous mosques, the main attraction of the town is the markets.

If you're approaching from Lanzhou, the bus station is just to the left of a large roundabout. To the left of the bus station are rows of market stalls. If you follow the road in front of the bus station, you'll pass a hotel about 100 metres down the road, on the left. Opposite the hotel is a bazaar. Continue down the street and pass a mosque on your left before crossing a bridge and entering a large square. To the right of the bridge, with its entrance facing the square, is the *Dongle Qiao Canting*, an extraordinary restaurant-cum-teahouse on several floors. Pop up the spiral staircase to the top terrace, where you can sip Muslim tea and chew *guazi* (melon seeds) or order other dishes such as *yangrou* (mutton) and *miantang* (noodle and meat soup).

Linxia does a thriving trade in spectacles made with ground crystal lenses and metal frames. Carved gourds, daggers and rugs are other local items in the market.

Getting There & Away

Recent policy changes appear to have put a stop to foreigners taking the bus. You may be referred to CITS to hire a taxi. If you are sold a bus ticket, there are plenty of buses from Lanzhou (west bus station) to Linxia, but it is worth remembering that buses from Linxia to Xiahe are scarce – there is an incredible overdemand for seats. If you want to include Linxia as part of a trip to Xiahe, you should break your journey in Linxia on the way back from Xiahe. It's easy to return to Lanzhou from Linxia; take any of the buses leaving the bus station from early morning until early afternoon.

Some travellers have found a bus connec-tion between Linxia and Xining. There are also buses from Linxia to Hezuo.

GANNAN – SOUTHERN GANSU

The southern part of Gansu Province, mostly occupied by Gannan Tibetan Autonomous Prefecture, is often referred to in Chinese as 'Gannan'. From the terraced fields of the loess plateau around Linxia, the landscape opens out beyond Xiahe in the south-west of the prefecture into vast grassland areas inhabited by Goloks (Tibetan nomads). Some of the heavily forested areas in the south-eastern part of the prefecture are also culturally Tibetan and have recently been opened to foreigners.

XIAHE

Xiahe is a monastery town which sprang up around Labrang Monastery, one of the six major Tibetan monasteries of the Gelukpa (Yellow Hat sect of Tibetan Buddhism). The others are Ganden, Sera and Drepung monasteries in the Lhasa area; Tashilhunpo Monastery in Shigatse; and Taersi Monastery in Huangzhong.

Xiahe is a great place for hiking in clean, peaceful surroundings. Take food, water, warm clothing and raingear. Follow the river or head up into the surrounding valleys.

You may be able to organise transport (ask at the Xiahe Binguan) or hitch-and-walk to smaller monasteries in Ganjia (28 km) or Sanke (14 km). Don't expect to get anywhere with rapidity: traffic in this region is mostly walking-tractors or horse-carts at infrequent intervals.

Labrang Monastery

The monastery was built in 1709 by the first Jamyang Shad-pa, who came from the nearby town of Ganjia.

The monastery contains six institutes (Institute of Esoteric Buddhism, Higher & Lower Institutes of Theology, Institute of Medicine, Institute of Astrology and Institute of Law). There are also numerous temple halls, Living Buddha residences and living quarters for the monks.

At its peak the monastery housed nearly

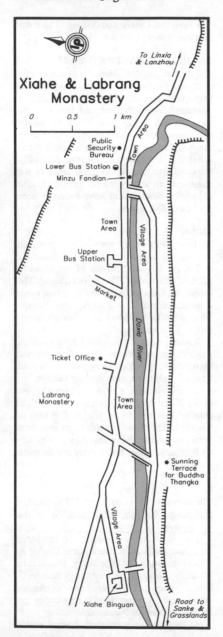

Xiahe & Labrang Monastery

To Linxia & Lanzhou

0   0.5   1 km

Public Security Bureau

Lower Bus Station

Minzu Fandian

Town Area

Village Area

Town Area

Upper Bus Station

Market

Daxia River

Ticket Office

Labrang Monastery

Town Area

Sunning Terrace for Buddha Thangka

Village Area

Xiahe Binguan

Road to Sanke & Grasslands

4000 monks, but there are probably less than 500 today – a token complement for what was once a powerhouse of learning. Most of the monks come from Qinghai, Gansu, Sichuan or Inner Mongolia. One monk said he received Y30 per month from the government; another monk had a taste for Coca-Cola, was learning how to bargain for foreign goods in English and loved roaming in a Landcruiser. There are three *tulkus* (Living Buddhas) in the area. One is in his 80s and lives at Ganjia; of the other two, one is in his 70s and the other in his 40s; both live at the monastery.

Many of the buildings look newly renovated. During the Cultural Revolution, monks and buildings took a heavy beating. In April 1985, the Institute of Esoteric Buddhism was razed in a fire caused by faulty electrical wiring. Apparently the fire burnt for a week and destroyed some priceless relics. Rebuilding has already started and the relics that were salvaged have been temporarily housed in another temple. As a result of the fire, monks are unwilling to use electric light anywhere in the monastery buildings, so take a torch (flashlight).

In the late afternoon, monks often sit on the grass beside the river for a 'jam-session' with trumpets and long, ceremonial horns.

Admission Tickets cost Y6 per person and are sold at a kiosk to the right of a large yard. The yard can be entered on the right-hand side of the main road – from the Minzu Fandian it's a two-km walk. The kiosk closes from noon to 2 pm for lunch and closes for the day at 4 pm. Postcards and brochures are on sale here.

Festivals There are important not only for the monks but also for the nomads, who stream into town from the grasslands in multicoloured splendour. Since the Tibetans use a lunar calendar, dates for individual festivals vary from year to year.

The Monlam (Great Prayer) Festival starts three days after the Tibetan New Year, which is usually in February or early March. On the

13th, 14th, 15th and 16th days of this month there are some spectacular ceremonies.

On the morning of the 13th, a *thangka* (sacred painting on cloth) of Buddha measuring over 30 metres by 20 metres is unfurled on the other side of the Daxia River from the hillside facing the monastery. This event is accompanied by processions, bathing rituals and prayer assemblies. On the 14th, there is an all-day session of Cham dances performed by 35 masked dancers with Yama, the King of Religion, playing the leading role. On the 15th, there is an evening display of butter lanterns and butter sculptures. On the 16th, the Maitreya statue is paraded around the monastery all day.

During the second month (usually starts in March or early April) there are several interesting festivals, especially those held on the seventh and eighth days.

The Fiend-Banishing Ceremony takes place on the seventh day and centres round a 'fiend' who is, in fact, a villager hired to play the part of a scapegoat. The fiend, his face painted white and black, is ceremoniously driven out to the other side of the river and is forbidden to enter the monastery during the next week. On the morning of the eighth day, hundreds of monks in full regalia take part in a grand parade to display the monastery's huge collection of treasures and the paraphernalia of the Living Buddhas.

Scriptural debates, ritual bathing, lighting of butter lamps, collective prayers and blessings take place at other times during the year to commemorate Sakyamuni, Tsong Khapa or individual generations of the Jiamuyang (Living Buddha).

Places to Stay

The up-market place to stay is the *Xiahe Binguan*, the former Summer Residence of the Living Buddha, a multicoloured haven of peace and architectural taste. It is miles away from the bus station (allow 45 minutes for the walk). To get there from the bus station continue straight down the main street, through the village and down to the river. A bed in an eight-bed dorm costs Y7.3; in a three-bed dorm it costs Y10. Staff are very friendly.

Tourism officials in Lanzhou are keen to cultivate Xiahe as a destination for the tour groups which usually stay at this hotel. Last year, approximately 6000 tourists passed through here.

Closer to the bus station and less expensive is the *Minzu Fandian*, just before the bridge in the centre of town. A bed in a four-bed room costs Y6 and a single is Y12. The only soul in this concrete box emanates from the Tibetan staff.

A budget hotel has opened next to the bus station. Turn right out of the bus station and then take the next left. The manager, a returnee Tibetan, is knowledgeable and speaks excellent English.

In the winter, when temperatures can drop to -23°C, wood for the stove in your room costs extra.

Places to Eat

The *Xiahe Binguan* has a restaurant serving good food. On the right-hand side of the bridge next to the Minzu Fandian is a noodle shop which does solid meals and is popular with the monks. There's a small bakery on the main street, just before the bus station, which sells fresh bread before the 6.30 am bus leaves.

Things to Buy

The main street has an abundance of shops and stalls selling patterned cloth, daggers, half-swords, yak-hair shoe-liners (keep feet warm), Dalai Lama pics, turquoise jewellery and trinkets. Don't take claims of authenticity too seriously, and bargain like everyone else. I was offered lynx skins and even a snow-leopard skin for Y3000 – whatever you do, don't buy these skins. If you do, you are contributing directly to the extermination of these rare beasts.

Getting There & Away

Most people used to reach Xiahe by bus from Lanzhou. The problem recently has been that the bus route has been forbidden for some reason and foreigners have been advised to contact CITS to take a taxi. When the bus is in favour again, book your ticket a day in advance. You might prefer to stay the night before departure at the Friendship Hotel, which is a lot closer to the bus station than the Lanzhou Hotel. The bus departs Lanzhou's west bus station (Xi Zhan) at 6.30 am and takes nine hours if you're lucky, 12 hours if you're not.

As our bus rumbled out of the bus station in the pre-dawn gloom, hawk-eyed staff spotted Tibetan stowaways clinging to the roof and sounded an alert which shook them off. After clambering over rough mountain terrain, the bus continues through valleys with fields of hemp, barley and beans; the occasional ruined monastery appears on a hillside with the odd snowcap towering in the background. The bus stops for lunch at Linxia.

Xiahe by Bus

Apart from the great scenery I found the trip memorable for several other reasons. The man sitting next to me was diligently extracting bogies which he then lined up carefully in exact rows of three on the rail in front of us. Each time passengers entered or left the bus, they unwittingly took the work of art with them.

The bus was totally overloaded and all the passengers standing in the aisle had to hit the floor when we passed through police checkpoints. At the third checkpoint, the police nabbed the driver and fined him Y5 for loading eight passengers too many (the other 15 had quickly sat down on the laps of the people in the back rows).

Local farmers had the bright idea of using traffic on the road to do some free threshing. Bundles of harvested corn were strewn across the road in stacks so high that passing vehicles were forced to hurdle these obstructions in a mad steeplechase. The resulting lead content of the grain must have been startling.

On the return journey, officials stopped the bus at another checkpoint and detained a man who was transporting large bales of sheepskins on the roof of the bus. Just before reaching Lanzhou, the bus driver had a face-off on a steep gradient with an oncoming truck driver. Neither party would budge from their respective positions in the middle of the road and were just getting down to fisticuffs when a truce was negotiated by drivers of the vehicles snarled up behind.

To depart Xiahe, buy your bus ticket a day in advance at the bus station. Although the Lanzhou bus is meant to leave at 6 am, the driver doesn't surface until later and everyone stands outside the gates in the freezing cold. Buses sometimes leave from the Minzu Fandian and you may be able to get a lift with a truck or Landcruiser returning to Linxia or Lanzhou. Traffic in other directions (Maqu, Luqu) seems to be slow. If you're heading towards places in south-eastern Gannan such as Têwo or Zhugqu, you'll probably have to backtrack to Hezuo.

Qinghai-Sichuan Highway

The Qinghai-Sichuan Highway runs from Xining to Chengdu. At Maniganggo the road joins the Sichuan-Tibet Highway (refer to the separate route description in the Sichuan Routes chapter).

Although places like Yushu may open soon, at present only Gonghe has been opened and it is still rare for individuals to be granted permits for further afield. If you stay long in one place, 'the men in green' may want to spoil the trip. Xining and Chengdu are both open cities at each end of the highway – a point worth raising to justify your presence in these remote areas. Keep moving, arrive late, leave early, and stay low on the outskirts of small towns. Take food and warm clothing. The bus from Xining to Yushu takes two days. From Xiwu (30 km from Yushu) to Chengdu allow three days.

XINING TO MANIGANGGO

Staff at the long-distance bus station in Xining have been instructed not to sell tickets to foreigners. They refer you to CITS who flip the idea away with the closed area argument. A local bus leaves from Xining for **Huangyuan** at 7 am from the north side of the roundabout on Shengli Lu. Huangyuan is a large town with shops, restaurants and a hotel on the main street. At the bottom of a short hill just before the town, the road forks right into Huangyuan and straight ahead for Daotanghe. After climbing out of a river

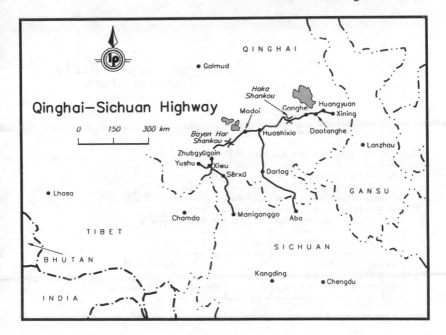

Qinghai–Sichuan Highway

valley, the route crosses the RiYue mountains at RiYue Shankou (3452 metres) about 10 km before Daotanghe.

Daotanghe is a junction for the roads to Golmud (via Heimahe on the southern edge of Qinghai Lake) and Yushu (via Madoi). There is a small shop, a restaurant, a truckers' hotel and a drowsy checkpoint here. The literal translation of Daotanghe is 'backflowing river'. Most rivers in China flow from west to east, but this one is an exception. According to legend, when the Chinese Princess Wen Cheng was en route to Tibet to marry King Songtsen Gampo she burst into tears when she saw her homeland blocked by Riyue Shan. The God of Rain was moved to send a shower. The tears and rain combined to form a stream which followed the Princess on her journey westwards.

The road continues for an hour out of the plateau and over another pass to **Gonghe**. Gonghe is a large county capital. If you favour a low profile, don't stay at the Guest-house (*Zhaodaisuo*) but try the seedier hostels opposite the bus station or get yourself dropped off at the entrance to town, just before the checkpoint (*Dianchazhan*), and try the Muslim hostel. Buses to Xining, Madoi and Yushu run daily. Try the trucks which stop outside the bus station or jump a walking tractor or a horse cart out of town from where you can flag down passing traffic.

Between Huangyuan and Gonghe no sight is more wondrous to the lonesome hitchhiker than the huge convoys of – rub your eyes and look again – brand new Mercedes trucks (tankers and flat beds) purring past. When one of these Rolls-Royces of transport in Qinghai actually stops to give you a ride, paradise is tangible. Forgotten are the long, backbreaking night rides in the back of a Jiefang coal truck.

From Gonghe the road runs up to another plateau to **Haka** which is a shabby collection of restaurants, shops and a hostel (trucks and

Qinghai–Sichuan Route Distance Chart

units used are km

Xining 西宁											
52	Huangyuan 湟源										
103	51	Daotanghe 倒淌河									
145	93	42	Gonghe 共和								
246	194	143	101	Haka Shankou 河卡山南							
420	368	317	275	174	Huashixia 花石峡						
495	443	392	350	249	75	Madoi 玛多					
616	564	513	471	370	196	121	Bayan Har Shankou 巴颜喀拉山口				
720	675	624	582	481	307	232	111	Zhubyugoin 竹节寺			
778	726	675	633	532	358	283	162	51	Xiwu 歇武		
869	817	766	724	623	449	374	253	142	91	Serxu 石渠	
1062	1010	959	917	816	642	567	446	335	284	193	Maniganggo 马尼干戈

buses stop here). From Haka to the pass over Haka Shan (3900 metres) is a short ride. The road twists and turns over the mountains while far below yak trains follow the old road which runs straight. From the pass you descend across a plateau to **Wenquan** (Hot Springs) which has comfortable hostels (one is run by the PLA) and restaurants. The highway then crosses Anyêmaqên Shan

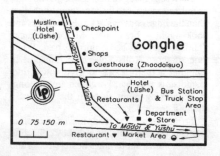

Gonghe

Muslim Hotel (Lüshe)
• Checkpoint
• Shops
■ Guesthouse (Zhaodaisuo)
Hotel (Lüshe)
Bus Station & Truck Stop Area
Restaurants
Department Store
To Huangyuan
To Xining
0 75 150 m
To Madoi & Yushu
Restaurant ▼ Market Area

going over a pass (5300 metres), past a large lake down to Huashixia which has a major checkpoint. From Huashixia there is a road branching off south past Mt Maqên Kangri (6282 metres) to Darlag and continuing into Aba (528 km) in Sichuan Province. From Aba there are buses to Chengdu.

About an hour after Huashixia you reach **Madoi**. This is a dull place at an altitude over 4000 metres dominated by a monstrous cinema which reportedly cost Y700 million to build. Armed guards patrol the roof of a prison near the government office compound. Shops here are uninteresting. The best place to stay is opposite the bus stop which also has a hotel. The truck stop is a five-minute walk down the street away from the cinema and then left. Trucks also stop outside the bus stop. Many trucks bypass Madoi altogether, so you may be better off walking a couple of km back to the main road. Goloks – the nomadic, Tibetan tribespeople from this area – dressed in wild outfits

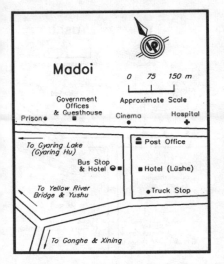

Madoi

interested in visiting the source area of the Yellow River. From Madoi to Gyaring on Ngoring Lake is about 44 km. Hitch a ride on a truck, arrange to hire a vehicle from the government offices or take a guide and a horse. Gyaring Hu Commune has a fish factory with a dormitory, reportedly the only place to stay near Gyaring. Roads in this area are frequently washed out. If you visit during November, there is a Frozen Fish Festival when truckloads of Tibetans come here to fish for scaleless Huang. From Ngoring Lake to Gyaring Lake is another 20 km and to reach the actual source you will need to mount a virtual expedition through the marshy Xingsu Lake area and up the Yueguzongliequ River. Recent research indicates that the real source may be the Kariqu River which rises from the eastern foot of the Bayan Har mountains – happy searching!

From Madoi the route continues up to the pass at Bayan Har Shankou (5082 metres), past Zhubgyügoin to **Xiwu**. Here the road forks: east to Sêrxü, straight ahead for **Yushu**. Security is tight in Yushu, so if Sichuan Province is your goal change transport here. Xiwu has a large, renovated monastery. From Xiwu to Sêrxü the road is currently under repair. Sêrxü is in Sichuan Province. There is no bus service so try the truck depot or the truckstop/hostel (*Tiemushe Lüguan*) for lifts. The highway

ride into town to watch foreigners, who are probably stranger than anything they see at the cinema.

The Yellow River Source Area
Madoi is of special importance as a base for those

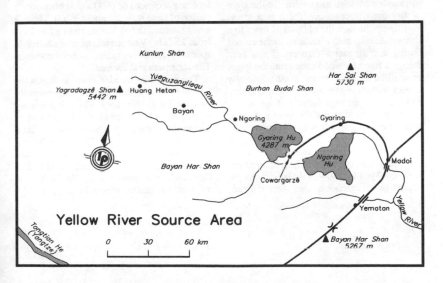

Yellow River Source Area

continues through Chola Shan to **Maniganggo** where it joins the Sichuan-Tibet Highway. From here you can travel to Lhasa via Chamdo (ask at the Chamdo Transport Company truckstop) or to Chengdu via Kangding (ask at the Sichuan Transport Company truckstop).

YUSHU (JYEKUNDO)

This is the capital of Yushu Autonomous Prefecture and worth the 30-km detour from Xiwu. However, the 'men in green' are super-fast at picking up nonpermit-holders. First you are questioned (one official speaks English), then your passport is confiscated; a written self-criticism follows and a bus ticket is arranged for the next bus back to Xining. If you have to wait a day, you will be allowed to wander the town accompanied by a Tibetan security official. Two letters are provided when you leave: one is a pass for hostels and checkpoints, the other is for Public Security in Xining where your passport is sent by special courier. Also included in the service are free rides around town in Public Security's motorcycle/sidecar combination complete with blue light.

Yushu (3700 metres), known in Tibetan as Jyekundo, lies in a picturesque river valley surrounded by high mountains. To the right of the department store there is a street leading up through the old part of town to a stream. A steep path climbs up to the ruined Dzong and Jiegusi Monastery. From here there are fine views of Yushu (note the large, prison-like structure to the north). Friendly monks will show you around the monastery which is undergoing total renovation.

The market down by the river is a good place to meet up with Tibetans keen to trade, barter or just laugh. Yushu, according to connoisseurs, is 'worm capital'. The worms are caterpillars collected during hibernation between April and July. July specimens are considered of inferior quality – the tail end.

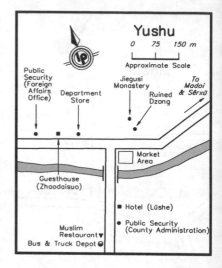

Boiled in wine, these caterpillars (Chinese: *DongchongCao*) are highly prized as a remedy for consumption and general debility. One jin (about 500 grams) equals 3000 broken specimens or 1800 whole ones (much preferred) and sells for about Y200. There is a huge annual fair at Yushu, lasting five days from 25 July. Vast crowds of nomads trek in specially for horse races, archery contests, Tibetan opera and dances.

The most comfortable place to stay is the *Guesthouse* (*Zhaodaisuo*), conveniently close to Public Security. There is a shabby hotel just off the street about 500 metres before the bus station. The bus station has a good Muslim restaurant. The bus to Xining leaves from here every other day at 7 am. Buy your tickets the day before. One foreigner who did obtain a permit for Yushu was a German naturalist researching asses...

Western Tibet & the Xinjiang Routes

Completed by the PLA between 1956 and 1957, the Xinjiang-Tibet Highway crosses the Kunlun mountains from Kashgar, and traverses the desolate Ngari (Ali) region. Now that the Qinghai-Tibet Highway has been turned into a newly asphalted speedway, there is even less traffic on this route, particularly between Shiquanhe (more commonly known as Ali) and Lhasa. From Lhasa to Kashgar (probably the best direction to travel the highway), a direct run averages nine days.

The road passes through the disputed territory of Aksai Chin and is one of the roughest in the world. Ngari, sometimes called the roof of the world, is very sparsely populated with little more than 50,000 inhabitants in an area of 30,000 sq km. This route is not officially open to foreigners; some have hitched unofficially from Lhasa to Kashgar in as little as 16 days, others have taken months. Plenty of foreigners have been fined travelling towards Lhasa from Kashgar, and Public Security's worries about safety are understandable in this instance.

This route should not be attempted without full preparations for high-altitude travel. At least two foreigners have died during the journey. One was thrown from the back of a truck when it hit a pothole; the other died of a combination of hypothermia and altitude sickness, also while riding on the back of a truck. Take a bulging food bag and clothing adequate for altitudes exceeding 5000 metres. One doughty American left Lhasa to hitch through this region with the largest, heaviest suitcase (full of goodies from Hong Kong) I have ever seen. But he made it and was last heard of in Ladakh.

Many of the truck drivers on this route carry rifles which they use to shoot game. Yecheng and Ali are the only two towns of any stature on the entire route. Not surprisingly, the 'men in green' are quick to pick up and fine the 'paperless'.

The road connection between China and Pakistan via the Karakoram Highway is described later in this chapter.

LHAZÊ TO ALI

For a description of the route from Lhasa to Lhazê see the Nepal Route chapter.

After Lhazê you have to cross the river by ferry to take the Xinjiang road in the direction of Coqên. The ferryman lives in the building on the other side and may help with a meal and arrange onward transportation. The road runs to **Raka**, then turns abruptly northwards past large glaciers to **Coqên**. After skirting Zhari Namco (Zhari Lake), the highway joins the main Amdo-Ali road at **Dongco**. Continuing through **Gêrzê**, the route climbs round the foot of Mt Nganglong Kangri (6596 metres), and passes **Gêgyai**, a town divided into two halves separated by about two km. The road then crosses the Sênggê Zangpo River (source of the Indus) and dips down into **Ali**. This is the prefectural capital – a bland, newly developed town with a geothermal power station. The local authorities are vigilant (various travellers have been fined for lacking permits) so the less time spent here the better.

To continue into Xinjiang, take the northern route out of Ali. However, the sights which are a real 'must' in the prefecture are reached by taking the southern road out of Ali towards Burang (435 km). The southern road passes through Gar to Namru which is the turn-off for **Zanda**. Allow one day to travel from Ali to Zanda which is the site of the Toling Monastery and a convenient base from which to visit the eerie ruins of the capital of the ancient Guge Kingdom at **Tsaparang**.

TSAPARANG

The persecution of Buddhism by King Lang Darma during the 9th century scattered the followers of Buddhism far away from Central Tibet. The kingdom of Guge, founded in 866, became a focal point for the

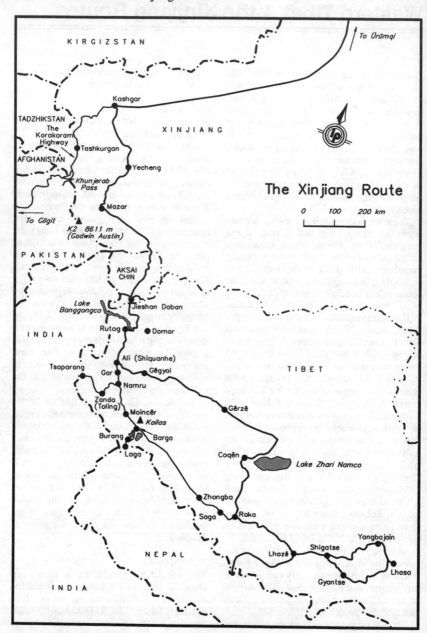

preservation and reintroduction of Buddhism. Yeshe O, a king of Guge who later abdicated to become a monk, sent the Lotsawa (translator) Rinchen Sangpo to India to study. On his return in 978, Rinchen Sangpo encouraged the revival of Buddhism and he is credited with building, amongst others, the monasteries at Tsaparang and Toling. Yeshe O, who had been captured and held to ransom by the king of Garlog, refused to be ransomed, and instead urged that the immense sum of gold collected for his release be used to bring the renowned Indian pandit Atisha to Tibet.

After much deliberation Atisha finally arrived in Tibet in 1040 and spent two years at Toling Monastery where he created a resurgence of interest in Buddhism which eventually spread all over Tibet. Although Central Tibet became, once again, the principal focus of Buddhism in Tibet, Tsaparang and Toling retained their importance within Western Tibet as political and religious centres until the 17th century.

According to some sources, a two-year siege by Kashmiris led to the fall of Tsaparang and the destruction of the Guge Kingdom. According to others, the King of Guge angered his lamas by favouring a Portuguese missionary priest, Father Andrade, who had arrived in 1624. Jealous of the favour, the lamas revolted during Father Andrade's absence, and in the ensuing factional fighting the kingdom of Guge tore itself apart. Today, more than 300 years later, all that remains is a huge complex of caves, living quarters and temples, some of it in an excellent state of preservation, the rest in ruins.

From **Namru** the road continues south through Moincêr to **Burang**. From Ali to Burang takes an average of two days with an overnight stop in Moincêr. Laga Monastery lies 29 km south of Burang but the main

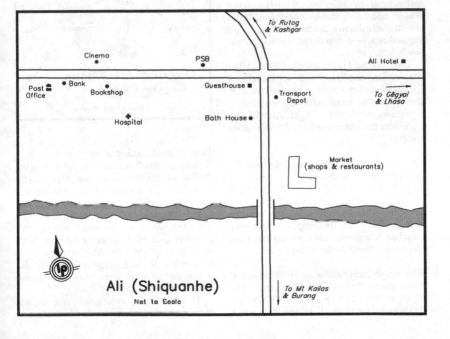

Ali (Shiquanhe)
Not to Scale

To Rutog & Kashgar

Cinema
PSB
Ali Hotel ■

Post Office
Bank
Bookshop
Guesthouse ■
Transport Depot
To Gêgyai & Lhasa

Hospital
Bath House ●

Market (shops & restaurants)

To Mt Kailas & Burang

attraction of Burang is its proximity to Mt Kailas and Lake Manasarovar – two of the most sacred sites in all Asia.

MT KAILAS & LAKE MANASAROVAR

For Hindus, Jains, Buddhists and adherents of Bon this region is the abode of the gods and has, for thousands of years, been a goal of utmost sanctity for pilgrims.

Mt Kailas (6714 metres), known in Tibet as Tise (the Peak) of Kang Rinpoche (Jewel of Snows), is the home of the Hindu god Shiva and his consort Devi; for Tibetans, it is the home of the god Demchog and his consort Dorje Phangmo. It is here, according to legend, that Milarepa, a great Tibetan Yogi and master of Tantric Buddhism, vied with Naro-Bonchung, a grand master of Bon, to prove the superiority of Buddhism. Many contests took place, but the final one was to see who could first reach the summit of Mt Kailas at the crack of dawn. Riding his *damaru* (ritual drum) Naro-Bonchung flew towards the peak only to be overtaken at the last second by Milarepa. Naro-Bonchung was so astonished that he let go of his drum which crashed down the mountain leaving a vertical scar – a distinctive feature of the south face.

Two lakes, Manasarovar (also called Mapam Tso) and Rakastal, lie at the southern foot of Mt Kailas. Rakastal is associated with the forces of darkness, whereas Manasarovar represents the forces of light. Also in this region are the sources of four of Asia's major rivers:

Senge-Khambab, 'river issuing from the lion's mouth' – the Indus;
Mapchu-Khambab, 'river issuing from the peacock's mouth' – the Karnali;
Tamchok-Khambab, 'river issuing from the horse's mouth – the Brahmaputra (Tsangpo);
Lanchen-Khambab, 'river issuing from the elephant's mouth' – the Sutlej.

Pilgrims perform *parikarama* (circumambulation in a clockwise direction) around Lake Manasarovar (4588 metres) and Mt Kailas.

Many Indian pilgrims approach on a trek

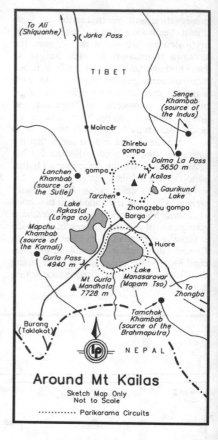

Around Mt Kailas

Sketch Map Only
Not to Scale
.... Parikarama Circuits

from Burang, taking about two days from Burang to Lake Manasarovar. After crossing the foot of Mt Gurla Mandhata (7728 metres) at the Gurla Pass, there is a superb panoramic view of the region before a descent to the lakes. During the circuit around Lake Manasarovar (total area about 350 sq km), pilgrims pick up pebbles or fill containers with the holy water. Both are prized gifts on their return. Ritual bathing in the lake is also performed to wash away sins. One circuit takes about three days (100 km).

The final and most arduous parikarama is that of Mt Kailas which takes between two and three days (55 km). It is said that those who complete this circuit 108 times are assured entry into nirvana.

The Kailas Circuit

Generally speaking, if you plan to do this circuit it's best to be totally self-sufficient, as if you were going bush – which you are!

Tibetans do the parikarama of Kailas in one day (12-14 hours). However, it takes most Westerners three days – and tiring ones at that. You need to be prepared with food and sleeping bag; in the warmer months you can possibly do without a tent or stove.

The starting point is Daerjing Lake (4500 metres) known as Tarchen. There is a place to stay *(Indian Pilgrim Resthouse)* run by a Tibetan called Dorje who speaks good English. There's no food. Prices are Y15 for a bed, Y5 for a concrete-floored room with nothing. Dorje will look after excess baggage while you do the circuit. You may be required to pay a circuit fee of up to Y60.

The path is very clear and starts just behind the resthouse. The following timings are for an average, fit walker. About 2½ to three hours from Tarchen is a gompa, just as you turn into a narrow river valley/canyon. During these first few hours you enjoy a stunning view across the plain to Rakas Tal and the snowcapped Himalaya in the distance.

From the first gompa to Zhirebu gompa is about five hours. Zhirebu is easy to miss as it's very small and you have to leave the path and cross the river to get to it. You can stay there on a kind of platform just inside the gate. At least it has a roof and three walls, providing some shelter. For Y1, the attendant may provide some tea and tsampa.

After Zhirebu you start climbing in earnest. Including rest stops, it takes about six hours to reach the top of the pass. There are many false summits – when you reach a place where there's a pile of cast-off clothes you are only halfway. The top of the pass is unmistakable, with the usual prayer flags. The pass is called Dolma La and lies at 5650 metres. The descent on the other side is rocky and steep, with a flattish section in the middle where the path at times is hard to follow. Just keep your eyes peeled for the chortens (piles of stones). It takes 1½ hours to come down to a beautiful grassy river valley. From here it's another 3½ to four hours to the next gompa. Near that gompa – 10 minutes or so further on – are a couple of caves.

It's a tiring section. One group of exhausted trekkers only walked for half an hour along the valley before reaching some nomads who took pity on them and gave them a spare tent supplied even with a stove for burning yak dung (very smoky if not properly dry!). Despite the tent it was still freezing.

From Zhongzebu gompa it's four to five hours back to Tarchen. Note this 15 km is basically downhill (a few ups) while the first 15 km is a gradual climb, hence the difference in time.

ALI TO KASHGAR

From Ali the Xinjiang-Tibet Highway runs north to Rutog, passes Lake Banggongco (renowned for its Bird Island) and crosses the Kunlun mountains over Lanek La Pass (5406 metres). This area around Aksai Chin is specially sensitive since it is the subject of a border dispute with India. India claims that 56,000 sq km of its territory is at present under Chinese control, a large chunk of that figure being in the Aksai Chin area. This bleak and uninhabited area is so remote that the Indian government did not find out the Chinese had built a road through it until two years after the event. Mazar is close to K2 (8611 metres) – the second highest peak in the world. The trek from Mazar to the base camp (4300 metres) on the Sarpo Laggo River takes six days. The trek ascends the Sumkwat Gorge, crosses the Aghil Pass (5300 metres), drops down to the Shaksgam River and continues along it until the junction with the Sarpo Laggo River.

From Mazar the highway crosses the Chiragsaldi Pass (5400 metres) and the Akazu Pass (3550 metres) to reach Yecheng. This is a large town with vigilant authorities who have fined foreigners between Y100

Xinjiang Route Distance Chart

units used are km

Lhasa 拉萨													
340	Shigatse 日喀则												
491	151	Lhazê 拉孜											
732	392	241	Raka 拉嘎										
974	634	483	242	Coqên 措勤									
1252	912	761	520	278	Gêrzê 改则								
1637	1297	1146	905	663	385	Gêgyai 革吉							
1749	1409	1258	1017	775	497	112	Ali (Shiquanhe) 狮泉河						
1866	1526	1375	1134	892	614	229	117	Rutog 日土					
2015	1675	1524	1283	1041	763	378	266	149	Domar 多玛				
2151	1811	1660	1419	1177	899	514	402	285	136	Jieshan Daban 界山大板			
2607	2267	2116	1875	1633	1355	970	858	741	592	456	Mazar 玛扎		
2856	2516	2365	2124	1882	1604	1219	1107	990	841	705	249	Yecheng 叶城	
3105	2765	2614	2373	2131	1853	1468	1356	1239	1090	954	498	249	Kashgar 喀什

From Lhazê the old Lhasa–Ladakh route (usually avoided by trucks heading for Xinjiang) runs parallel with the Himalayas to Burang.

and Y150 for lacking permits and then turned them back (this applies especially for those coming from Kashgar). From Yecheng it is a flat run around the Takla Makan Desert to Kashgar.

KASHGAR

Kashgar, called Kashi in Chinese, was once a major halt for caravans on the Silk Road. It is now a prosperous commercial centre with a population composed of Uigur, Tajik and Kirgiz nationalities. Here it is the Han Chinese who are in the minority. The Uighur phrase list at the end of this chapter may help when negotiating for transport to or from Kashgar.

Off Limits?
Whether or not you will be able to visit Kashgar by the time you read this is uncertain. Serious anti-Chinese rioting broke out in April 1990. Apparently, several Chinese were killed by an Uigur mob and troops were rushed into Kashgar. Foreigners were kicked out so there would be no witnesses to the crackdown that followed. The border with Pakistan was closed due to 'landslides'. No one but the Chinese government knows just how many were arrested or killed. The Chinese have remained tight-lipped about the whole affair, and the outside world will probably never know exactly what happened.

Kashgar

0   0.5   1 km

Sunday
Market
Area

Main
Bazaar
Area

East
Lake

To Pakistan

Renmin Xilu   Renmin Donglu

To Yecheng & Hotan

Kezil River

1 Oasis Hotel
2 Seman Hotel
3 Friendship Hotel
4 Public Security Bureau
5 Chini Bagh Hotel
6 CAAC
7 Id Kah Mosque
8 CITS
9 Bank of China
10 Post Office
11 Mao Statue
12 Local Bus station
13 Long-Distance Bus Station
14 Renmin Park & Zoo
15 Abakh Hoja Tomb
16 Kashgar Guesthouse
17 Saytalasrahan's Tomb

1 绿洲宾馆	10 邮局
2 色满宾馆	11 毛泽东塑像
3 友谊宾馆	12 市公共汽车站
4 公安局外事科	13 长途汽车站
5 其尼巴合宾馆	14 人民公园
6 中国民航	15 香妃墓
7 艾提尕清真寺	16 喀什噶尔宾馆
8 中国国际旅行社	17 赛衣提艾里艾斯拉罕墓
9 中国银行	

The effect on travellers is that if you're coming from Ürümqi, both Kashgar and the Pakistani border can only be reached by taking an expensive CITS tour. Ironically, travellers coming from Pakistan are still getting into Kashgar without a tour.

Prices announced by CITS were as follows: from Ürümqi, Y1700 for a two-day trip to Kashgar (flying both ways). To cross the Pakistani border with a two-day stop-off in Kashgar will cost Y3000. These prices can probably be bargained down somewhat, especially if you can form a small group with other travellers. Prices include transport, hotels and a guide. Arrangements are to be made with CITS in Ürümqi. Unfortunately, this particular CITS office is a bastion of avarice and incompetence – you might be able to negotiate more favourable terms with CTS in the Overseas Chinese Hotel in Ürümqi or the Xinjiang Overseas Tourist Corporation (☎ 78691, 23782) (*xīnjiāng hǎiwài lüyóu zǒng gōngsī*), 32 Xinhua Nanlu also in Ürümqi. Many travellers trying to book trips to Kashgar have expressed extreme dissatisfaction with the Ürümqi CITS office.

Information
CITS The office (☎ 3156) is just off of Jiefang Beilu (see map).

Money The Bank of China (☎ 2461) is on Renmin Xilu near the post office. The money-changing brigade will pursue you all over Kashgar. Cash US dollars are snapped up for Sino-Pakistani trade and by Kashgaris preparing for pilgrimage to Mecca.

CAAC This office (☎ 2113) is on Jiefang Beilu north of the Id Kah Mosque (see map).

Maps Fairly accurate maps of Kashgar are available from some of the hotels. There's one (in Chinese) in the waiting hall of the long-distance bus station which may help you orientate yourself.

Things to See
The Bazaar The bazaar area lies around the Id Kah Mosque and square. Merchants and dealers beckon, haggle, swear and doze. Items for sale include carpets; pewter, brass, and copper articles; Yengisar daggers; fresh and dried fruits; local tobacco sold with papers (the local gazette torn into thin strips) to roll your own; and imported and smuggled cigarettes.

An astounding sight, not to be missed, is the Sunday animal market in a large field about half an hour's walk east of the main bazaar. Amidst clouds of dust and the thunder of hooves, a biblical-looking event takes place. Donkeys, horses, camels, Karakoram goats, fat-tailed sheep, cattle – the market has them all. Camel carts lurch off carrying door-frames and window-frames...

Since many of the locals make the pilgrimage to Mecca, there is a good market for money changing in the bazaar. Dress as you would for any Muslim country. Western women clad in shorts, T-shirts or thin blouses have been molested by cheeky or irate locals.

The Id Kah Mosque The mosque, recently renovated, has a strong central Asian atmosphere. A strange assortment of beggars, pilgrims and mullahs takes refuge in the shady courtyard. During the Korban Festival (late August-early September) a band of musicians perches precariously on top of the portal, whilst a wild assortment of nationalities gyrate below.

The Abakh Khoja Tomb To reach this tomb takes about an hour on foot from the Kashgar Guesthouse. The tomb of Xiang Fei, a concubine of the Emperor Qianlong, and those of her relatives are in the mosque. The cemetery behind the mosque has some holes in the graves with the occasional bone poking through. Tickets cost Y0.50 and a drowsy guide provides a laconic tour: 'concubine mother...concubine father...concubine brother...other brother...'

Places to Stay

If you are forced to visit Kashgar on a CITS group tour, you won't have much choice about where you stay – CITS will make all the arrangements for accommodation and you'll be required to pay in advance. If you manage to get in as an individual traveller, you can choose from the few places that accept foreigners.

The *Seman Hotel* (☎ 2129, 2060) (*sèmǎn bīnguǎn*) is in the former Russian consulate on the western edge of town. It's a pleasant place to stay, with relaxing grounds. A double with bath costs Y35 – check to make sure the plumbing works. A bed in the dormitory costs Y10. At the moment, this is probably the best place to stay.

The *Kashgar Guesthouse* (☎ 2367, 2368) (*kāshí gě'ěr bīnguǎn*) is the top-rated hotel in town and is up to the same good standard of any other basic Chinese tourist hotel further east. The problem with this place is that it's far from the town centre – the main intersection is a good hour's walk away, and there's no bus. You can usually wave down a jeep or a truck, or hitch a lift on a donkey cart. Double rooms in building No 1 go for Y100 (with shower and toilet). A bed in a four-bed room in one of the other buildings is Y12, but the building is a real echo chamber. There's a post office, dining rooms, souvenir shops and a small store (just inside the front gate) which sells bottled fruit.

There are three other hotels in Kashgar that are supposed to take foreigners, but at the time of writing this they were either closed or 'temporarily off limits' and filled with Han Chinese plainclothes police. The following information is supplied in case things change for the better.

The *Chini Bagh Hotel* (☎ 2291, 2103) (*qínîbāhé bīnguan*) in the former British consulate used to be popular with the Pakistani traders commuting along the Karakoram Highway. Doubles without bath cost Y30; a bed in a chaotic six-bed room costs Y10. The shower block is a slime pit. Barely a trace of the colonial grandeur is left. There are rumours that this hotel will be torn down soon.

The *Oasis Hotel* (*lüzhōu bīnguǎn*) is opposite the Seman Hotel. Assuming they reopen to foreigners, dorm beds cost Y12 in a four-bed room. No showers – use those at the Seman Hotel.

The *Friendship Hotel* (*yǒuyì bīnguǎn*) is no longer friendly to foreigners. It's near the Id Kah Mosque. Dorms are Y15 and doubles are Y50.

Places to Eat

You won't starve in Kashgar, but restaurant city it ain't. The *Kashgar Guesthouse* serves Chinese meals for Y25 each!

For a wide variety of Uigur foods, pop into the food market close to the Id Kah Mosque. There you can try shish kebab, rice & mutton, fried fish, *samsa* (rectangles of crisp pastry enclosing fried mince-meat) and fruit. To the left of the mosque is a teahouse with a balcony above the bustling crowds. Flat bread and shish kebab are sold at the huddle of stalls on the main road, just west of the big square opposite the Mao statue. There are a couple of excellent ice cream stalls here too – very cold and very vanilla. There are more ice cream stalls in the Id Kah Square, and you should find eggs and roast chicken being sold near the main intersection at night.

Bottled and canned fruit are available from the large food store opposite the Id Kah Square on the main north-south road. There's a smaller store next to the cinema on the main intersection selling the same. You can buy eggs near the long-distance bus station; the ones painted red are hard-boiled.

The *Oasis Café* serves good Western food and is underneath the Friendship Hotel. However, this restaurant now charges Western prices. The *Seman Restaurant*, across the street from the Seman Hotel, isn't bad but you can eat more cheaply in the market areas.

Getting There & Away

Air There are daily flights from Kashgar to Ürümqi, and the fare is Y435. CAAC is on the main street north of the Id Kah Mosque. The flight takes slightly under two hours.

Bus At the time of writing this, CITS was saying foreigners can only go to Kashgar by air. However, if you manage to get into Kashgar, it's possible that you can still depart by bus, at least to Ürümqi. If Kashgar opens up again to individual travellers, bus trips to/from other destinations should be possible. There are buses from the Kashgar long-distance bus station to Ürümqi, Daheyan, Aksu, Maralbixi, Khotan, Yengisar, Payziwat, Yopuria, Makit, Yakam and Kargilik.

There is a daily bus to Ürümqi via Aksu, Korla and Toksun. Tickets for the bus can only be bought one day before departure and the bus is scheduled to depart Kashgar at 8 am. The trip takes three days.

The bus to Turpan actually goes to Daheyan, stopping overnight at Aksu and Korla and going straight through Toksun on to Daheyan. The trip takes three days. Daheyan is a small railway town on the Lanzhou-Ürümqi line, and to get to nearby Turpan there are three buses a day. See the Daheyan section for details.

The baggage stored on the roof of the bus is not accessible during the trip. Take a small bag of essentials with you on board. Be warned that buses don't always run on schedule. You could take four days to do the trip, driving anything between eight and 14 hours a day depending on breakdowns or other factors.

Korla and Aksu were once officially open to foreigners – they are now closed again but this could change any time. The town of Yanqi, 52 km north of Korla, is a possible stopover (by train or bus) for a visit to Buddhist caves in the area or to the nearby lake, Bagragh Kol. From Yanqi to the lakeside centre of Bohu is about 12 km. Access to the lake from Bohu could involve a mud-wading expedition, but the fishing villages might be worth a visit. Prices charged for transport can be as high as Y100 per day for a motorised three-wheeler – bargaining is advised. Korla has bus and train connections with Daheyan (Turpan station), Ürümqi and Yining. Aksu has bus and air connections. The major problem with stopping off on the way

between Kashgar and Ürümqi is that you will need great patience to commandeer a seat in buses already packed to the gills.

Getting Around

The city buses are of no use; to get around you have to walk or hire a bike, donkey cart or jeep. The most common transport in Kashgar is bicycle or donkey cart, and there's also the odd horse-drawn cart.

Bikes can be hired from the Oasis Hotel, but there have been numerous stories of cheating, 'misplaced' deposits and lost identity documents. It's probably better to try the bike rental close to the Seman Hotel (ask at the hotel for directions). There is another bike rental in a white building inside the courtyard of the large yellow building to the left of the Mao statue.

Jeeps are available for hire at CITS and at the Kashgar Guesthouse. Be prepared to bargain down to a reasonable price.

KARAKORAM HIGHWAY

This highway over the Khunjerab Pass (4800 metres) was opened to foreigners in May 1986 – it closed again in April 1990. The official excuse was landslides, but the real reason was a political earthquake. However, in August of the same year it opened again but only for individual travel from Pakistan to Kashgar – from Kashgar to Pakistan requires an expensive CITS tour! If the highway is opened again to individuals, you can go from Kashgar as far as Pirali (Chinese border checkpoint) just for the trip (or some hiking en route) without crossing the border.

For centuries this route was used by caravans plodding down the Silk Road. Back in 400 AD, the Chinese pilgrim Fa Xian recorded feelings of vertigo: 'The way was difficult and rugged, running along a bank exceedingly precipitous. When one approached the edge of it, his eyes became unsteady; and if he wished to go forward in the same direction, there was no place on which he could place his foot, and beneath were the waters of the river called the Indus'. 'Khunjerab' translates as 'valley of blood', a reference to local bandits who

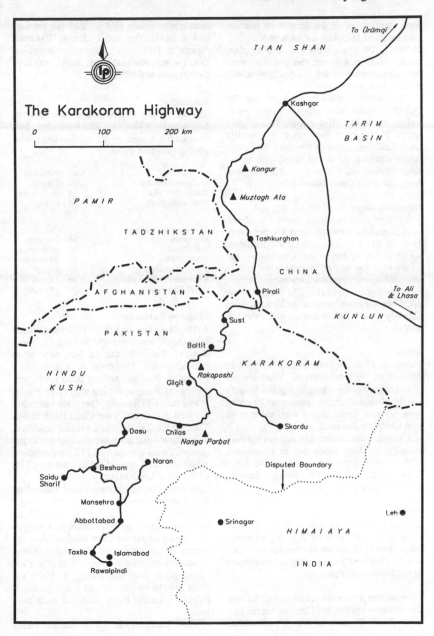

The Karakoram Highway

0   100   200 km

To Ürümqi

TIAN SHAN

Kashgar

TARIM BASIN

▲ Kongur

▲ Muztagh Ata

PAMIR

TADZHIKSTAN

Tashkurghan

CHINA

To Ali & Lhasa

AFGHANISTAN

Pirali

Sust

KUNLUN

PAKISTAN

Baltit

KARAKORAM

HINDU KUSH

Gilgit   ▲ Rakaposhi

Dasu

Chilas   Skardu

Besham   ▲ Nanga Parbat

Naran   Disputed Boundary

Saidu Sharif

Mansehra

Abbottabad

Leh ●

Taxila   Islamabad   Srinagar   HIMALAYA

Rawalpindi   INDIA

took advantage of the terrain to plunder caravans and slaughter the merchants.

Nearly 20 years were required to plan, push, blast and level the present road between Islamabad and Kashgar; over 400 roadbuilders died.

The section between Kashgar and the Pakistan border still needs a few more years before it can be called a road. It is mighty rough. Facilities en route are being steadily improved, but remember to take sufficient warm clothing, food and drink with you – once stowed on the roof of the bus your baggage is not easily accessible.

Information

For information or advice, contact the Pakistan Tourism Development Corporation, H-2, St 61, F – 7/4, Islamabad, Pakistan. CITS in Ürümqi has no maps, no knowledge of the highway and no interest other than to sell you an outrageously expensive tour.

A separate guide, *The Karakoram Highway – a travel survival kit* by John King (Lonely Planet Publications), gives the full story.

Visas

Pakistani visas are compulsory for visitors from most Western countries. Visas are *not* given at the border: Hong Kong and Beijing are the closest places to obtain your Pakistan visa, so plan ahead if you want to enter or exit China on this road.

Chinese visas can be obtained in your own country, in Hong Kong and in Islamabad. The Chinese Embassy in Islamabad takes between one and five days to issue the visa and charges Rs 70.

Border

Opening & Closing Times These are officially given as 1 May and 31 October respectively. However, the border can open late or close early depending on conditions at the Khunjerab Pass.

Formalities These are performed at Sust on the Pakistan border; the Chinese border post is at Pirali. Pirali now has a post office,

restaurants, hotels (Y4 to Y10 per person) and a bank. You can't change Pakistan rupees at Pirali, only Western currencies. Don't worry, Kashgar street marketeers love cash rupees and US dollars.

Routing

The Karakoram Highway stretches between Islamabad and Kashgar. The following chart provides a rough guide to distances and average journey times:

	km	duration
Kashgar-Tashkurgan	280	7 hours
Tashkurgan-Pirali	84	90 minutes
Pirali-Khunjerab	35	1 hour
Sino-Pakistan border		
Khunjerab-Sust	86	2¼ hours
Sust-Passu	35	45 minutes
Passu-Gulmit	14	20 minutes
Gulmit-Karimabad	37	1 hour
Karimabad (Hunza)-Gilgit	98	2 hours
Gilgit-Rawalpindi	631	18 hours

China to Pakistan

At the time of writing this CITS (in collusion with Public Security) was forcing travellers heading for Pakistan to buy expensive package tours. However, it pays to shop around. In Kashgar, several other tour agencies have sprung up selling trips to the border at less than CITS prices. One such operation is based in the rear of the Chini Bagh Hotel. The best thing to do is talk to other travellers in Kashgar – the rates are cheaper for larger groups. Prices quoted by CITS vary wildly – Y500 to Y2000 depending on what the CITS staff ate for lunch that day.

In case the rules change and individual travel again becomes possible, you can get to the border cheaply by bus. Buses for Pakistan leave from the bus station in Kashgar, but weekly departure dates are flexible – the normal departure day is Wednesday. Some buses only go as far as Pirali and charge Y15; others go to Sust and charge Y150. It's a good idea to traipse around hotels to see if Pakistani traders have chartered their own bus.

From Kashgar, the bus crosses the Pamir

Plateau (3000 metres) before overnighting just short of the foothills of Kongur mountain (*gōnggé'ér shān*), which is 7719 metres, and nearby Muztag-Ata mountain (*mùshìtăgé shān*) at 7546 metres. The journey on the next day passes through stunning scenery: high mountain pastures with grazing camels and yaks tended by Tajiks in yurts (Mongolian-style tents). Some travellers have stayed in yurts beside Karakol Lake (*kălākùlì hú*), close to both these mountains. Sven Hedin, the Swedish explorer, nearly drowned in this lake!

The bus spends the second night at Tashkurgan (*tăshìkù'ěrgān*), a predominantly Tajik town which could be used as a base to explore the nearby ruined fort, local cemeteries and surrounding high country. From Tashkurgan (3600 metres) the road climbs higher to Pirali, which wouldn't be worth a stop if it wasn't the Chinese checkpost. If you're on a Pakistani bus, you'll have no need to change buses; if you've taken the local bus from Kashgar, you'll need to change to a Pakistani bus from Pirali onwards.

Pakistan to China

The situation is awfully confused out there, but at the time of writing this, individual travellers from Pakistan were managing to get across the border into Kashgar and then on to Ürümqi by bus. However, going the other direction seems to be impossible except with a ridiculously expensive CITS tour.

From Rawalpindi to Gilgit there are five buses daily. An ordinary coach costs Rs 85; deluxe will cost Rs 120. If you can't stand the pace of the bus ride, the flight between Rawalpindi and Gilgit is good value at Rs 180.

From Gilgit to Sust, there's a NATCO (Northern Areas Transportation Company) bus which costs Rs 22; buy your ticket on the morning of departure at 7 am – the bus leaves at 9 am. The tourist hotel at Sust charges Rs 25 for a bed in the dormitory.

From Sust to Pirali, there's a bus for Rs 160 or US$10. At Pirali everyone changes to a Chinese bus to Kashgar. This bus stops overnight at Tashkurgan. Trucks offer lifts (negotiate the price); ditto for jeeps. Tashkurgan to Kashgar takes aeons over an atrocious boulder-strewn road.

UIGHUR PHRASE LIST

Personal Pronouns

I
   mān   مەن

You
   sān/siz/silā   سەن، سىز، سىلا

He
   u   ئۇ

She
   u   ئۇ

It
   u   ئۇ

We
   biz   بىز

You (plural)
   silār/sizlār   سىلەر، سىزلەر

They
   ular   ئۇلار

Question Words

Where
   nārdā/kāyārda/kāyār/nā
   نە رده ، قەيەرده ، قەيەر ، نا

When
   kaqan   قاچان

Why
   nemixka/nema üqūn
   نىمىشقا، نېمە ئۈچۈن

Greetings & Civilities

Peace be with you!
   Aman bolung!   ئامان بولۇڭ!

Have a safe trip!
   Sapiringizgā ak yol tilāymān!
   سەپىرىڭىزگە ئاق يول تىلەيمەن!

Small Talk

Yes
   bolidu/makul   بولىدۇ، ماقۇل

No
   yak/ āmās/bolmaydu
   ياق، ئەمەس، بولمايدۇ

Hello
hāy/hoy   هەي ، هاي ، هوي
Goodbye
hox/hāyr-hox   خوش ، خەير - خوش
OK
bolidu/makul   بولىدۇ، ماخۇل
Good
yahxi/ubdan/isil/bālān
ياخشى، ئۇبدان، ئىسىل، بالەن
Thank you
rāhmat/hāxkalla
رەخمەت ، هەشكەللە
Where are you from?
Siz nārdin kāldingiz
سىز نەردىن كەلدىڭىز؟
I'm from...
Mān...din...   مەن ...... دىن ......
Britain
Angliyā/Birtaniyā
ئەنگلىيە ، برتانىيە
America
America   ئامرىكا
Canada
Canada   كانادا
Australia
Awistiraliyā   ئاۋستىرالىيە
What's your name?
Ismingiz nimā?   ئىسمىڭىز نىمە ؟
My name is ...
Ismim...   ئىسمىم ......
I don't understand
Mān qüxānmidim/mān uhmudum
مەن چۈشەنمىدىم، مەن ئۇخمۇدۇم

Getting Around
Where is the ...?
...nārdā?   نە ردە
truck stop
maxina bekiti   ماشىنا بېكىتى
bus station
aptubus bekiti   ئاپتوبۇس بېكىتى
I want to take the bus to Kashgar
Mān Kāxkārghā baridghan aptubuska qikattim
مەن قەشقە رگە بارىدىغان ئاپتوبۇسقا چىقاتتىم
How much is the ticket?
Billāt bahasi kanqā?
بىللەت باھاسى قانچە ؟

When does the bus leave?
Aptubus kaqan mangidu?
ئا پتوبۇس قاچان ماڭىدۇ؟
Xinjiang time?
Xinjiang waktimu?
شىنجىاڭ ۋاقتىمۇ؟
Beijing time?
Beijing waktimu?
بېيجىڭ ۋاقتىمۇ؟
Where are you going?
Siz nārgā barisiz?
سىز نەگە بارىسىز؟
When are you going?
Siz kaqan mangisiz?
سىز قاچان ماڭىسىز؟
Have you got a spare seat?
Box orun barmu?
بوش ئورۇن بارمۇ؟
How much do you want from here to Kashgar?
Bu yārdin Kaxkārghā kānqā pul alisiz?
بۇ يەردىن قەشقە رگە قانچە پۇل ئالىسىز؟
Have a cigarette!
Tamaka qikāmsiz?
تاماكا چىكەمسىز؟
I don't smoke!
Mān tamaka qākmāymān
مەن تاماكا چەكمەيمەن .
What are we doing now?
Hazir nemā ix kiliwatisiz?
ھازىر نىمە ئىش قىلىۋاتىسىز؟
The truck's broken down!
Maxina bozulup kaldi
ماشىنا بۇزۇلۇپ قالدى .
Is it OK if I take a photo?
Mān bir rāsimgā tartiwalsam bolamdu?
مەن بىر رەسىمگە تارتىۋالسام بولامدۇ؟
What's the name of this place?
Bu yārning ismi nemā?
بۇ يەرنىڭ ئىسمى نىمە؟
How far is it from here to...?
U...bu yārdin kānqā yirak?
ئۇ ... بۇ يەردىن قانچە يىراق؟

Accommodation
Where is the ...hotel?
...mehmanhanisi nārdā?
...... مېهمانخانىسى نە ردە؟

Guest house
mehmanhana   مېهمانخانا

toilet
hala/hajāthana/ oburna/ tarāthana/   خالا، هاجەتخانا، ئوبۇرنا، تاراتخانا

I need one bed
manga bir kawat lazim   ماڭا بىر كارۋات لازىم.

two beds
ikki karwat   ئىككى كارۋات

What is the price for the bed?
karwatning bahasi kanqā?   كارۋاتنىڭ باھاسى قانچە؟

I want something cheaper
Bir az ārzanrakni alattim   بىر ئاز ئەرزانراقنى ئالاتتىم.

This is fine
Bu yahxikan/bu bolidikan   بۇ ياخشىكەن، بۇ بولىدىكەن.

Is there any hot water?
Issik su barmu?   قىسسىق سۇ بارمۇ؟

Is there a place to wash/bathroom
Munqa barmu?/Yuyundighan jay barmu?   مۇنچا بارمۇ؟ يۇيۇندىغان جاي بارمۇ؟

Food

I'm hungry
korsughum eqip kātti   قورسۇغۇم ئېچىپ كەتتى.

Do you have...?
Sizda...barmu?   سىزدە .... بارمۇ؟

food
yimaklik   يىمەكلىك

meat
gox   گۆش

mutton
koy goxi   قوي گۆشى

bread
holka/nan   بولكا، نان،

eggs
tuhum   تۇخۇم

vegetables
sāy/koktat   سەي، كۆكتات

rice
gürüx   گۈرۈش

tea
qay   چاي

(boiled water)
kaynak su   قاينات سۇ

I'm a vegetarian
Mān gox yimāymān   مەن گۆش يېمەيمەن.

Health

I feel...cold
Mān zukam bolup kalghandāk his kilwatimān   مەن زۇكام بولۇپ قالغاندەك ھىس قىلىۋاتىمەن

tired
harmak/qarqimak   ھارماق، چارچىماق

I don't feel well
Mijāzim yok/halim box   مىجەزىم يوق، ھالىم بوش

I've got a...headache
Bexim aghirip kaldi   بېشىم ئاغرىپ قالدى.

stomach problems
Axkazinim aghirip kaldi   ئاشقازىنىم ئاغرىپ قالدى.

I need a doctor
Manga bir dohtur lazim   ماڭا بىر دوختۇر لازىم.

Days of the Week

This week
bu hāptā   بۇ ھەپتە

Next week
kilār hāptā   كېلەر ھەپتە

Monday
duxānbā   دۈشەنبە

Tuesday
sāyxānbā   سەيشەنبە

Wednesday
qarxānba   چارشەنبە

Thursday
pāyxānbā   پەيشەنبە

Friday
jüma/azna   جۈمە، ئازنا

Saturday
xānba   شەنبە

Sunday
yākxānbā   يەكشەنبە

Time

Morning
  qüxtin burun چۈشتىن بۇرۇن
Evening
  kāq/ahximi كەچ ، ئاخشىمى
Yesterday
  tönügün تۈنۈگۈن
Today
  bügün بۈگۈن
Tomorrow
  ātā ئەتە
Now
  hazir ھازىر

Numbers

1 *bir* بىر
2 *ikki* ئىككى
3 *üq* ئۈچ
4 *tört* تۆرت
5 *bāx* بەش
6 *altā* ئالتە
7 *yāttā* يەتتە
8 *sākkiz* سەككىز
9 *tokkuz* توققۇز
10 *on* ئون
20 *yigirmā* يىگىرمە
30 *ottuz* ئوتتۇز
40 *kirik* قىرىق
50 *āllik* ئەللىك
60 *atmix* ئاتمىش
70 *yātmix* يەتمىش
80 *sāksān* سەكسەن
90 *toksan* توقسان
100 *yüz* يۈز
1000 *bir ming* بىر مىڭ

Place Names

Urumqi
  ürümqi ئۈرۈمچى
Türfan
  turpan تۇرپان
Kumul
  kumul قۇمۇل
(Chinese version commonly used: Hami)
Korla
  korla كورلا
Kuche
  kuqa كۇچا
Aksu
  aksu ئاقسۇ
Kashgar
  kaxkar قەشقەر
Tashkurgan
  taxkorghan تاشقورغان
Khunjirap
  kunjirap قۇنجىراپ
Yarkand
  yārkān يەركەن
(Chinese version commonly used: Shache)
Ali
  ali ئالى
Tibet
  tibāt تىبەت
Pakistan
  pakistan پاكىستان
India
  hindistan ھىندىستان
China
  zhong guo جۇڭگو
Xinjiang
  xinjiang شىنجاڭ

Glossary

Unless otherwise noted, terms are in Tibetan (rendered phonetically). Some Sanskrit terms have been emphasised because they are already well known in the West.

(T) = Tibetan
(S) = Sanskrit

Amdo – formerly north-eastern part of Tibet, now subsumed under Qinghai Province.
Amitabha (S) – Buddha of endless life; *Opame* (T).

Atisha (S) – Atisha Dipankara Srijnana, Indian Buddhist teacher who visited Tibet in 1042 and re-established Buddhism there.
Avalokitesvara (S) – the Bodhisattva of Compassion; *Chenrezig* (T).

Balpo – Nepal, Nepalese; also *Balyul*.
Barkhor – inner pilgrim-circuit in Lhasa.
Bodhisattva (S) – a being who compassionately refrains from entering Nirvana in order to save others. Worshipped as a deity in Mahayana and Vajrayana Buddhism.
Bodpa – a Tibetan.
Bon – animist religion in Tibet before arrival of Buddhism.
Bumpa – ceremonial water pot.

Cham – masked dance.
Champa – Buddha of the Future, or *Maitreya Buddha* (S).
Chang – Tibetan beer, brewed from barley and millet.
Chang-Tang – the northern steppes of Tibet.
Chenrezig – the patron saint of Tibet; *Avalokitesvara* (S).
Chikyab Khenpo – Lord Chamberlain.
Choi – teaching; *Dharma* (S).
Chomolongma – goddess mother of the world: Mt Everest.
Chorten – a small temple representing the Buddha's mind; *Stupa* (S).
Chotrimpa – the monk responsible for monastic discipline.

Chuba – a heavy cloak made from sheepskin or woollen cloth.

Deva (S) – male god; *Lha* (T).
Devi (S) – goddess, usually consort of Shiva. In Tibet, Lhamo (T) is the most eminent goddess, protectress of Lhasa and the Gelukpa order.
Dolma – One of the most important Vajrayana goddesses, consort of Avalokitesvara; *Tara* (S). *Dolmachangmo* (Green Tara) and *Dolmakarmo* (White Tara).
Dorje – thunderbolt symbol.
Dorje Phagmo – Thunderbolt Sow; Tibet's only female incarnation.
Dranyen – the Tibetan lute.
Dri – female yak.
Drilbu – ritual bell, with half a Dorje as a handle.
Drokpa – nomad, dweller of the black tent.
Drölma Lhakang – monastery where Atisha resided.
Drukyul – 'Dragon Land': Bhutan.
Drungyik Chemo – secretary-general.
Dukhang – a hall of assembly for the monks.
Dung – conch horn.
Dzo – a cross between cattle and female yaks.
Dzong – fort; also, district headquarters.
Dzongpon – district commissioner.

Gau – portable shrine.
Gelong – the third grade of monk (requires a minimum age of 30 and observance of 250 rules).
Genja – spiked fiddle.
Gelukpa – founded by Tsongkhapa in the 14th century; known as the Yellow Hat Sect; also *Gelugpa*.
Geshe – a doctor of divinity.
Getsul – the second grade of monk.
Gompa – lamasery or monastery, literally 'place of meditation'.
Gonkhang – an inner chapel.
Guge – kingdom founded in Western Tibet during 9th century.

Guru (S) – master or teacher.

Gyagar – India: 'Region of the White World'

Gyaltsab – regent.

Gyaltsan – cylindrical victory banners.

Gyalwa Rinpoche – 'Victorious One', the name most Tibetans give the Dalai Lama.

Gyanag – China: 'Region of the Black World'.

Gyatso – ocean.

Gyumang – hammer dulcimer.

Jokhang – main temple in Lhasa, also *Tsuglag Khang*.

Kagyupa – religious order founded by Marpa, 11th century.

Kalachakra (S) – a Vajrayana text and deity, 'Wheel of Time'.

Kalon – minister

Kangling – human bone trumpet.

Kanjur-Lhakang – a library in a monastery.

Karmapa – a suborder of the Kagyupa, with abbots distinguished by their black hats.

Kashag – the council of ministers.

Kiang – wild asses.

Kham – Eastern Tibet.

Khampa – inhabitant of Eastern Tibet.

Khenpo – the equivalent to an abbot, he directs the teaching, presides over the assembly and liturgical acts, and monitors the education of monks.

Khata – ceremonial white scarf.

Khorlo – wheel, symbolises setting into motion of the teaching; *Chakra* (S), psychic centre.

Kjangchag – full prostration.

Korlam – clockwise circuit of sacred places.

Kyorpon – the monk who checks students memorised scriptural passages.

Lama – general term for a monk, or more specifically for a fully ordained monk who has become a master.

Lamaism – Tibetan Buddhism.

Lhakhang – temple or chapel.

Lhap-tsug – pile of stones marking top of a pass, *Obo*.

Lingkhor – outer pilgrim circuit in Lhasa.

Losar – New Year.

Lu – water spirits.

Mahakala (S) – a Vajrayana god, protector of the tent; *Gonpo* (T).

Mandala – a symbol of the mind and body of Buddha which is used in meditation.

Mani – the mantra *Om Mani Padme Hum*, of Avalokitesvara, his Tibetan incarnation. Generally translated as 'Hail Jewel in the the lotus'.

Manichorkor – prayer-wheel.

Manjusri (S) – one of the most important Buddhist deities, Bodhisattva of Wisdom; *Jampeyang* (T).

Mantra (S) – prayer formula or chant.

Momo – steamed tsampa dough, usually with meat in the middle, like dumplings.

Namdrel – the study of logic (one of the five groups of study).

Namchuwangdan – an intricate monogram often depicted on the exterior wall of a monastery. It is a mantra that represents the human body in microcosmic form.

Nechung Chogyal – State Oracle.

Nirvana (S) – personal or self liberation, the state beyond sorrow.

Norbulinka – summer residence of the Dalai Lama in Lhasa.

Nyingmapa – a religious order founded around the 10th to 11th centuries by combining various older sects and traditions.

Oumah – the study of the path between extremes.

Padmasambhava (S) – great master of the Tantra, founder of the Nyingmapa order.

Parchin – the second group of study in the study of logic (the comparative study of Buddhist scriptures).

Piwang – two stringed fiddle.

Po – Tibet (also *Bod, Bodyul, and Khawachan* – *'Land of Snow'*).

Rapjung – the first of three grades of monk; wears brownish-red robes.

Rinpoche – blessed, or jewel.

Sakyamuni (S) – title of Gautama Buddha, 5th century BC, also sage of Sakya tribe.
Sakyapa – religious order founded 11th century, Red Hat Sect.
Silon – prime minister.
Sunyata – the study of nonexistence or voidness.

Terma – secret doctrines.
Thamzing – struggle sessions (public torture and humiliation).
Thangka – painting on cloth, often sacred.
Torma – dough effigies used as offerings.
Tsampa – roasted barley-flour, a staple food in Tibet.

Tsatsa – votive plaques.
Tsipon – departmental head.
Tsokchen – main assembly hall.
Tsong Khapa – great reformer of Tibetan Buddhism and founder of the Gelukpa order. Lived 1357-1419.
Tso Ngombo – Kokonor, or Qinghai Lake.
Tulku – a living Buddha.

Yak – male Tibetan ox.
Yama – Hindu God of death; in Tibet, Lord of the Dead and King of Religion.
Yidam – in Tantric Buddhism, a god who protects and guides the individual, family or monastery.

Index

Guides to the Indian Subcontinent

Bangladesh - a travel survival kit
This practical guide – the only English-language guide to Bangladesh – encourages travellers to take another look at this often-neglected but beautiful land.

India - a travel survival kit
Widely regarded as *the* guide to India, this award-winning book has all the information to help you make the most of the unforgettable experience that is India.

Karakoram Highway the high road to China - a travel survival kit
Travel in the footsteps of Alexander the Great and Marco Polo on the Karakoram Highway, following the ancient and fabled Silk Road. This comprehensive guide also covers villages and treks away from the highway.

Kashmir, Ladakh & Zanskar - a travel survival kit
Detailed information on three contrasting Himalayan regions in the Indian state of Jammu and Kashmir – the narrow valley of Zanskar, the isolated 'little Tibet' of Ladakh, and the stunningly beautiful Vale of Kashmir.

Pakistan - a travel survival kit
Discover 'the unknown land of the Indus' with this informative guidebook – from bustling Karachi to ancient cities and tranquil mountain valleys.

Sri Lanka - a travel survival kit
Some parts of Sri Lanka are off-limits to visitors, but this guidebook uses the restriction as an incentive to explore other areas more closely – making the most of friendly people, good food and pleasant places to stay – all at reasonable cost.

Tibet - a travel survival kit
The fabled mountain-land of Tibet was one of the last areas of China to become accessible to travellers. This guide has full details on this remote and fascinating region, including the border crossing to Nepal.

Trekking in the Indian Himalaya
All the advice you'll need for planning and equipping a trek, including detailed route descriptions for some of the world's most exciting treks.

Trekking in the Nepal Himalaya
Complete trekking information for Nepal, including day-by-day route descriptions and detailed maps – a wealth of advice for both independent and group trekkers.

Also available:
Hindi/Urdu phrasebook, *Nepal* phrasebook, and *Sri Lanka* phrasebook.

Dear traveller

Prices go up, good places go bad, bad places go bankrupt...and every guidebook is inevitably outdated in places. Fortunately, many travellers write to us about their experiences, telling us when things have changed. If we reprint a book between editions, we try to include as much of this information as possible in a Stop Press section. Most of this information has not been verified by our own writers.

We really enjoy hearing from people out on the road, and apart from guaranteeing that others will benefit from your good and bad experiences, we're prepared to bribe you with the offer of a free book for sending us substantial useful information.

Thank you to everyone who has written and, to those who haven't, I hope you do find this book useful – and that you let us know when it isn't.

Tony Wheeler

Tibet has not been an easy place to visit, and was virtually closed to independent travellers since the 1987 riots. The Chinese authorities from summer of 1992 have once again been allowing independent travellers to visit Tibet without having to go on an organised pre-paid package tour. Making it much easier and cheaper to visit Tibet.

Meanwhile, any Tibetans who are actively supporting independence for their country are still being imprisoned. Ecologically the country is being ruined at the expense of progress and development.

A traveller reported a new place to stay in Tingri. The *Mt Everest Mountain View Hotel*, is very basic, has no electricity, and costs Y10 per person. The only meals they cook are momos and instant noodle soup. If hitchhiking, never pay in advance. The rate is about Y1RMB per 10 km.

Visas & Permits
A Chinese visa and a Tibetan permit are required to enter Tibet. PSB in Shigatse is a good place for getting permits. They didn't give permits for the Everest area in 1992.

Money & Costs
The bank at the Chinese border with Nepal keeps unreliable opening hours. One traveller reported that he could not exchange any money; as a result he was allowed to take FEC out of the country but not RMB.

Getting There & Away
Travelling in and out of Tibet by plane, bus or hitching is easy now. There is a regular bus between Lhasa and Golmud, taking two days, which includes sleeping during two nights in a hotel. The Chinese bus goes right through with no stops, taking thirty hours. In Lhasa the Yak Hotel can book you on the Japanese bus.

There are four buses per week form Lhasa to the Nepal border via Zhangmu. The journey takes four days.

Travellers' Tips
It is very easy to hitch up the Golmud Road to Lhasa, and most people seem to come that way. The cost of the journey is no more then Y300 RMB, and it takes takes from 30 hours to four days. It is necessary to walk around two or three check points, but at night the driver may just hide you in the back of the truck. One should hitch at night to start with as trucks are afraid to stop during the day – there are also a few trucks leaving Golmud during the day. It is illegal for the driver to take you and he can get a Y500 RMB fine or even his truck taken from him.

Robert Wilkinson – USA

Lonely Planet Guidebooks

Lonely Planet guidebooks cover every accessible part of Asia as well as Australia, the Pacific, South America, Africa, the Middle East, Europe and parts of North America. There are five series: *travel survival kits*, covering a country for a range of budgets; *shoestring guides* with compact information for low-budget travel in a major region; *walking guides*; *city guides* and *phrasebooks*.

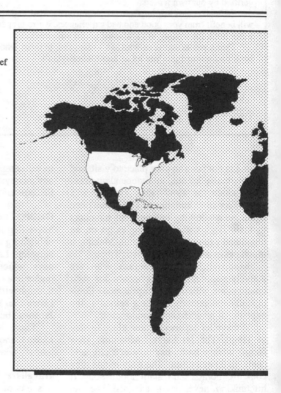

Australia & the Pacific
Australia
Bushwalking in Australia
Islands of Australia's Great Barrier Reef
Fiji
Micronesia
New Caledonia
New Zealand
Tramping in New Zealand
Papua New Guinea
Papua New Guinea phrasebook
Rarotonga & the Cook Islands
Samoa
Solomon Islands
Sydney city guide
Tahiti & French Polynesia
Tonga
Vanuatu

South-East Asia
Bali & Lombok
Bangkok city guide
Myanmar (Burma)
Burmese phrasebook
Cambodia
Indonesia
Indonesia phrasebook
Malaysia, Singapore & Brunei
Philippines
Pilipino phrasebook
Singapore city guide
South-East Asia on a shoestring
Thailand
Thai phrasebook
Vietnam, Laos & Cambodia

North-East Asia
China
Mandarin Chinese phrasebook
Hong Kong, Macau & Canton
Japan
Japanese phrasebook
Korea
Korean phrasebook
North-East Asia on a shoestring
Taiwan
Tibet
Tibet phrasebook
Tokyo city guide

West Asia
Trekking in Turkey
Turkey
Turkish phrasebook
West Asia on a shoestring

Middle East
Egypt & the Sudan
Egyptian Arabic phrasebook
Iran
Israel
Jordan & Syria
Yemen

Indian Ocean
Madagascar & Comoros
Maldives & Islands of the East Indian Ocean
Mauritius, Réunion & Seychelles